the
world
electric power
industry

Source References

In addition to sources listed with the national accounts, in PART II, Section Two of this volume, these sources were used in the preparation of tables in the APPENDIX

Table 1: United Nations. *Demographic yearbook.* (Population data)

Table 2: United Nations. *The growth of world industry.*

Central Statistical Office. *Industrial statistics of Finland.*
Staatlichen Zentralverwaltung für Statistik. *Statistiches jahrbuch.* (East Germany)
Ministère du Développement. Service Centrale des Statistiques. *Annuaire statistique du Maroc.* (Morocco)
Department of Statistics. *Report on the census of industrial production.* (Singapore)
Bureau of Statistics. *Statistical yearbook of South Africa.*
Department of Commerce. Bureau of the Census. *Census of mineral industries.* (United States)
Ministry of Labour and Mines. *Annual report of the mines department.* (Zambia)

Table 4: United Nations. ECE. *Half-yearly bulletin of electric energy statistics for Europe.*

Instituto Costarricense de Electricidad. *Memoria.* (Costa Rica)
Economic Planning Agency. *Economic studies.* (Japan)
Ministère de l'Economie Nationale. Service de la Statistique Generale. *Bulletin mensuel.* (Lebanon)
Department of Statistics. *Monthly abstract of statistics.* (New Zealand)
Ministerio de Hacienda. *Boletin informativo.* (Uruguay)

Table 6: Dominion Bureau of Statistics. *Electric power statistics.* (Canada)
East African Common Services Organization. *Economic and statistical review.* (Kenya and Uganda)
Comisión Federal de Electricidad. *Estadísticas de explotación divisiones CFE.* (Mexico)
Central Statistical Office. *Monthly digest of statistics.* (Mozambique and Rhodesia)
United Nations. ECE. *Half-yearly bulletin of electric energy statistics for Europe.* (Europe and the United States)

Table 8: United Nations. ECE. *Annual bulletin of electric energy statistics for Europe.*
UNIPEDE. *Statistiques.*
US. Federal Power Commission. *Hydroelectric plant construction cost and annual production expenses. (supplement.)* Figures for the United States are author's estimates based on this source.

Table 9: United Nations. *Monthly bulletin of statistics.*
————. ECE. *Half-yearly bulletin of electric energy statistics for Europe.*
Ministerio de Hacienda. *Boletin informativo.* (Uruguay)

ADDENDA AND CORRIGENDA

Regional Titles

Account on page 121 should be headed: *UNDERDEVELOPED WORLD*

Account on page 129 should be headed: *EAST EUROPE*

Country Names

	formerly			formerly
CONGO (KINSHASA) . .	Congo (Leopoldville)	SABAH . . .	North Borneo
GUYANA	British Guiana	SOMALIA . .	British & Italian Somaliland
MALAGASY	Madagascar	TANZANIA . .	Tanganyika & Zanzibar
MALAWI	Nyasaland	ZAMBIA . . .	Northern Rhodesia
RHODESIA	Southern Rhodesia		

Deviation from Calendar Year - Qualification of Data

	fiscal year	special notes
AFGHANISTAN	beginning 20 March	
AUSTRALIA	ending 30 June	Capacity & fuel consumption data should be shifted one column to the right. Lignite here includes South Australian coal.
BARBADOS	ending 30 June	
BRITISH HONDURAS		1958-1962 data: Belize only.
BURMA	ending 30 September	
CHILE		Fuel consumption data include fuels consumed by some industrial producers.
DENMARK	beginning 1 April	
ETHIOPIA	ending 10 September	
FINLAND		Fuel consumption totals should be shifted one column to the right.
GUYANA		Data exclude sugar estates.
INDIA	beginning 1 April	
INDONESIA		Industry consumption: public service plus large industrial establishments only.
IRAN	beginning 21 March	
IRELAND	beginning 1 April	
JAPAN	beginning 1 April	
LIBYA		Industry revenue/kwh: Tripolitania only.
MALAYA	ending 31 August	
MALTA	beginning 1 April	
MAURITIUS		Data exclude power generated by sugar mills for own use.
MOROCCO		1958-1963 data: l'Office Nationale de l'Electricité only.
NEW GUINEA	ending 30 June	
NEW ZEALAND	beginning 1 April	
PANAMA CANAL ZONE	ending 30 June	Transport consumption: Panama Canal Co.
PAPUA	ending 30 June	
SOMALIA		Data incomplete.
SOUTH AFRICA	beginning 1 July	
SWITZERLAND	ending 30 September	
TANZANIA		Data for Tanganyika only.
USSR		Nuclear capacity excludes Troitsk plant (status as generating plant not known).
WESTERN SAMOA		Data for Apia district only.

(over)

N. B. GUYOL

the
world
electric power
industry

UNIVERSITY OF CALIFORNIA PRESS

BERKELEY AND LOS ANGELES 1969

This study was conducted at the University of California, Berkeley, California, under a grant from Resources for the Future, Inc., and under the auspices of the University's Department of Geography and Institute of International Studies.

University of California Press

Berkeley and Los Angeles, California

University of California Press, Ltd.

London, England

Acknowledgments

This study would not have been possible without the assistance of Resources for the Future, the cooperation of the Federal Power Commission of the United States, and the past efforts of various national and international agencies and professional organizations engaged in energy research. Extensive and intensive use has been made of the publications of the Statistical Office of the United Nations, the Energy Division of the Economic Commission for Europe, the Economic Commission for Asia and the Far East, the Economic Commission for Latin America, the Statistical Office of the European Community, the International Union of Producers and Distributors of Electric Energy, the World Power Conference, the Union for Coordination of Electricity Production and Transmission, and the International Railway Union—and of the publications of the many national agencies and organizations dealing with electric power, economics, and statistics.

Thanks are due to the librarians who were kind enough to make available the facilities of the following libraries: Economic and Social Affairs, United Nations, New York; Economic Commission for Europe, Geneva; Edison Electric Institute, New York; Federal Power Commission and the United States Department of State, Washington, D.C.; University of California, Berkeley; and Standard Oil Company of California, San Francisco.

Thanks are due also to many individuals who assisted in the search for or interpretation of data, including especially Mr. James Dilloway (ECE); Mr. Arthur Ramsdell (UN STATISTICAL OFFICE); Mr. Kristian Laading (OECD); Messrs. F. Stewart Brown, Haskell Wald, and Lester Landerkin (FPC); Mrs. Berenice Mitchell (US BUREAU OF MINES); Mr. George Brenk (STANDARD OIL COMPANY OF CALIFORNIA); Mr. V. Paretti (EEC); and Mr. A. Runacres (UK ELECTRICITY COUNCIL).

Finally, thanks are due to those who helped to set up and conduct the project—especially Professor James Parsons of the Department of Geography, and Mrs. Cleo Stoker of the Institute of International Studies, University of California, Berkeley—and to those who participated directly in the preparation of this report, including Mr. Kenneth Gillespie, who is responsible for the graphics; Miss Marsha Bratten; Mr. James Harris; Mr. and Mrs. J. A. McFadden; Mrs. Leonard Weiss; Mr. and Mrs. D. L. Stannard; and my most demanding colleagues, collaborators, and critics, Melinda and Dorothy Guyol.

We would appreciate comments, corrections, or additional data that might contribute to an updated version of this publication.

N.B.G.

Contents

Tables

Chapter V

Chapter VI

Illustrations

Methods

This study is based on systematic surveys of the electric power industry in 162 countries—all the countries for which the necessary data could be found, and all but perhaps a dozen of the countries which produce or consume as much as ten million kilowatt hours per year. These data, most of which appear in the country tables in Part II of this study, are taken or derived arithmetically from sources believed to be reliable—official national publications, publications of the United Nations and its regional commissions, the World Power Conference, UNIPEDE, UCPTE, and other sources listed in the bibliography. In cases of disagreement among sources, the author has exercised his own judgment as to which figures are closer to the truth.

In a few countries, end uses of electricity are distinguished only by the categories "high-tension" and "low-tension." The former has been treated in this study as equivalent to industrial consumption, the latter as equivalent to consumption in the domestic sector.

Loss (or loss and use), as shown in this study, is usually taken from published sources, but may be simply the difference between supply and reported consumption.

In a few cases—the Portuguese colonies in particular—data on sales are available, but not data on production. In these cases, losses have been estimated and added to sales to arrive at production. In the case of Mozambique, exports also have been added to sales in calculating production.

A special problem arises in connection with regional and world data on gross and net production and supply. It will be noted that, in many of the country tables, either gross or net figures appear, but not both. In compiling regional and world summaries, the appropriate figure has been used when available, but in the absence of one, the other has been substituted for it. The net totals shown for particular regions and the world therefore consistently exceed the true net totals, and the gross totals shown are consistently below the true gross totals.

Some of the country data which appear in Tables 1 and 3 of the Appendix are the author's estimates, entered when needed to arrive at reasonable totals for particular regions and the world. Regional and world totals, to a corresponding extent, are estimated.

Terms Used in the Electricity Accounts

CAPACITY: As used here, nominal or nameplate rating of generators as of the end of the year indicated.

GROSS PRODUCTION: Total output of power plants, including power used in station operations.

NET PRODUCTION: Output, excluding power used in station operation.

HYDROELECTRICITY: Power generated from falling water, including electricity produced by pumped storage plants (plants which generate power, usually during periods of peak demands, from water pumped into elevated reservoirs, usually during off-peak periods).

CONVENTIONAL THERMAL ELECTRICITY: Electricity generated in power plants using conventional fuels (commercial or non-commercial). This includes electricity generated in diesel and gas turbine plants as well as steam plants.

NUCLEAR ELECTRICITY: Electricity generated in power plants which derive their energy from nuclear fuels.

GEOTHERMAL ELECTRICITY: Power generated from volcanic steam.

UTILITIES: Electricity supply systems operated primarily as suppliers of power for public use (as distinguished from industrial and transportation agencies generating primarily for their own use).

NET IMPORTS: Total imports minus total exports.

GROSS SUPPLY: Gross production plus net imports.

NET SUPPLY (= gross consumption): Net production plus net imports.

CONSUMPTION: Net supply, excluding own use and loss; power delivered to consumers.

TRANSPORTATION: Railways, tramways, trolleybuses, and subways.

INDUSTRY: Mining and manufacturing, including consumption in electric boilers.

DOMESTIC SECTOR: Households, commercial establishments, public buildings and grounds, street lighting, and miscellaneous uses.

LOSS (and use): Losses in transmission and distribution, plus the input of pumped storage plants. Where only gross production and supply figures are shown, includes also consumption by plant auxiliaries.

Explanatory Note and Abbreviations

kw kilowatt (1,000 watts)

mw megawatt (1,000 kw)

kwh kilowatt hour

mwh megawatt hour (1,000 kwh)

twh terawatt hour (kilowatt hour $\times$ 10^9)

kv kilovolt (1,000 volts)

Tcal teracalorie (1 kilogram calorie $\times$ 10^9) = approximately 4 Btu $\times$ 10^9

— nil or negligible

-- data not available

e partially estimated; error probably less than 10%

( ) data enclosed in parentheses are estimates in which the potential error is large. Their primary purpose is to fill gaps in regional data. They are not intended to represent conditions in particular countries with any precision, and should be used in this fashion only with reservations.

COUNTRIES are listed under their names as of 1967; where a name is new, the former name is indicated on the appropriate country data-sheet.

THE YEARS referred to are, in most cases, calendar years. Deviations from calendar years are indicated on the country data-sheets, but have been disregarded in running totals for various regions.

POPULATION data represent mid-year populations in 1964 of countries as defined (including enclaves).

GROWTH RATES shown as percentages are calculated as compounded annually.

SUBDIVISIONS OF INDUSTRY, when referred to, correspond more or less with ISIC categories grouped as follows: food, beverages, and tobacco (20-22); textiles, clothing, footwear, and leather goods (23, 24, and 29); wood products and furniture, paper and paper products (25-27); chemicals, fuels, and rubber (30-32); basic metals (34); non-metallic mineral products (33); metal products, machinery and equipment (35-38); printing, publishing, and other manufacturing (28 and 39).

PART I

SOURCES AND USES OF THE WORLD'S ELECTRICITY, 1964

(TWH - Electric or Thermal)

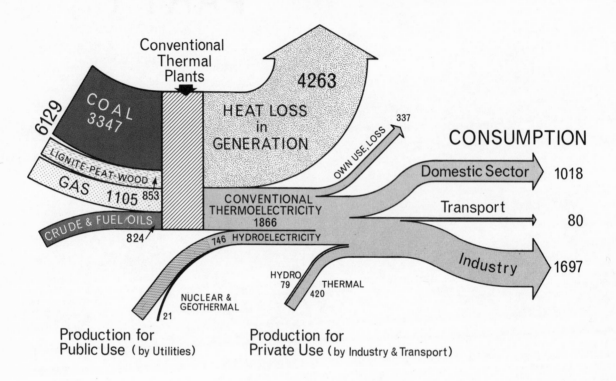

Introduction

Electricity is one of the better forms of energy. It is efficient, easy to live with, and easy to use. It converts to heat, light, or power with little loss of energy; it consumes no oxygen and gives off no smoke; it can be had in the precise quantity required for any given purpose; and it can be turned on or off, instantly and at will, with no effort on the part of the user. Electricity is the most versatile of all the energy sources. It can be turned into light of any desired intensity. It can be converted into power in the minute quantities required for electronic controls or in the tremendous quantities required to operate nuclear diffusion plants. It can be transformed into heat of any desired temperature or used to remove heat when cold is wanted. It can be used to separate elements electrolytically and thus supply us with such metals as aluminum and pure copper.

Electricity provides all of the energy used in telecommunications; it produces most of the world's stationary power, an important part of the world's heat and mobile power, and virtually all of the world's artificial light. It is, in short, one of the most effective instruments available to us for increasing productivity and for altering relationships between man and his environment.

Every country uses electricity. Nearly every country has a clearly defined electric power industry—an industry important enough and well enough developed to be reported upon officially at least once each year.

But the data that appear in national reports on the electric power industries of different countries do not fit into a single pattern, so it is difficult to compare the industry of one country with that of another. It is even more difficult to combine data on several countries and thus arrive at a composite picture of the electric power industry in the world, or in any major region of the world except West Europe and the non-Communist portion of the Far East.

An attempt has been made in the present study to correct this situation by collecting data on the electric power industry in every country of the world, putting these data in comparable forms, and combining them to produce certain regional and world aggregates.

This study consists mainly of statistical data on the electric power industry in particular countries, selected regions, and the world, plus observations concerning variations in certain characteristics of the industry from one region to another and from one country to another.

Because the electric power industry is important not only in its own right but also because of its role in human affairs, the study has been carried beyond the confines of the industry proper, into an exploration of certain factors affecting or affected by the industry. Attention has been given especially to relationships between the quantities of electricity consumed and the amount of work performed, in the economy as a whole and in particular sectors of the economy.

The focal point of the study is the year 1964—the most recent year for which adequately inclusive, internationally comparable data are currently available. To put the year 1964 into perspective, and to gain some insight into the dynamics of the industry, the study also reviews developments in the industry during the period 1958 to 1964.

The countries whose national power industries form the composite world industry are so diverse as to seem hand-picked in proof of diversity—from Norway to New Zealand, from Mexico to India, from Greenland to South Africa. The smallest country in area is Gibraltar; the largest is the Soviet Union. Populations vary from the five thousand who live on the islands of St. Pierre and Miquelon to the seven hundred million who live in Mainland China. Any quantitative measure of their differences holds to a pattern of two extremes separated by a very long range. Their kilowatt hour shares in the world's supply of electricity, in 1964, ranged from six million to a million million.

This diversity influenced the content and determined the arrangement of the study. The first two chapters of the text describe the electric power industry in terms of its structure in the world—the world whole and selected regions of the world. The next three chapters describe the differing patterns of the industry, from country to country and from region to region. The final chapter explores the dynamics of the industry as reflected in changes during the period 1958 to 1964.

Chapter 1
The Structure of the Industry
in the World

The flow chart in the frontispiece portrays certain important aspects of the world electric power industry in the year 1964. The electricity pictured in the chart represents virtually all the electricity generated in stationary power plants anywhere in the world in that year.

The chart traces the flow of electricity from producer to consumer in lines whose width is proportional to the quantities of energy involved. At the left end of the chart are the fuels used in generating conventional thermal electricity. Hydroelectricity is drawn into the supply, as are nuclear and geothermal electricity, and transfers from industrial producers (at the bottom of the chart). Losses and plants' own use are extracted at the top, and the electricity remaining is delivered, at the right end of the chart, to the three major categories of consumer—industry, transport, and the domestic sector.

The chart is an aggregate, a statistical montage, of the electric power industries in some 162 countries. The magnitude of the quantities shown is not immediately apparent, for the necessary abbreviation provided by the terawatt hour has lopped nine digits from each figure. In terms to which we are more accustomed, the electricity represented in the chart amounts to 3,132,900 million kwh, or an average of 972 kwh for each of the world's 3,224 million people.

Fuels consumed

The conventional fuels consumed by utilities in generating electricity are shown, in the terawatt hour electricity equivalents, at the left end of the flow chart. The dominance of coal here is unchallenged: alone, it provides more than half the energy consumed by utilities. With its close relatives, lignite and peat, coal provides more than two-thirds of all power plant input. Gas—mainly natural gas—provides 18% of the energy consumed by electric utilities, petroleum fuels 13%. A small but interesting fraction of the input of utility power plants is supplied by relatively exotic fuels, such as charcoal, paddy husk, fuelwood, sawdust, and sulphite liquor.

The fuel requirements of the electric power plants put the industry in a prominent role in world fuel markets. In 1964, they consumed 27% of the world's coal and lignite, 12% of the world's natural gas, and 5% of the world's oil. Altogether, consumption by the electric power industry represented 14% of the world's entire supply of fuels.

Production

World output of electricity in 1964 amounted to something over 3,100 billion kwh. Nearly three-quarters of this total was thermo-electric power generated in conventional steam or internal combustion plants. Practically all the remainder was hydroelectricity, generated by falling water. Nuclear fuels were responsible for one-half of one percent of the total; volcanic steam, converted to electricity in geo-thermal power plants, for one-tenth of one percent.

Utilities generated 84% of the electricity produced in 1964. The balance was generated by industrial establishments and railways. These auto-producers consumed most of their own output as well as large quantities of electricity purchased from utilities, but they also provided power *to* utilities—about one-tenth of their total output in 1964.

Deliveries and consumption

Eighty-nine percent of the electricity generated in 1964 was delivered to consumers. Eleven percent was used in plant operations or lost in transmission and distribution. Of the electricity that reached consumers, somewhat more than half was supplied to industry, a bit less than one-third to the domestic sector, and two and one-half percent to transportation.

CONSUMPTION OF ELECTRICITY IN 1964

sectors	%
industrial	54.2
domestic	32.5
transport	2.5
net consumption	89.2
own use (incl. pumping) + loss in transmission	10.8
gross consumption	100.0

Industrial sector

Electricity is the principal source of industrial power, an important source of heat and process energy, and the sole source of industrial light. The lion's share of the electricity used in industry—an estimated 91%—is used in manufacturing. The rest is used in mining.

The different branches of manufacturing use quite different amounts of electricity. Two industry groups, combined, use more than half of all the electricity consumed in industry—the chemical industries (including fuels), and the crude metals industries. Use in other branches ranges downward from 10% of the total to a minimum—in the food, beverage, and tobacco group—of just under 5%.

Use in mining averages 48 kwh per capita, use in manufacturing 478 kwh per capita. In sub-groups of manufacturing, use ranges from an average of 152 kwh per capita in the chemicals and fuels industries to 23 kwh in the food, beverage, and tobacco industries.

The distribution of electricity within industry is discussed in detail in Chapter Three.

Domestic sector

Approximately 1,000 billion kwh, or 316 kwh per capita, are consumed in the domestic sector. Something over half the electricity delivered to this sector is consumed in households, most of the remainder in commercial establishments. The balance is distributed among many uses such as street lighting, agriculture, and the operation of public buildings and grounds.

Consumption of electricity in the domestic sector, and certain related factors, are examined in Chapter Three.

Transport sector

Most of the electricity consumed in transportation is used in the operation of railways. The remainder is used in urban transport—in trams, trolleybuses, and subways. Electricity is used also in the operation of certain pipelines, but little information is available on the quantities so used. On a per capita basis, use in transportation averages only 25 kwh annually.

The use of electricity in transportation is considered in detail in Chapter Three.

Certain important aspects of the world electric power industry are not reflected in the flow chart, mainly because they are national or regional phenomena that, on a world basis, average out to insignificance. Among these are international trade in electricity; nature and utilization of electric power plants; ownership of electric power facilities; variations—diurnal, weekly, and seasonal—in electricity demand and supply; electricity prices; availability and costs of electric service; and efficiency of fuel use. These aspects of the industry are examined in Chapters Three, Four, and Five.

The world electricity situation is summarized statistically in Table 1.

TABLE 1.   WORLD:
SUMMARY OF THE ELECTRICITY SITUATION IN 1964

	million KW	%
Capacity		
Gross total	733.7	100.0
Hydro	209.7	28.6
Conventional Thermal	520.0	70.8
Nuclear	3.5	0.5
Geothermal	0.5	0.1

	twh	%
Production		
Gross total	3132.9	100.0
Net total	3071.6	98.0
Hydro	825.2	26.4
Conventional Thermal	2286.7	72.9
Nuclear	17.1	0.6
Geothermal	3.9	0.1
Net import	0.2	

	twh	%
Supply		
gross	3133.1	100.0
net	3071.8	98.0
Consumption		
total	2795.2	89.2
transport	79.5	2.5
domestic sector	1018.5	32.5
industry	1697.2	54.2
Lost (incl. some own use)	276.6	8.8

	million MT	000 Tcals
Fuels consumed by utilities		
Coal	511.3	2878.3
Lignite and peat	270.2	734.5
Oil fuels	68.8	708.7
Gases		950.2
Other fuels		0.8
Total:		5272.5

Chapter 2
Seven Regions and Four Worlds

For purposes of analysis, the world has been divided into seven geographic regions: North America, West Europe, East Europe and the Soviet Union, Africa, Asia, Oceania, and Latin America. These regions are basically continents, modified slightly to obtain greater economic or politico-economic homogeneity.

For other views of the world, countries have been regrouped into two pairs of worlds: first, on the basis of economic status, into developed and underdeveloped worlds; second, on the basis of politico-economic systems, into the free enterprise and Communist worlds.

Each of the seven regions and four worlds is defined and described in this chapter, and the structure of the electric power industry in each is summarized. Structural detail is elaborated in subsequent chapters, in the discussion of various aspects of the world electric power industry.

Regional and world comparisons are made throughout the text in paragraphs, tables, graphs, and maps.

NORTH AMERICA

40% of the world electric power industry
 7% of the world's population

This region consists essentially of Canada and the United States, two economically developed countries with very high levels of electricity consumption. The region also includes Greenland, and St. Pierre and Miquelon.

The structure of production in North America differs a little from that of the world; hydro's share in total output is somewhat smaller and the share of conventional thermal electricity correspondingly larger. The pattern of fuel use reflects an unusually heavy reliance on natural gas. The structure of consumption differs significantly from that of the world as a whole. A very small share of the electricity supply is used in transportation, a relatively large share in

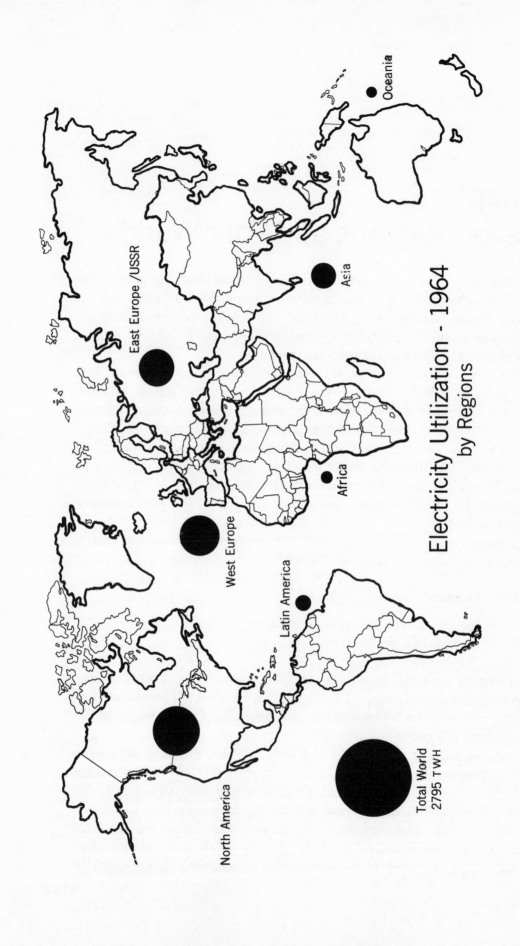

Electricity Utilization - 1964
by Regions

Oceania

Asia

East Europe /USSR

Africa

West Europe

Latin America

North America

Total World
2795 TWH

the domestic sector. Industry takes somewhat less than half the total.

Only 10% of capacity is in the hands of establishments producing primarily for private use; 90% is utility owned. In Canada, practically all utilities are publicly owned; in the United States, most are privately owned. The continental portion of the region is served by extensive, internationally connected networks through which electricity is made available to practically the entire population.

North America's consumption of electricity, on a per capita basis, is much larger than that of the world as a whole: five times as large in industry, eight times as large in the domestic sector.

Per capita consumption of electricity in 1964:

	kwh
industry	2788
domestic sector	2487
transport	24
total	5299

A statistical summary of the electricity situation in North America is given in Table 2.

TABLE 2. NORTH AMERICA:
SUMMARY OF THE ELECTRICITY SITUATION IN 1964

	million KW	%
Capacity		
Gross total	267.5	100.0
Hydro	63.2	23.6
Conventional thermal	203.4	76.0
Nuclear	0.9	0.4
Geothermal	—	
	twh	%
Production		
Gross total	(1218.8)	100.0
Net total	1218.8	
Hydro	293.7	24.1
Conventional thermal	921.4	75.6
Nuclear	3.5	0.3
Geothermal	0.2	—
Net import	0.9	

TABLE 2 (Continued)

	twh	%
Supply		
gross	(1219.7)	100.0
net	1219.7	
Consumption		
total	1120.4	91.8
transport	5.0	0.4
domestic sector	525.8	43.1
industry	589.6	48.3
Lost (incl. some own use)	99.3	8.2

	million MT	000 Tcals	
Fuels consumed by utilities			
Coal	208.1	1389.2	64%
Lignite	2.1	8.3	—
Oil fuels	15.7	164.5	8%
Gases		613.2	28%
Total		2175.2	100%

WEST EUROPE

24% of the world electric power industry
10% of the world's population

The West Europe region comprises three distinct sub-regions. The first is the European Economic Community, a rather highly developed and closely knit group of six countries operating, in the main, under free enterprise economies: Belgium, France, Italy, Luxembourg, the Netherlands, and West Germany. The second, Other North Europe, consists of nine relatively prosperous countries adjacent to the European Community and bound to it by economic ties of varying strength: Austria, Denmark, Finland, Iceland, Ireland, Norway, Sweden, Switzerland, and the United Kingdom. The third sub-region, Other South Europe, includes six countries or other political entities situated within western Europe but characterized by lower levels of economic development: Gibraltar, Greece, Malta, Portugal, Spain, and Yugoslavia.

Sub-regional shares in the world electric power industry more or less parallel their economic differences: 12% of the world industry is concentrated in the European Economic Community, 10% in Other North Europe and 2% in Other South Europe.

Of West Europe's electricity, one-third is generated in hydro-electric plants, nearly two-thirds in conventional thermal plants. Nuclear and geothermal facilities produce less than 2% of the total supply. Conventional thermal electricity is obtained mainly from coal and lignite, produced within the region, and fuel oils extracted from imported crudes.

Private generation is relatively important in this area: industry and transportation provide more than a fifth of West Europe's total output. Most West European countries have complete networks, and all except certain island countries have interties with their neighbors.

The region's consumption pattern corresponds rather closely with that of the world as a whole, but its consumption per capita is more than twice the world average.

Per capita consumption of electricity in 1964:

	kwh
industry	1196
domestic sector	710
transport	69
total	1975

Table 3 summarizes the electric power industry in West Europe. Statistical data for the three sub-regions are given in Part II.

TABLE 3.   WEST EUROPE:
SUMMARY OF THE ELECTRICITY SITUATION IN 1964

Capacity	million KW	%
Gross total	201.3	100.0
Hydro	75.2	37.4
Conventional thermal	123.5	61.4
Nuclear	2.3	1.1
Geothermal	0.3	0.1
Production	twh	%
Gross total	779.3	100.0
Net total	742.9	95.3
Hydro	257.5	33.0
Conventional thermal	507.7	65.2
Nuclear	11.6	1.5
Geothermal	2.5	0.3
Net import	−0.9	—

TABLE 3 (Continued)

	twh	%
Supply		
gross	778.4	100.0
net	742.0	95.3
Consumption		
total	671.0	86.2
transport	23.6	3.0
domestic sector	241.2	31.0
industry	406.2	52.2
Lost (incl. some own use)	71.0	9.1

	million MT	000 Tcals	
Fuels consumed by utilities			
Coal	110.5	633.9	62%
Lignite and peat	74.2	158.3	16%
Oil fuels	20.7	208.0	20%
Gases		22.4	2%
Other		0.5	—
Total		1023.1	100%

EAST EUROPE/USSR

20% of the world electric power industry
10% of the world's population

This region comprises Albania, Bulgaria, Czechoslovakia, East Germany, Hungary, Poland, Romania, and the Soviet Union. The region is bound together by politico-economic ties as well as geography.

Water power is less important here than in the world as a whole. Conventional thermal facilities—fueled largely by domestically-produced coal, lignite, and natural gas—produce 86% of the region's electricity.

Utilities control nearly three-fourths of all generating capacity, and produce a little more than three-fourths of the total output. Extensive, interconnected networks provide power to a large percentage of the population. This is the only region in which all electric power facilities are publicly owned.

The structure of consumption is quite unlike that of West Europe or the world as a whole: industry's share in the electricity supply is larger and the domestic sector's share only half as large. Transportation uses 6% of the region's total supply, as against 3% in West Europe.

Per capita consumption of electricity in East Europe/USSR in 1964 was almost twice the world average:

	kwh
industry	1272
domestic sector	312
transport	115
total	1699

The region's electric power industry is summarized in Table 4. Separate data for East Europe are given in Part II.

TABLE 4.   EAST EUROPE/USSR:
SUMMARY OF THE ELECTRICITY SITUATION IN 1964

	million KW	%
Capacity		
Gross total	137.4	100.0
Hydro	24.7	18.0
Conventional thermal	112.4	81.8
Nuclear	0.3	0.2
Geothermal	—	

	twh	%
Production		
Gross total	616.0	100.0
Net total	604.3	98.1
Hydro	83.7	13.6
Conventional thermal	530.3	86.1
Nuclear	2.0 E	0.3 E
Geothermal	—	
Net import	0.1	

	twh	%
Supply		
gross	616.1	100.0
net	604.4	98.1
Consumption		
total	558.9	90.7
transport	37.7	6.1
domestic sector	102.8	16.7
industry	418.4	67.9
Lost (incl. some own use)	45.5	7.4

TABLE 4 (Continued)

	million MT	000 Tcals	
Fuels consumed by utilities			
Coal	86.2	283.8	25%
Lignite and peat	176.1	524.5	47%
Oil fuels	4.0	37.9	3%
Gases		272.9	25%
Other fuels		0.3	—
Total		1119.4	100%

AFRICA

1.6% of the world electric power industry
9.4% of the world's population

The countries that make up this region are bound together mainly by geography. Except for South Africa, which is well along in the developmental process, most of the region is underdeveloped in respect of both the total economy and the electric power industry.

Twenty-five percent of Africa's power is produced in hydro-electric plants, the remainder in conventional thermal plants. Neither nuclear nor geothermal facilities have been developed in this region. In most of Africa, thermal electric power is generated principally from imported oil, but in South Africa, which produces the bulk of the continent's conventional thermal power, and in Rhodesia and Nigeria, domestically-produced coal is the source of practically all the thermal electricity produced.

Production is largely in the hands of utilities, although a few countries with specialized, power-intensive industries — such as Cameroon, the Congo (Kinshasa) and Ghana — depend primarily upon private production. Outside of South Africa, networks are limited in extent and provide power to only a very small fraction of the total population.

The structure of consumption is unlike that of the world industry: transport's share in the total is larger, industry's share much larger. The industrial sector consumes three times as much as does the domestic sector in the continent as a whole, and in South Africa, five times as much.

Per capita consumption in South Africa is high—almost twice the world average of 867 kwh—but in the continent as a whole it is very low.

Per capita consumption of electricity in 1964:

	kwh
industry	112
domestic sector	34
transport	7
total	153

The structure of Africa's electric power industry in 1964 is summarized in Table 5.

TABLE 5.   AFRICA:
SUMMARY OF THE ELECTRICITY SITUATION IN 1964

	million KW	%
Capacity		
Gross total	13.8	100.0
Hydro	3.4	24.6
Conventional thermal	10.4	75.4
Nuclear	—	—
Geothermal	—	—

	twh	%
Production		
Gross total	53.7	100.0
Net total	51.6	96.1
Hydro	12.2	22.7
Conventional thermal	41.5	77.3
Nuclear	—	—
Geothermal	—	—
Net import	—	—

	twh	%
Supply		
gross	53.7	100.0
net	51.6	96.1
Consumption		
total	46.6	86.8
transport	2.1	3.9
domestic sector	10.4	19.4
industry	34.1	63.5
Lost (incl. some own use)	5.0	9.3

TABLE 5 (Continued)

Fuels consumed by utilities	million MT	000 Tcals	
Coal	19.0	104.8	83%
Oil fuels	1.8	18.7	15%
Gases		2.1	2%
Total		125.6	100%

ASIA

10% of the world electric power industry
55% of the world's population

Asia, as defined here, stretches from Turkey to Japan, taking in the entire Middle East, Southeast Asia, and all of the Asian Peoples Republics. Except for Japan, which has shown a remarkable development—both in its total economy and in its electric power industry—the region is one of slight economic development and modest levels of electricity production and consumption.

Hydroelectricity, with a share of more than 36% in total output, is relatively important here. The remainder comes from conventional thermal plants, there being no significant development of either nuclear or geothermal facilities in the region as of 1964. Thermal electricity is generated mainly from domestically produced coal and lignite, but oil fuels, imported or produced mainly from imported crudes, constitute some 32% of the input of thermal electric power plants. Some crude is used directly as power plant fuel in Japan.

The situation of the electric power industry in Asia is partially obscured by the absence of reliable data on the Asian Peoples Republics—Mainland China in particular. The data that are available indicate that utilities control something better than 90% of all Asia's generating capacity, and yield a corresponding share of Asia's electricity. Japan and China (Taiwan) have highly developed networks; elsewhere, service is provincial or local for the most part, reaching but a small fraction of the region's population.

Asia, *without* Japan, has 52% of the world's population — but has only a 4.3% share of the world's electric power. Per capita consumption of electricity in Asia, even with Japan included, is only slightly above that of Africa. Structures of consumption in Asia and Africa differ mainly in their ratios of industrial and domestic use: Asia delivers a smaller share of its electricity to industry, and a larger share to the domestic sector.

Per capita consumption of electricity in Asia in 1964:

	kwh
industry	104
domestic sector	47
transport	5
total	156

A statistical summary of the electricity situation in Asia is given in Table 6. Separate data, also for Asia but excluding the Asian Peoples Republics, are given in Part II.

TABLE 6.   ASIA:
SUMMARY OF THE ELECTRICITY SITUATION IN 1964

	million KW	%
Capacity		
Gross total	75.2	100.0
Hydro	28.5	37.9
Conventional thermal	46.7	62.1
Nuclear	—	—
Geothermal	—	—

	twh	%
Production		
Gross total	323.6	100.0
Net total	313.7	96.9
Hydro	118.0	36.5
Conventional thermal	205.6	63.5
Nuclear	—	—
Geothermal	—	—
Net import	—	—

	twh	%
Supply		
gross	323.6	100.0
net	313.7	96.9
Consumption		
total	279.5	86.4
transport	8.7	2.7
domestic sector	83.5	25.8
industry	187.3	57.9
Lost (incl. some own use)	34.2	10.5

TABLE 6 (Continued)

Fuels consumed by utilities	million MT	000 Tcals	
Coal	78.0	397.5	66%
Lignite	2.4	6.6	1%
Oil fuels	18.0	189.0	32%
Gases		6.9	1%
Total		600.0	100%

OCEANIA

1.3% of the world electric power industry
0.5% of the world's population

The electric power industry in this region is concentrated almost entirely in Australia and New Zealand, although there are a number of interesting industries in some of the lesser islands, especially New Caledonia. The population is small, but the area covered is very large. It is a relatively prosperous, developed area, with a highly developed electric power industry.

The structure of the industry here differs markedly from the structure in other regions. The division of production between hydro and thermal is similar to that of the world as a whole, but geothermal facilities—with nearly 3% of all output—are more important than in other regions. Conventional thermal power is generated almost entirely from domestically produced coal and lignite.

Practically all utilities in the region are publicly owned. In both Australia and New Zealand there are extensive networks which supply electricity to virtually the entire population. New Zealand boasts one of the world's three geothermal power plants, and a submarine cable by which the systems of its two islands are interconnected.

In consumption, the domestic sector is dominant. In 1964 Oceania was the only region to use more electricity—total and per capita—for domestic purposes than for industrial purposes. New Caledonia has one of the highest levels of electricity consumption per capita in the world.

The region's per capita consumption in 1964 was high:

	kwh
industry	918
domestic sector	1125
transport	45
total	2088

The electricity situation in Oceania in 1964 is summarized in Table 7.

TABLE 7. OCEANIA:
SUMMARY OF THE ELECTRICITY SITUATION IN 1964

	million KW	%
Capacity		
Gross total	11.1	100.0
Hydro	4.1	37.4
Conventional thermal	6.8	60.9
Nuclear	—	—
Geothermal	0.2	1.7

	twh	%
Production		
Gross total	43.3	100.0
Net total	- -	- -
Hydro	15.0	34.7
Conventional thermal	27.1	62.5
Nuclear	—	—
Geothermal	1.2	2.8
Net import	—	—

	twh	%
Supply		
gross	43.3	100.0
net	- -	- -
Consumption		
total	35.8	82.7
transport	0.8	1.8
domestic sector	19.3	44.6
industry	15.7	36.3
Lost (incl. some own use)	7.5	17.3

	million MT	000 Tcals	
Fuels consumed by utilities			
Coal	8.1	59.0	58%
Lignite	15.4	36.8	36%
Oil fuels	0.6	6.2	6%
Gases		—	
Total		102.0	100%

LATIN AMERICA

3.0% of the world electric power industry
7.4% of the world's population

This is an enormous area, extending from the Rio Grande, on the border between the United States and Mexico, to Tierra del Fuego. It is perhaps best classified as a developing area, rather than developed or underdeveloped.

The structure of production in Latin America is unusual. Almost half of the electricity supply is generated in hydroelectric plants, only 54% in conventional thermal plants. As of 1964, there were no nuclear or geothermal plants in operation. Thermal electricity is generated mainly from oil fuels and natural gas; coal, domestic and imported, constitutes only 8% of the fuel consumed in the generation of electric power.

Electrical service in this area is limited. Outside of Chile, such networks as exist cover relatively small areas. Much of the region depends entirely upon local facilities, and it is estimated that less than half the people are supplied with electricity.

Per capita consumption in Latin America in 1964 was less than half that of the world as a whole—and twice that of Africa or Asia:

	kwh
industry	193
domestic sector	150
transport	7
total	350

The structure of the industry in Latin America is summarized statistically in Table 8.

TABLE 8.   LATIN AMERICA:
SUMMARY OF THE ELECTRICITY SITUATION IN 1964

	million KW	%
Capacity		
Gross total	27.4	100.0
Hydro	10.6	38.6
Conventional thermal	16.8	61.4
Nuclear	—	
Geothermal	—	

Production	twh	%
Gross total	98.2	100.0
Net total	97.0	98.8
Hydro	45.1	45.9
Conventional thermal	53.1	54.1
Nuclear	—	—
Geothermal	—	—
Net import	0.1	—

Supply	twh	%
gross	98.3	100.0
net	97.1	98.8
Consumption		
total	83.0	84.4
transport	1.6	1.6
domestic sector	35.5	36.1
industry	45.9	46.7
Lost (incl. some own use)	14.1	14.4

Fuels consumed by utilities	million MT	000 Tcals	
Coal	1.4	10.1	8%
Oil fuels	8.0	84.4	66%
Gases		32.7	26%
Total		127.2	100%

DEVELOPED WORLD

90% of the world electric power industry
29% of the world's population

The developed world, for the purposes of this study, includes North America, the European Communities, Other North Europe, East Europe and the Soviet Union, Oceania, Japan, and the Union of South Africa.

In the developed world, the electric power industry is structured in much the same fashion as it is in the world as a whole. Eighty-four percent of the industry is owned by utilities, 16% by industry and transport. Hydroelectricity represents one-quarter of the electricity generated, thermal electricity three-quarters. All of the world's nuclear power and all of its geothermal power are generated in the developed portions of the world.

Half of all electricity distributed in the developed world is consumed by industry, one-third is used in the domestic sector, and 2.6% is used in transport. For fuels, the developed world depends to some extent on fuel oils and gases, but coal and lignite represent 70% of all input.

Per capita consumption of electricity in the developed world in 1964:

	kwh
industry	1610
domestic sector	994
transport	79
total	2683

The structure of the electric power industry in the developed world is shown in Table 9.

TABLE 9. DEVELOPED WORLD:
SUMMARY OF THE ELECTRICITY SITUATION IN 1964

	million KW	%
Capacity		
Gross total	646.5	100.0
Hydro	172.4	26.7
Conventional thermal	470.1	72.7
Nuclear	3.5	0.5
Geothermal	0.5	0.1

	twh	%
Production		
Gross total	2816.5	100.0
Net total	(2760.7)	98.0
Hydro	685.7	24.3
Conventional thermal	2109.8	74.9
Nuclear	17.1	0.6
Geothermal	3.9	0.2
Net import	1.4	

	twh	%
Supply		
gross	2817.9	100.0
net	(2762.1)	98.0
Consumption		
total	2529.6	89.8
transport	74.7	2.6
domestic sector	937.4	33.3
industry	1517.5	53.9
Lost (incl. some own use)	232.5	8.2

	million MT	000 Tcals	
Fuels consumed by utilities			
Coal	447.7	2570.2	55%
Lignite	257.4	694.3	15%
Oil fuels	51.6	528.7	11%
Gases		908.4	19%
Other fuels		0.8	
Total		4702.4	100%

UNDERDEVELOPED WORLD

10% of the world electric power industry
71% of the world's population

For the purposes of this study, the underdeveloped world includes
Latin America, Other South Europe, Africa (except South Africa),
and Asia (except Japan). Some of the countries within these regions
might well be classified as developing, rather than as underdeveloped, and there are other obvious imperfections in the groupings,
but such shifts as might be made would have very little effect on
the totals and proportions shown.

In the underdeveloped world, the industry's structure is quite different from that prevailing in the developed world. Utilities control
a larger share of the total industry (87%), private producers only
13%. There is a relatively heavy dependence on hydro, 43% of all
capacity and 44% of all output originating in water power plants.
The remaining supply comes entirely from conventional thermal
plants, there being neither nuclear nor geothermal facilities in the
underdeveloped world.

Oil fuels play an unusual role in the underdeveloped world. They
are responsible for only one-third of all output, but they are the
single, or principal, power plant fuel in most underdeveloped countries.

The pattern of distribution varies only slightly from that of the developed world; industries consume 57% of the supply, the domestic sector 26%, and transportation 1.5%.

Per capita consumption of electricity in the underdeveloped world in 1964:

	kwh
industry	79
domestic sector	35
transport	2
total	116

A statistical summary of the electricity situation in the underdeveloped world is given in Table 10.

TABLE 10.   UNDERDEVELOPED WORLD:
SUMMARY OF THE ELECTRICITY SITUATION IN 1964

	million KW	%
Capacity		
Gross total	87.2	100.0
Hydro	37.3	42.8
Conventional thermal	49.9	57.2
Nuclear	—	
Geothermal	—	
	twh	**%**
Production		
Gross total	316.4	100.0
Net total	(310.9)	98.3
Hydro	139.5	44.1
Conventional thermal	176.9	55.9
Nuclear	—	
Geothermal	—	
Net import	−1.2	
	twh	**%**
Supply		
gross	315.2	100.0
net	(309.7)	98.2
Consumption		
total	265.6	84.2
transport	4.8	1.5
domestic sector	81.1	25.7
industry	179.7	57.0
Lost (incl. some own use)	44.1	14.0

	million MT	000 Tcals	
Fuels consumed by utilities			
Coal	63.6	308.1	54%
Lignite	12.8	40.2	7%
Oil fuels	17.2	180.0	32%
Gases		41.8	7%
Total		570.1	100%

FREE ENTERPRISE WORLD

77% of the world electric power industry
67% of the world's population

The free enterprise world, in this study, includes North America, Latin America (except Cuba), West Europe (except Yugoslavia), Oceania, Africa, the Middle East, and the non-Communist Far East.

The structure of the electric power industry in the free enterprise world is very similar to that of the world as a whole—especially in respect of installed capacity and production. The consumption pattern differs somewhat, however, with transportation using only 1.7% of the supply and industry 50%. The domestic sector's share of the total rises to 37% in this area.

Per capita consumption of electricity in 1964 in the free enterprise world:

	kwh
industry	567
domestic sector	420
transport	19
total	1006

The structure of the industry in the free enterprise world is shown in Table 11.

TABLE 11.   FREE ENTERPRISE WORLD:
SUMMARY OF THE ELECTRICITY SITUATION IN 1964

	million KW	%
Capacity		
Gross total	575.4	100.0
Hydro	176.8	30.7
Conventional thermal	394.9	68.6
Nuclear	3.2	0.6
Geothermal	0.5	0.1

TABLE 11 (Continued)

	twh	%
Production		
Gross total	2431.3	100.0
Net total	(2382.3)	98.0
Hydro	710.4	29.2
Conventional thermal	1701.9	70.0
Nuclear	15.1	0.6
Geothermal	3.9	0.2
Net import	−0.2	

	twh	%
Supply		
gross	2431.1	100.0
net	(2382.1)	98.0
Consumption		
total	2160.5	88.9
transport	41.4	1.7
domestic sector	901.6	37.1
industry	1217.5	50.1
Lost (incl. some own use)	221.6	9.1

	million MT	000 Tcals	
Fuels consumed by utilities			
Coal	378.4	2370.4	61%
Lignite	88.2	192.6	5%
Oil fuels	64.0	662.4	17%
Gases		677.1	17%
Other fuels		0.5	
Total		3903.0	100%

Communist World

23% of the world electric power industry
33% of the world's population

The Communist world, in this study, includes the Soviet Union; the East European countries of Albania, Bulgaria, Czechoslovakia, East Germany, Hungay, Poland, and Romania; the Asian Peoples Republics of Mainland China, North Korea, Mongolia, and North Vietnam; plus Cuba and Yugoslavia.

In the Communist world, the industry is structured quite differently from the pattern observed in both the free enterprise world and the world as a whole. Here, hydroelectric facilities provide only 16.4% of total production, conventional thermal facilities 83.3%. The share of nuclear facilities in the total is estimated at only 0.3%, and, as of 1964, there were no known geothermal plants in the Communist world.

Differences in the pattern of consumption between the Communist world and other areas are outstanding, with transportation taking nearly 5.5% of the electricity supply, the domestic sector only 17%. More than two-thirds of the supply goes to industry.

Per capita consumption of electricity in 1964 in the Communist world:

	kwh
industry	445
domestic sector	109
transport	35
total	589

A summary of the electric power situation in the Communist world as of 1964 is given in Table 12.

TABLE 12. COMMUNIST WORLD:
SUMMARY OF THE ELECTRICITY SITUATION IN 1964

	million KW	%
Capacity		
Gross total	158.3	100.0
Hydro	32.9	20.8
Conventional thermal	125.1	79.0
Nuclear	0.3	0.2
Geothermal	—	
	twh	%
Production		
Gross total	701.6	100.0
Net total	(689.3)	98.2
Hydro	114.8	16.4
Conventional thermal	584.8	83.3
Nuclear	2.0	0.3
Geothermal	—	
Net import	0.4	

TABLE 12 (Continued)

	twh	%
Supply		
gross	702.0	100.0
net	(689.7)	98.2
Consumption		
total	634.7	90.4
transport	38.1	5.4
domestic sector	116.9	16.7
industry	479.7	68.3
Lost (incl. some own use)	55.0	7.8

Fuels consumed by utilities	million MT	000 Tcals	
Coal	132.9	507.9	37%
Lignite	182.0	541.9	40%
Oil fuels	4.8	46.3	3%
Gases		273.1	20%
Other fuels		0.3	
Total		1369.5	100%

Chapter 3
Electricity Consumption

Most of the world's electricity is consumed in three relatively developed portions of the world: North America takes 40% of the total; West Europe uses 24%, and 20% is used in East Europe. Asia, with its tremendous population, gets only 10%, and Latin America, Africa, and Oceania together, only 6%.

TABLE 13.
ELECTRICITY CONSUMPTION, 1964,
by Region, Economic Level, and Politico-economic System

Area	Quantity Consumed (twh)	Share of World Total (%)
North America	1120	40.1
West Europe	671	24.0
East Europe/USSR	559	20.0
Asia	279	10.0
Latin America	83	3.0
Africa	47	1.6
Oceania	36	1.3
World	2795	100.0
Developed World	2530	90.5
Underdeveloped World	265	9.5
Free Enterprise World	2160	77.3
Communist World	635	22.7

The developed countries, as a group, consume 90% of the world's electricity, the underdeveloped countries less than 10%. On a politico-economic basis, the free enterprise world gets 77% of the total supply, the Communist world 23%.

The distribution of electricity consumption in 1964 is shown in Table 13 and Figure 3.

31

DISTRIBUTION OF
ELECTRICITY CONSUMPTION - 1964

Percentages of World Total

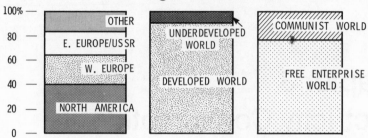

In total consumption of electricity, these countries lead the world:

Country	twh consumed
United States	999.1
USSR	426.4
Japan	158.0
United Kingdom	157.0
West Germany	142.4
Canada	121.2
France	88.4
Italy	66.9
East Germany	44.4
Sweden	39.4

Geographic variations in total consumption of electricity are interesting, but they tend to obscure something of even greater interest—the availability of electricity to people within different areas, which is indicated by electricity consumption per capita.

TABLE 14.
PER CAPITA CONSUMPTION OF ELECTRICITY, 1964,
by Region, Economic Level, and Politico-economic System

Area	kwh
North America	5299
Oceania	2088
West Europe	1975
East Europe/USSR	1699
Latin America	350

Area	kwh
Asia	156
Africa	153
World	867
Developed World	2683
Underdeveloped World	116
Free Enterprise World	1006
Communist World	589

Figure 4 is a world map showing variations from country to country in per capita levels of electricity consumption. A relationship between electricity consumption per capita and levels of economic activity will be noted at once: the heavily shaded areas in the map are the productive and relatively prosperous portions of the world, while the unshaded areas are those which have developed least economically. In between are countries that might be classified as developing. Detailed data on total and per capita use in various countries of the world in the year 1964 are given in Appendix Table 1.

Particularly worth noting are the sub-regional variations within West Europe, and the levels of consumption in Japan and South Africa in comparison with those of other countries in Asia and Africa.

The full range of consumption is somewhat wider than the map suggests. It extends from 10,433 kilowatt hours per capita, in Norway, to only a few kilowatt hours per capita in the least developed countries of Africa and Asia.

These six countries have the highest levels of electricity consumption per capita.

Country	kwh
Norway	10,433
Canada	6,290
New Caledonia	5,547
Luxembourg	5,246
United States	5,200
Sweden	5,141

Levels of consumption per capita are influenced by the availability of electric service, as well as by other factors. Figure 5 shows that service is almost universally available in countries previously identified as having very high levels of consumption, but available to a relatively small fraction of the population in most areas characterized by very low levels of consumption.

There are significant differences in the structure of electricity demands from one region to another. Patterns of consumption in the several regions are compared statistically in Table 15.

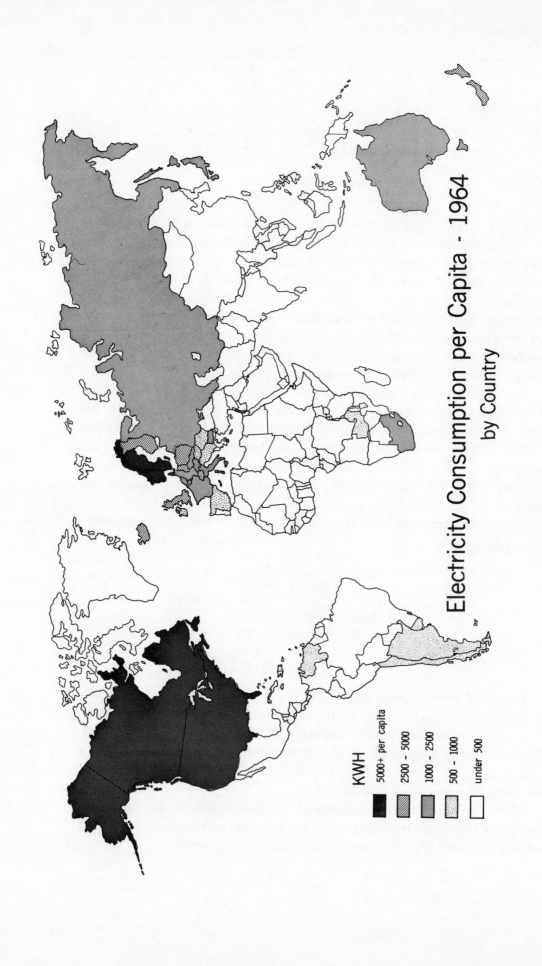

Electricity Consumption per Capita - 1964
by Country

KWH

5000+ per capita
2500 - 5000
1000 - 2500
500 - 1000
under 500

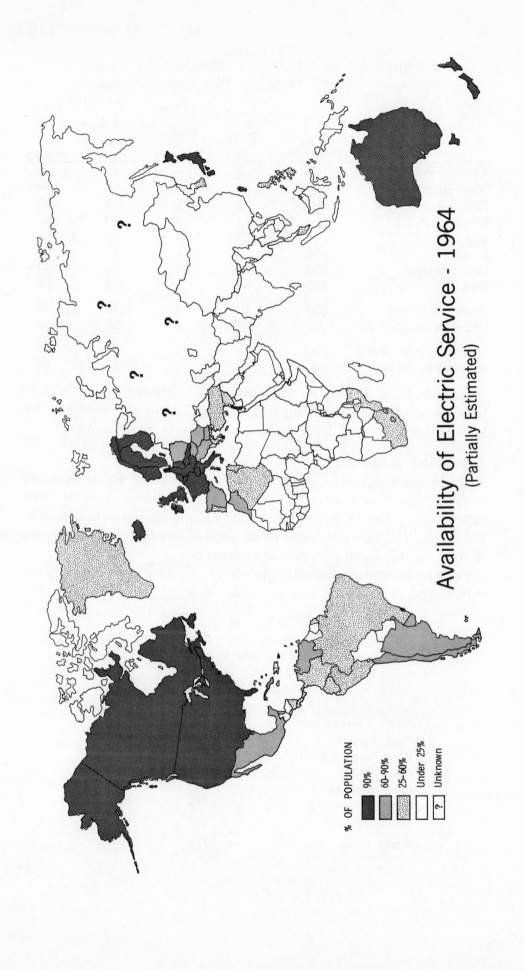

Availability of Electric Service - 1964
(Partially Estimated)

% OF POPULATION

90%
60-90%
25-60%
Under 25%
? Unknown

TABLE 15.
STRUCTURE OF ELECTRICITY CONSUMPTION, 1964,
by Region, Economic Level, and Politico-economic System

| | | | Percentages | | |
| | | | | Net Consumption | |
Area	Gross Consumption	Own Use + Loss	Transport	Domestic Sector	Industry
North America	100	9	—	43	48
West Europe	100	14	3	31	52
East Europe/USSR	100	9	6	17	68
Africa	100	13	4	19	64
Asia	100	13	3	26	58
Oceania	100	17	2	45	36
Latin America	100	15	2	36	47
World	100	10	3	33	54
Developed World	100	10	3	33	54
Underdeveloped World	100	15	2	26	57
Free Enterprise World	100	11	2	37	50
Communist World	100	10	5	17	68

Some light is thrown on the reasons for differences in the distribution of electricity among different sectors of the economy by examination of actual levels of consumption in each sector.

Domestic Sector

World consumption of electricity in the domestic sector amounts to more than 1,000 terawatt hours annually. North America uses 52% of this, West Europe 24%, East Europe and the USSR 10%. This leaves 150 terawatt hours to be divided among all the countries of Asia, Africa, Latin America and Oceania.

The distribution of domestic electricity among the various regions is indicated in Figure 6, and in Table 16.

TABLE 16.
ELECTRICITY CONSUMPTION IN THE DOMESTIC SECTOR, 1964,
by Region, Economic Level, and Politico-economic System

Area	Quantity Consumed (twh)	Share of World Total (%)
North America	526	51.6
West Europe	241	23.7
East Europe/USSR	103	10.1
Asia	84	8.2
Latin America	36	3.5
Oceania	19	1.9
Africa	10	1.0
World	1019	100.0

Area	Quantity Consumed (twh)	Share of World Total (%)
Developed World	938	92.1
Underdeveloped World	81	7.9
Free Enterprise World	902	88.5
Communist World	117	11.5

DISTRIBUTION OF ELECTRICITY CONSUMPTION IN THE DOMESTIC SECTOR - 1964

Percentages of World Total

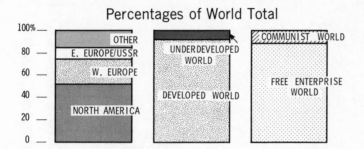

From the point of view of economic development, the developed countries together, with 29% of the world's population, consume 92% of the world's electricity, leaving only 8% to be divided among a total of 2.3 billion people—71% of the world's total population.

On a politico-economic basis, the free enterprise world is heavily favored, consuming eight times as much electricity in the domestic sector as does the Communist world.

Variations from one region to another in the per capita use of electricity in the domestic sector are shown in Figure 7 and in Table 17. The range of consumption extends from nearly 2,500 kwh in North America to an average of only 34 kwh per capita in Africa, with other regions falling between these two extremes.

TABLE 17.
PER CAPITA CONSUMPTION OF ELECTRICITY IN THE DOMESTIC SECTOR, 1964,
by Region, Economic Level, and Politico-economic System

Area	kwh
North America	2487
Oceania	1125
West Europe	710
East Europe/USSR	312

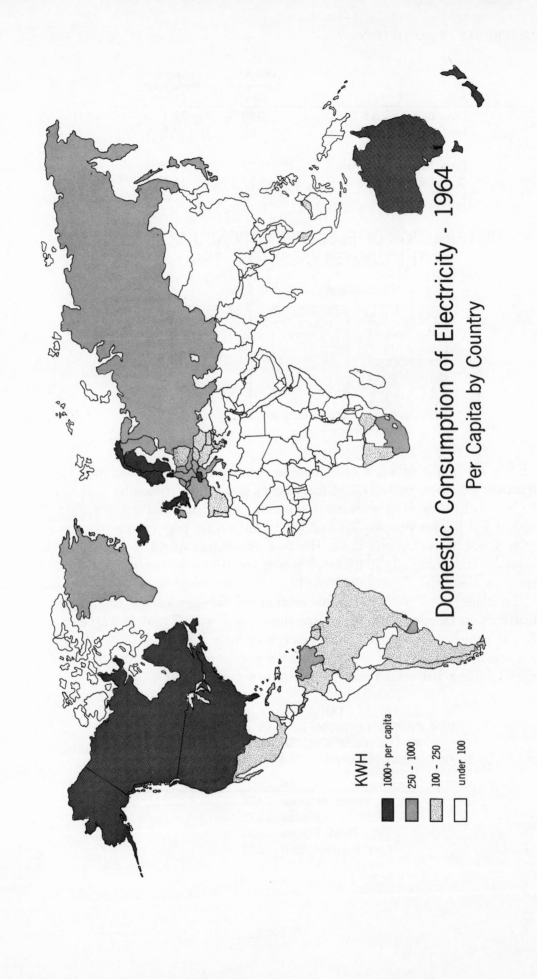

Domestic Consumption of Electricity - 1964

Per Capita by Country

KWH

1000+ per capita

250 - 1000

100 - 250

under 100

TABLE 17 (Continued)

Area	kwh
Latin America	150
Asia	47
Africa	34
World	316
Developed World	994
Underdeveloped World	35
Free Enterprise World	420
Communist World	109

The range of per capita consumption among countries extends from 3,500 kilowatt hours in Norway down to a single kilowatt hour in Nepal. The highest levels of consumption are in these countries:

Country	kwh
Norway	3534
USA	2526
Bermuda	2417
New Zealand	2244
Canada	2097
Iceland	1725
Sweden	1624
Switzerland	1574
UK	1491

The patterns brought out in the table and in the map suggest again a relationship between levels of economic activity and levels of electricity use in the domestic sector. This relationship is explored a little further in Table 18, which makes a direct comparison of gross domestic product per capita and electricity consumption per capita.

TABLE 18.
CONSUMPTION OF ELECTRICITY IN THE DOMESTIC SECTOR
Related to Gross Domestic Product in 93 Countries, 1964

Reporting Countries (ranked by GDP)	Gross Domestic Product ($ US per capita)	Electricity Consumed (kwh per capita)
United States	3014	2526
Sweden	2032	1624
Canada	2002	2097
Switzerland	2002	1578
Iceland	1857	1725
Denmark	1848	1064
Australia	1774	1192
New Zealand	1774	2244
Luxembourg	1735	536
Norway	1546	3534

TABLE 18 (Continued)

Reporting Countries (ranked by GDP)	Gross Domestic Product ($ US per capita)	Electricity Consumed (kwh per capita)
Germany, West	1541	719
France	1534	494
United Kingdom	1480	1491
Belgium	1458	459
Finland	1446	588
Netherlands	1264	741
Israel	1053	763
Austria	1031	724
Puerto Rico	1005	833
Italy	916	375
Venezuela	887	269
Ireland	779	641
Japan	736	568
Argentina	703	(241)
Trinidad and Tobago	660	149
Libya	600	77
Uruguay	560	300
Greece	532	183
Spain	528	169
South Africa	526	(295)
Chile	513	158
Singapore	504	250
Cyprus	501	320
Panama	448	190
Jamaica	437	172
Mexico	424	130
Malta	380	185
Costa Rica	366	282
Barbados	357	87
Gabon	349	35
Portugal	341	126
Nicaragua	299	61
Guatemala	288	37
Guyana	281	46
Dominican Republic	272	67
Malaysia, Western	264	103
Colombia	263	(138)
Liberia	251	48
El Salvador	246	66
Turkey	245	30
Sabah	235	39
Peru	233	57

TABLE 18 (Continued)

Reporting Countries (ranked by GDP)	Gross Domestic Product ($ US per capita)	Electricity Consumed (kwh per capita)
Ghana	232	23
Philippines	228	51
Iran	223	42
Rhodesia	223	204
Mauritius	220	68
Algeria	206	35
Ivory Coast	206	22
Jordan	198	45
Honduras	194	27
Sarawak	194	34
Brazil	193	140
Ecuador	192	63
Tunisia	192	27
Paraguay	190	22
China (Taiwan)	189	97
Zambia	181	70
Morocco	175	31
Senegal	168	19
Bolivia	141	45
Ceylon	137	18
Sierra Leone	133	19
Central African Republic	120	8
Cambodia	115	(9)
Thailand	112	16
Sudan	96	8
Vietnam, South	95	25
India	95	12
Pakistan	95	11
Korea, South	89	19
Togo	88	4
Kenya	86	28
Haiti	84	14
Gambia	77	12
Niger	76	(2)
Uganda	74	10
Congo (Kinshasa)	72	7
Tanzania (excluding Zanzibar)	67	5
Nepal	63	1
Nigeria	62	5
Burma	60	(7)
Ethiopia	46	5

Source: UN. **Mo. bull. of stats.** (for gross domestic product.)

The relationships brought out in the table should be and are less than perfect, for levels of electricity consumption in the domestic sector, though influenced by levels of living, are influenced too by climate, the availability and cost of electricity, and the availability and cost of alternate sources of energy.

The influences of cost and availability on consumption levels in the domestic sector are best understood by reference to levels of consumption for *residential* purposes, for these reflect direct encounters between consumers and the variables that determine quantity of use. The individual purchaser of residential electricity is directly and personally concerned with the availability and cost of electricity, and with the cost of competitive service, if any, as well as with his ability to pay for the service he needs.

Table 19 shows the relationship in a number of countries between domestic and residential consumption per capita.

TABLE 19.
RESIDENTIAL CONSUMPTION OF ELECTRICITY
Related to Consumption of Electricity in the Domestic Sector
in 53 Countries, 1964

Reporting Countries (ranked by total kwh)	Quantity Consumed Per Capita	
	Domestic Sector Total (kwh)	Residential Only (kwh)
Norway	3534	2962
United States	2526	1237
New Zealand	2244	1813
Canada	2097	1414
Sweden	1725	1116
Iceland	1624	730
Switzerland	1578	947
United Kingdom	1491	966
Australia	1192	862
Denmark	1064	438
Netherlands	741	366
Austria	724	361
Germany, West	719	377
Ireland	641	369
Germany, East	589	283
Finland	588	236
Japan	568	204
Luxembourg	536	197
France	494	234
Belgium	459	268

Reporting Countries (ranked by total kwh)	Quantity Consumed Per Capita	
	Domestic Sector Total (kwh)	Residential Only (kwh)
Italy	375	193
Hong Kong	365	116
Czechoslovakia	343	154
Cyprus	320	103
Costa Rica	282	221
Singapore	250	93
Hungary	230	98
Yugoslavia	198	136
Panama	190	74
Greece	183	116
Poland	183	76
Spain	169	93
Brunei	134	123
Mexico	130	44
Portugal	126	74
Romania	118	45
Malaya	103	21
China (Taiwan)	97	65
Dominican Republic	67	38
El Salvador	66	31
Nicaragua	61	31
Sabah	39	23
Guatemala	37	21
Algeria	35	13
Sarawak	34	17
Honduras	27	12
Vietnam, South	25	13
Korea, South	19	7
Ceylon	18	8
Thailand	16	9
India	12	5
Pakistan	11	3
Nigeria	5	5

Transportation

Electricity consumption in transportation amounts to 80 twh per annum. Of this total, nearly half is used in East Europe and the Soviet Union, the remainder mainly in Western Europe. Asia takes 11% of the supply, and North America only 6%. Africa, Oceania, and Latin America together consume only 6% of the world total.

Ninety-four percent of the electricity consumed in transportation is used in the developed world, only 6% in the underdeveloped world. The Communist world gets 48%, the free enterprise world 52%.

Of particular interest here are the very large quantities of electricity used for transportation in the Soviet Union and Japan—33 twh and 7 twh respectively, together constituting more than half of all the electricity that goes into transportation annually.

The distribution of electricity consumption in transportation among different regions is shown in Table 20, and in Figure 8.

TABLE 20.
ELECTRICITY CONSUMPTION IN TRANSPORTATION, 1964,
by Region, Economic Level, and Politico-economic System

Area	Quantity Consumed (twh)	Share of World Total (%)
East Europe/USSR	37.7	47.4
West Europe	23.6	29.7
Asia	8.7	10.9
North America	5.0	6.3
Africa	2.1	2.7
Latin America	1.6	2.0
Oceania	0.8	1.0
World	79.5	100.0
Developed World	74.7	94.0
Underdeveloped World	4.8	6.0
Free Enterprise World	41.4	52.1
Communist World	38.1	47.9

DISTRIBUTION OF ELECTRICITY CONSUMPTION
IN TRANSPORTATION - 1964

Percentages of World Total

On a per capita basis, the pattern of electricity use in transportation is quite different. Highest levels are attained in four European countries with great water power resources — Switzerland, Sweden, Austria, and Norway; in the Soviet Union, with its extensive network of electrified railways; and in Czechoslovakia and South Africa. Each of these countries consumes more than 100 kwh per capita in transportation, most of this in rail transportation. Details on these and other countries are given in Table 21.

TABLE 21.
PER CAPITA CONSUMPTION OF ELECTRICITY IN TRANSPORTATION
in 43 Countries, 1964

Reporting Countries	kwh
Switzerland	281
Sweden	230
Austria	156
USSR	145
Norway	117
Czechoslovakia	111
South Africa	107
Luxembourg	97
France	95
West Germany	90
Belgium	74
Japan	74
Australia	66
Italy	66
Netherlands	61
East Germany	57
United Kingdom	44
Poland	42
Hungary	41
Bulgaria	30
Spain	30
Cuba	27
United States	26
Denmark	22
Portugal	19
Argentina	18
New Zealand	17
Chile	15
Romania	14
Uruguay	11

TABLE 21 (Continued)

Reporting Countries	kwh
Brazil	10
Yugoslavia	10
Finland	7
Morocco	5
Hong Kong	5
Greece	5
United Arab Republic	4
Algeria	3
Congo (Kinshasa)	3
India	3
Tunisia	2
Turkey	2
Peru	1

Levels of electricity use in railway operations are determined in part by degree of railway electrification and in part by volume of traffic handled. The high level of per capita consumption in Switzerland is attributable to a combination of dense traffic and fully electrified railways. There is a high level of electrification also in Morocco, but traffic there is light, and electricity consumption per capita low. Most of the countries characterized by relatively high levels of railway electrification are also countries in which rail traffic is relatively heavy. Details on electricity consumption by railways are shown in relation to levels of railway electrification in Table 22.

TABLE 22.
RAILWAY CONSUMPTION OF ELECTRICITY
Related to Electrification of Rail Traffic in Selected Countries, 1964

Reporting Countries	Railways	Electricity Consumed* (kwh per capita)	Electrification Level (percent of all traffic)
Switzerland	Swiss Federal Railways	227	100
Sweden	Swedish State Railways	162	93
Austria	Austrian Federal Railways	103	69
USSR	(national railway system)	102†	37
South Africa	South African Railways	81	36
Luxembourg	Luxembourg National Railways	79	50
France	French National Railways	75	66
Czechoslovakia	Czechoslovak State Railways	69	40

Reporting Countries	Railways	Electricity Consumed* (kwh per capita)	Electrification Level (percent of all traffic)
Norway	Norwegian State Railways (1963)	62	64
Belgium	Belgian National Railway Company	53	49
Netherlands	Netherlands Railways	53	73
Italy	Italian State Railways	52	88
West Germany	German Federal Railway	51	45
Japan	Japanese National Railways	34	54
Poland	Polish State Railways	30	22
UK	British Railways	27	22
East Germany	German State Railway	26	12
Hungary	Hungarian State Railways (1965)	21	16
Spain	Spanish National Railway System	17	36
Denmark	Danish State Railways	12	9
Portugal	Portuguese Railway Company	9	30
USA	Class I Railways	8	2
Yugoslavia	Yugoslav Railways	5	6
Morocco	Moroccan, E. Moroccan and Tangiers-Fez Railways	4	69
Algeria	Algerian National Railway Company	3	29
Turkey	Turkish State Railways	1	3

*In most cases, for traction only.
†Estimated (at 70% of total use in transportation).
Source: International Union of Railways. **International railway statistics.**

Little is known about the use of electricity in pipelines, but the magnitude of this form of use is suggested by the volume of TVA sales to a single gas transmission system in fiscal 1965—821 million kwh (*Annual Report of the Tennessee Valley Authority, 1965*). Aggregate use of electricity for pipeline operations in the United States is certainly in the billions of kwh.

Industry

Fifty-four percent of the world's electric power, or 1,700 twh, is used in industry. Of this, nearly 150 twh are used in mining, roughly 1,550 twh in manufacturing.

The geographic pattern of industrial use corresponds more or less with the pattern of total electricity use.

TABLE 23.

ELECTRICITY CONSUMPTION IN INDUSTRY, 1964,

by Region, Economic Level, and Politico-economic System

Area	Quantity Consumed (twh)	Share of World Total (%)
North America	590	34.8
East Europe/USSR	418	24.6
West Europe	406	23.9
Asia	187	11.0
Latin America	46	2.7
Africa	34	2.0
Oceania	16	1.0
World	1697	100.0
Developed World	1517	89.4
Underdeveloped World	180	10.6
Free Enterprise World	1217	71.7
Communist World	480	28.3

More than a third of the total is consumed in North America, one-quarter in Western Europe, and one-quarter in East Europe and the Soviet Union. The developed countries, together, take 89% of the total, leaving only 11% for the whole underdeveloped world. The free enterprise world gets 72% of the total, the Communist world 28%.

These percentage shares in the world's consumption of electricity for industrial purposes are shown graphically in Figure 9.

DISTRIBUTION OF ELECTRICITY CONSUMPTION IN INDUSTRY - 1964

Percentages of World Total

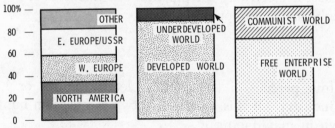

Three-quarters of the electricity used by industry is consumed in these ten countries:

Country	twh
USA	508.7
USSR	317.8
Japan	95.8
West Germany	95.1
Canada	80.8
UK	73.8
France	59.8
Italy	44.4
East Germany	33.4
Poland	25.4

On a per capita basis, industrial requirements of electricity range from an average of nearly 2,800 kwh in North America downward through somewhat less than half as much in Europe and the Soviet Union, a third as much in Japan and Oceania, and not much more than 100 kwh per capita in Asia and Africa. In the underdeveloped countries as a group, consumption averages only 79 kwh per capita annually.

TABLE 24.
PER CAPITA CONSUMPTION OF ELECTRICITY IN INDUSTRY, 1964,
by Region, Economic Level, and Politico-economic System

Area	kwh
North America	2788
East Europe/USSR	1272
West Europe	1196
Oceania	918
Latin America	193
Africa	112
Asia	105
World	526
Developed World	1609
Underdeveloped World	79
Free Enterprise World	567
Communist World	445

Variations in consumption per capita from one country to another are shown in Figure 10, opposite. Again, the range from country to country is wider than it is from region to region. Norway and New Caledonia use more than 5,000 kwh per capita in industry—Luxembourg, the Netherlands Antilles, and Canada more than 4,000 kwh per capita. At the other end of the scale are many countries whose

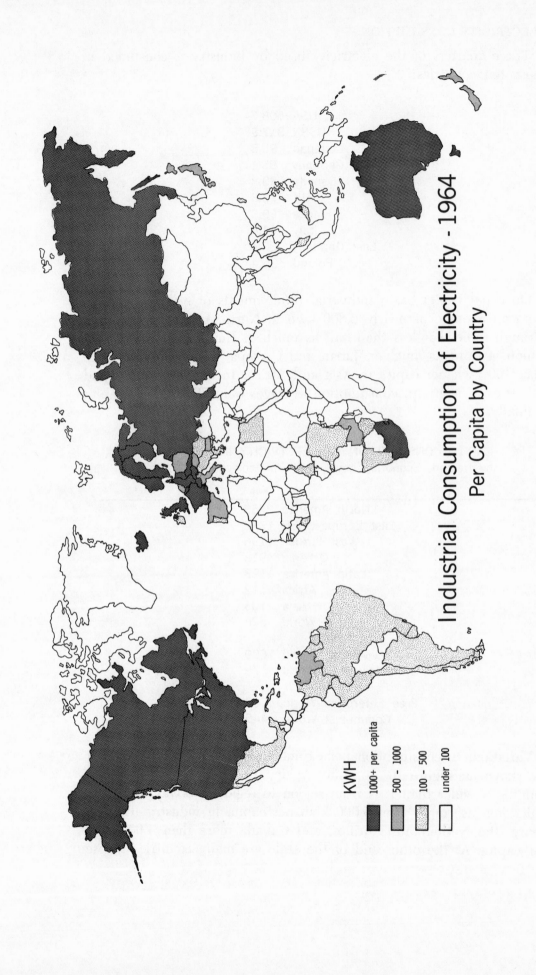

Industrial Consumption of Electricity - 1964

Per Capita by Country

KWH

1000+ per capita

500 - 1000

100 - 500

under 100

industrial use averages less than 20 kwh per capita, and some, like Cambodia, Sudan, and Malawi, that consume 5 kwh per capita or less.

Variations here, as in the domestic sector, are related to levels of economic activity. The relationship — and deviations therefrom — is shown in Table 25, which relates estimated net value of industrial production to electricity consumption in industry in the year 1964.

TABLE 25.
INDUSTRIAL CONSUMPTION OF ELECTRICITY
Related to Industrial Production in 64 Countries, 1964

Reporting Countries (ranked by IP)	Industrial Production ($US per capita)	Electricity Consumed (kwh per capita)
United States	1021	2648
Luxembourg	764	4613
Germany, West	693	1632
Canada	676	4193
France	609	1236
United Kingdom	604	1360
Denmark	573	431
Netherlands	509	875
Belgium	506	1388
Norway	462	6782
Austria	426	1177
Finland	418	2017
Italy	330	868
Trinidad and Tobago	301*	629
Venezuela	298*	528
Israel	293	488
Puerto Rico	261	341
Argentina	253	(271)
Ireland	248	296
South Africa	203	1175
Surinam	175*	207
Spain	158	518
Portugal	147	302
Mexico	137	203
Uruguay	134*	206
Jamaica	115	209
Iraq	114*	92
Greece	112	196
Zambia	108	629
Cyprus	105	126

TABLE 25 (Continued)

Reporting Countries (ranked by IP)	Industrial Production ($US per capita)	Electricity Consumed (kwh per capita)
Malta and Gozo	102	160
Panama	87	98
Guyana	84	206
Liberia	75	127
Iran	64*	38
Peru	63	216
Rhodesia	58	247
Costa Rica	51*	94
Nicaragua	51	83
Guatemala	46	35
Malaysia, Western	46*	106
China (Taiwan)	45	335
El Salvador	44*	(51)
Ecuador	42	36
Mauritius	42	36
Turkey	40	92
Morocco	40	51
Bolivia	37	76
Tunisia	33	61
Paraguay	32*	30
Barbados	32	116
Honduras	29*	23
Syria	24	54
Jordan	18*	18
Thailand	15*	14
Cambodia	13*	(1)
Vietnam, South	12	7
Burma	11*	(12)
Kenya	9	19
Uganda	8	30
Togo	8*	11
Sudan	6*	2
Tanzania (excluding Zanzibar)	5	11
Malawi	3*	5

*Partially estimated.

Source: Calculated from data on gross domestic product and its origin as
reported in UN. **Yearbook of national accounts statistics.**

Wide deviations from the "normal" relationship can be attributed mainly to differences in the structure of industry. The relatively low levels of industrial production in Norway, Luxembourg, and Canada in respect of their levels of electricity consumption are attributable to the heavy emphasis placed on metals and chemical industries. The high return per unit of energy invested in Denmark and Puerto Rico, in contrast, reflects the emphasis placed in these areas on light industry.

Since the particular uses of electricity in industry have a considerable bearing on the relationship between energy utilization and industrial product, the distribution of electricity among various branches of industry — shown in Table 26 and Figure 11 — may be of special interest. The distribution shown was estimated on the basis of total electricity utilization in industry, and detailed end-use data on its utilization in 65 countries, of which 25 are developed and 40 underdeveloped. It has not been possible to obtain such data for the Soviet Union, Australia, or New Zealand, among the developed countries, or for any of the countries of Communist Asia. This sample represents 76% of the electricity used in industry in the developed

THE USES OF ELECTRICITY IN INDUSTRY - 1964
Percentage Distribution of 1697 Terawatt Hours

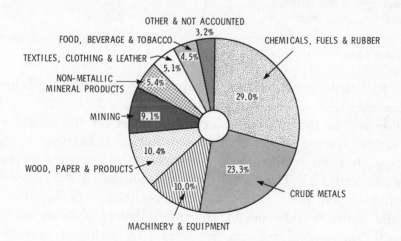

countries, and 42% of the electricity used in industry in the under-developed countries.

One hundred and fifty-four twh are consumed in the production of minerals, nearly 500 twh in the production of chemicals, fuels, and related products. Crude metals take nearly 400 twh per annum. And then there is a sharp drop-off to the less energy-intensive industries, from machinery and equipment down to the food, beverage, and tobacco industries.

TABLE 26.
INDUSTRIAL CONSUMPTION OF ELECTRICITY,
BY INDUSTRY GROUP, 1964

Industry Group	Reported by 65 Countries (twh)	Shares in Industry Consumption (%)	Actual Total Consumption and Estimated Shares (twh)
All Industry	1227	100.0	1697
Mining	106	9.1	154
Manufacturing	1121	90.9	1543
Chemicals, fuels, and rubber	363	29.0	493
Crude metals	289	23.3	396
Machinery and equipment	127	10.0	170
Wood, paper, and products	130	10.4	176
Non-metallic mineral products	63	5.4	91
Textiles, clothing, and leather	58	5.1	86
Food, beverage, and tobacco	54	4.5	76
Other and not accounted	37	3.2	55

For details and sources of data see Table 2 of the Appendix.

There is a striking contrast in the quantities of energy consumed in various subdivisions of industry in the developed countries on the one hand, and in the underdeveloped countries on the other.

Another interesting aspect of this distribution is brought to light by relating electricity utilization in subdivisions of industry to population, as in Table 27. The table's first column shows the quantities of electricity used per capita in each subdivision of industry to supply the entire world's needs, at current levels of economic development. The second column indicates how much is needed to support the levels of production that obtain only in the developed countries, and column three shows how little is now used in the underdeveloped countries of the world. The differences are shown graphically in Figure 12.

TABLE 27.
PER CAPITA CONSUMPTION OF ELECTRICITY IN INDUSTRY, BY INDUSTRY GROUP, 1964

Industry Group	World (kwh)	Developed World (kwh)	Underdeveloped World (kwh)
Chemicals and fuels	152	487	14
Crude metals	123	385	15
Machinery and equipment	53	172	3
Wood, paper, and products	55	175	5
Non-metallic minerals	28	81	7
Textiles, clothing, and leather	27	69	9
Food, beverage, and tobacco	23	69	5
Other and not accounted	17	42	7
All manufacturing	478	1480	65
Mining	48	129	14
All Industry	526	1609	79

ELECTRICITY USE PER CAPITA
TOTAL POPULATION - 1964
Divisions of Industry at Different Levels
of Economic Development

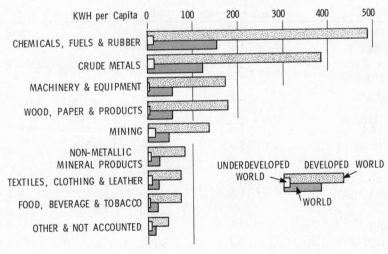

Electricity Prices

An attempt has been made, in connection with individual country surveys, to indicate the average prices paid for electricity sold—to households, to industrial consumers, to railways, and to all users. Prices have been calculated, in most cases, on the basis of average revenues received from sales to the groups indicated. The one exception here is in the prices indicated for electricity used for lighting. These have been taken from ILO surveys of average retail prices for certain commodities purchased for household consumption.

It is obvious that these figures do not tell the whole story, because average prices are made up, in most cases, of a composite of relatively high prices to small-scale consumers and relatively low prices to those who consume large quantities of electricity. Such differences are especially significant in the industrial sector, where certain very large-scale consumers, such as electrochemical and electrometallurgical plants, normally pay only a fraction as much for their power as do small-scale industries. The data presented here should be viewed with these reservations in mind.

Average costs of electricity consumed in households range from a minimum of 0.7¢ or so, in Norway, to more than 10¢ per kwh in some of the less developed countries.

TABLE 28.
AVERAGE COST OF RESIDENTIAL ELECTRICITY
in Selected Countries, 1964*

Country	U.S.¢ per kwh	Country	U.S.¢ per kwh
Norway (1962)	0.7	Afghanistan	2.3
Bolivia	1.2	Zambia	2.3
New Zealand	1.3	Brazil	2.3
Sweden	1.3		
Uruguay	1.5	USA	2.4
		Ecuador	2.5
Kuwait	1.7	Rhodesia	2.5
Philippines	1.7	Faeroe Islands	2.5
Canada	1.8	Puerto Rico	2.6
China (Taiwan)	1.9		
Costa Rica	1.9	Netherlands	2.6
		Iceland (1965)	2.8
Spain	2.0	Chile	2.9
United Kingdom	2.1	South Korea	3.0
South Africa (1961)	2.1	Ceylon	3.1
Australia	2.2		
Colombia	2.2	El Salvador	3.1
		Fiji Islands	3.1
Denmark	2.2	Romania	3.3
Peru (one company)	2.2	Japan	3.4

Country	U.S.¢ per kwh	Country	U.S.¢ per kwh
Mexico	3.4	Mauritius	4.6
		Gambia	4.6
Turkey (1962)	3.5		
Western Samoa	3.5	Belgium	4.7
UAR (1964/65)	3.6	Malaya	4.7
West Germany	3.6	Panama	4.9
India	3.6	Nepal	4.9
		Singapore	4.9
Ghana (1962/63)	3.7		
Finland (1962)	3.7	Luxembourg	4.9
Cyprus	3.7	Thailand	5.3
Jamaica	3.7	Sabah	5.8
Italy	3.7	Honduras	5.9
		Malagasy (1961)	6.0
Brunei	4.2		
Dominican Republic	4.3	Nicaragua	6.3
France	4.3	Venezuela	6.3
Trinidad	4.3	Paraguay	6.6
Uganda	4.4	Libya (1961)	7.0
		Sarawak	7.9
USSR	4.4		
Nigeria	4.4	Burma	12.2
Guatemala	4.5	Laos	13.2

*Except as indicated.

TABLE 29.
AVERAGE COST OF ELECTRICITY FOR RESIDENTIAL LIGHTING
in Selected Countries, 1966

Country	U.S.¢ per kwh	Country	U.S.¢ per kwh
Kuwait	0.6	Zambia	2.3
Colombia	0.7	Austria	2.4
New Zealand	0.9	China (Taiwan.)	2.4
Uruguay	1.2	India	2.5
Costa Rica	1.8	Turkey	2.5
Canada	2.0	Japan	2.8
Kenya	2.0	Guatemala	3.0
Denmark	2.0	Iceland	3.0
Sweden	2.1	Israel	3.0
Australia	2.2	Peru	3.2
Cyprus	2.2	Philippines	3.3
Ghana	2.3	Bulgaria	3.4
Ireland	2.3	Finland	3.4
Rhodesia	2.3	Iraq	3.4
United Kingdom	2.3	Jamaica	3.5

TABLE 29 (Continued)

Country	U.S.¢ per kwh	Country	U.S.¢ per kwh
Thailand	3.6	Cuba	7.0
Brazil	3.9	Malta	7.0
Congo (Kinshasa)	3.9	Virgin Islands	7.0
Singapore	3.9	Windward Islands	7.0
USA (Chicago)	4.0	Paraguay	7.1
Netherlands	4.1	St. Pierre and Miquelon	7.3
Syria	4.1	Leeward Islands	7.6
Angola	4.2	Mozambique	7.7
Ceylon	4.2	Jordan	7.8
Mexico	4.2	Belgium	7.9
Venezuela	4.2	Morocco	7.9
Vietnam, South	4.5	Panama	8.0
Spain	4.6	France	8.1
Pakistan	4.6	Brunei	8.2
Barbados	4.7	Libya	8.4
Bermuda	4.7	Hungary	8.5
Nigeria	4.7	Burma	8.7
Hong Kong	4.8	Guyana	8.8
Guam	5.0	Lebanon	8.8
Puerto Rico	5.0	Malaya	8.8
Argentina	5.3	Trinidad	8.8
Nicaragua	5.5	New Caledonia	8.9
Aden	5.6	Upper Volta	8.9
Iran	5.6	Chad	9.3
Sudan	5.7	Martinique	9.5
Falkland Islands	5.8	Czechoslovakia	9.7
Netherlands Antilles	5.8	Sarawak	9.8
Bahama Islands	5.9	British Honduras	9.8
South Korea	5.9	Ivory Coast	10.1
Rwanda	6.0	Malagasy	10.5
Chile	6.0	Tanzania	11.2
Dominican Republic	6.0	Guadeloupe	11.3
Ethiopia	6.0	Sabah	11.4
Honduras	6.0	Gibraltar	11.7
Greece	6.1	Haiti	12.0
Fiji Islands	6.3	Central African Republic	12.2
Italy	6.4	Reunion	12.2
West Germany	6.5	French Polynesia	12.3
U.A.R.	6.9	Sierra Leone	12.6
Portugal	6.9	Togo	12.9

Country	U.S.¢ per kwh	Country	U.S.¢ per kwh
Dahomey	13.4	Gabon	15.4
Yugoslavia	13.6	Mauritania	15.4
Cameroon	13.8	Senegal	15.4
Congo (Brazzaville)	13.8	Mali	16.2
Mauritius	14.3	Niger	21.1
		Poland	22.5

It is difficult to generalize concerning the geographic pattern of prices, except to note that average prices of more than 5¢ per kwh are confined largely to the least developed countries of the world. It must be observed at the same time, however, that there are some underdeveloped countries in which the cost of residential power is very low—in the range of 1¢ to 3¢ per kwh, and there are not, in fact, many developed countries which can boast such low rates. In most of the developed countries, the average costs of residential electricity range from 3¢ to 5¢ per kwh.

The cost of electricity to railways ranges from a minimum of roughly 0.6¢ per kwh, in Norway, to 2.1¢ per kwh, in Czechoslovakia. Lowest prices obtain in certain countries whose principal energy resource is water power—Norway, Sweden, Portugal, and Switzerland —while at the bottom of the list, with relatively high power prices, are countries with meager water power resources—Czechoslovakia, the Netherlands, Tunisia, Belgium, and Luxembourg.

TABLE 30.
COST OF ELECTRICITY USED IN RAIL TRANSPORT
in Selected Countries, 1964*

Country	U.S.¢ per kwh
Norway	0.6
Portugal	0.7
Italy	0.7
Spain	0.7
Sweden	0.8
Yugoslavia	1.0
Denmark	1.0
South Africa	1.1
France	1.2
Austria	1.2
Switzerland	1.2
Poland	1.3
USA	1.3
West Germany	1.3
Australia (1964/65)	1.3

TABLE 30 (Continued)

Country	U.S.¢ per kwh
Turkey	1.5
Algeria	1.6
United Kingdom	1.6
Belgium	1.7
Luxembourg	1.7
Tunisia	1.8
Morocco	1.8
Netherlands	1.9
Czechoslovakia	2.1

*Except as indicated.

The average cost of electricity to industry in a fairly broad selection of countries around the world is indicated in Table 31. The countries have been ranked according to the relative costs of electricity.

TABLE 31.
AVERAGE COST OF INDUSTRIAL POWER
in Selected Countries, 1964*

Country	U.S.¢ per kwh	Country	U.S.¢ per kwh
Norway	0.4	Mexico	1.4
South Africa (mining)	0.6	New Zealand	1.5
Canada	0.6	Brazil (1962)	1.5
Sweden	0.8	Italy	1.5
Faeroe Islands	0.8	Puerto Rico	1.5
China (Taiwan)	0.9	Singapore	1.5
USA	0.9	Ireland	1.6
Philippines	0.9	Chile (1962)	1.6
Finland	1.0	United Kingdom	1.6
UAR	1.0	Belgium	1.7
India	1.1	Zambia	1.7
Spain	1.1	Peru (one company)	1.7
Denmark	1.1	West Germany	1.8
Japan	1.2	Luxembourg	1.8
Rhodesia	1.2	Australia	1.8
France	1.3	Cyprus	1.9
Trinidad	1.3	Malaya	1.9
South Korea	1.3	Iceland	2.0
Kuwait	1.3	Dominican Republic	2.0
Netherlands	1.4	Costa Rica	2.0

Country	U.S.¢ per kwh	Country	U.S.¢ per kwh
Nepal	2.0	Brunei	2.9
Ecuador (1961)	2.0	Nicaragua	3.0
Hong Kong (1962)	2.0	Uganda	3.1
Senegal (1961)	2.0	Sabah	3.4
Afghanistan (1962)	2.3	Indonesia (1961)	3.4
Guatemala	2.4	Venezuela	3.5
Thailand	2.4	Mauritius	3.5
Turkey (1962)	2.4	Sarawak	3.6
Panama	2.5	Ghana	3.7
Romania	2.5	Sudan	4.0
Ceylon	2.5	Burma	4.1
Honduras	2.6	Nigeria	4.3
Jamaica	2.6	Gambia	4.6
El Salvador	2.6	Paraguay (1961)	5.1
Uruguay (1962)	2.7	Cambodia	5.5
		Libya (Tripolitania)	5.6

*Except as indicated.

On a national basis, the costs of power to industry range upward from 0.4¢ per kwh. The list is headed by countries with abundant water power resources, such as Norway, Canada, Sweden, and China (Taiwan), but includes also certain other countries abundantly supplied with low-cost fuels, such as South Africa and the United States. At the bottom of the list, with industrial power costs of 4¢ and upwards, are principally those countries deficient in energy, most of which are only slightly developed economically.

The costs of industrial power in most of the developed countries and in some of the less developed countries as well average less than 2¢ per kwh. In none of the developed countries for which we have data do industrial power costs exceed 2¢ per kwh.

The costs of electric power to particular users are determined not only by the overall costs of producing electricity, but also by pricing policy in different countries. Some countries, in order to encourage the development of industry, offer electricity to industry at relatively low prices, offsetting any potential losses here by raising prices on electricity sold to other sectors of the economy. France, for example, provides power to industrial consumers at only 1.3¢ per kwh, but to residential consumers, it prices power at 4.3¢ per kwh. The United Kingdom, in contrast, sells power to industrial users at an average cost of 1.6¢ per kwh, and charges residential users only 2.1¢ per kwh.

Prices may vary widely, too, within particular countries—from one part of the country to another, and from one subdivision of industry to another. This can be illustrated by reference to the United States, where data are available on average costs of electricity in different areas and in each of the different subdivisions of industry. Regional costs are compared in Table 32, and costs in the several subdivisions of industry in Table 33.

TABLE 32.
AVERAGE COST OF INDUSTRIAL POWER IN THE UNITED STATES,
by Geographic Area, 1964

Area	U.S.¢ per kwh
East South Central	0.5
Pacific	0.7
Mountain	0.7
West South Central	0.8
South Atlantic	0.9
East North Central	1.0
Middle Atlantic	1.0
West North Central	1.2
New England	1.4

Source: U.S. Department of Commerce. Bureau of the Census.
Annual survey of manufactures.

TABLE 33.
AVERAGE COST OF INDUSTRIAL POWER IN THE UNITED STATES,
by Industry Branch, 1964

Industry Branch	U.S.¢ per kwh
Chemicals and allied products	0.6
Primary metals	0.7
Petroleum and coal products	0.8
Paper and allied products	0.9
Textiles	0.9
Stone, clay, and glass products	1.0
Transportation equipment	1.0
Electrical machinery	1.1
Rubber and plastics products	1.1
Tobacco manufactures	1.2
Food and kindred products	1.3
Lumber and wood products	1.3
Miscellaneous manufacturing	1.3
Machinery, except electrical	1.3
Instruments and related products	1.3
Fabricated metal products	1.4
Printing and publishing	1.4
Furniture and fixtures	1.5
Apparel and related products	1.6
Leather and leather products	1.7

Source: U.S. Department of Commerce. Bureau of the Census.
Annual survey of manufactures.

Chapter 4
Electricity Supplies

Of the 3,100 twh of electricity produced and consumed in the world, 74% is obtained from thermal electric plants, 26% from hydro plants. Practically all thermal output comes from conventional plants; the combined output of nuclear and geothermal facilities amounts to considerably less than 1% of the world's electricity supply.

Differences in sources of electricity from one region to another are brought out in Figure 13, following, and Table 34, below. It will be noted that there is no continental area in which hydro is dominant. It approaches equality with thermal electric power only in Latin America, where its share represents 46% of total output.

TABLE 34.
STRUCTURE OF ELECTRICITY PRODUCTION, 1964,
by Region, Economic Level, and Politico-economic System

| Area | Percentages | | | |
	Gross Production	Hydro	Conventional Thermal	Geothermal and Nuclear
East Europe/USSR	100	13.6	86.1	0.3e
Africa	100	22.7	77.3	—
North America	100	24.1	75.6	0.3
West Europe	100	33.0	65.2	1.8
Asia	100	36.5	63.5	—
Oceania	100	34.7	62.5	2.8
Latin America	100	45.9	54.1	—
World	100	26.4	72.9	0.7
Developed World	100	24.3	74.9	0.8
Underdeveloped World	100	44.1	55.9	—
Free Enterprise World	100	29.2	70.0	0.8
Communist World	100	16.4	83.3	0.3

There are a number of countries in which practically all electricity is generated in hydroelectric plants, such as Norway, Switzerland, and Portugal, in Europe; Cameroon, Uganda, the Congo (Kinshasa), and Rhodesia, in Africa; New Zealand and New Caledonia in

63

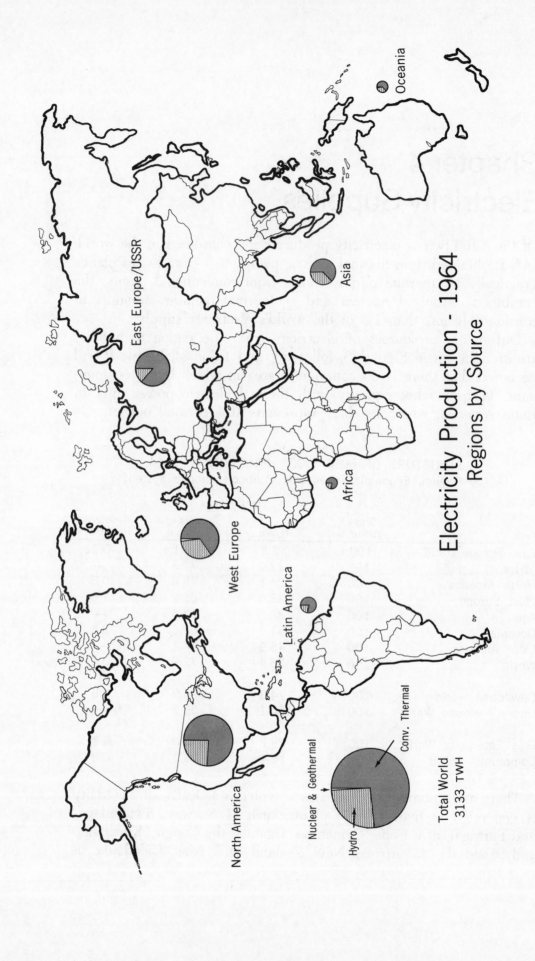

Electricity Production - 1964
Regions by Source

Oceania

East Europe/USSR

Asia

Africa

West Europe

Latin America

North America

Nuclear & Geothermal

Hydro

Conv. Thermal

Total World
3133 TWH

Oceania, and a scattering of countries elsewhere. There are others that depend almost entirely upon conventional thermal plants—such as Belgium, the Netherlands, Denmark, South Africa, and practically all the countries of the Middle East. But sources tend to be somewhat diversified in most countries, as they are in most regions.

A little over a third of the world's hydroelectricity is produced in North America, a bit less than a third in West Europe. Asia produces 14% of the total (mainly in Japan); East Europe and the Soviet Union produce 10% (mainly in the Soviet Union); Latin America, Oceania, and Africa together produce less than 9%. Most of the world's hydro (83%) is produced in the developed world, an even larger share (86%) in the free enterprise world. Regional shares in the output of hydroelectricity are shown in Table 35 and in Figure 14.

TABLE 35.
PRODUCTION OF HYDROELECTRICITY, 1964,
by Region, Economic Level, and Politico-economic System

Area	Quantity Consumed (twh)	Share of World Total (%)
North America	294	35.6
West Europe	257	31.1
Asia	118	14.3
East Europe/USSR	84	10.2
Latin America	45	5.5
Oceania	15	1.8
Africa	12	1.5
World	825	100.0
Developed World	686	83.1
Underdeveloped World	139	16.9
Free Enterprise World	710	86.1
Communist World	115	13.9

Hydroelectricity is normally subject to the vagaries of rainfall and runoff; the extent to which it is influenced by these factors, in spite of steps taken to modify water flows, is shown in Table 36.

TABLE 36.
SEASONAL VARIATIONS IN HYDRO PRODUCTION. 1964*

Country	$\dfrac{\text{month of max. daily average}}{\text{month of min. daily average}}$ = ratio
South Korea (1965)	8.17
Ivory Coast	6.00
Ireland	5.72
Algeria	4.33
Romania	3.44

TABLE 36 (Continued)

Country	$\dfrac{\text{month of max.}}{\text{month of min.}} \dfrac{\text{daily average}}{\text{daily average}}$ = ratio
UK	2.86
Lebanon	2.75
Portugal (1965)	2.70
Venezuela (1963)	2.56
Poland	2.54
Costa Rica	2.50
Malaya	2.50
Yugoslavia	2.31
Czechoslovakia	2.29
France	2.15
Cuba	2.00
Austria	1.96
Greece (1965)	1.93
West Germany	1.85
Luxembourg (pumped)	1.80
Japan	1.80
Spain	1.78
Australia	1.75
Turkey	1.71
Philippines	1.68
New Zealand (1965)	1.61
Norway	1.55
Italy	1.53
Sweden	1.45
Switzerland	1.38
Chile	1.35
Iceland (1965)	1.33
Nigeria	1.33
Morocco	1.30
Finland	1.29
Uruguay	1.27
Mexico (1965)	1.25
USA	1.25
Uganda	1.23
Rhodesia	1.13
Canada	1.10

*Except as indicated.

Forty percent of the world's conventional thermal electricity is produced in North America, 22% in West Europe, and 23% in East Europe and the Soviet Union. More than 92% of the total is produced in the developed world, a bit less than three-quarters of the total in the free enterprise world.

DISTRIBUTION OF HYDRO-ELECTRICITY PRODUCTION - 1964

Percentages of World Total

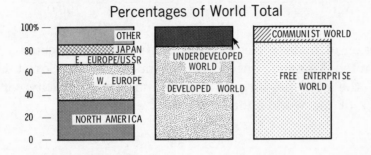

TABLE 37.
PRODUCTION OF CONVENTIONAL THERMAL ELECTRICITY, 1964,
by Region, Economic Level, and Politico-economic System

Area	Quantity Consumed (twh)	Share of World Total (%)
North America	921	40.3
East Europe/USSR	530	23.2
West Europe	508	22.2
Asia	206	9.0
Latin America	53	2.3
Africa	42	1.8
Oceania	27	1.2
World	2287	100.0
Developed World	2110	92.3
Underdeveloped World	177	7.7
Free Enterprise World	1702	74.4
Communist World	585	25.6

Output of geothermal power is confined to Italy, New Zealand, and the United States. These three countries together produce close to 4 twh annually, with Italy, the senior producer in this field, responsible for nearly two-thirds of all output.

68   ELECTRICITY SUPPLIES

TABLE 38.

PRODUCTION OF GEOTHERMAL ELECTRICITY, 1964,
by Country

Country	Quantity (million kwh)	Percentage of World Total
Italy	2527	64.4
New Zealand	1194	30.4
USA	204	5.2
World	3925	100.0

Production of nuclear electricity is confined to nine countries, led by the United Kingdom, the U. S. A., Italy, and the Soviet Union. Together, the nine produce 17 twh of nuclear electricity, or one-half of 1% of the world's total output of electricity.

TABLE 39.

PRODUCTION OF NUCLEAR ELECTRICITY, 1964,
by Country

Country	Quantity (million kwh)	Percentage of World Total
United Kingdom	8346	49.0
USA	3343	19.6
Italy	2401	14.1
USSR	(2000)*	11.7
France	655	3.9
Canada	141	0.8
West Germany	104	0.6
Belgium	51	0.3
Japan	2	—
World	17043	100.0

*Excluding Troitsk. Estimated on the basis of 300 MW of capacity.

Fuel Consumption in the Generation of Electricity

More than 500 million tons of coal, 250 million tons of lignite, nearly 70 million tons of distillate and residual fuel oils, and about 100 billion cubic meters (3.5 trillion cubic feet) of natural gas are used annually in the generation of electric power. To these must be added lesser quantities of peat (about 20 million metric tons), fuel wood (a few million tons), and such exotic fuels as charcoal, paddy husk, sulphite liquor, and sawdust.

Regional shares in fuel consumption are shown in Table 40—in teracalories and coal equivalents.

TABLE 40.
CONSUMPTION OF FUELS IN THE GENERATION OF ELECTRICITY
BY UTILITIES, 1964

Area	Energy content (000 Tcal)	Coal equivalent (million MT)
North America	2175.2	310.8
East Europe/USSR	1119.4	160.0
West Europe	1023.1	146.2
Asia	600.0	85.7
Latin America	127.2	18.2
Africa	125.6	17.9
Oceania	102.0	14.6
World	5272.5	753.4
Developed World	4702.4	671.9
Underdeveloped World	570.1	81.5
Free Enterprise World	3903.0	557.7
Communist World	1369.5	195.7

Coal and lignite are the principal sources of power for public use, not only in the world as a whole, but also in most regions of the world. Only in Latin America and the Middle East, both rich in oil and gas but poor in coal, are other sources of energy more important than coal.

The relative importance of different fuels in the several regions is indicated in Table 41, and in Figure 15.

TABLE 41.
STRUCTURE OF FUEL CONSUMPTION
IN THE GENERATION OF ELECTRICITY BY UTILITIES, 1964,
by Region, Economic Level, and Politico-economic System

Area	Percentages			
	Total	Coal, Lignite, and Peat	Oil Fuels	Gases
North America	100	64	8	28
West Europe	100	78	20	2
East Europe/USSR	100	72	3	25
Asia	100	67	32	1
Latin America	100	8	66	26
Africa	100	83	15	2
Oceania	100	94	6	—
World	100	69	13	18
Developed World	100	70	11	19
Underdeveloped World	100	61	32	7
Free Enterprise World	100	66	17	17
Communist World	100	77	3	20

FUELS CONSUMED IN ELECTRIC POWER PLANTS BY REGION - 1964

(Utilities only)

Million Tcals

TOTAL

COAL

LIGNITE, PEAT, ETC.

FUEL OILS

GASES

Northern America

Developed World

Underdeveloped World

West Europe

East Europe/USSR

Asia

Oceania

Africa

Communist World

Free Enterprise World

Latin America

Very large quantities of coal and lignite are consumed in three areas: North America (210 million tons), West Europe (185 million tons), and East Europe/USSR (an estimated 262 million tons). West Europe's total includes fairly substantial quantities of lignite, while consumption in East Europe and the Soviet Union includes large quantities of lignite and rather substantial quantities of peat, an important source of electric power in the Soviet Union.

Close to 70 million tons of oil are consumed in the generation of electric power by utilities. West Europe, with consumption of 21 million tons, is the principal user of fuel oil, followed by Asia (18 million tons) and North America (16 million tons).

The use of natural gas for generating electricity is highly concentrated, with 65% of the world total being used in North America, and most of the remainder in East Europe and the Soviet Union.

Transfers

The production of electricity in many countries is divided between utilities producing for public distribution and private interests producing mainly for their own consumption. Approximately 16% of the world's electricity is produced by industrial and transportation establishments. Not all this electricity is retained by the producers, however. Data available concerning the year 1964 indicate that approximately 10% of the electricity produced by private industry is supplied to public networks.

In countries with great water power resources, privately generated electricity is normally surplus hydro, generated during periods of heavy runoff by such industries as aluminum and pulp and paper. In certain coal producing countries, like Germany, France, and Belgium, and certain oil producing countries in the Middle East, it is commonly an indirect form of marketing another form of energy.

The extent of this business is indicated by data on transfers of privately generated power to public networks, shown in Table 42. It will be noted that private producers of electricity furnish power to public utilities in all the countries listed.

TABLE 42.

PRIVATE GENERATION AND TRANSFERS OF ELECTRICITY, 1964,*

in Selected Countries (million kwh)

Country	Transfers to Public Supply	Private Generation
West Germany	23,743	61,287
France	11,236	28,178
East Germany (1965)	5,780	22,274
Canada	4,750	32,098
United Kingdom	3,392	18,251
United States	3,346	99,751
USSR (1962)	2,336	84,079
Czechoslovakia	1,739	7,748
Belgium	1,221	8,501
Australia	1,151	2,093
Norway (1962)	905	13,355
Philippines	778	850
Japan	706	21,432
Switzerland	499	3,399
Bulgaria	461	1,112
Poland	330	6,456
Austria	307	3,450
Luxembourg	139	1,411
Spain	139	1,793
Brazil	137	4,051
Yugoslavia	132	1,470
China (Taiwan)	127	157
Netherlands	125	4,570
Hungary	106	1,201
Chile	86	2,532
Algeria	29	243
Turkey	28	577
India	26	3,586
Denmark	24	893
Greece	15	65
Ireland	9	137
Brunei	4	58
Portugal	2	265
Thailand	2	79

*Except as indicated.

Trade

Some three dozen countries engage in international trade in electricity. Most of these are European countries, but there is a fairly brisk trade in Africa, mainly between Zambia and its neighbors, and in North America, between the United States and its neighbors. Altogether, around 35 twh of electricity enter international trade annually.

In Europe, practically all countries are interconnected with one or more neighbors; but the principal flows of electricity are seasonal flows, within each of two blocs — the NORDEL group, consisting of Denmark, Finland, Norway, and Sweden, in which there is a substantial movement of surplus hydro from Norway to the other three members of the bloc during the period of winter surpluses; and EEC and its trading partners — Austria, Spain, Switzerland, and the United Kingdom. Trade here is based mainly on summer surpluses in Austria and Switzerland and winter surpluses in Spain.

Trade in Africa is based almost entirely on the availability of year-round surpluses of hydro at a few large installations: Kariba, in Rhodesia; Le Marinel, in the Congo; Owen Falls, in Uganda; and Revué, in Mozambique.

In North America, trade is based principally upon winter surpluses of hydroelectricity in Canada.

In East Europe and the Soviet Union, there is a considerable interchange of power, which, on balance, consists mainly of exports from Poland and the Soviet Union to other members of the COMECON group. There is no significant international trade in electricity in Asia, Oceania, or Latin America.

Data on international movements of electricity in the year 1964 are shown in Figure 16. Monthly data on international trade in electricity in the year 1964 are given in Table 6 of the Appendix.

TABLE 43.

INTERNATIONAL MOVEMENT OF ELECTRICITY, 1964*

(million kwh)

	Import	Export	Net Import
NORDEL			
Denmark	858	39	819
Finland	702	6	696
Norway	116	1507	−1391
Sweden	1433	1638	−205
	3109	3190	−81

SEASONAL VARIATIONS OF INTERNATIONAL TRADE IN ELECTRICITY - 1964
Net Imports in Mil KWH/day

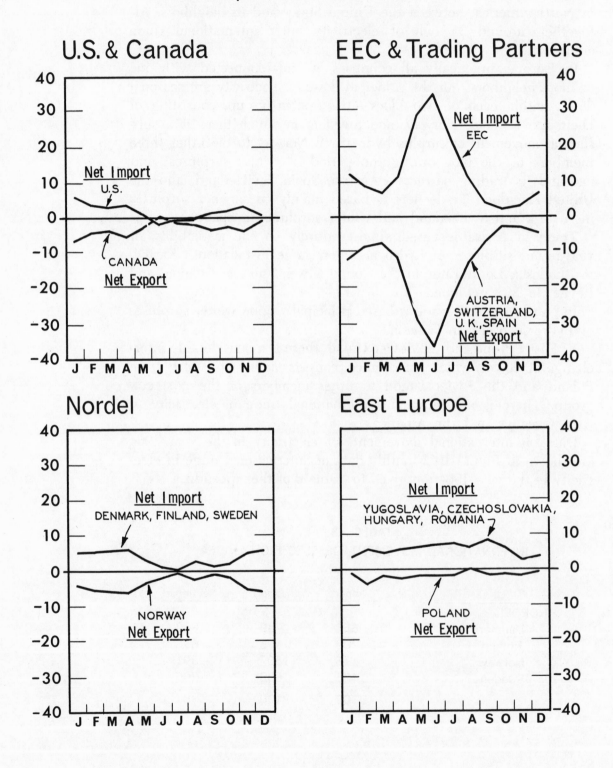

TABLE 43 (Continued)

	Import	Export	Net Import
EEC			
Belgium	360	709	−349
France	3795	1567	2228
West Germany	6272	5312	960
Italy	1756	754	1002
Luxembourg	1489	796	693
Netherlands	50	32	18
	13722	9170	4552
EEC trading partners			
Austria	993	3701	−2708
Spain (and Andorra)	172	1735	−1563
Switzerland	3518	4682	−1164
UK	83	294	−211
	4766	10412	−5646
Other West Europe			
Greece	8	23	−15
Portugal	43	55	−12
Yugoslavia	429	87	342
	480	165	315
COMECON			
Bulgaria	3	26	−23
Czechoslovakia	1618	916	702
East Germany	835e	688	147
Hungary	1159	78	1081
Poland	739	1297	−558
Romania	113	109	4
USSR	79e	1379	−1300
	4546	4493	53
Africa			
Congo (Kinshasa)	—	198	−198
Mozambique	—	102	−102
Rhodesia	102	1853	−1751
Uganda	—	178	−178
Kenya	180	—	180
Tanzania	—	6	−6
Zambia	2033	—	2033
	2315	2337	−22
America			
Canada	3121	4159	−1038
Mexico	121	—	121

TABLE 43 (Continued)

	Import	Export	Net Import
USA	6208	4253	1955
Panama	—	8	−8
Canal Zone	8	—	8
	9458	8420	1038

*Except as indicated.

Chapter 5
Electric Plant and
Plant Utilization

Properly speaking, electric utility plant includes facilities for the generation, transmission, and distribution of electricity. All three are important components of the total system. In terms of capital investment, generating facilities loom largest, representing roughly half of all investment on the average; distribution facilities normally represent 30% to 40% of the total investment, and transmission facilities the remainder.

Most of the discussion that follows deals with generating facilities, although some attention has been given to transmission of electricity. Little has been said about distribution facilities, mainly because of difficulties in collecting pertinent data. This aspect of the electric power industry, and the related questions of horizontal and vertical integration of facilities, certainly merit more attention than they have received.

Generating Plant

Installed capacity of world generating facilities amounted to 734 million KW in the year 1964, of which conventional thermal facilities represented 70.8%, hydro facilities 28.6%, and nuclear and geothermal facilities together 0.6%.

TABLE 44.
INSTALLED CAPACITY OF ELECTRIC POWER PLANTS, 1964,
by Type

	Quantity (mil KW)	Share of Total Capacity (%)
Hydro	209.7	28.6
Geothermal	0.5	0.1
Nuclear	3.5	0.5
Conventional Thermal	520.0	70.8
Total	733.7	100.0

The geographical distribution of the world's installed capacity is shown in Table 45. The pattern here is substantially the same as the pattern of production, with more than 60% of the total concentrated in North America and West Europe. Eighty-eight percent is concentrated in the developed world, 78% in the free enterprise economies.

TABLE 45.
INSTALLED CAPACITY, 1964,
by Region, Economic Level, and Politico-economic System

Area	Capacity (mil KW)	Share of World Total (%)
North America	267.5	36.5
West Europe	201.3	27.4
East Europe/USSR	137.4	18.7
Asia	75.2	10.3
Latin America	27.4	3.7
Africa	13.8	1.9
Oceania	11.1	1.5
World	733.7	100.0
Developed World	646.5	88.1
Underdeveloped World	87.2	11.9
Free Enterprise World	575.4	78.4
Communist World	158.3	21.6

Since the subject of distribution was examined at some length in the chapter on production, the discussion here can be usefully limited to certain other aspects of the electric power industry, such as the ownership of electric power facilities, plant characteristics, and certain aspects of plant utilization.

Ownership

In considering ownership, one distinction needs to be made immediately—namely, between plants generating primarily for public consumption, which we refer to as utilities, and plants producing electricity primarily for private consumption. Eighty-four percent of the world's generating capacity falls in the first category, only 16% in the second.

So far as utilities are concerned, ownership is divided between public and private interests, with public interests dominating in some areas, private interests in others.

In North America, for example, public authorities are dominant in Canada, where they control 88% of all utility capacity. In the United States, by contrast, three-quarters of all utility capacity is privately owned.

The pattern is similarly variegated in West Europe. Here, public interests are dominant in most countries, but generating capacity in Belgium, Spain, and Portugal is mainly in private ownership. The situation in Germany is somewhat obscure, because the form is the form of private enterprise, but ownership appears to rest with government.

In East Europe and the Soviet Union, all utilities are state owned. In Africa, ownership again is very much mixed, with utilities in most of the continent now publicly owned, but private ownership still dominant in most of the former French colonies, in East Africa, and apparently also in the Spanish and Portuguese possessions in Africa.

Japanese utilities are almost entirely privately owned. Elsewhere in Asia, most utilities are government owned, as are practically all utilities in Oceania.

The ownership pattern in Latin America is definitely mixed. Utilities in Mexico and Uruguay are entirely government owned, as are utilities in a number of smaller countries, such as Guyana, Puerto Rico, and Cuba. Elsewhere in Latin America they are, in the main, privately owned, or of mixed government and private ownership.

The pattern of ownership throughout the world at the end of 1964 — as nearly as we are able to appraise it — is shown in Figure 17.

The ownership of plants generating primarily for private consumption also varies a good deal from one area to another—both in the nature of the facilities owned and in the nature of the operators. In France, Germany, Belgium, and the Netherlands, for example, the coal industry is a leading private producer of power. The aluminum industry is a major source of private power in Austria and the United States. The aluminum and paper industries are major sources of private power in the Scandinavian countries and Canada. In the Middle East and Venezuela, the petroleum companies lead in the production of power for private consumption, and in the Congo, Chile, and Peru, it is the copper companies that are dominant. Throughout the world, the iron and steel industry is an important producer of electricity for private consumption, and there are many countries in which the railways have developed their own facilities for generating electricity.

Hydroelectric Plant

Certain industries which depend heavily upon low-cost power—the electrochemical and electrometallurgical industries in particular — have been prominent in the development of water power resources, and own a significant share of all hydroelectric capacity. The bulk

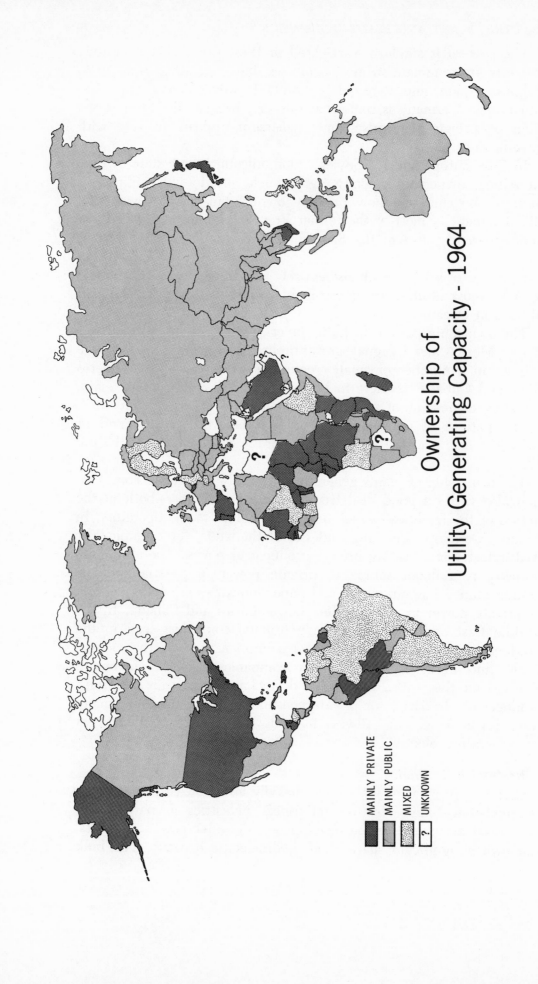

Ownership of
Utility Generating Capacity - 1964

MAINLY PRIVATE
MAINLY PUBLIC
MIXED
? UNKNOWN

of the world's hydro capacity, however, and practically every large hydroelectric plant—including every hydro plant of more than 500 MW in the United States—is publicly owned.

An important element of most large hydro installations is the associated storage capacity. This capacity enables the producer of power to compensate for seasonal variations in the flow of water, and seasonal or other variations in the demand for electricity. The amount of storage capacity available varies a good deal from one country to another, as does the relation between storage capacity and output of hydroelectricity. In some cases, such as Owen Falls (in Uganda) and Kariba (in Rhodesia), storage capacity exceeds a normal year's output of electricity. In most countries, it represents only a fraction of the hydroelectricity produced in the course of a year.

Unfortunately, it has not been possible to obtain data on storage capacity expressed in mwh for some of the more important producers of hydroelectricity, such as the United States, Canada, and the Soviet Union. Storage capacities for other countries are shown, in relation to electricity production in the year 1964, in Table 46.

TABLE 46.
HYDROELECTRIC STORAGE CAPACITY AND POWER GENERATION
in Selected Countries, 1964*

Country	Seasonal Storage Capacity (mil kwh)	Output (mil kwh)	Storage Capacity (percent of output in 1964)
Norway	24,514	43,864	56
Sweden	16,230	43,022	38
Rhodesia (1965)	8,500	3,864	220
Spain	7,139	20,646	35
Italy	6,382	39,328	16
France	6,016	35,218	17
Switzerland	5,970	22,663	26
Brazil	5,759	22,097	26
Portugal	2,040	4,220	48
Finland	2,000	8,501	24
New Zealand	1,963	7,753	25
Uganda	1,680	521	322
Yugoslavia	1,300	7,575	17
Bugaria	1,242	1,471	84
United Kingdom	1,183	4,022	29
Austria	1,112	13,179	8
Morocco	1,003	1,171	86
Turkey	918	1,652	56
Greece	709	749	95
Uruguay	705	1,267	56

TABLE 46 (Continued)

Country	Seasonal Storage Capacity (mil kwh)	Output (mil kwh)	Storage Capacity (percent of output in 1964)
Romania	547	585	94
Czechoslovakia	499	2,727	18
West Germany	337	12,102	3
Algeria	209	284	74
Ireland	61	784	8
Ceylon	44	338	13
Iceland	25	656	4
Poland	20	726	3
Tunisia	20	38	53
Belgium	7	115	6
Luxembourg	5	805	1

*Except as indicated.

Part of the storage capacity listed in Table 46 is pumped storage capacity—that is, hydroelectric power especially created to meet peak demands by lifting and storing water during off-peak hours. Lifting power is commonly provided by thermal electric generating capacity during off-peak hours. A good example here is the Vianden plant in Luxembourg, which utilizes off-peak thermal power imported from Germany to lift water into the storage pond at Vianden—water which is subsequently released and used to generate hydroelectricity for re-export to Germany.

The extent to which pumped storage is employed throughout the world is indicated by data on consumption of electricity for pumping purposes. Output of pumped storage is roughly equivalent to two-thirds of the input indicated in Table 47.

TABLE 47.
ELECTRICITY CONSUMED IN PUMPED STORAGE OPERATIONS
in Selected Countries, 1964
(million kwh)

Country	Input
West Germany	1,466
Luxembourg	1,040
Brazil	954
USA	728
Austria	667
United Kingdom	589
Italy	509
Switzerland	390
Czechoslovakia	194
Japan	161

Country	Input
France	151
Sweden	95
Uruguay	49
Poland	32
Bulgaria	12
Yugoslavia	3

Sources: FPC. **Hydroelectric plant construction cost and annual production expenses, 1964.**
   UN. ECE. **Ann. bull. of elec. energy stat.**
   UNIPEDE. **Statistiques.**

Thermoelectric Plants

The world's 520 million KW of conventional thermal capacity consists mainly of steam power plants, but includes also a significant amount of diesel and gas turbine capacity.

World steam plant capacity, which totals something over 500 million KW, is distributed among a very large number of plants, ranging in size from less than 5 KW to more than 1.5 million KW (the latter at the Frimmersdorf plant in Germany and the Kingston plant of TVA in the United States). More than half of the world's steam capacity is concentrated in plants of 100 MW or more. In the United States alone, the capacity of such plants amounts to 157 million KW. Europe claims about 50 million KW, Asia about 22 million, Oceania 3 million, and Latin America over 4 million. In South Africa, the capacity of plants of 100 MW or more totals approximately 4 million KW.

World diesel capacity amounts to something over 10 million KW, mostly in units of less than 10 KW. The bulk of this capacity is located in a few highly developed countries, where it is used primarily for peaking. The United States, for example, has approximately 3,000 MW of diesel capacity, Canada 255 MW, Australia approximately 150 MW, and West Germany 200 MW (in 1965). But diesel plants are also widely used in less developed areas, often as the principal if not the only source of electricity. They are the sole source of electricity in many of the African states and a good many of the small, island states. And they are a major source of electricity in some of the larger, underdeveloped countries. Argentina, for example, has a diesel capacity of half a million KW in the public supply system, and as much again in industrial plants. India operates over 300 MW of diesel capacity.

Another important use of diesel plants is in connection with mining operations, especially in isolated regions. Much of the electricity used in the production of copper in Chile and Peru is generated in diesel plants, as is the power used in producing alumina in Guinea, gold in Ghana, and oil in Brunei.

The aggregate capacity of the world's gas turbine plants appears to be in the vicinity of 3,000 MW, located mainly in the developed countries, where it is used principally for peaking. At the end of 1965, some 380 MW of gas turbine capacity were installed in the European Community—a figure which may be compared with a diesel capacity in that area of only 146 MW. The capacity of gas turbines in Canada, 413 MW at the end of 1964, also exceeds that of diesel engines. In the Far East, plants with an aggregate capacity of 127 MW are in operation, and in the United Kingdom capacity totals 74 MW. Several plants are known to be in operation in the Soviet Union, including one at Kharkov and possibly two others at Shatsk.

There are only three geothermal plants in the entire world: the Larderello plant in Italy, with a capacity of 331 MW; the Wairakei plant in New Zealand, with a capacity of 192 MW; and The Geysers plant in California, USA, with a capacity of 27 MW. Of particular interest concerning these plants is their very high rate of output— 7,800 hours per KW in Italy, more than 6,500 hours per KW in New Zealand, and 7,000 hours per KW in the United States.

Nuclear plants have now gained a firm foothold in the world, particularly in the United Kingdom, which can claim more than half the world's 3,494 MW nuclear capacity. More than 90% of the world's nuclear capacity is concentrated in the twelve large plants listed.

TABLE 48.
THE TWELVE LARGEST NUCLEAR POWER PLANTS
IN OPERATION IN 1964*

Plant		Net Output Capacity (MW)
Hinkley Point—A	UK	524
Trawsfynydd	UK	500
Hunterston—A	UK	322
Bradwell	UK	300
Berkeley	UK	276
Indian Point—1	USA	270
Enrico Fermi	Italy	247
Calder Hall	UK	200
Chinon—2	France	200
Latina	Italy	200
Dresden—1	USA	200
Novo Voronezh	USSR	196

*Excluding Troitsk, in the USSR, whose size and status as a producer of electricity is not certain.
Source: IAEA. Bulletin. Vol. 10, No. 1, 1968.

An important source of electricity in a dozen countries or so is the combined heat and power station, which provides heat, as well as electricity, to the district in which it is located. This particular type of operation is highly developed in the Soviet Union and in certain North European and East European countries. There are some combined heat and power stations in the USA, but data concerning their operations are not available.

TABLE 49.
OUTPUT OF POWER AND HEAT IN COMBINED STATIONS
in Selected Countries, 1964*

Country	Electricity (million kwh)	Heat (Tcal)
USSR (1961)	68,443	151,019
East Germany	24,436	104,255
Poland	10,859	35,109
Czechoslovakia (ps only)	4,892	23,194
West Germany	2,600	11,630
Belgium (1961)	2,507	915
Denmark (ps only)	1,100	3,960
Sweden	545	2,447
Austria	330	623
United Kingdom	162	1,113
Finland	180	1,110
Switzerland (1965)	33	338

*Except as indicated.
Source: ECE. **Situation and future prospects of Europe's electric power industry**.

Another form of combined operation that deserves comment is the power and desalination plant, which has gained a foothold in certain countries seriously deficient in fresh water. According to the United Nations study, *Water Desalination in Developing Countries,* the capacity of such combined stations, as of 1961, was as shown in Table 50.

TABLE 50.
POWER AND WATER CAPACITY OF DESALINATION PLANTS
OPERATING IN 1961*

Country	Capacity	
	Electric (MW)	Water (M³/day)
Southwest Africa	64.0	564
Netherlands Antilles	22.5	16,700
Bahamas	11.1	5,455
Iran	3.0	1,364
Virgin Islands-USA (1962)	3.0	1,136
Kuwait	1.4	27,273

*Except as indicated.
Source: UN. **Water desalination.**

Transmission Facilities

Transmission networks vary considerably from one region to another in coverage, degree of integration and length of lines.

North America, for example, is pretty well covered by the networks of its many systems, most of which are interconnected with neighboring networks. Interconnection extends across national boundaries, to provide for interchange at many points between Canada and the United States, and at least limited interchange between the United States and Mexico.

Each of the countries of West Europe also has its own rather comprehensive network and is connected with each of its neighbors, in some cases by submarine cable (Sweden and Denmark are so interconnected, as are Britain and France).

The East European countries, too, boast fairly comprehensive networks, and extensive integration with each other through COMECON. The Soviet Union is served by a number of large regional networks —some interconnected and some in process of interconnection.

In Africa, there are extensive regional networks in the Union of South Africa, Algeria, and Morocco. Rhodesia also has a fairly extensive network. Elsewhere in Africa, networks appear to be limited, serving mainly as direct channels from a few large-scale producers, such as Kariba in Rhodesia and Le Marinel in the Congo, to the Zambian mines; and from Owen Falls in Uganda to the Nairobi area in Kenya.

Japan and China (Taiwan) appear to be the only countries in Asia served by nationwide, high-tension networks, but there are important provincial networks in other Asian countries, including India, Malaya, and West Pakistan.

Australia is served by extensive State networks, plus the Snowy Mountains Scheme. New Zealand has integrated networks on each of the two islands—networks now interconnected by submarine cable.

In Latin America, much of Chile is supplied by a single network, as are a number of the small countries and islands in the Caribbean area, but most of the countries of Latin America are supplied by a combination of provincial networks and local supply systems.

A crude picture of the extent of transmission networks within particular areas is provided in Table 51, which simply shows the aggregate length of high-tension lines in service in 1964. Unfortunately, the data available concerning most of the countries in Latin America are not current and therefore not properly comparable with data from other areas.

TABLE 51.
HIGH-TENSION TRANSMISSION LINES IN USE, 1964*
(length in kilometers)

United States	263,945	Portugal	2,232
USSR	167,300	Netherlands	1,939
Canada	70,592	Denmark	1,664
Italy	39,465	Belgium	1,624
West Germany	39,210	Rhodesia & Zambia (1961)	1,450
Japan	35,767	Thailand	1,377
United Kingdom	29,796	Morocco (1961)	1,194
France	27,585	China (Taiwan)	1,084
India	22,757	Algeria	900
Spain	19,350	Burma (1963)	763
Sweden	18,663	South Korea	725
Poland	16,107	Philippines (NPC only)	698
East Germany	14,850	Cyprus	525
Australia	13,128	Ethiopia (1961)	418
Czechoslovakia	10,599	Nigeria (1961)	404
New Zealand	8,650	Kenya (1961)	400
Yugoslavia	8,525	Puerto Rico	388
Finland	7,711	Malaya	385
South Africa	6,950	Iran (1962)	326
Norway	5,941	Ceylon	322
Romania	5,641	Congo (Kinshasa)	285
Austria	4,546	Uganda (1961)	265
Switzerland	4,252	South Vietnam	263
Pakistan (1963)	3,877	Sudan (1961)	180
Bulgaria	3,836	Afghanistan (1962)	160
Hungary	3,737	Iceland	51
Ireland	3,277	Luxembourg	18
Turkey	2,712	Hong Kong	8
Greece	2,363		

*Except as indicated.

Sources: Europe. UN. ECE. **The situation and future prospects of Europe's electric power supply industry.**
Asia. UN. ECAFE. **Elec. power.**
Africa. UN. ECA. **Situation, trends & prospects.**
Canada. Dominion Bureau of Statistics. **Electric power statistics.**
South Africa. Electrical Supply Commission (ESCOM). **Annual report.**

Plant Utilization

The electric power industry is a capital-intensive industry. Its economic efficiency depends to an unusual degree upon fullness of plant utilization—that is, the number of kwh extracted from each KW of installed capacity in the course of a year. This varies a good deal, because it depends in part on the firmness of demand, and in part on the margin maintained between peak demands and total plant capacity.

On a long-term basis, demands for electricity are characterized by an almost unwavering growth, year after year; but on a less-than-year basis, demands fluctuate rather wildly — partly in response to man's habits of work and play, and partly in response to climate and related factors. There are, in fact, three pronounced rhythms of demand—diurnal, weekly, and seasonal.

The widest fluctuations are those associated with night and day, or, more specifically, with hours of work, social activity, and sleep. Minimum demands, which normally fall between the hours of midnight and six a.m., represent between two-thirds and one-third of peak demands. But the amplitude of fluctuations is wider in winter than it is in summer; principally because of differences in the amount of sunlight available in the two periods.

Variations in the magnitude of fluctuations from one country to another are shown in Table 52. At the head of this list are countries whose variations are smallest; at the bottom of the list are those with the widest fluctuations during the twenty-four hour day. Heading the list are two distinct groups of countries. First are those like Norway, Austria, Sweden, and Finland, that are relatively rich in water power resources and possess highly-developed electrochemical or electrometallurgical industries, and that firm up demands by diverting electricity to consumption in electric boilers. The second group comprises principally Communist countries in which loads are firmly regulated by load shedding or other controls on the utilization of electricity during periods of maximum demand. Near the bottom of the list are a number of countries, such as Denmark, the United Kingdom, and Ireland, in which demands in the domestic sector — the variable component of total demands — outweigh demands in the industrial sector — the stable component.

TABLE 52.
DIURNAL VARIATIONS IN DEMANDS FOR ELECTRICITY
in Selected Countries, 1964*
(minimum as percent of peak load)

Norway	79
Austria	71
Bulgaria	68
East Germany	68
Romania	67
Czechoslovakia	65
Sweden	64

TABLE 52 (Continued)

Finland	60
France	60
Yugoslavia	59+
Poland	59
Panama Canal Zone	58
Belgium	57
Hungary	55
Italy	55
Puerto Rico	54
Malaya (central network)	53
Switzerland	52
West Germany	46
Spain	46
Chile (interconnected system)	44±
Ireland	43
Netherlands	43
Singapore (1965)	42±
Portugal	40
United Kingdom	40
Greece	39
Cyprus	33
Ceylon	32
Uruguay	32
Denmark	31
Mauritius	29±
Peru	29
Colombia (one company)	26

---

*Except as indicated.

Sources:
UNIPEDE. **L'écon. élec.**
UN. ECE. **Elec. power situation.**
Ceylon. Department of Government Electrical Undertakings.
  Administration report of the Acting General Manager.
Chile. Empresa Nacional de Electricidad, S.A. **Producción y
  consumo de energía en Chile.**
Colombia. Empresas Publicas de Medellin. **Informes y balance.**
Cyprus. Electricity Authority of Cyprus. **Annual report and
  accounts.**
Malaya. Central Electricity Board of the Federation of Malaya.
  Annual report.
Mauritius. Central Electricity Board. **Annual report and ac-
  counts.**
Panama Canal Zone. US. FPC. **Power system statement.**
Puerto Rico. US. FPC. **Power system statement.**
Singapore. City Council. **Annual report of the Electricity De-
  partment.**
Uruguay. Administración General de las Usinas Eléctricas y los
  Teléfonos del Estado. **Producción de energía eléctrica.**

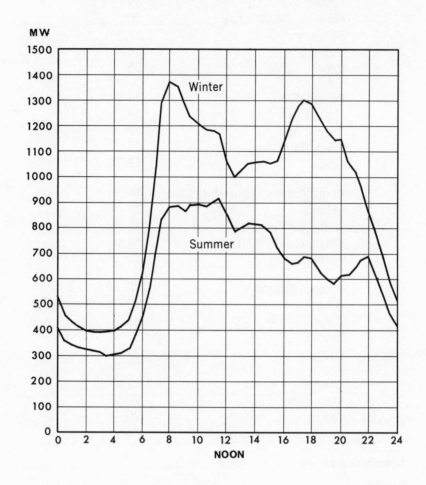

DIURNAL VARIATIONS IN ELECTRICITY
CONSUMPTION - DENMARK (1961–62)

It might be noted in passing that most of the countries that stand at the head of the list make some use of pumped storage facilities, thereby reducing the gap between peak and minimum loads.

Weekly fluctuations in electricity demands are also associated with man's work habits, and the fact that in most of the world the work week consists of five or six days followed by one or two days of rest. An interesting study of load variations during the week was presented by Mr. Daniel Jung, in a paper on the distribution of electricity consumption presented at the UNIPEDE Congress in June 1964. A simplified version of the data presented in this paper is shown below, with differences from one working day to another disregarded. Of particular interest here is the consistency with which Sunday loads approximate two-thirds of workday loads in five of the six countries represented in the table.

TABLE 53.
WEEKLY FLUCTUATIONS IN ELECTRIC LOADS*, 1964†

Country	Working Days	Saturdays	Sundays
Austria (1962)	1.0	0.87	0.68
France	1.0	0.89	0.65
West Germany	1.0	0.83	0.65
Italy	1.0	1.00	0.64
Switzerland	1.0	0.87	0.68
UK (1962/63)	1.0	0.83	0.75

*Coefficients, with average working day taken as 1.0.
†Except as indicated.
After the system developed by Daniel Jung, "Distribution of electricity consumption through the year: weighting of daily consumptions and seasonal variation." UNIPEDE, Madrid Congress, 1964.

A graphic illustration of weekly variations in loads, based on data from one region of the United States, is given in Figure 19.

The extent to which demands for electricity vary from one *season* to another is indicated in Figure 20. Amplitude of variation is expressed here as an index number, based, in the Northern Hemisphere, on the ratio of consumption in the months of January and December to consumption in the months of July and August in the same year. For countries in the Southern Hemisphere, the index is inverted.

The map does not show the full range of seasonal variation. This is brought out in Table 54, in which are shown all countries where winter demands vary by more than 20% above or more than 10% below summer demands.

The list is headed by the United Kingdom and Ireland, where winter loads are more than 60% higher than are summer loads. The three countries at the top of the list are, in fact, maritime states, characterized especially by cool summers in which air conditioning

WEEKLY VARIATIONS IN ELECTRIC LOADS
U.S.A., Region I, December [a]

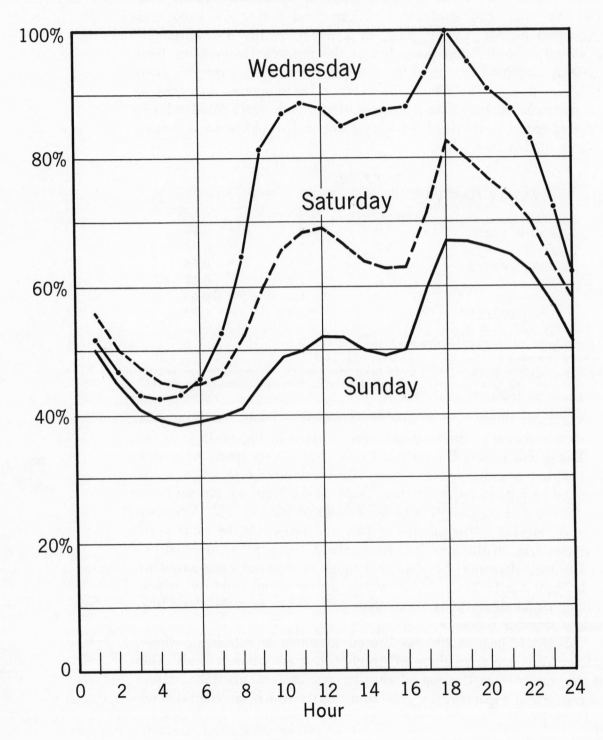

a 1960. Source: Federal Power Commission.

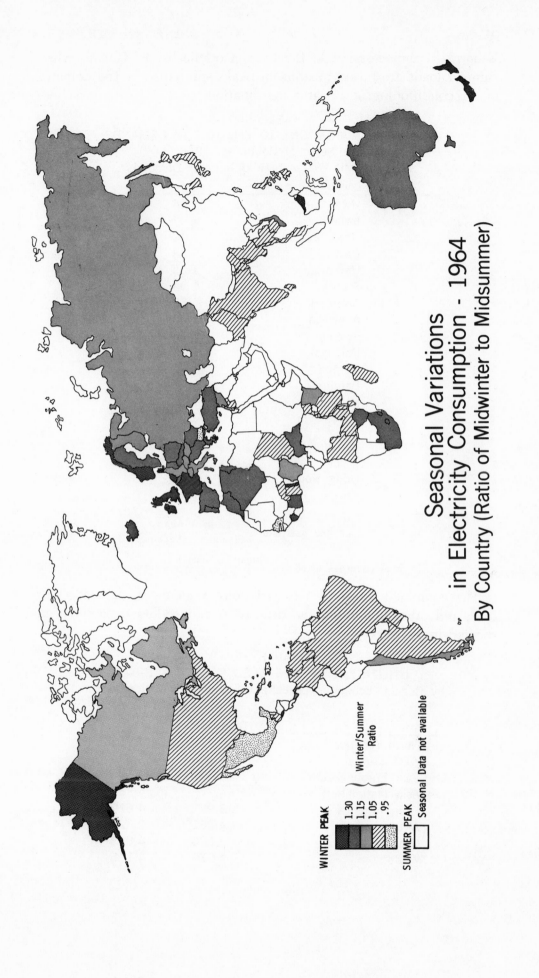

Seasonal Variations
in Electricity Consumption - 1964
By Country (Ratio of Midwinter to Midsummer)

WINTER PEAK

1.30
1.15
1.05
.95

} Winter/Summer
Ratio

SUMMER PEAK

Seasonal Data not available

is normally unnecessary. At the bottom of the list is Kuwait, where summer loads are raised to unusual peaks—probably by the demands of air conditioning and water desalination.

TABLE 54.
SEASONAL VARIATIONS IN ELECTRICITY DEMANDS
in Selected Countries, 1964
Ratio of Mid-Winter to Mid-Summer Demands*

Country	Ratio
UK	1.64
Ireland	1.62
New Zealand	1.42
Norway	1.38
Netherlands	1.35
France	1.34
Denmark	1.32
Australia	1.29
Sweden	1.28
Portugal	1.27
Iceland	1.25
Belgium	1.25
Poland	1.22
Yugoslavia	1.21
Lebanon	0.89
Israel	0.83
Hong Kong	0.80
Kuwait	0.65

*In New Zealand and Australia $= \dfrac{\text{July} + \text{August}}{\text{January} + \text{December}}$

In other countries listed $= \dfrac{\text{January} + \text{December}}{\text{July} + \text{August}}$

The combined effect of the variations in demand, capacity margins, and other factors on the utilization of installed capacity is indicated in Table 55.

TABLE 55.
UTILIZATION OF INSTALLED CAPACITY, 1964,
by Region, Economic Level, and Politico-economic System

Area	kwh produced per KW	
	Total Capacity	Hydro Capacity
North America	4,778	4,812
West Europe	4,100	3,633
East Europe/USSR	4,991	3,501
Asia (estimated)	4,712	4,358
Latin America	3,901	4,679
Africa	4,061	3,723
Oceania	4,230	4,023
World*	4,576	4,145

| | kwh produced per KW | |
Area	Total Capacity	Hydro Capacity
Developed World	4,651	4,144
Underdeveloped World*	3,868	4,148
Free Enterprise World	4,514	4,282
Communist World*	4,819	3,545

*Excluding Communist Asia

Details concerning utilization of capacity in particular countries are given in Appendix Table 7.

Levels of plant use are affected also by type of plant. Output per KW of hydro capacity depends in part on availability of water. It also depends upon whether hydro is used for peaking purposes or base load operations. In countries which use hydro for base load operations, such as Norway, Sweden, Iceland, and Finland, output per KW is frequently above 5,000 hours annually. In general, these are countries rich in water resources which depend primarily on hydro for their electricity. Where hydro facilities provide a relatively small part of the total supply, they are more likely to be used for peaking purposes, and output per KW therefore comparatively low. (See Figure 21.)

Fuel Efficiency

In systems which depend heavily on conventional thermal electric power, a major factor in plant economics is the efficiency with which fuels are used to generate electricity.

There is much variation here, from country to country and from plant to plant. Country-by-country data, given in Table 56, show a range of from 36.5% in Japan to 21.3% in India, with countries for which data are available more or less equally distributed through this range. The figures shown, although based on fuel consumption measured in kilogram calories or Btu's per kilowatt hour generated, are not strictly comparable; they do not all refer to the same period of time, nor are they equally inclusive. Some, for example, refer to all thermal plants, including diesel stations, while others deal only with the efficiency of steam power plants.

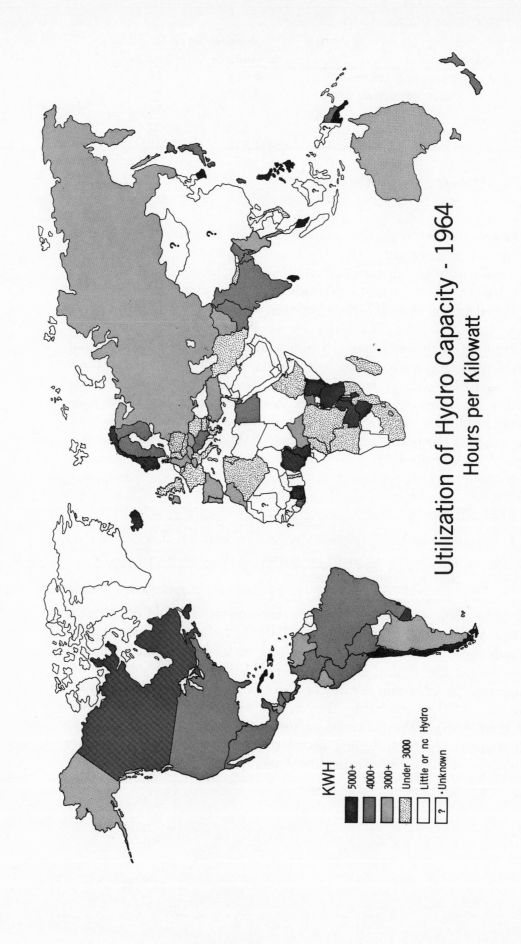

Utilization of Hydro Capacity - 1964
Hours per Kilowatt

KWH

- 5000+
- 4000+
- 3000+
- Under 3000
- Little or no Hydro
- ? · Unknown

TABLE 56.
AVERAGE THERMAL EFFICIENCIES OF UTILITY ELECTRIC PLANTS
in Selected Countries, 1964*

Japan	36.5
Italy	34.3
France	33.1
USA	32.5
China (Taiwan)	32.0
Netherlands	32.0
West Germany	30.8
Belgium	30.1
Denmark	30.1
Austria	29.3
USSR	28.7
Iceland	28.7
Thailand	28.6
Romania	28.5
U.K.	27.6
Poland	26.9
Singapore	26.8
Spain	25.2
New Zealand	24.6
Yugoslavia	24.4
Czechoslovakia	24.1
Luxembourg	24.1
Turkey	24.0
Greece	23.9
Australia	23.9
Portugal	23.6
Argentina (1962)	23.1
Cyprus	22.8
Hungary	22.6
Ireland	22.0
India (1963)	21.3

*Except as indicated.

Concerning countries not listed in the table, little can be said about fuel efficiencies—either because the quantities of fuel consumed are not known precisely, or because the quality of the fuels consumed is not accurately known. For countries which depend primarily on diesel plants, it is probably safe to assume that efficiencies are, for the most part, in the range of 25% to 35%. For countries with small steam plants operating on an intermittent basis, efficiencies are likely to fall somewhat below the range indicated in Table 56.

Data on efficiencies of particular plants indicate that the range is in fact much wider than is shown by the table, being closely associated with plant size, age, and technical characteristics. The influence of plant size, for example, is well illustrated by the following data on fuel efficiencies in steam plants of various size categories in the United Kingdom.

TABLE 57.

RELATIONSHIP OF FUEL EFFICIENCY TO PLANT SIZE*

(Illustrated by UK Data for 1964/65)

Average Efficiency of Fuel Use	Plant Size (MW)
11.8	Under 5
10.4	5 - 10
12.6	10 - 15
11.6	15 - 20
14.9	20 - 25
18.8	25 - 50
22.0	50 - 75
22.4	75 - 100
23.6	100 - 150
24.6	150 - 200
27.3	200 - 250
27.0	250 - 300
29.0	300 - 400
32.5	400 - 500
32.4	500 - 600
33.7	600+

*Steam plants only.

Source: Ministry of Power. **Statistical digest, 1965.**

The *economic* efficiency of thermoelectric plants varies with plant size, as indicated in Table 58.

TABLE 58.

GENERATING COSTS*

Related to

SIZES OF CONVENTIONAL STEAM PLANTS

(Illustrated by UK Data for 1964/65)

Size of Plant (MW)	US¢/kwh sent out
under 5	2.8
5 - 10	4.6
10 - 15	3.2
15 - 20	3.6
20 - 25	2.5

Size of Plant (MW)	US¢/kwh sent out
25 - 50	1.6
50 - 75	1.1
75 - 100	1.1
100 - 150	1.0
150 - 200	0.9
200 - 250	0.8
250 - 300	0.9
300 - 400	0.7
400 - 500	0.6
500 - 600	0.6
600 +	0.6

*Excluding capital charges.

Source: Ministry of Power. **Statistical digest, 1965.**

Chapter 6
Trends

The dynamic nature of the electric power industry is reflected in historical data on electricity production since the turn of the century:

1900	(approximately)	5	twh
1913		54	twh
1920		122	twh
1929		288	twh
1937		447	twh
1950		951	twh
1958		1914	twh

Between 1958 and 1964, output increased a further 1,200 twh, or at an average rate of 8.6% annually.

Demands

Growth was universal, and universally rapid. On a regional basis, it ranged from 6.8% per annum in North America to 12.8% per annum in Asia, attaining an average of better than 8% per annum in all but the most highly developed economies. Phenomenal rates of development were attained in some of the least developed countries — in some, average rates of more than 20% per year.

TABLE 59.
TRENDS IN GROSS CONSUMPTION OF ELECTRICITY, 1958-1964

Area	Average Annual Increase (%)
Asia	12.8
East Europe/USSR	11.0
Oceania	8.9
West Europe	8.3

Area	Average Annual Increase (%)
Latin America	8.1
Africa	8.0
North America	6.8
World	8.5
Developed World	8.3
Underdeveloped World	10.4
Free Enterprise World	7.8
Communist World	11.0

Domestic demands played a major role in the growth of the industry, rising by an average of more than 9.5% per annum, and actually out-pacing total growth in most of the major consuming areas. Even in Norway, where consumption in the domestic sector already exceeded 5,000 kwh per capita at the beginning of the period, it increased by more than 7.5% per annum during the period 1958 through 1964.

In the United States, despite vigorous competition from other sources of energy—natural gas in particular—electricity consumption in the domestic sector rose by 8.3% per annum during the period 1958 through 1964. In the Soviet Union, where consumption in the domestic sector was relatively low at the beginning of the period (about 160 kwh per capita), consumption rose by an average of better than 15% per year.

TABLE 60.
TRENDS IN DOMESTIC CONSUMPTION OF ELECTRICITY, 1958-1964,
by Region, Economic Level, and Politico-economic System

Area	Percent/year
East Europe/USSR	13.8
Asia	12.7
West Europe	10.6
Oceania	9.0
Latin America	8.6
Africa	8.0
North America	8.0
World	9.6
Underdeveloped World	10.1
Developed World	9.5
Communist World	13.4
Free Enterprise World	9.1

Transportation played a variable role in the development of demands for electricity. In East Europe and the Soviet Union, the needs of transportation rose by an average of 18.6% per year between 1958 and 1964; in Africa and Asia, they rose by more than 9.5% per year.

Trends were somewhat mixed in West Europe, with electricity consumption by railways tending to increase, consumption in urban transportation tending to decrease. On balance, West Europe showed a net increase averaging 4.7% per year.

In North America, Oceania, and Latin America, the use of electricity in transportation decreased between 1958 and 1964. In the United States, there was a significant decline in the use of electricity by railways during this period, apparently associated with the decline in passenger rail traffic. (Here, in contrast with practices elsewhere, passenger rather than freight service had been electrified.) Outside the United States, decline in the use of electricity in transportation has been associated mainly with urban travel.

Use of electricity for urban transportation has been increasing in some of the less developed countries of Southern Europe, and in a number of the Communist countries — especially Czechoslovakia, Poland, and Romania.

The divergent trends of electricity use in urban transportation appear to be related to the development of automotive transportation, which was more rapid in the West than in the East.

More than half the increase in the world's consumption of elec-

TABLE 61.

TRENDS IN THE USE OF ELECTRICITY
IN TRANSPORTATION, 1958-1964,

by Region, Economic Level, and Politico-economic System

Area	Percent/year
East Europe/USSR	18.6
Asia	9.6
Africa	9.6
West Europe	4.7
Latin America	−0.7
Oceania	−1.4
North America	−2.4
World	9.6
Developed World	10.0
Underdeveloped World	3.9
Free Enterprise World	4.3
Communist World	18.6

tricity must be attributed to the rising requirements of industry. Between 1958 and 1964, there was a spectacular increase in industry's use of electricity in a number of underdeveloped areas, especially those associated or formerly associated with France. In nine of these —Togo, Guinea, Ivory Coast, Upper Volta, Central African Republic, New Caledonia, Dahomey, French Polynesia, and Niger — the consumption of electricity in industry appears to have increased by an average of more than 30% per annum.

On a regional basis, rates of growth ranged from a minimum of 6% per annum, in North America, to 13.4% in Asia.

TABLE 62.
TRENDS IN INDUSTRIAL CONSUMPTION OF ELECTRICITY, 1958-1964,
by Region, Economic Level, and Politico-economic System

Area	Percent/year
Asia	13.4
East Europe/USSR	10.9
Oceania	9.1
Latin America	8.0
Africa	7.7
West Europe	7.5
North America	6.0
World	8.3
Developed World	8.0
Underdeveloped World	10.7
Free Enterprise World	7.3
Communist World	10.9

In spite of all these differences in rates of growth from one sector of the economy to another, there was relatively little change in the overall structure of electricity consumption between 1958 and 1964. Industry's share of the total declined slightly, from 55% to 54%, while the share of the domestic sector rose from 31% to 33%. These changes are hardly discernible in Figure 22, which shows the development of demands for electricity between 1958 and 1964.

Supplies

The growth of demands for electricity was matched by a rapid expansion of production, from both established and new sources. There were large increases in output of hydroelectricity, for example, especially in Africa, Oceania, and the underdeveloped world as a whole.

DEVELOPMENT OF
ELECTRICITY CONSUMPTION, 1958-1964
By Use

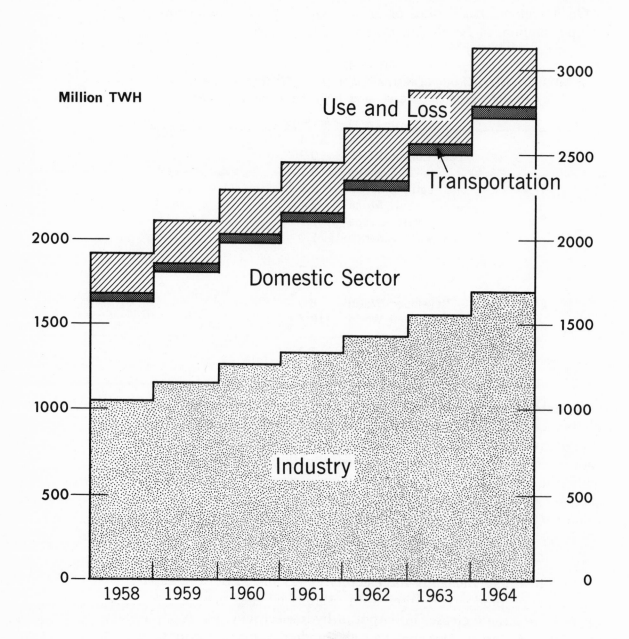

Million TWH

Use and Loss

Transportation

Domestic Sector

Industry

TABLE 63.
TRENDS IN PRODUCTION OF HYDROELECTRICITY, 1958-1964,
by Region, Economic Level, and Politico-economic System

Area	Percent/year
Africa	14.2
Oceania	9.4
East Europe/USSR	8.3
Latin America	6.1
Asia	5.3
West Europe	4.7
North America	3.8
World	5.0
Developed World	4.3
Underdeveloped World	9.4
Free Enterprise World	4.6
Communist World	8.5

Amazing gains were made in output of conventional thermal electricity during the period 1958 to 1964. In Asia, output rose by an average of 19.6% per year, while gains in East Europe/USSR, West Europe, and Latin America averaged better than 10% per year. Spectacular increases occurred in Japan and Italy, where there was a definite switch from hydro to thermal facilities. In Japan, production of conventional thermal power rose at a rate of better than 28% per year between 1958 and 1964, and in Italy it averaged only a bit less than 28% per year.

TABLE 64.
TRENDS IN PRODUCTION
OF CONVENTIONAL THERMAL ELECTRICITY, 1958-1964,
by Region, Economic Level, and Politico-economic System

Area	Percent/year
Asia	19.6
East Europe/USSR	11.4
West Europe	10.1
Latin America	10.1
Oceania	7.9
North America	7.7
Africa	6.8
World	9.9
Developed World	9.8
Underdeveloped World	11.5
Free Enterprise World	9.5
Communist World	11.5

Production of geothermal power more than doubled between 1958 and 1964, rising at an average rate of 12.5% per annum. It was during this period that the new plants at Wairakei in New Zealand, and The Geysers in California, came on stream.

Output of nuclear power soared from a mere half-billion kwh in 1958 to over 17 billion in 1964. More than half this development took place in the United Kingdom, most of the remainder in West Europe, the USA, and the Soviet Union. (The 17 billion kwh figure includes an estimate of 2 billion kwh for the Soviet Union—an estimate based on the reported capacities of the plants at Beloyarsk [94 MW net] and Novo Voronezh [196 MW net]. Such data as are available concerning nuclear electricity production in the USSR suggest that the Troitsk plant may be used for other purposes than the production of electricity.)

The net effect of differential rates of growth in output of hydro, conventional thermal, geothermal, and nuclear power was a significant change in the structure of production, reflected mainly in a decline in hydro's share in total output, and increases in the shares of conventional thermal, nuclear, and geothermal in the total. Hydro's share fell from 32% to 26% between 1958 and 1964, while the share of conventional thermal in the total rose from 68% to 73%, and the shares of the other two sources together rose from 0.1% to 0.7%.

TABLE 65.

CHANGES IN THE

STRUCTURE OF ELECTRICITY PRODUCTION, 1958-1964,

by Region, Economic Level, and Politico-economic System

Area	Percentage Shares in Total Production					
	Hydro		Conv. Thermal		Other	
	1958	1964	1958	1964	1958	1964
North America	28.4	24.1	71.6	75.6	—	0.3
West Europe	40.3	33.0	59.2	65.2	0.5	1.8
East Europe/USSR	15.8	13.6	84.2	86.1	—	(0.3)
Africa	16.4	22.7	83.6	77.3	—	—
Asia	55.2	36.5	44.8	63.5	—	—
Oceania	34.0	34.6	66.0	62.6	—	2.8
Latin America	51.4	45.9	48.6	54.1	—	—
World	32.1	26.3	67.8	73.0	0.1	0.7
Developed World	30.6	24.3	69.3	74.9	0.1	0.8
Underdeveloped World	47.0	44.1	53.0	55.9	—	—
Free Enterprise World	35.3	29.2	64.5	70.0	0.2	0.8
Communist World	18.8	16.4	81.2	83.3	—	(0.3)

CHANGES IN THE STRUCTURE OF
ELECTRICITY PRODUCTION, 1958-1964

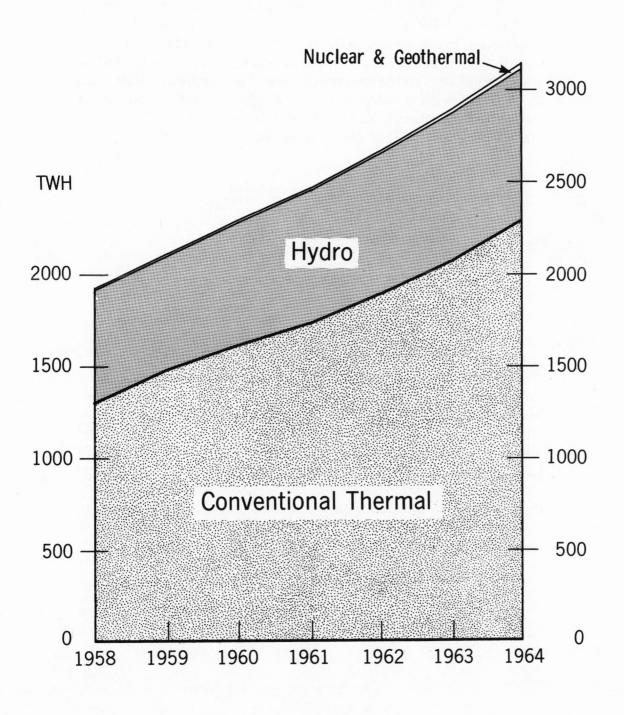

Changes in Fuel Consumption by Electric Utilities

The tremendous increase in output of conventional thermal power during the period between 1958 and 1964 was accompanied by a nearly proportionate increase in fuel use by electric utilities. On an energy-content basis, the rate of increase averaged 8.9% per annum, as compared with a 9.9% increase in output of conventional thermal power.

Each of the different fuels was consumed in greater quantity in 1964 than in 1958. Coal consumption rose from 341 to 511 million metric tons, lignite consumption from 158 to 270 millions tons. The use of oil fuels more than doubled, increasing from 33 to 69 million metric tons, and gas consumption more than doubled, rising from about 50,000 million cubic meters to roughly 100,000 million cubic meters. Annual rates of increase ranged from just under 7%, in the case of coal, to 13.5%, in the case of fuel oils.

	Average Annual Increase 1958-1964 (%)
Coal	6.9
Lignite, Peat, and Wood	9.1
Fuel Oils	13.5
Gas	12.8
Other	12.2
Total	8.9

Regional patterns of change were particularly interesting. Coal, the traditional source of thermal electric power, made important gains throughout the world. Gas made very large gains percentagewise, but in absolute terms, its contributions to the electricity supply were outstanding only in North America and East Europe/USSR. Fuel oils, not an important source of electricity before 1964 except in Latin America, achieved considerable importance in West Europe and Asia. Consumption of oil for power generation increased more than four-fold in the European Communities, and ten-fold in Japan.

Changes in the structure of fuel consumption in the generation of electric power by utilities are shown in Table 66 and Figure 24.

TABLE 66.
FUEL USE BY ELECTRIC UTILITIES
in 1958 and 1964

Fuel	1958		1964	
	Quantity (000 Tcal)	Share of Total (Percentage)	Quantity (000 Tcal)	Share of Total (Percentage)
Coal	1936.8	61	2878.3	55
Lignite and Peat	434.0	14	734.5	14
Fuel Oils	332.2	10	708.7	13
Gas	461.0	15	950.2	18
Other Fuels	0.4	—	0.8	—
All Fuels	3164.4	100	5272.5	100

International Trade in Electricity

International trade in electricity developed even more rapidly than did consumption during the period 1958 to 1964, rising at a rate of 17% per annum. From a total of only 15 twh in 1958, movement across international boundaries reached 38 twh in 1964.

The largest part of this increase occurred in West Europe, where international trade rose from 9 twh to 23 twh per annum. Percentage-wise, the largest increase took place in the East Europe/USSR region, following establishment of the COMECON network. There was also a substantial growth in Africa, following the completion of Kariba and the resulting flow of electricity from Rhodesia to Zambia.

TABLE 67.
DEVELOPMENT OF INTERNATIONAL TRADE
IN ELECTRICITY, 1958-1964:
Total Exports* (twh)

	1958	1964
West Europe	8.8	22.9
North America	4.9	8.5
East Europe/USSR	0.7	4.5
Africa	0.8	2.3
World	15.2	38.2

*Sum of reported exports by particular countries.

A development of special interest took place in Europe during this period—namely, the construction of a submarine interconnection between Britain and France.

Country-by-country data on the growth of net international trade are given in Table 5 of the Appendix.

TRENDS IN WORLD CONSUMPTION
OF FUELS IN ELECTRIC POWER PLANTS
1958-1964

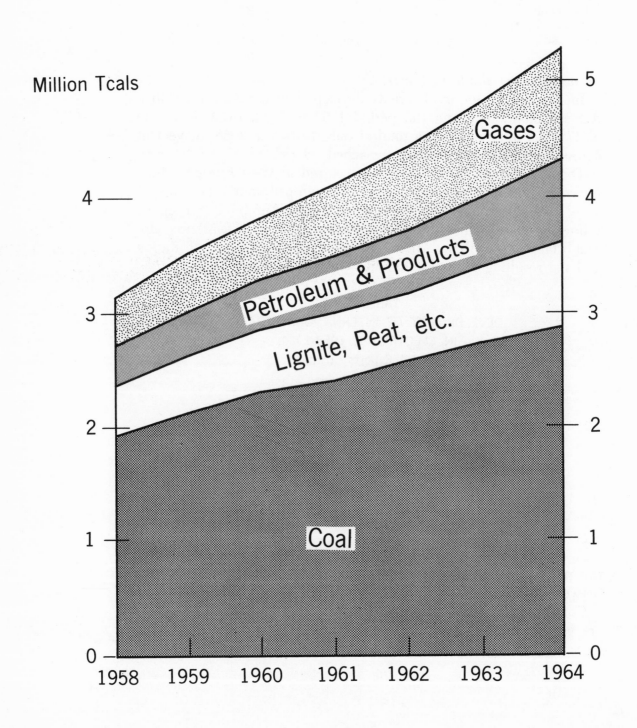

Plant

Installed capacity, like production, rose steadily and rapidly during the period of 1958 to 1964, although not quite as rapidly as did production. Net additions to installed capacity increased by an average of more than 45,000 MW per year, of which one-quarter was new hydro capacity, about three-quarters new conventional thermal capacity. Additions to nuclear capacity averaged 545 MW per annum during the period, additions to geothermal capacity about 43 MW per annum.

TABLE 68.
TRENDS IN INSTALLED CAPACITY
OF ELECTRIC POWER PLANTS, 1958-1964

	Average Annual Increase (000 MW)	Annual Growth Rate (%)
Total	45.4	8.0
Hydro	11.8	7.1
Conventional Thermal	33.0	8.3
Nuclear	0.6	58.3
Geothermal	0.04	11.1

The distribution of additions to capacity was similar to that of increases in production and consumption. In terms of physical quantity, they were largest in North America, where additions to capacity averaged 14.7 million KW annually, and next largest in Europe, where they averaged 11 million KW per annum. Rates of increase, however, were much higher in Asia and East Europe/USSR than they were in the western countries. Asia's growth, in fact, was nearly twice as rapid as growth in North America and Western Europe.

TABLE 69.
GROWTH OF TOTAL INSTALLED CAPACITY, 1958-1964,
by Region, Economic Level, and Politico-economic System

Area	Average Annual Increase (%)
Asia	11.0
East Europe/USSR	10.8
Latin America	9.4
Oceania	8.0
North America	6.9
West Europe	6.8
Africa	6.8
World	8.0

TABLE 69 (Continued)

Area	Average Annual Increase (%)
Developed World	7.9
Underdeveloped World	9.0
Free Enterprise World	7.5
Communist World	10.2

One-third of the world's hydro capacity was installed during this period, 40% of its conventional thermal and geothermal capacities, and 95% of its nuclear capacity. These changes in aggregate capacity were accompanied by significant changes in the sizes of both generating units and plants — hydro, conventional thermal, and nuclear.

In the case of generating units for hydroelectric plants, for example, the size of the largest units in use increased from 115 MW, at Kuibyshev, to 225 MW, at Bratsk. In Canada, the maximum size increased from 114 to 148.5 MW; in the U.S., from 100 MW to 150 MW.

There were substantial increases, too, in the maximum sizes of electric power *plants*. For many years, the Grand Coulee (USA), with a capacity of 1,974 MW, was by far the largest hydroelectric plant in the world. It is still the largest plant in the United States. In 1958, however, Kuibyshev, with a capacity of 2,300 MW became the world's largest hydroelectric plant, and since then two larger plants have been built, both in the Soviet Union: Volgagrad, with a capacity of 2,563 MW, and Bratsk, whose capacity has now reached 4,500 MW.

The scale of operations also changed substantially elsewhere—in Africa, by the construction of Kariba, with a capacity of 705 MW; in the Far East, by the completion of India's Bhakra hydro plant, with five 90 MW units and a total capacity of 450 MW; in Latin America, with the construction of Brazil's Furnas, with a capacity of 1,250 MW; and in West Europe, with the construction of Aldeadavila, whose 718 MW make it the largest hydro plant in that region.

Australia got its first large hydro plants with the completion of Tumut No. 1 (320 MW) in 1959, and Tumut No. 2 (280 MW) in 1962.

The development of both units and plants was even more dramatic in connection with the generation of thermal electric power. The largest units in service outside of the United States in 1958 were 150 MW units in the Soviet Union and in West Europe. By 1964, the size of the largest units had increased to 300 MW in the Soviet Union and Canada, to 550 MW in the United Kingdom, and to 200 MW in Asia. In the United States, the maximum size of thermal units increased from 335 MW, in 1958, to 700 MW, in 1964. At the end of 1964, there were in operation in the United States some 52 units of 300 MW or more capacity.

Thermal plant sizes also increased tremendously. The Frimmers-dorf plant in Germany, the world's largest thermal electric plant in 1964, had only 588 MW of capacity in 1958, but had increased to 2,078 MW by the end of 1964. Russia's largest thermal plant at that time had a capacity of 610 MW, or substantially less than the largest US plant—TVA's Kingston plant, with a capacity of 1,600 MW—at that time the largest thermal electric plant in the world.

The maximum capacity of nuclear plants—90 MW at the beginning of 1958—rose to 524 MW (net) with the completion in 1964 of the Hinkley Point plant in Great Britain.

Changes in Ownership

The long-term trend toward public ownership of utilities continued during the period 1958 to 1964. In some cases, changes were effected by public acquisition of utility properties: the purchase by the Mexican government of properties formerly owned by the Mex Light and Foreign Power Groups; the purchase by the Argentine government of SEGBA shares; confiscation by the Cuban government of the assets of Cia. Cubana de Electricidad; purchase by the Colombian government of the property of Cia. Colombiana de Electricidad; the acquisition by Eletrobras of the properties of Brazilian Electric Power Company and American and Foreign Power Company; the transfer to ENEL of Italy's privately owned utilities; and the transfer of utility properties to governments in relatively small countries in Asia and Africa.

The public's share in the utility industry was increased also by the relatively rapid development of publicly owned facilities in comparison with those that are privately owned. In India, for example, government's share in the total capacity of the utility industry rose from 62% in 1958 to 78% in 1964; and in Chile, ENDESA increased its share in the total utility industry from 63% in 1958 to 70% in 1964, simply by expanding more rapidly than did the privately owned portion of the industry. There appear to have been no significant changes in the balance of ownership in the two strongholds of private enterprise—the US and Japan.

Chapter 7
Geographic Coverage
of this Survey

Historical data on installed capacity and on production, trade, and consumption of electricity in most of the countries of the world, and, in many cases, data on the uses of electricity and the fuels used to generate electricity, are provided in this portion of the survey. Unfortunately, it has not been possible to obtain the complete geographic coverage sought. Thus, there are about a dozen countries for which no data whatsoever have been uncovered; among these are Bhutan, Botswana, Cayman Islands, Gilbert and Ellice Islands, Maldive Islands, Mauritius dependencies, Muscat and Oman, Sikkim, South Arabia (protectorate), Tonga, Trucial Oman, Turks and Caicos Islands, West Irian, and Yemen.

Only a modicum of data have been found for another two dozen countries. These countries are listed below, together with their estimated production of electricity in the year 1964 (except as otherwise indicated).

Country	Production (million kwh)
British Solomon Islands	2
Burundi	15
Cape Verde Islands	3
Channel Islands (1965)	224
Comores Island	0.6
Cook Islands (1960)	approx. 1
Falkland Islands (1966)	1.6
Isle of Man (1965)	84
Lesotho (formerly Basutoland)	2.7
Leeward Islands (1962)	13
Mauritania	5
New Hebrides	6.4
Ocean Island (1960)	3.4
Portuguese Timor	0.7
Qatar (1961)	62

Country	Production (million kwh)
St. Helena (1960)	0.1
Seychelles Islands	1
Spanish Guinea	9.4
Spanish Sahara and Ifni	1.5
Swaziland (1960)	2.4
Windward Islands (1962)	approx. 16

Certain enclaves which do not appear in the list of countries have been treated as part of their host countries—Monaco, for example, is shown with France, San Marino and the Holy See with Italy, Lichtenstein with Switzerland, and Andorra with Spain. The Spanish data also include the Canary Islands and Spanish North Africa (principally Ceuta and Melilla).

In the case of the Asian Peoples Republics, the only data available are those dealing with total production of electricity, and for Mainland China they appear to be neither accurate nor up-to-date. For this part of the world a single table has therefore been prepared, incorporating those production data that seem acceptable, and adding to them estimates for subjects and areas otherwise unrepresented. The sources of data and methods of estimate employed are indicated on the pages dealing with the Asian Peoples Republics.

PART II
SECTION ONE

World and Regional Electricity Accounts

WORLD

SUPPLY AND USE (million kwh)	1958	1959	1960	1961	1962	1963	1964
PRODUCTION (Utilities & industries)							
Total (Gross)	1 914 322	2 108 220	2 296 647	2 460 650	2 665 082	2 881 085	3 132 852
(Net)	1 884 382	2 074 487	2 259 014	2 419 246	2 617 487	2 828 253	3 071 566
Hydro	613 575	631 092	684 015	723 714	761 390	798 155	825 172
Conventional thermal	1 298 337	1 473 447	1 607 374	1 729 683	1 893 975	2 067 683	2 286 712
Nuclear	474	1 433	2 737	4 376	6 510	11 648	17 043
Geothermal	1 936	2 248	2 521	2 877	3 207	3 599	3 925
PRODUCTION (Utilities only)							
Total (Gross)	1 570 663	1 741 006	1 900 981	2 044 574	2 221 970	2 414 005	2 630 151
(Net)	--	--	--	--	--	--	--
Hydro	547 093	563 407	609 605	649 292	684 531	722 028	745 960
Conventional thermal	1 021 465	1 175 119	1 288 197	1 390 428	1 530 437	1 679 717	1 866 232
Nuclear	169	232	658	1 977	3 795	8 661	14 034
Geothermal	1 936	2 248	2 521	2 877	3 207	3 599	3 925
NET IMPORTS	857	-1 741	650	-1 221	-1 110	432	209
SUPPLY (Gross)	1 915 179	2 106 479	2 297 297	2 459 429	2 663 972	2 881 517	3 133 061
(Net)	1 885 239	2 072 746	2 259 664	2 418 025	2 616 377	2 828 685	3 071 775
CONSUMPTION	1 687 180	1 859 416	2 030 745	2 172 793	2 353 834	2 570 478	2 795 149
Transport	45 906	49 802	54 856	58 977	64 538	73 689	79 501
Domestic sector	588 860	648 115	707 187	770 389	854 330	936 507	1 018 493
Industry	1 052 414	1 161 499	1 268 702	1 343 427	1 434 966	1 560 282	1 697 155
LOSS AND USE	198 059	213 330	228 919	245 232	262 543	258 207	276 626
PLANT (thousand kw)							
CAPACITY (Utilities & industries)							
Total	461 640	504 347	545 874	586 381	629 026	685 903	733 725
Hydro	138 820	149 736	162 118	174 284	186 514	199 548	209 664
Conventional thermal	322 305	353 772	382 618	410 765	440 117	483 206	520 017
Nuclear	222	477	759	919	1 908	2 606	3 494
Geothermal	293	362	379	413	487	543	550
CAPACITY (Utilities only)							
Total	373 779	412 168	447 122	483 079	521 026	571 745	616 803
Hydro	125 844	136 357	148 190	156 147	171 892	184 044	194 217
Conventional thermal	247 531	275 287	298 154	325 960	347 252	385 126	419 181
Nuclear	111	162	399	559	1 395	2 032	2 855
Geothermal	293	362	379	413	487	543	550
FUEL CONSUMPTION (Utilities only)							
Coal (mmt)	340 880	375 380	405 097	425 032	453 817	486 203	511 287
Lignite & peat (mmt)	157 814	181 222	195 615	206 857	222 754	242 289	270 176
Fuel oils (mmt)	32 560	36 000	41 547	48 061	52 494	57 649	68 755
Gases (Tcals)	451 423	531 437	578 461	636 323	711 964	834 323	950 231
Total (Tcals)	3 154 798	3 533 625	3 835 825	4 106 634	4 417 411	4 834 595	5 272 527
RESERVOIR STORAGE CAPACITY (million kwh)	52 307	55 725	62 451	64 217	70 130	77 185	83 180

SUPPLY AND USE (million kwh)	1958	1959	1960	1961	1962	1963	1964
PRODUCTION (Utilities & industries)							
Total (Gross)	1 741 093	1 907 405	2 073 887	2 216 786	2 398 639	2 591 155	2 816 498
(Net)	1 714 099	1 876 866	2 039 625	2 179 187	2 355 476	2 542 752	2 760 694
Hydro	532 204	540 748	583 766	614 856	643 005	665 707	685 669
Conventional thermal	1 206 479	1 362 976	1 484 863	1 594 677	1 745 917	1 910 201	2 109 861
Nuclear	474	1 433	2 737	4 376	6 510	11 648	17 043
Geothermal	1 936	2 248	2 521	2 877	3 207	3 599	3 925
PRODUCTION (Utilities only)							
Total (Gross)	1 424 560	1 569 794	1 709 537	1 833 242	1 990 918	2 161 363	2 350 896
(Net)	--	--	--	--	--	--	--
Hydro	474 789	482 244	518 583	549 000	575 044	597 672	615 629
Conventional thermal	947 666	1 085 070	1 187 775	1 279 388	1 408 872	1 551 431	1 717 308
Nuclear	169	232	658	1 977	3 795	8 661	14 034
Geothermal	1 936	2 248	2 521	2 877	3 207	3 599	3 925
NET IMPORTS	300	−1 899	303	−1 439	−1 275	1 054	1 358
SUPPLY (Gross)	1 741 393	1 905 506	2 074 190	2 215 347	2 397 364	2 592 209	2 817 856
(Net)	1 714 399	1 874 967	2 039 928	2 177 748	2 354 201	2 543 806	2 762 052
CONSUMPTION	1 540 419	1 689 015	1 841 304	1 966 747	2 128 495	2 326 080	2 529 559
Transport	42 073	46 094	50 902	54 806	60 264	69 124	74 679
Domestic sector	543 430	597 068	650 628	707 898	785 483	861 965	937 387
Industry	954 916	1 045 853	1 139 774	1 204 043	1 282 748	1 394 991	1 517 493
LOSS AND USE	173 980	185 952	198 624	211 001	225 706	217 726	232 493
PLANT (thousand kw)							
CAPACITY (Utilities & industries)							
Total	409 600	447 690	483 018	517 864	554 452	605 639	646 517
Hydro	117 582	126 668	135 787	145 463	154 561	165 459	172 419
Conventional thermal	291 503	320 183	346 093	371 069	397 496	437 031	470 054
Nuclear	222	477	759	919	1 908	2 606	3 494
Geothermal	293	362	379	413	487	543	550
CAPACITY (Utilities only)							
Total	329 992	364 523	394 242	424 679	457 387	502 963	541 141
Hydro	106 183	114 849	123 560	128 801	141 504	151 502	158 392
Conventional thermal	223 405	249 150	269 904	294 906	314 001	348 886	379 344
Nuclear	111	162	399	559	1 395	2 032	2 855
Geothermal	293	362	379	413	487	543	550
FUEL CONSUMPTION (Utilities only)							
Coal (mmt)	307 430	329 293	353 766	370 998	396 681	426 873	447 726
Lignite & peat (mmt)	152 676	176 211	190 345	199 755	214 465	231 618	257 366
Fuel oils (mmt)	22 708	25 167	29 962	35 373	38 547	42 386	51 576
Gases (Tcals)	443 084	520 921	595 954	615 632	686 545	799 547	908 467
Total (Tcals)	2 869 635	3 174 975	3 440 091	3 665 165	3 938 602	4 319 482	4 702 518
RESERVOIR STORAGE CAPACITY (million kwh)	43 736	46 294	50 670	53 435	58 517	64 977	68 113

UNDERDEVELOPED WORLD, UNDERDEVELOPED WEST AND COMMUNIST ASIA

SUPPLY AND USE (million kwh)	1958	1959	1960	1961	1962	1963	1964
PRODUCTION (Utilities & industries)							
Total (Gross)	173 229	200 815	222 760	243 864	266 443	289 930	316 354
(Net)	170 283	197 621	219 389	240 059	262 011	285 501	310 872
Hydro	81 371	90 344	100 249	108 858	118 385	132 448	139 503
Conventional thermal	91 858	110 471	122 511	135 006	148 058	157 482	176 851
Nuclear	–	–	–	–	–	–	–
Geothermal	–	–	–	–	–	–	–
PRODUCTION (Utilities only)							
Total (Gross)	146 103	171 212	191 444	211 332	231 052	252 642	279 255
(Net)	--	--	--	--	--	--	--
Hydro	72 304	81 163	91 022	100 292	109 487	124 356	130 331
Conventional thermal	73 799	90 049	100 422	111 040	121 565	128 286	148 924
Nuclear	–	–	–	–	–	–	–
Geothermal	–	–	–	–	–	–	–
NET IMPORTS	557	158	347	218	165	–622	–1 149
SUPPLY (Gross)	173 786	200 973	223 107	244 082	266 608	289 308	315 205
(Net)	170 840	197 779	219 736	240 277	262 176	284 879	309 723
CONSUMPTION	146 761	170 401	189 441	206 046	225 339	244 398	265 590
Transport	3 833	3 708	3 954	4 171	4 274	4 565	4 822
Domestic sector	45 430	51 047	56 559	62 491	68 847	74 542	81 106
Industry	97 498	115 646	128 928	139 384	152 218	165 291	179 662
LOSS AND USE	24 079	27 378	30 295	34 231	36 837	40 481	44 133
PLANT (thousand kw)							
CAPACITY (Utilities & industries)							
Total	52 040	56 657	62 856	68 517	74 574	80 264	87 208
Hydro	21 238	23 068	26 331	28 821	31 953	34 089	37 245
Conventional thermal	30 802	33 589	36 525	39 696	42 621	46 175	49 963
Nuclear	–	–	–	–	–	–	–
Geothermal	–	–	–	–	–	–	–
CAPACITY (Utilities only)							
Total	43 787	47 645	52 880	58 400	63 639	68 782	75 662
Hydro	19 661	21 508	24 630	27 346	30 388	32 542	35 825
Conventional thermal	24 126	26 137	28 250	31 054	33 251	36 240	39 837
Nuclear	–	–	–	–	–	–	–
Geothermal	–	–	–	–	–	–	–
FUEL CONSUMPTION (Utilities only)							
Coal (mmt)	33 450	46 087	51 331	54 034	57 136	59 330	63 561
Lignite & peat (mmt)	5 138	5 011	5 270	7 102	8 289	10 671	12 810
Fuel oils (mmt)	9 852	10 833	11 585	12 688	13 947	15 263	17 179
Gases (Tcals)	8 339	10 516	12 507	20 691	25 419	34 776	41 764
Total (Tcals)	285 163	358 650	395 734	441 469	478 809	515 113	570 009
RESERVOIR STORAGE CAPACITY (million kwh)	8 571	9 431	11 781	10 782	11 613	12 208	15 067

FREE ENTERPRISE WORLD

SUPPLY AND USE (million kwh)	1958	1959	1960	1961	1962	1963	1964
PRODUCTION (Utilities & industries)							
Total (Gross)	1 538 891	1 678 491	1 821 783	1 935 843	2 083 877	2 243 575	2 431 301
(Net)	1 515 103	1 651 694	1 791 846	1 902 993	2 045 624	2 201 685	2 382 327
Hydro	543 085	557 385	602 692	632 737	654 182	685 576	710 421
Conventional thermal	993 396	1 117 425	1 213 833	1 295 853	1 419 978	1 543 752	1 701 912
Nuclear	474	1 433	2 737	4 376	6 510	10 648	15 043
Geothermal	1 936	2 248	2 521	2 877	3 207	3 599	3 925
PRODUCTION (Utilities only)							
Total (Gross)	1 287 069	1 407 675	1 531 572	1 636 671	1 765 302	1 907 672	2 072 213
(Net)	--	--	--	--	--	--	--
Hydro	478 955	491 946	530 552	560 659	579 814	611 823	633 567
Conventional thermal	806 009	913 249	997 841	1 071 158	1 178 486	1 284 589	1 422 687
Nuclear	169	232	658	1 977	3 795	7 661	12 034
Geothermal	1 936	2 248	2 521	2 877	3 207	3 599	3 925
NET IMPORTS	973	–1 771	576	–1 215	–1 220	424	–186
SUPPLY (Gross)	1 539 864	1 676 720	1 822 359	1 934 628	2 082 657	2 243 999	2 431 115
(Net)	1 516 076	1 649 923	1 792 422	1 901 778	2 044 404	2 202 109	2 382 141
CONSUMPTION	1 361 100	1 485 512	1 616 847	1 715 407	1 847 623	1 992 269	2 160 447
Transport	32 183	33 122	34 895	36 122	38 108	39 960	41 410
Domestic sector	534 011	584 698	636 005	691 073	764 758	830 528	901 603
Industry	794 906	867 692	945 947	988 212	1 044 757	1 121 781	1 217 434
LOSS AND USE	154 976	164 411	175 575	186 371	196 781	209 840	221 694
PLANT (thousand kw)							
CAPACITY (Utilities & industries)							
Total	373 180	406 704	437 890	467 920	499 145	542 383	575 403
Hydro	121 272	129 401	138 750	148 190	157 271	167 674	176 732
Conventional thermal	251 398	276 469	298 007	318 403	339 484	371 865	394 932
Nuclear	217	472	754	914	1 903	2 301	3 189
Geothermal	293	362	379	413	487	543	550
CAPACITY (Utilities only)							
Total	312 246	343 319	370 660	398 771	426 930	465 970	498 531
Hydro	109 203	116 937	125 671	130 876	143 484	153 298	162 418
Conventional thermal	202 644	225 863	244 216	266 928	281 569	310 402	333 013
Nuclear	106	157	394	554	1 390	1 727	2 550
Geothermal	293	362	379	413	487	543	550
FUEL CONSUMPTION (Utilities only)							
Coal (mmt)	256 754	272 495	291 813	304 461	329 086	356 659	378 375
Lignite & peat (mmt)	53 579	59 870	63 203	68 165	73 823	78 731	88 183
Fuel oils (mmt)	28 794	32 923	38 198	44 355	48 670	53 460	63 982
Gases (Tcals)	376 122	450 815	491 975	528 857	574 943	627 634	677 166
Other fuels (Tcals)	371	214	284	407	360	329	543
Total (Tcals)	2 394 848	2 622 995	2 841 530	3 040 705	3 293 945	3 584 496	3 903 071
RESERVOIR STORAGE CAPACITY (million kwh)	51 523	54 478	60 356	62 285	67 909	73 820	79 528

SUPPLY AND USE (million kwh)	1958	1959	1960	1961	1962	1963	1964
PRODUCTION (Utilities & industries)							
Total (Gross)	375 431	429 729	474 864	524 807	581 205	637 510	701 551
(Net)	369 279	422 793	467 168	516 253	571 863	626 568	689 239
Hydro	70 490	73 707	81 323	90 977	107 208	112 579	114 751
Conventional thermal	304 941	356 022	393 541	433 830	473 997	523 931	584 800
Nuclear	(included in	conventional	thermal)			1 000e	2 000e
Geothermal	—	—	—	—	—	—	—
PRODUCTION (Utilities only)							
Total (Gross)	283 594	333 331	369 409	407 903	456 668	506 333	557 938
(Net)	--	--	--	--	--	--	--
Hydro	68 138	71 461	79 053	88 633	104 717	110 205	112 393
Conventional thermal	215 456	261 870	290 356	319 270	351 951	395 128	443 545
Nuclear	(included in	conventional	thermal)			1 000e	2 000e
Geothermal	—	—	—	—	—	—	—
NET IMPORTS	-116	30	74	-6	110	8	395
SUPPLY (Gross)	375 315	429 759	474 938	524 801	581 315	637 518	701 946
(Net)	369 163	422 823	467 242	516 247	571 973	626 576	689 634
CONSUMPTION	326 080	373 904	413 898	457 386	506 211	578 209	634 702
Transport	13 723	16 680	19 961	22 855	26 430	33 729	38 091
Domestic sector	54 849	63 417	71 182	79 316	89 572	105 979	116 890
Industry	257 508	293 807	322 755	355 215	390 209	438 501	479 721
LOSS AND USE	43 083	48 919	53 344	58 861	65 762	48 367	54 932
PLANT (thousand kw)							
CAPACITY (Utilities & industries)							
Total	88 460	97 643	107 984	118 461	129 881	143 520	158 322
Hydro	17 548	20 335	23 368	26 094	29 243	31 874	32 932
Conventional thermal	70 907	77 303	84 611	92 362	100 633	111 341	125 085
Nuclear	5	5	5	5	5	305	305
Geothermal	—	—	—	—	—	—	—
CAPACITY (Utilities only)							
Total	61 533	68 849	76 462	84 308	94 096	105 775	118 272
Hydro	16 641	19 420	22 519	25 271	28 408	30 746	31 799
Conventional thermal	44 887	49 424	53 938	59 032	65 683	74 724	86 168
Nuclear	5	5	5	5	5	305	305
Geothermal	—	—	—	—	—	—	—
FUEL CONSUMPTION (Utilities only)							
Coal (mmt)	84 126	102 885	113 284	120 571	124 731	129 544	132 912
Lignite & peat (mmt)	104 235	121 352	132 412	138 692	148 931	163 558	181 993
Fuel oils (mmt)	3 766	3 077	3 349	3 706	3 824	4 189	4 773
Gases (Tcals)	75 301	80 622	86 486	107 466	137 021	206 689	273 065
Other fuels (Tcals)	—	7	—	—	—	—	259
Total (Tcals)	759 950	910 630	994 295	1 065 929	1 123 466	1 250 099	1 369 456
RESERVOIR STORAGE CAPACITY (million kwh)	784	1 237	2 095	1 932	2 221	3 365	3 597

SUPPLY AND USE (million kwh)	1958	1959	1960	1961	1962	1963	1964
PRODUCTION (Utilities & industries)							
Total (Gross)	(824 298)	(902 263)	(958 673)	(995 241)	(1 064 028)	(1 133 693)	(1 218 770)
(Net)	824 298	902 263	958 673	995 241	1 064 028	1 133 693	1 218 770
Hydro	234 324	238 541	255 398	259 549	276 136	272 822	293 646
Conventional thermal	589 809	663 534	702 724	733 906	785 500	857 404	921 436
Nuclear	(165)	(188)	(518)	(1 692)	(2 292)	(3 299)	(3 484)
Geothermal	–	–	33	94	100	168	204
PRODUCTION (Utilities only)							
Total (Gross)	(722 966)	(794 884)	(844 546)	(883 681)	(946 915)	(1 010 406)	(1 086 909)
(Net)	--	--	--	--	--	--	--
Hydro	211 633	215 796	228 999	234 484	249 922	243 868	261 944
Conventional thermal	511 168	578 900	614 996	647 411	694 601	763 071	821 277
Nuclear	165	188	518	1 692	2 292	3 299	3 484
Geothermal	–	–	33	94	100	168	204
NET IMPORTS	–524	–474	–620	–509	–797	–850	+917
SUPPLY (Gross)	(823 774)	(901 789)	(958 053)	(994 732)	(1 063 231)	(1 132 843)	(1 219 687)
(Net)	823 774	901 789	958 053	994 732	1 063 231	1 132 843	1 219 687
CONSUMPTION	750 829	823 643	877 260	910 576	974 285	1 038 946	1 120 383
Transport	5 777	5 567	5 425	5 276	5 234	5 043	5 030
Domestic sector	329 465	362 477	390 271	417 203	454 682	483 482	525 799
Industry	415 587	455 599	481 564	488 097	514 369	550 421	589 554
LOSS AND USE	72 945	78 146	80 793	84 156	88 946	93 897	99 304
PLANT (thousand kw)							
CAPACITY (Utilities & industries)							
Total	179 333	196 144	209 585	223 324	234 562	255 078	267 523
Hydro	45 776	49 434	51 823	55 321	57 501	61 028	63 212
Conventional thermal	133 452	146 605	157 453	167 549	176 356	193 254	203 358
Nuclear	105	105	297	442	692	769	926
Geothermal	–	–	12	12	13	27	27
CAPACITY (Utilities only)							
Total	157 363	174 293	186 998	200 815	212 141	231 761	244 191
Hydro	41 941	45 199	47 195	46 737	52 920	56 098	58 273
Conventional thermal	115 317	128 989	139 494	153 624	158 516	174 867	184 965
Nuclear	105	105	297	442	692	769	926
Geothermal	–	–	12	12	13	27	27
FUEL CONSUMPTION (Utilities only)							
Coal (mmt)	142 071	153 479	160 979	166 095	177 235	194 855	208 058
Lignite & peat (mmt)	688	593	933	1 181	1 445	1 533	2 130
Fuel oils (mmt)	12 523	13 287	13 759	14 091	14 152	14 689	15 667
Natural gas (Tcals)	358 538	426 913	458 987	483 183	523 217	566 788	612 627
Total (Tcals)	1 442 774	1 594 363	1 684 877	1 747 992	1 863 129	2 028 881	2 175 163
RESERVOIR STORAGE CAPACITY (million kwh)	--	--	--	--	--	--	--

WEST EUROPE

SUPPLY AND USE (million kwh)	1958	1959	1960	1961	1962	1963	1964
PRODUCTION (Utilities & industries)							
Total (Gross)	482 875	517 347	571 280	615 745	669 138	720 161	779 334
(Net)	463 848	496 351	548 552	590 838	640 273	689 058	742 945
Hydro	194 984	200 814	228 029	236 521	240 443	261 456	257 515
Conventional thermal	285 652	313 209	338 928	374 248	422 131	448 932	507 735
Nuclear	309	1 245	2 219	2 684	4 218	7 346	11 557
Geothermal	1 930	2 079	2 104	2 292	2 346	2 427	2 527
PRODUCTION (Utilities only)							
Total (Gross)	369 567	394 536	438 808	474 226	517 885	563 340	608 739
(Net)	--	--	--	--	--	--	--
Hydro	167 277	172 098	195 729	202 548	205 407	229 237	226 315
Conventional thermal	200 356	220 315	240 835	269 101	308 629	327 314	371 347
Nuclear	4	44	140	285	1 503	4 362	8 550
Geothermal	1 930	2 079	2 104	2 292	2 346	2 427	2 527
NET IMPORTS	578	-1 855	509	-1 288	-1 101	406	-860
SUPPLY (Gross)	483 453	515 492	571 789	614 457	668 037	720 567	778 474
(Net)	464 426	494 496	549 061	589 550	639 172	689 464	742 085
CONSUMPTION	413 495	442 720	491 799	529 121	575 328	621 059	670 947
Transport	17 834	18 524	19 725	20 388	21 836	23 022	23 547
Domestic sector	131 857	142 082	158 765	175 392	200 892	225 787	241 178
Industry	263 804	282 114	313 309	333 341	352 600	372 250	406 222
LOSS AND USE	50 931	51 776	57 262	60 429	63 844	68 405	71 138
PLANT (thousand kw)							
CAPACITY (Utilities & industries)							
Total	135 444	146 050	156 063	165 509	177 504	190 095	201 353
Hydro	52 433	55 193	58 685	62 024	66 379	70 885	75 233
Conventional thermal	82 606	90 197	96 634	102 703	109 602	117 366	123 538
Nuclear	112	367	457	472	1 211	1 520	2 251
Geothermal	293	293	287	310	312	324	331
CAPACITY (Utilities only)							
Total	106 304	115 233	123 315	130 952	141 086	151 478	162 326
Hydro	46 359	49 104	52 497	55 350	59 340	63 634	67 941
Conventional thermal	59 651	65 784	70 434	75 180	80 736	86 562	92 430
Nuclear	1	52	97	112	698	958	1 624
Geothermal	293	293	287	310	312	324	331
FUEL CONSUMPTION (Utilities only)							
Coal (mmt)	77 366	78 994	84 229	89 716	100 208	105 629	110 483
Lignite & peat (mmt)	45 492	50 465	53 071	57 957	62 663	67 175	74 156
Fuel oils (mmt)	6 374	8 243	9 288	11 010	13 820	15 039	20 699
Gases (Tcals)	8 797	12 763	19 839	24 286	25 436	25 150	22 366
Total (Tcals)	610 481	651 225	696 679	768 460	866 958	922 994	1 023 181
RESERVOIR STORAGE CAPACITY (million kwh)	47 149	50 497	56 163	58 196	64 178	70 024	75 019

SUPPLY AND USE (million kwh)	1958	1959	1960	1961	1962	1963	1964
PRODUCTION (Utilities & industries)							
Total (Gross)	238 780	255 823	283 505	302 988	328 770	355 941	385 924
(Net)	227 633	243 528	270 106	288 149	311 743	337 972	364 964
Hydro	82 079	82 694	100 230	93 901	88 383	103 174	87 568
Conventional thermal	154 767	171 006	181 031	206 510	237 482	249 464	292 618
Nuclear	4	44	140	285	559	876	3 211
Geothermal	1 930	2 079	2 104	2 292	2 346	2 427	2 527
PRODUCTION (Utilities only)							
Total (Gross)	159 873	171 913	192 285	204 558	222 730	243 478	263 194
(Net)	--	--	--	--	--	--	--
Hydro	71 692	72 146	86 840	80 362	75 484	90 172	76 235
Conventional thermal	86 247	97 644	103 201	121 619	144 341	150 003	181 221
Nuclear	4	44	140	285	559	876	3 211
Geothermal	1 930	2 079	2 104	2 292	2 346	2 427	2 527
NET IMPORTS	2 993	2 866	4 103	4 369	3 236	4 341	4 552
SUPPLY (Gross)	241 773	258 689	287 608	307 357	332 006	360 282	390 476
(Net)	230 626	246 394	274 209	292 518	314 979	342 313	369 516
CONSUMPTION	207 573	223 095	248 687	265 746	286 789	310 607	337 695
Transport	10 398	11 093	11 951	12 397	13 432	14 339	14 711
Domestic sector	51 643	56 089	62 725	69 623	79 122	89 185	98 477
Industry	145 532	155 913	174 011	183 726	194 235	207 083	224 507
LOSS AND USE	23 053	23 299	25 522	26 772	28 190	31 706	31 821
PLANT (thousand kw)							
CAPACITY (Utilities & industries)							
Total	66 371	71 979	77 259	81 233	85 756	92 862	99 262
Hydro	23 922	24 757	26 262	27 413	28 352	29 848	31 047
Conventional thermal	42 155	46 877	50 613	53 398	56 970	62 308	67 136
Nuclear	1	52	97	112	122	382	748
Geothermal	293	293	287	310	312	324	331
CAPACITY (Utilities only)							
Total	46 433	50 726	54 436	56 992	60 018	65 310	71 504
Hydro	21 356	22 154	23 640	24 372	25 006	26 500	27 612
Conventional thermal	24 783	28 227	30 412	32 198	34 578	38 104	42 813
Nuclear	1	52	97	112	122	382	748
Geothermal	293	293	287	310	312	324	331
FUEL CONSUMPTION (Utilities only)							
Coal (mmt)	25 774	26 743	26 665	28 403	32 728	31 977	34 305
Lignite & peat (mmt)	37 226	41 921	44 283	46 145	49 645	52 595	58 386
Fuel oils (mmt)	2 126	2 243	2 246	3 954	5 740	7 158	11 665
Gases (Tcals)	6 146	9 614	15 833	20 442	21 647	21 293	18 615
Total (Tcals)	258 186	280 959	287 212	326 508	376 545	397 005	463 305
RESERVOIR STORAGE CAPACITY (million kwh)	9 374	10 065	11 329	11 565	11 824	12 522	12 747

SUPPLY AND USE (million kwh)	1958	1959	1960	1961	1962	1963	1964
PRODUCTION (Utilities & industries)							
Total (Gross)	215 851	230 893	254 588	275 722	299 439	317 181	340 980
(Net)	208 745	222 995	246 019	266 603	288 789	305 254	327 299
Hydro	94 362	95 861	102 620	117 007	125 012	124 308	136 757
Conventional thermal	121 184	133 831	149 889	156 316	170 768	186 403	195 877
Nuclear	305	1 201	2 079	2 399	3 659	6 470	8 346
Geothermal	—	—	—	—	—	—	—
PRODUCTION (Utilities only)							
Total (Gross)	183 763	194 700	216 290	235 728	257 429	276 103	296 708
(Net)	--	--	--	--	--	--	--
Hydro	77 951	78 667	84 804	97 603	103 898	106 214	117 901
Conventional thermal	105 812	116 033	131 486	138 125	152 587	166 403	173 468
Nuclear	—	—	—	—	944	3 486	5 339
Geothermal	—	—	—	—	—	—	—
NET IMPORTS	-2 228	-4 421	-3 347	-5 346	-3 966	-2 740	-4 164
SUPPLY (Gross)	213 623	226 472	251 241	270 376	295 473	314 441	336 816
(Net)	206 517	218 574	242 672	261 257	284 823	302 514	323 135
CONSUMPTION	183 503	195 219	216 402	233 551	255 278	272 743	291 288
Transport	6 319	6 527	6 788	6 932	7 299	7 474	7 470
Domestic sector	74 259	79 185	88 856	97 499	112 535	126 078	130 784
Industry	102 925	109 507	120 758	129 120	135 444	139 191	153 034
LOSS AND USE	23 014	23 355	26 270	27 706	29 545	29 771	31 847
PLANT (thousand kw)							
CAPACITY (Utilities & industries)							
Total	59 395	63 787	67 858	72 421	78 921	83 458	86 705
Hydro	22 167	23 655	25 110	26 807	29 544	31 827	33 697
Conventional thermal	37 117	39 817	42 388	45 254	48 288	50 493	51 505
Nuclear	111	315	360	360	1 089	1 138	1 503
Geothermal	—	—	—	—	—	—	—
CAPACITY (Utilities only)							
Total	51 218	55 311	59 047	63 267	69 431	73 555	76 678
Hydro	18 960	20 475	21 870	23 504	26 182	28 256	30 175
Conventional thermal	32 258	34 836	37 177	39 763	42 673	44 723	45 627
Nuclear	—	—	—	—	576	576	876
Geothermal	—	—	—	—	—	—	—
FUEL CONSUMPTION (Utilities only)							
Coal (mmt)	49 006	49 779	55 400	58 254	64 224	70 677	71 918
Lignite & peat (mmt)	3 667	4 229	4 087	5 037	5 394	5 414	5 336
Fuel oils (mmt)	3 368	5 431	6 555	6 484	6 964	6 904	7 633
Gases (Tcals)	2 598	3 085	3 950	3 778	3 784	3 831	3 643
Total (Tcals)	329 030	354 078	393 380	409 035	448 260	487 585	505 822
RESERVOIR STORAGE CAPACITY (million kwh)	32 385	34 059	36 323	39 115	44 009	48 538	51 095

OTHER SOUTH EUROPE

SUPPLY AND USE (million kwh)	1958	1959	1960	1961	1962	1963	1964
PRODUCTION (Utilities & industries)							
Total (Gross)	28 244	30 631	33 187	37 035	40 929	47 039	52 430
(Net)	27 470	29 828	32 427	36 086	39 741	45 832	50 682
Hydro	18 543	22 259	25 179	25 613	27 048	33 974	33 190
Conventional thermal	9 701	8 372	8 008	11 422	13 881	13 065	19 240
Nuclear	–	–	–	–	–	–	–
Geothermal	–	–	–	–	–	–	–
PRODUCTION (Utilities only)							
Total (Gross)	25 931	27 923	30 233	33 940	37 726	43 759	48 837
(Net)	--	--	--	--	--	--	--
Hydro	17 634	21 285	24 085	24 583	26 025	32 851	32 179
Conventional thermal	8 297	6 638	6 148	9 357	11 701	10 908	16 658
Nuclear	–	–	–	–	–	–	–
Geothermal	–	–	–	–	–	–	–
NET IMPORTS	-187	-300	-247	-311	-371	-1 195	-1 248
SUPPLY (Gross)	28 057	30 331	32 940	36 724	40 558	45 844	51 182
(Net)	27 283	29 528	32 180	35 775	39 370	44 637	49 434
CONSUMPTION	22 419	24 406	26 710	29 824	33 261	37 709	41 964
Transport	1 117	904	986	1 059	1 105	1 209	1 366
Domestic sector	5 955	6 808	7 184	8 270	9 235	10 524	11 917
Industry	15 347	16 694	18 540	20 495	22 921	25 976	28 681
LOSS AND USE	4 864	5 122	5 470	5 951	6 109	6 928	7 470
PLANT (thousand kw)							
CAPACITY (Utilities & industries)							
Total	9 678	10 284	10 946	11 855	12 827	13 775	15 386
Hydro	6 344	6 781	7 313	7 804	8 483	9 210	10 489
Conventional thermal	3 334	3 503	3 633	4 051	4 344	4 565	4 897
Nuclear	–	–	–	–	–	–	–
Geothermal	–	–	–	–	–	–	–
CAPACITY (Utilities only)							
Total	8 653	9 196	9 832	10 693	11 637	12 613	14 144
Hydro	6 043	6 475	6 987	7 474	8 152	8 878	10 154
Conventional thermal	2 610	2 721	2 845	3 219	3 485	3 735	3 990
Nuclear	–	–	–	–	–	–	–
Geothermal	–	–	–	–	–	–	–
FUEL CONSUMPTION (Utilities only)							
Coal (mmt)	2 586	2 472	2 164	3 059	3 256	2 975	4 260
Lignite & peat (mmt)	4 599	4 315	4 701	6 775	7 624	9 166	10 434
Fuel oils (mmt)	880	569	487	572	1 116	977	1 401
Gases (Tcals)	53	64	56	66	5	26	108
Total (Tcals)	22 894	16 188	16 087	32 917	42 153	38 404	54 054
RESERVOIR STORAGE CAPACITY (million kwh)	5 390	6 373	8 511	7 516	8 345	8 964	11 177

SUPPLY AND USE (million kwh)	1958	1959	1960	1961	1962	1963	1964
PRODUCTION (Utilities & industries)							
Total (Gross)	94 293	103 473	114 180	124 404	134 670	143 062	157 045
(Net)	88 378	96 887	106 767	116 172	125 742	132 611	145 371
Hydro	5 388	4 750	6 267	6 269	6 938	6 376	6 322
Conventional thermal	88 905	98 723	107 913	118 135	127 732	136 686	150 723
Nuclear	–	–	–	–	–	–	–
Geothermal	–	–	–	–	–	–	–
PRODUCTION (Utilities only)							
Total (Gross)	60 279	68 776	78 341	87 053	95 981	103 697	115 657
(Net)	--	--	--	--	---	--	--
Hydro	4 988	4 441	5 939	5 978	6 664	6 115	6 063
Conventional thermal	55 291	64 335	72 402	81 075	89 317	97 582	109 594
Nuclear	–	–	–	–	–	–	–
Geothermal	–	–	–	–	–	–	–
NET IMPORTS	59	130	197	121	461	1 103	1 353
SUPPLY (Gross)	94 352	103 603	114 377	124 525	135 131	144 165	158 398
(Net)	88 437	97 017	106 964	116 293	126 203	133 714	146 724
CONSUMPTION	80 017	88 195	97 266	105 815	114 413	120 981	132 534
Transport	2 078	2 450	2 907	3 359	3 757	4 176	4 793
Domestic sector	14 609	17 133	19 859	21 387	23 420	24 722	27 101
Industry	63 330	68 612	74 500	81 069	87 236	92 083	100 640
LOSS AND USE	8 420	8 822	9 698	10 478	11 790	12 733	14 190
PLANT (thousand kw)							
CAPACITY (Utilities & industries)							
Total	20 683	22 514	24 117	26 026	27 953	30 364	33 756
Hydro	1 724	2 014	2 235	2 620	2 883	3 073	3 410
Conventional thermal	18 959	20 500	21 882	23 406	25 070	27 291	30 346
Nuclear	–	–	–	–	–	–	–
Geothermal	–	–	–	–	–	–	–
CAPACITY (Utilities only)							
Total	12 733	14 323	15 732	17 446	19 202	21 392	24 491
Hydro	1 615	1 922	2 146	2 538	2 801	2 995	3 327
Conventional thermal	11 118	12 401	13 586	14 908	16 401	18 397	21 164
Nuclear	–	–	–	–	–	–	–
Geothermal	–	–	–	–	–	–	–
FUEL CONSUMPTION (Utilities only)							
Coal (mmt)	25 351	28 377	30 816	32 919	34 738	35 912	36 194
Lignite & peat (mmt)	42 980	48 390	55 535	61 021	66 418	73 616	86 061
Fuel oils (mmt)	485	376	359	490	465	610	874
Natural gas (Tcals)	12 846	16 456	16 803	17 419	19 178	22 474	25 601
Total (Tcals)	412 099	478 268	514 887	555 032	594 440	691 990	776 250
RESERVOIR STORAGE CAPACITY (million kwh)	328	521	1 369	996	932	2 076	2 308

AFRICA

SUPPLY AND USE (million kwh)	1958	1959	1960	1961	1962	1963	1964
PRODUCTION (Utilities & industries)							
Total (Gross)	33 462	36 251	39 743	43 225	45 585	49 172	53 694
(Net)	32 078	34 712	38 085	41 199	43 626	47 066	51 574
Hydro	5 512	6 058	7 522	9 533	10 665	11 070	12 224
Conventional thermal	27 950	30 193	32 221	33 692	34 920	38 102	41 470
Nuclear	–	–	–	–	–	–	–
Geothermal	–	–	–	–	–	–	–
PRODUCTION (Utilities only)							
Total (Gross)	27 777	30 116	33 991	37 289	39 285	41 951	47 324
(Net)	--	--	--	--	--	--	--
Hydro	3 129	3 479	5 043	7 027	8 026	8 756	9 940
Conventional thermal	24 648	26 637	28 948	30 262	31 259	33 195	37 384
Nuclear	–	–	–	–	–	–	–
Geothermal	–	–	–	–	–	–	–
NET IMPORTS	355	–4	–10	–3	–	–32	–22
SUPPLY (Gross)	33 817	36 247	39 733	43 222	45 585	49 140	53 672
(Net)	32 433	34 708	38 075	41 196	43 626	47 034	51 552
CONSUMPTION	29 593	31 656	34 867	37 762	40 105	42 494	46 618
Transport	1 228	1 418	1 582	1 728	1 854	1 961	2 128
Domestic sector	6 530	7 101	7 723	8 067	8 506	9 385	10 393
Industry	21 835	23 137	25 562	27 967	29 745	31 148	34 097
LOSS AND USE	2 840	3 052	3 208	3 434	3 521	4 540	4 934
PLANT (thousand kw)							
CAPACITY (Utilities & industries)							
Total	9 211	9 921	11 052	11 889	12 688	13 221	13 744
Hydro	1 600	1 833	2 570	2 856	3 159	3 283	3 344
Conventional thermal	7 611	8 088	8 482	9 033	9 529	9 938	10 400
Nuclear	–	–	–	–	–	–	–
Geothermal	–	–	–	–	–	–	–
CAPACITY (Utilities only)							
Total	8 082	8 717	9 775	10 483	11 240	11 677	12 080
Hydro	1 557	1 789	2 528	2 811	3 099	3 223	3 283
Conventional thermal	6 525	6 928	7 247	7 672	8 141	8 454	8 797
Nuclear	–	–	–	–	–	–	–
Geothermal	–	–	–	–	–	–	–
FUEL CONSUMPTION (Utilities only)							
Coal (mmt)	14 848	17 141	16 521	16 745	17 254	18 005	19 028
Lignite & peat (mmt)	–	–	–	–	–	–	–
Fuel oils (mmt)	1 026	1 179	1 331	1 548	1 535	1 693	1 780
Gases (Tcals)	–	–	–	1 416	1 990	1 968	2 060
Total (Tcals)	93 385	98 909	105 359	110 088	113 140	118 918	125 568
RESERVOIR STORAGE CAPACITY (million kwh)	2 310	2 310	2 310	2 306	2 306	2 282	2 928

SUPPLY AND USE (million kwh)	1958	1959	1960	1961	1962	1963	1964
PRODUCTION (Utilities & industries)							
Total (Gross)	156 806	189 805	218 163	244 190	263 472	293 501	323 579
(Net)	154 242	186 319	213 551	239 260	257 026	285 599	313 717
Hydro	86 635	91 474	91 418	105 711	104 230	115 459	118 018
Conventional thermal	70 171	98 331	126 745	138 479	159 242	178 039	205 559
Nuclear	–	–	–	–	–	3	2
Geothermal	–	–	–	–	–	–	–
PRODUCTION (Utilities only)							
Total (Gross)	141 284	172 117	198 220	222 444	239 443	265 739	294 555
(Net)	--	--	--	--	--	--	--
Hydro	80 916	85 585	85 913	100 030	98 794	109 660	110 834
Conventional thermal	60 368	86 532	112 307	122 414	140 649	156 079	183 721
Nuclear	–	–	–	–	–	–	–
Geothermal	–	–	–	–	–	–	–
NET IMPORTS		–	–	–	–	–	–
SUPPLY (Gross)	156 806	189 805	218 163	244 190	263 472	293 501	323 579
(Net)	154 242	186 319	213 551	239 260	257 026	285 599	313 717
CONSUMPTION	133 420	162 098	187 308	210 262	226 700	253 698	279 468
Transport	5 001	5 349	5 873	6 498	7 064	7 812	8 662
Domestic sector	40 636	46 943	50 532	59 064	66 311	74 577	83 545
Industry	87 783	109 806	130 903	144 700	153 325	171 309	187 261
LOSS AND USE	20 822	24 221	26 243	28 998	30 326	31 901	34 249
PLANT (thousand kw)							
CAPACITY (Utilities & industries)							
Total	40 263	45 714	50 987	55 627	61 688	68 678	75 185
Hydro	17 369	18 855	21 438	23 468	25 470	27 084	28 458
Conventional thermal	22 894	26 859	29 549	32 159	36 218	41 582	46 715
Nuclear	–	–	–	–	–	12	12
Geothermal	–	–	–	–	–	–	–
CAPACITY (Utilities only)							
Total	35 768	40 835	45 628	50 146	55 450	61 926	68 411
Hydro	16 446	17 973	20 501	22 500	24 481	26 035	27 411
Conventional thermal	19 322	22 862	25 127	27 646	30 969	35 891	41 000
Nuclear	–	–	–	–	–	–	–
Geothermal	–	–	–	–	–	–	–
FUEL CONSUMPTION (Utilities only)							
Coal (mmt)	38 221	52 052	62 047	65 521	69 076	74 067	77 968
Lignite & peat (mmt)	539	696	569	327	665	1 505	2 376
Fuel oils (mmt)	4 071	4 830	8 359	12 015	13 238	15 138	18 006
Gases (Tcals)	969	1 606	2 328	4 143	5 125	5 350	6 843
Total (Tcals)	239 489	318 197	406 242	465 387	497 974	546 701	599 927
RESERVOIR STORAGE CAPACITY (million kwh)	871	748	960	960	962	962	962

SUPPLY AND USE (million kwh)	1958	1959	1960	1961	1962	1963	1964
PRODUCTION (Utilities & industries)							
Total (Gross)	25 933	28 175	30 830	33 083	35 119	39 249	43 285
(Net)	(25 933)	(28 175)	(30 830)	(33 083)	(35 119)	(39 249)	(43 285)
Hydro	8 789	9 558	9 854	11 023	12 179	13 961	15 018
Conventional thermal	17 138	18 448	20 592	21 569	22 179	24 284	27 073
Nuclear	—	—	—	—	—	—	—
Geothermal	6	169	384	491	761	1 004	1 194
PRODUCTION (Utilities only)							
Total (Gross)	24 228	26 464	28 900	31 209	33 281	37 173	40 944
(Net)	--	--	--	--	--	--	--
Hydro	8 673	9 439	9 793	10 959	12 107	13 866	14 942
Conventional thermal	15 549	16 856	18 723	19 759	20 413	22 303	24 808
Nuclear	—	—	—	—	—	—	—
Geothermal	6	169	384	491	761	1 004	1 194
NET IMPORTS	—	—	—	—	—	—	—
SUPPLY (Gross)	25 933	28 175	30 830	33 083	35 119	39 249	43 285
(Net)	(25 933)	(28 175)	(30 830)	(33 083)	(35 119)	(39 249)	(43 285)
CONSUMPTION	21 540	23 304	25 568	27 576	29 214	32 703	35 745
Transport	846	786	780	777	774	760	776
Domestic sector	11 426	12 566	13 738	14 957	15 828	17 596	19 256
Industry	9 268	9 952	11 050	11 842	12 612	14 347	15 713
LOSS AND USE	4 393	4 871	5 262	5 507	5 905	6 546	7 540
PLANT (thousand kw)							
CAPACITY (Utilities & industries)							
Total	7 011	7 621	8 450	9 256	9 676	10 232	11 115
Hydro	2 323	2 680	2 887	3 418	3 508	3 733	4 159
Conventional thermal	4 688	4 872	5 483	5 747	6 006	6 307	6 764
Nuclear	—	—	—	—	—	—	—
Geothermal	—	69	80	91	162	192	192
CAPACITY (Utilities only)							
Total	6 658	7 291	8 051	8 952	9 354	9 884	10 964
Hydro	2 296	2 653	2 860	3 391	3 481	3 706	4 132
Conventional thermal	4 362	4 569	5 111	5 470	5 711	5 986	6 640
Nuclear	—	—	—	—	—	—	—
Geothermal	—	69	80	91	162	192	192
FUEL CONSUMPTION (Utilities only)							
Coal (mmt)	6 130	6 576	6 620	6 942	6 949	7 807	8 108
Lignite & peat (mmt)	9 517	10 826	11 083	12 435	13 463	14 360	15 453
Fuel oils (mmt)	530	531	472	382	399	523	595
Natural gas (Tcals)	—	—	—	10	20	35	34
Total (Tcals)	68 993	72 425	79 792	82 899	88 582	94 639	102 049
RESERVOIR STORAGE CAPACITY (million kwh)	1 649	1 649	1 649	1 759	1 752	1 841	1 963

SUPPLY AND USE (million kwh)	1958	1959	1960	1961	1962	1963	1964
PRODUCTION (Utilities & industries)							
Total (Gross)	61 304	65 794	71 504	77 151	83 795	89 829	98 243
(Net)	60 254	64 668	70 282	75 842	82 398	88 559	97 002
Hydro	31 465	32 267	34 614	35 986	38 855	41 152	45 068
Conventional thermal	29 839	33 527	36 890	41 165	44 940	48 677	53 175
Nuclear	–	–	–	–	–	–	–
Geothermal	–	–	–	–	–	–	–
PRODUCTION (Utilities only)							
Total (Gross)	45 372	48 936	53 685	58 739	63 984	69 281	77 121
(Net)	--	--	--	--	--	--	--
Hydro	25 828	26 765	29 084	31 085	33 771	36 667	40 561
Conventional thermal	19 544	22 171	24 601	27 654	30 213	32 614	36 560
Nuclear	–	–	–	–	–	–	–
Geothermal	–	–	–	–	–	–	–
NET IMPORTS	389	462	604	532	536	605	121
SUPPLY (Gross)	61 693	66 256	72 108	77 683	84 331	90 434	98 364
(Net)	60 643	65 130	70 886	76 374	82 934	89 164	97 123
CONSUMPTION	52 220	56 060	60 906	64 877	70 695	76 097	83 054
Transport	1 724	1 731	1 780	1 764	1 670	1 715	1 665
Domestic sector	21 672	23 389	25 822	28 194	31 104	33 058	35 521
Industry	28 824	30 940	33 304	34 919	37 921	41 324	45 868
LOSS AND USE	8 423	9 070	9 980	11 497	12 239	13 067	14 069
PLANT (thousand kw)							
CAPACITY (Utilities & industries)							
Total	16 054	17 116	18 899	20 652	22 494	25 185	27 465
Hydro	6 732	7 017	7 699	8 211	8 992	9 632	10 597
Conventional thermal	9 322	10 099	11 200	12 441	13 502	15 553	16 868
Nuclear	–	–	–	–	–	–	–
Geothermal	–	–	–	–	–	–	–
CAPACITY (Utilities only)							
Total	11 442	12 034	13 240	14 949	16 313	18 577	20 756
Hydro	5 525	5 790	6 392	7 145	7 851	8 523	9 599
Conventional thermal	5 917	6 244	6 848	7 804	8 462	10 054	11 157
Nuclear	–	–	–	–	–	–	–
Geothermal	–	–	–	–	–	–	–
FUEL CONSUMPTION (Utilities only)							
Coal (mmt)	826	942	855	953	1 357	1 428	1 448
Lignite & peat (mmt)	–	–	–	–	–	–	–
Fuel oils (mmt)	4 936	5 551	5 732	6 051	6 285	7 157	8 034
Gases (Tcals)	7 317	8 846	10 123	15 066	18 299	27 432	32 753
Total (Tcals)	64 920	73 726	76 294	85 273	93 791	112 577	127 246
RESERVOIR STORAGE CAPACITY (million kwh)	–	–	–	–	–	–	–

PART II
SECTION TWO
National Electricity Accounts
Aden to Zambia

GEOGRAPHIC COVERAGE

Detailed information on electricity supply and demand covering, insofar as possible, the years 1958 through 1964, are given on pages 139-298 for each of the following countries.

Aden	Congo (Brazzaville)	Guyana
Afghanistan	Congo (Kinshasa)	
Albania	Costa Rica	Haiti
Algeria	Cuba	Honduras
American Samoa	Cyprus	Hong Kong
Angola	Czechoslovakia	Hungary
Argentina		
Asian Peoples	Dahomey	Iceland
Republics*	Denmark	India
Australia	Dominican Republic	Indonesia
Austria		Iran
	Ecuador	Iraq
Bahamas	El Salvador	Ireland
Bahrain	Ethiopia	Israel
Barbados		Italy
Belgium	Faeroe Islands	Ivory Coast
Bermuda	Fiji Islands	
Bolivia	Finland	Jamaica
Brazil	France	Japan
British Honduras	French Guiana	Jordan
Brunei	French Polynesia	
Bulgaria	French Somaliland	Kenya
Burma		Korea, North*
	Gabon	Korea, South
Cambodia	Gambia	Kuwait
Cameroon	Germany, East	
Canada	Germany, West	Laos
Central African	Ghana	Lebanon
Republic	Gibraltar	Liberia
Ceylon	Greece	Libya
Chad	Greenland	Luxembourg
Chile	Guadeloupe	
China (Mainland)*	Guam	Macao
China (Taiwan)	Guatemala	Malagasy
Colombia	Guinea	Malawi

------

*Asian Peoples Republics includes: China (Mainland); Korea, North; Mongolia and Vietnam, North.

Malaya	Peru	Switzerland
Mali	Philippines	Syria
Malta	Poland	
Martinique	Portugal	Tanzania
Mauritius	Portuguese Guinea	Thailand
Mexico	Puerto Rico	Trinidad
Mongolia*		Togo
Morocco	Reunion	Tunisia
Mozambique	Rhodesia	Turkey
	Romania	
Nauru	Rwanda	Uganda
Nepal	Ryukyu Islands	USSR
Netherlands		United Arab Republic
Netherlands Antilles	Sabah	United Kingdom
New Caledonia	St. Pierre-Miquelon	United States
New Guinea,	St. Thomas-Prince	Upper Volta
Australia	Sarawak	Uruguay
New Zealand	Saudi Arabia	
Nicaragua	Senegal	Venezuela
Niger	Sierra Leone	Vietnam, North*
Nigeria	Singapore	Vietnam, South
Norway	Somalia	Virgin Islands
	South Africa	
Pakistan	Southwest Africa	Western Samoa
Panama	Spain	
Panama Canal Zone	Sudan	Yugoslavia
Papua	Surinam	
Paraguay	Sweden	Zambia

*Asian Peoples Republics includes: China (Mainland); Korea, North; Mongolia and Vietnam, North.

ADEN

SUPPLY AND USE (million kwh)	1958	1959	1960	1961	1962	1963	1964	1965
PRODUCTION (Utilities & industries)								
Total (Gross)	119	132	144	160	163	183	205	
(Net)	--	--	--	--	--	--	--	
Hydro	—	—	—	—	—	—	—	
Conventional thermal	119	132	144	160	163	183	205	
Nuclear	—	—	—	—	—	—	—	
Geothermal	—	—	—	—	—	—	—	
PRODUCTION (Utilities only)								
Total (Gross)	57	66	74	82	81	90	106	
(Net)	--	--	--	--	--	--	--	
Hydro	—	—	—	—	—	—	—	
Conventional thermal	57	66	74	82	81	90	106	
Nuclear	—	—	—	—	—	—	—	
Geothermal	—	—	—	—	—	—	—	
NET IMPORTS	—	—	—	—	—	—	—	
SUPPLY (Gross)	119	132	144	160	163	183	205	
(Net)	--	--	--	--	--	--	--	
CONSUMPTION	--	--	--	--	--	--	--	
Transport	—	—	—	—	—	—	—	
Domestic sector	--	--	--	--	--	--	--	
Industry	--	--	--	--	--	--	--	
LOSS AND USE	--	--	--	--	--	--	--	

PLANT (thousand kw)

CAPACITY (Utilities & industries)	1958	1959	1960	1961	1962	1963	1964	1965
Total	43	44	45	45	45	51	51	
Hydro	—	—	—	—	—	—	—	
Conventional thermal	43	44	45	45	45	51	51	
Nuclear	—	—	—	—	—	—	—	
Geothermal	—	—	—	—	—	—	—	
CAPACITY (Utilities only)								
Total	14	18	18	18	18	24	24	
Hydro	—	—	—	—	—	—	—	
Conventional thermal	14	18	18	18	18	24	24	
Nuclear	—	—	—	—	—	—	—	
Geothermal	—	—	—	—	—	—	—	

FUEL CONSUMPTION (Utilities only)

	1958	1959	1960	1961	1962	1963	1964	1965
Total (Tcals)	--	--	--	--	--	--	--	
RESERVOIR STORAGE CAPACITY (million kwh)	—	—	—	—	—	—	—	

SUPPLEMENTARY DATA FOR 1964

Transmission lines, 100 kv+ (km) : —
Households served (thousands) : 23 (1961)
Revenues per kwh (U.S. cents) — Total:
  Residential: Railways:
  Industry: Lighting: 5.6
Population (thousands) : 231

Other characteristics of plants and systems:

    Aden's power is generated by the Government Electricity Department in the steam plant at Aden. Power is also generated privately by the British Petroleum refinery, Little Aden. Service is available to only a small portion of the total population.

Sources of data:
Benn Bros. *Elec. undertakings.*
UN. *Stat. yrbk.*

SUPPLY AND USE (million kwh)	1958	1959	1960	1961	1962	1963	1964	1965
PRODUCTION (Utilities & industries)								
Total (Gross)	53	84	118	126	158	181	204	
(Net)	--	--	--	--	--	--	--	
Hydro	49	79	111	116	149	169	--	
Conventional thermal	4	5	7	10	9	12	--	
Nuclear	—	—	—	—	—	—	—	
Geothermal	—	—	—	—	—	—	—	
PRODUCTION (Utilities only)								
Total (Gross)	35	68	102	107	131	142	--	
(Net)	--	--	--	--	--	--	--	
Hydro	34	67	98	104	127	139	--	
Conventional thermal	1	1	4	3	4	3	--	
Nuclear	—	—	—	—	—	—	—	
Geothermal	—	—	—	—	—	—	—	
NET IMPORTS	—	—	—	—	—	—	—	
SUPPLY (Gross)	53	84	118	126	158	181	204	
(Net)	--	--	--	--	--	--	--	
CONSUMPTION	--	--	--	--	--	--	--	
Transport	—	—	—	—	—	—	—	
Domestic sector	--	--	--	--	--	--	--	
Industry	34	--	--	--	--	45	--	
LOSS AND USE	--	--	--	--	--	--	--	

PLANT (thousand kw)

	1958	1959	1960	1961	1962	1963	1964	1965
CAPACITY (Utilities & industries)								
Total	40	45	49	59	61	61	--	
Hydro	34	37	38	48	48	47	--	
Conventional thermal	6	8	11	11	13	14	--	
Nuclear	—	—	—	—	—	—	—	
Geothermal	—	—	—	—	—	—	—	
CAPACITY (Utilities only)								
Total	32	36	36	37	38	38	--	
Hydro	29	32	32	33e	33	33	--	
Conventional thermal	3	4	4	4e	5	5	--	
Nuclear	—	—	—	—	—	—	—	
Geothermal	—	—	—	—	—	—	—	

FUEL CONSUMPTION (Utilities only)

	1958	1959	1960	1961	1962	1963	1964	1965
Total (Tcals)	--	--	--	--	--	--	--	
RESERVOIR STORAGE CAPACITY (million kwh)	--	--	--	--	--	--	--	

SUPPLEMENTARY DATA FOR 1964

Transmission lines, 100 kv+ (km): (1962) 160
Households served (thousands): --
Revenues per kwh (U.S. cents) — Total:
  Residential: 2.3   Railways:
  Industry: 2.3   Lighting:
Population (thousands): 15380

Sources of data:
  Benn Bros. *Elec. undertakings.*
  UN. *Stat. yrbk.*
  UN. ECAFE. *Elec. power.*

Other characteristics of plants and systems:

  Power development is planned by the Ministry of Industry and Mines, which also executes major hydroelectric projects. Power plants above 500 KW are owned and operated by the Afghan Electric Company, in which the government has a 70% holding. Service is provided to a relatively small fraction of the total population, mainly through local production and distribution facilities.

ALBANIA

SUPPLY AND USE (million kwh)	1958	1959	1960	1961	1962	1963	1964	1965
PRODUCTION (Utilities & industries)								
Total (Gross)	150	175	194	227	242	258	288	
(Net)	--	--	182	212	--	--	--	
Hydro	87	119	121	108	118	168	203	
Conventional thermal	63	56	73	119	124	90	85	
Nuclear	—	—	—	—	—	—	—	
Geothermal	—	—	—	—	—	—	—	
PRODUCTION (Utilities only)								
Total (Gross)	--	150	170	200	215	--	--	
(Net)	--	--	--	--	--	--	--	
Hydro	--	--	--	--	--	--	--	
Conventional thermal	--	--	--	--	--	--	--	
Nuclear	—	—	—	—	—	—	—	
Geothermal	—	—	—	—	—	—	—	
NET IMPORTS	—	—	—	—	—	—	—	
SUPPLY (Gross)	--	--	194	227	--	--	--	
(Net)	--	--	182	212	--	--	--	
CONSUMPTION	--	--	152	181	--	--	--	
Transport	—	—	—	—	—	—	—	
Domestic sector	--	--	31	41	--	--	--	
Industry	--	--	121	140	--	--	--	
LOSS AND USE	--	--	30	31	--	--	--	

PLANT (thousand kw)

CAPACITY (Utilities & industries)	1958	1959	1960	1961	1962	1963	1964	1965
Total	--	--	--	--	--	--	--	
Hydro	--	--	--	--	--	--	--	
Conventional thermal	--	--	--	--	--	--	--	
Nuclear	—	—	—	—	—	—	—	
Geothermal	—	—	—	—	—	—	—	
CAPACITY (Utilities only)								
Total	--	--	--	--	--	--	--	
Hydro	--	--	--	--	--	--	--	
Conventional thermal	--	--	--	--	--	--	--	
Nuclear	—	—	—	—	—	—	—	
Geothermal	—	—	—	—	—	—	—	

FUEL CONSUMPTION (Utilities only)

	1958	1959	1960	1961	1962	1963	1964	1965
Total (Tcals)	--	--	--	--	--	--	--	
RESERVOIR STORAGE CAPACITY (million kwh)	--	--	--	--	--	--	--	

SUPPLEMENTARY DATA FOR 1964

Transmission lines, 100 kv+ (km): --
Households served (thousands): --
Revenues per kwh (U.S. cents) — Total:
  Residential: Railways:
  Industry: Lighting:
Population (thousands): 1814

Other characteristics of plants and systems:

There is little information available concerning electric power systems in Albania. Generating facilities are presumably government-owned. The level of consumption per capita in the domestic sector indicates that electricity is supplied to a relatively small fraction of the total population.

Sources of data:
UN. *Stat. yrbk.*
Komisionit të planit të shtetit, Drejtoria e statistikës.
  Vjetari statistikor i RPSH.

SUPPLY AND USE (million kwh)	1958	1959	1960	1961	1962	1963	1964	1965
PRODUCTION (Utilities & industries)								
Total (Gross)	1114	1198	1335	1538	1332	1256	1342	
(Net)	1103	1186	1318	1516	1311	1231	1318	
Hydro	408	403	348	253	264	256	284	
Conventional thermal	706	795	987	1285	1068	1000	1058	
Nuclear	–	–	–	–	–	–	–	
Geothermal	–	–	–	–	–	–	–	
PRODUCTION (Utilities only)								
Total (Gross)	1114	1192	1325	1387	1156	1088	1099	
(Net)	1103	1180	1308	1365	1135	1063	1095	
Hydro	408	403	348	253	264	256	284	
Conventional thermal	706	789	977	1134	892	832	815	
Nuclear	–	–	–	–	–	–	–	
Geothermal	–	–	–	–	–	–	–	
NET IMPORTS	–5	6	7	–	–	–	–	
SUPPLY (Gross)	1109	1204	1342	1538	1332	1256	1342	
(Net)	1098	1192	1325	1516	1311	1231	1318	
CONSUMPTION	969	1051	1176	1364	– –	1049	1178	
Transport	55	48	51	55	47	44	36	
Domestic sector	378	420	473	– –	– –	414	405	
Industry	536	583	652	– –	– –	591	737	
LOSS AND USE	129	141	149	152e	– –	182	140	
PLANT (thousand kw)								
CAPACITY (Utilities & industries)								
Total	433	446	452	509e	509e	509	474	
Hydro	186	186	186	134	134	134	138	
Conventional thermal	247	260	266	375	375	375	336	
Nuclear	–	–	–	–	–	–	–	
Geothermal	–	–	–	–	–	–	–	
CAPACITY (Utilities only)								
Total	433	434	439	434	434	434	363	
Hydro	186	186	186	134	134	134	138	
Conventional thermal	247	248	253	300	300	300	225	
Nuclear	–	–	–	–	–	–	–	
Geothermal	–	–	–	–	–	–	–	
FUEL CONSUMPTION (Utilities only)								
Coal (mmt)	325	171	96	19	–	–	–	
Fuel oil (mmt)	– –	170	– –	191	56	39	28	
Natural gas (Tcals)	– –	– –	– –	1416	1990	1968	2060	
Total (Tcals)	– –	– –	– –	– –	– –	– –	– –	
RESERVOIR STORAGE CAPACITY (million kwh)	211	211	211	208	208	208	209	

SUPPLEMENTARY DATA FOR 1964

Transmission lines, 100 kv+ (km): 900
Households served (thousands): 520
Revenues per kwh (U.S. cents) — Total:
  Residential: Railways: 1.6
  Industry: Lighting:
Population (thousands): 11645

Other characteristics of plants and systems:

L'Electricité et Gaz de l'Algérie, a public agency, is responsible for the production, transmission and distribution of electricity in Algeria. It operates an extensive network which serves perhaps one-quarter of the Algerian population.

Sources of data:
UN. *Stat. yrbk.*
UN. ECA. *Situation, trends & prospects.*
UNIPEDE. *Statistiques.*
Electricité et Gaz de l'Algérie. *Rapport de gestion.*
Directeur Generale des Plan des Etudes Economiques.
  Service de Statistique Generale. *Annuaire statistique de l'Algérie.*
——— . *Bulletin mensuel de statistique générale.*

AMERICAN SAMOA

SUPPLY AND USE (million kwh)	1958	1959	1960	1961	1962	1963	1964	1965
PRODUCTION (Utilities & industries)								
Total (Gross)	5.9	6.4	6.9	7.2	11	--	--	
(Net)	--	--	--	--	--	--	--	
Hydro	—	—	—	—	—	—	—	
Conventional thermal	5.9	6.4	6.9	7.2	11	--	--	
Nuclear	—	—	—	—	—	—	—	
Geothermal	—	—	—	—	—	—	—	
PRODUCTION (Utilities only)								
Total (Gross)	5.9	6.4	6.9	7.2	11	--	--	
(Net)	--	--	--	--	--	--	--	
Hydro	—	—	—	—	—	—	—	
Conventional thermal	5.9	6.4	6.9	7.2	11	--	--	
Nuclear	—	—	—	—	—	—	—	
Geothermal	—	—	—	—	—	—	—	
NET IMPORTS	—	—	—	—	—	—	—	
SUPPLY (Gross)	5.9	6.4	6.9	7.2	11	--	--	
(Net)	--	--	--	--	--	--	--	
CONSUMPTION	--	--	--	--	--	--	--	
Transport	--	--	--	--	--	--	--	
Domestic sector	--	--	--	--	--	--	--	
Industry	--	--	--	--	--	--	--	
LOSS AND USE	--	--	--	--	--	--	--	

PLANT (thousand kw)

CAPACITY (Utilities & industries)	1958	1959	1960	1961	1962	1963	1964	1965
Total	2.5	2.5	2.5	2.5	3.5	--	--	
Hydro	—	—	—	—	—	—	—	
Conventional thermal	2.5	2.5	2.5	2.5	3.5	--	--	
Nuclear	—	—	—	—	—	—	—	
Geothermal	—	—	—	—	—	—	—	
CAPACITY (Utilities only)								
Total	2.5	2.5	2.5	2.5	3.5	--	--	
Hydro	—	—	—	—	—	—	—	
Conventional thermal	2.5	2.5	2.5	2.5	3.5	--	--	
Nuclear	—	—	—	—	—	—	—	
Geothermal	—	—	—	—	—	—	—	

FUEL CONSUMPTION (Utilities only)

	1958	1959	1960	1961	1962	1963	1964	1965
Total (Tcals)	--	--	--	--	--	--	--	
RESERVOIR STORAGE CAPACITY (million kwh)	—	—	—	—	—	—	—	

SUPPLEMENTARY DATA FOR 1964

Transmission lines, 100 kv+ (km):   —
Households served (thousands):   (1961) 1
Revenues per kwh (U.S. cents) — Total:
  Residential: Railways:
  Industry: Lighting:
Population (thousands):   23

Other characteristics of plants and systems:

    Electricity is generated and distributed by the Department of Public Works of the government of American Samoa.

Sources of data:
UN. *Stat. yrbk.*
Governor of American Samoa. *Annual report.*

143

ANGOLA

SUPPLY AND USE (million kwh)	1958	1959	1960	1961	1962	1963	1964	1965
PRODUCTION (Utilities & industries)								
Total (Gross)	117	123	143	184	196	215	260	
(Net)	--	--	--	--	--	--	--	
Hydro	72	91	111	150	161	178	225	
Conventional thermal	45	32	32	34	35	37	35	
Nuclear	—	—	—	—	—	—	—	
Geothermal	—	—	—	—	—	—	—	
PRODUCTION (Utilities only)								
Total (Gross)	72	77	95	129	141	185	232	
(Net)	--	--	--	--	--	--	--	
Hydro	48	66	85	125e	136e	153e	207e	
Conventional thermal	24	11	10	(4)	(5)	(32)	(25)	
Nuclear	—	—	—	—	—	—	—	
Geothermal	—	—	—	—	—	—	—	
NET IMPORTS	—	—	—	—	—	—	—	
SUPPLY (Gross)	117	123	143	184	196	215	260	
(Net)	--	--	--	--	--	--	--	
CONSUMPTION	--	109	118	153	168	185	232	
Transport	--	--	--	--	--	--	--	
Domestic sector	--	49	43	51	--	--	--	
Industry	55c	60	75	102	--	--	--	
LOSS AND USE	--	14	25	31	--	--	--	

PLANT (thousand kw)

	1958	1959	1960	1961	1962	1963	1964	1965
CAPACITY (Utilities & industries)								
Total	68	72	88	88	262	334	334	
Hydro	27	28	28	28	199	262	259	
Conventional thermal	41	44	60	60	63	72	75	
Nuclear	—	—	—	—	—	—	—	
Geothermal	—	—	—	—	—	—	—	
CAPACITY (Utilities only)								
Total	37	38	38	38	202	--	--	
Hydro	24	24	24	24	188	--	--	
Conventional thermal	13	14	14	14	14	--	--	
Nuclear	—	—	—	—	—	—	—	
Geothermal	—	—	—	—	—	—	—	

FUEL CONSUMPTION (Utilities only)

	1958	1959	1960	1961	1962	1963	1964	1965
Total (Tcals)	--	--	--	--	--	--	--	
RESERVOIR STORAGE CAPACITY (million kwh)	--	--	--	--	--	--	--	

SUPPLEMENTARY DATA FOR 1964

Transmission lines, 100 kv+ (km) : --
Households served (thousands) :   18
Revenues per kwh (U.S. cents) — Total:
   Residential: Railways:
   Industry: Lighting:
Population (thousands) :   5084

Other characteristics of plants and systems:

Angola's electricity is generated mainly by Companhia Eléctrica do Lobito e Benguela, of mixed ownership, Serviço Autonomo de Luz e Agua de Luanda, and various municipal systems. Service is largely local in character, and apparently available only to a small part of the population.

Sources of data:
Benn Bros. *Elec. undertakings.*
Inst. de Est. *Anuário estatístico do ultramar.*
UN. *Stat. yrbk.*
US. FPC. *World power data.*
Direcção dos Serviços de Economia e Estatística Geral.
   Anuário estatístico.

ARGENTINA

SUPPLY AND USE (million kwh)	1958	1959	1960	1961	1962	1963	1964	1965
PRODUCTION (Utilities & industries)								
Total (Gross)	9418	9544	10459	11547	11887	12449	13752	
(Net)	--	--	--	--	--	--	--	
Hydro	665	770	927	1086	1167	1186	1236	
Conventional thermal	8753	8774	9532	10461	10720	11263	12516	
Nuclear	—	—	—	—	—	—	—	
Geothermal	—	—	—	—	—	—	—	
PRODUCTION (Utilities only)								
Total (Gross)	7374	7373	7864	8620	8756	9144	10167	
(Net)	--	--	--	--	--	--	--	
Hydro	665	770	870	1025	1104	1111	1167	
Conventional thermal	6709	6603	6994	7595	7652	8033	9000	
Nuclear	—	—	—	—	—	—	—	
Geothermal	—	—	—	—	—	—	—	
NET IMPORTS	—	—	—	—	—	—	—	
SUPPLY (Gross)	9418	9544	10459	11547	11887	12449	13752	
(Net)	--	--	--	--	--	--	--	
CONSUMPTION	8030	8327	9015	9774	10087	--	--	
Transport	381	392	415	439	392	--	--	
Domestic sector	2998	3097	(3700)	4416	4678	--	--	
Industry	4651	4838	4900e	4919	5017	--	--	
LOSS AND USE	1388	1217	1444	1773	1800	--	--	

PLANT (thousand kw)

	1958	1959	1960	1961	1962	1963	1964	1965
CAPACITY (Utilities & industries)								
Total	2947	3166	3474	3721	3995	4686	5091	
Hydro	278	316	340	346	357	363	374	
Conventional thermal	2669	2850	3134	3375	3638	4323	4717	
Nuclear	—	—	—	—	—	—	—	
Geothermal	—	—	—	—	—	—	—	
CAPACITY (Utilities only)								
Total	2178	2228	2287	2495	2649	3184	3541	
Hydro	260	293	317	322	333	341	347	
Conventional thermal	1918	1935	1970	2173	2316	2843	3194	
Nuclear	—	—	—	—	—	—	—	
Geothermal	—	—	—	—	—	—	—	

FUEL CONSUMPTION (Utilities only)

	1958	1959	1960	1961	1962	1963	1964	1965
Coal (mmt)	269	339	238	244	295	--	--	
Fuelwood (mmt)	10	7	2	2	2	--	--	
Diesel oil (mmt)	138	278	268	302	325	258	309	
Fuel oil (mmt)	1880	1908	1920	1872	1671	1675	2037	
Natural gas (Tcals)	62	49	336	3451	4744	--	--	
Total (Tcals)	--	--	--	--	--	--	--	
RESERVOIR STORAGE CAPACITY (million kwh)	--	--	--	--	--	--	--	

SUPPLEMENTARY DATA FOR 1964

Transmission lines, 100 kv+ (km) :   --
Households served (thousands) :   --
Revenues per kwh (U.S. cents) — Total: (1962) 3.0
   Residential: Railways:
   Industry: Lighting: 3.3
Population (thousands):   22019

Sources of data:
Benn Bros. *Elec. undertakings.* UN. *Stat. yrbk.*
UN. ECLA. *Estud. econ.* _____. *Estud. sobre la eléc.*
_____. *Stat. bull.* US. *Foreign serv. desp.*
Dirección General del Gas del Estado. *Boletín estadístico*
   anual. _____. *Gas del estado; aspectos de su obra*
   presente y futura.
Dirección Nacional de Energía y Combustibles.
   Combustibles. _____. *Energía eléctrica.*

Other characteristics of plants and systems:

   Argentina's electric power facilities, which until recently were about equally divided between public and private owners, appear now to be predominantly under public ownership as a result of the purchase by the Argentine government of the Servicios Eléctricos del Gran Buenos Aires. These properties, and the properties of Agua y Energía Eléctrica, provide altogether an installed capacity of 2.5 million KW. The Argentine supply system consists of a number of regional networks, plus numerous generating plants serving only their own localities. The number of meters in service indicates that about half the people of Argentina are supplied with electricity.

SUPPLY AND USE (million kwh)	1958	1959	1960	1961	1962	1963	1964	1965
PRODUCTION (Utilities & industries)								
Total (Gross)	35842	50232	56501	59838	62987	65438	68165	
(Net)	--	--	--	--	--	--	--	
Hydro	14313	16612	18139	19918	21445	22266	23393	
Conventional thermal	(21529)	(33620)	(38362)	(39920)	(41542)	(43172)	(44772)	
Nuclear	—	—	—	—	—	—	—	
Geothermal	—	—	—	—	—	—	—	
PRODUCTION (Utilities only)								
Total (Gross)	35842	50232	56501	59838	62987	65438	68165	
(Net)	--	--	--	--	--	--	--	
Hydro	14313	16612	18139	19918	21445	22266	23393	
Conventional thermal	21529	33620	38362	39920	41542	43172	44772	
Nuclear	—	—	—	—	—	—	—	
Geothermal	—	—	—	—	—	—	—	
NET IMPORTS								
SUPPLY (Gross)	(35842)	(50232)	(56501)	(59838)	(62987)	(65438)	(68165)	
(Net)	--	--	--	--	--	--	--	
CONSUMPTION	(32000)	(45000)	(51000)	(54000)	(57000)	(59000)	(61000)	
Transport	—	—	—	—	—	—	—	
Domestic sector	(4800)	(6700)	(7600)	(8100)	(8500)	(8900)	(9000)	
Industry	(27200)	(38300)	(43400)	(45900)	(48500)	(50100)	(52000)	
LOSS AND USE	(3842)	(5232)	(5501)	(5838)	(5987)	(6438)	(7165)	
PLANT (thousand kw)								
CAPACITY (Utilities & industries)								
Total	11358	12938	13800	14700	15500	16100	16900	
Hydro	3858	4438	4900	5500	5900	6100	6400	
Conventional thermal	7500	8500	8900	9200	9600	10000	10500	
Nuclear	—	—	—	—	—	—	—	
Geothermal	—	—	—	—	—	—	—	
CAPACITY (Utilities only)								
Total	--	--	--	--	--	--	--	
Hydro	--	--	--	--	--	--	--	
Conventional thermal	--	--	--	--	--	--	--	
Nuclear	—	—	—	—	—	—	—	
Geothermal	—	—	—	—	—	—	—	
FUEL CONSUMPTION (Utilities only)								
Total (Tcals)	--	--	--	--	--	--	--	
RESERVOIR STORAGE CAPACITY (million kwh)	--	--	--	--	--	--	--	

SUPPLEMENTARY DATA FOR 1964

Transmission lines, 100 kv + (km) :   - -
Households served (thousands) :   - -
Revenues per kwh (U.S. cents) — Total: —
  Residential: –   Railways: –
  Industry: –   Lighting: –
Population (thousands) :   721,000

Other characteristics of plants and systems:

    For this area, the data available deal only with total production of electricity in North Korea, the Mongolian Peoples Republic and North Vietnam, 1958 through 1964, and mainland China in 1958 and 1964. The division of production between hydro and thermal power is the author's estimate, as are data on the consumption and end-uses of electricity.

Sources of data:

Direction de la Documentation. "Le développement économique de la République Populaire du Mongolie." *Notes et études documentaires.* No. 3312.

UN. *Stat. yrbk.*

US. Congress. Joint Economic Committee. *An economic profile of Mainland China; studies prepared for the Committee. Vol. 1: General economic setting. The economic sectors.*

Wu, Yuan-Li. *Economic development and the use of energy resources in Communist China.*

AUSTRALIA

SUPPLY AND USE (million kwh)	1958	1959	1960	1961	1962	1963	1964	1965
PRODUCTION (Utilities & industries)								
Total (Gross)	19796	21199	23199	24814	26275	29279	32519	
(Net)	--	--	--	--	--	--	--	
Hydro	3428	3819	4036	4662	4968	6674	6898	
Conventional thermal	16368	17380	19163	20152	21307	22605	25621	
Nuclear	—	—	—	—	—	—	—	
Geothermal	—	—	—	—	—	—	—	
PRODUCTION (Utilities only)								
Total (Gross)	18200	19556	21449	23056	24550	27394	30426	
(Net)	--	--	--	--	--	--	--	
Hydro	3338	3724	3998	4621	4917	6599	6840	
Conventional thermal	14862	15832	17451	18435	19633	20795	23586	
Nuclear	—	—	—	—	—	—	—	
Geothermal	—	—	—	—	—	—	—	
NET IMPORTS	—	—	—	—	—	—	—	
SUPPLY (Gross)	19796	21199	23199	24814	26275	29279	32519	
(Net)	--	--	--	--	--	--	--	
CONSUMPTION	16645	17700	19390	20865	21969	24464	26880	
Transport	802	740	734	731	729	716	731	
Domestic sector	7847e	8518e	9406	10252	10834	12029	13279	
Industry	7996	8442	9250	9882	10406	11719	12870	
LOSS AND USE	3151	3499	3809	3949	4306	4815	5639	

PLANT (thousand kw)

	1958	1959	1960	1961	1962	1963	1964	1965
CAPACITY (Utilities & industries)								
Total	5531	5953	6665	7215	7499	7983	8498	
Hydro	1126	1423	1553e	1857e	1881e	2073e	2169e	
Conventional thermal	4405	4530e	5112e	5358e	5618e	5910e	6329e	
Nuclear	—	—	—	—	—	—	—	
Geothermal	—	—	—	—	—	—	—	
CAPACITY (Utilities only)								
Total	5201	5645	6314	6959	7227	7686	8407	
Hydro	1105	1402	1532	1836	1860	2052	2148	
Conventional thermal	4096	4243	4782	5123	5367	5634	6259	
Nuclear	—	—	—	—	—	—	—	
Geothermal	—	—	—	—	—	—	—	

FUEL CONSUMPTION (Utilities only)	1958	1959	1960	1961	1962	1963	1964	1965
Coal (mmt)	5879	6213	6010	6330	6602	7201	7513	
Coke (mmt)	49	40	25	16	18	4	1	
Lignite (mmt)	9517	10826	11083	12435	13463	14360	15453	
Lignite briquettes (mmt)	112	322	918	952	721	723	628	
Fuelwood (mmt)	109	112	127	120	147	177	165	
Diesel oil (mmt)	71	68	69	68	56	59	63	
Fuel oil (mmt)	363	359	292	193	221	331	383	
Natural gas (Tcals)	—	—	—	10	19	33	32	
Total (Tcals)	--	--	--	--	--	--	--	
RESERVOIR STORAGE CAPACITY (million kwh)	--	--	--	--	--	--	--	

SUPPLEMENTARY DATA FOR 1964

Transmission lines, 100 kv+ (km) :   13128
Households served (thousands) :   2972
Revenues per kwh (U.S. cents) — Total: 2.1
  Residential: 2.2   Railways: 1.3
  Industry: 1.8   Lighting: 1.8
Population (thousands) : (1964) 11136

Sources of data:
UN. *Stat. yrbk.*
UN. ECAFE. *Elec. power.*
UNIPEDE. *Statistiques.*
Electricity Supply Association of Australia.
  Statistics of the electricity supply industry in Australia.

Other characteristics of plants and systems:

Electricity is generated and distributed mainly by agencies of the several state governments (Commissions, Authorities or Trusts), and the Snowy Mountains Hydro Electric Authority, an instrument of the Commonwealth government which provides for the needs of the Capital Territory and sells the remainder of the power available to New South Wales and Victoria. Most of the populated portions of Australia are served by regional networks, but many isolated communities obtain power from local generating plants. About ninety-five per cent of the Australian population is supplied with electricity.

147

AUSTRIA

SUPPLY AND USE (million kwh)	1958	1959	1960	1961	1962	1963	1964	1965
PRODUCTION (Utilities & industries)								
Total (Gross)	13559	14791	15965	16628	17807	18440	20363	
(Net)	13237	14412	15573	16185	17294	17873	19884	
Hydro	10617	10976	11882	11664	12127	11955	13179	
Conventional thermal	2942	3815	4083	4964	5680	6485	7184	
Nuclear	—	—	—	—	—	—	—	
Geothermal	—	—	—	—	—	—	—	
PRODUCTION (Utilities only)								
Total (Gross)	10854	11905	12938	13490	14585	15153	16913	
(Net)	10620	11620	12644	13153	14190	14709	16434	
Hydro	9117	9549	10345	10162	10617	10532	11726	
Conventional thermal	1737	2356	2593	3328	3968	4621	5187	
Nuclear	—	—	—	—	—	—	—	
Geothermal	—	—	—	—	—	—	—	
NET IMPORTS	−1364	−1933	−1903	−1948	−2099	−1693	−2708	
SUPPLY (Gross)	12195	12858	14062	14680	15708	16747	17655	
(Net)	11873	12479	13670	14237	15195	16180	17176	
CONSUMPTION	10007	10639	11614	12196	12974	13777	14841	
Transport	818	864	941	951	1032	1089	1122	
Domestic sector	3046	3241	3570	3886	4342	4757	5227	
Industry	6143	6534	7103	7359	7600	7931	8492	
LOSS AND USE	1866	1840	2056	2041	2221	2403	2335	

PLANT (thousand kw)

	1958	1959	1960	1961	1962	1963	1964	1965
CAPACITY (Utilities & industries)								
Total	3788	4033	4088	4269	4723	5031	5536	
Hydro	2834	2928	2946	3036	3183	3320	3736	
Conventional thermal	954	1105	1142	1233	1540	1711	1800	
Nuclear	—	—	—	—	—	—	—	
Geothermal	—	—	—	—	—	—	—	
CAPACITY (Utilities only)								
Total	3013	3252	3297	3404	3822	4104	4601	
Hydro	2488	2585	2603	2686	2829	2961	3367	
Conventional thermal	525	667	694	718	993	1143	1234	
Nuclear	—	—	—	—	—	—	—	
Geothermal	—	—	—	—	—	—	—	

FUEL CONSUMPTION (Utilities only)

	1958	1959	1960	1961	1962	1963	1964	1965
Coal (mmt)	34	18	38	38	68	97	127	
Low grade coal (mmt)	—	—	—	—	62	—	—	
Lignite (mmt)	1099	1562	1335	2087	2154	2241	2419	
Fuel oils (mmt)	13	35	40	87	190	293	376	
Natural gas (Tcals)	2598	3085	3950	3724	3731	3796	3596	
Manufactured gas (Tcals)	—	—	—	54	53	35	36	
Total (Tcals)	5695	7632	8212	10684	12168	13581	14749	
RESERVOIR STORAGE CAPACITY (million kwh)	1004	1017	1088	1024	1024	1099	1112	

SUPPLEMENTARY DATA FOR 1964

Transmission lines, 100 kv+ (km): 4546
Households served (thousands): 2340
Revenues per kwh (U.S. cents) — Total:
  Residential: Railways: 1.2
  Industry: Lighting: 2.2
Population (thousands):   7215

Sources of data:
  UCPTE. *Réseau.* UN. *Stat. yrbk.*
  UN. ECE. *Ann. bull. of elec. energy stat.*
  ———. *Elec. power situation.*
  ———. *Org. of elec. power services.*
  UNIPEDE. *L'écon. élec.*
  ———. *Réseaux de transport.*
  ———. *Statistiques.*

Other characteristics of plants and systems:

Completely integrated service is provided by eight "Land" companies, four municipal undertakings, and six special companies. All service has been nationalized. Significant quantities of power are also generated by the railways and in various industries - - the iron and steel industry and the aluminum industry in particular. Electricity is available to virtually the entire population of Austria. There is a considerable exchange of power between West Germany and Austria, keyed mainly to Austria's summer surplus and winter shortage of hydroelectricity.

BAHAMAS

SUPPLY AND USE (million kwh)	1958	1959	1960	1961	1962	1963	1964	1965
PRODUCTION (Utilities & industries)								
Total (Gross)	52	65	76	89	101	113	123	
(Net)	--	--	--	--	--	--	--	
Hydro	—	—	—	—	—	—	—	
Conventional thermal	52	65	76	89	101	113	123	
Nuclear	—	—	—	—	—	—	—	
Geothermal	—	—	—	—	—	—	—	
PRODUCTION (Utilities only)								
Total (Gross)	52	65	76	89	101	113	123	
(Net)	--	--	--	--	--	--	--	
Hydro	—	—	—	—	—	—	—	
Conventional thermal	52	65	76	89	101	113	123	
Nuclear	—	—	—	—	—	—	—	
Geothermal	—	—	—	—	—	—	—	
NET IMPORTS	—	—	—	—	—	—	—	
SUPPLY (Gross)	52	65	76	89	101	113	123	
(Net)	--	--	--	--	--	--	--	
CONSUMPTION	--	--	--	--	--	--	--	
Transport	—	—	—	—	—	—	—	
Domestic sector	--	--	--	--	--	--	--	
Industry	--	--	--	--	--	--	--	
LOSS AND USE	--	--	--	--	--	--	--	

PLANT (thousand kw)								
CAPACITY (Utilities & industries)								
Total	13	14	24	25	27	33	33	
Hydro	—	—	—	—	—	—	—	
Conventional thermal	13	14	24	25	27	33	33	
Nuclear	—	—	—	—	—	—	—	
Geothermal	—	—	—	—	—	—	—	
CAPACITY (Utilities only)								
Total	13	14	24	25	27	33	33	
Hydro	—	—	—	—	—	—	—	
Conventional thermal	13	14	24	25	27	33	33	
Nuclear	—	—	—	—	—	—	—	
Geothermal	—	—	—	—	—	—	—	

FUEL CONSUMPTION (Utilities only)

	1958	1959	1960	1961	1962	1963	1964	
Total (Tcals)	--	--	--	--	--	--	--	
RESERVOIR STORAGE CAPACITY (million kwh)	—	—	—	—	—	—	—	

SUPPLEMENTARY DATA FOR 1964

Transmission lines, 100 kv+ (km) : —
Households served (thousands) : (1963) 16
Revenues per kwh (U.S. cents) — Total: 4.1
   Residential: Railways:
   Industry: Lighting: 4.1
Population (thousands) :   134

Other characteristics of plants and systems:

Electricity in the Bahamas is generated and distributed through the Bahamas Electricity Corporation, which is publicly owned. Power appears to be supplied to about half the population. It is generated entirely from imported distillate and residual fuel oils.

Sources of data:

Benn Bros. *Elec. undertakings.*
UN. *Non-self-gov. terr.; summaries.*
————. *Stat. yrbk.*
Bahamas Electricity Corp. *Report and accounts, 1956-1966.*
United Kingdom. Colonial Office. *Bahamas* (Annual report).

BAHRAIN

SUPPLY AND USE (million kwh)	1958	1959	1960	1961	1962	1963	1964	1965
PRODUCTION (Utilities & industries)								
Total (Gross)	187	192	210	229	256	265	298	
(Net)	--	--	--	--	--	--	--	
Hydro	—	—	—	—	—	—	—	
Conventional thermal	187	192	210	229	256	265	298	
Nuclear	—	—	—	—	—	—	—	
Geothermal	—	—	—	—	—	—	—	
PRODUCTION (Utilities only)								
Total (Gross)	41	45	57	73	95	115	134	
(Net)	--	--	--	--	--	--	--	
Hydro	—	—	—	—	—	—	—	
Conventional thermal	41	45	57	73	95	115	134	
Nuclear	—	—	—	—	—	—	—	
Geothermal	—	—	—	—	—	—	—	
NET IMPORTS	—	—	—	—	—	—	—	
SUPPLY (Gross)	187	192	210	229	256	265	298	
(Net)	--	--	--	--	--	--	--	
CONSUMPTION	--	--	--	--	--	--	--	
Transport	—	—	—	—	—	—	—	
Domestic sector	--	--	--	--	--	--	--	
Industry	146e	147e	153e	156e	162e	150e	164e	
LOSS AND USE	--	--	--	--	--	--	--	

PLANT (thousand kw)

	1958	1959	1960	1961	1962	1963	1964	1965
CAPACITY (Utilities & industries)								
Total	48	54	60	65	65	65	70	
Hydro	—	—	—	—	—	—	—	
Conventional thermal	48	54	60	65	65	65	70	
Nuclear	—	—	—	—	—	—	—	
Geothermal	—	—	—	—	—	—	—	
CAPACITY (Utilities only)								
Total	15	21	27	32	32	32	37	
Hydro	—	—	—	—	—	—	—	
Conventional thermal	15	21	27	32	32	32	37	
Nuclear	—	—	—	—	—	—	—	
Geothermal	—	—	—	—	—	—	—	

FUEL CONSUMPTION (Utilities only)

	1958	1959	1960	1961	1962	1963	1964	1965
Total (Tcals)	--	--	--	--	--	--	--	
RESERVOIR STORAGE CAPACITY (million kwh)	—	—	—	—	—	—	—	

SUPPLEMENTARY DATA FOR 1964

Transmission lines, 100 kv+ (km):   —
Households served (thousands): (1961) 23
Revenues per kwh (U.S. cents) — Total: (1961) 2.1
  Residential: Railways:
  Industry: Lighting:
Population (thousands): 177

Sources of data:
  Benn Bros. *Elec. undertakings.*
  UN. *Stat. yrbk.*
  ———. *Water desalination.*
  Belgrave, James H.D. *Welcome to Bahrain.*

Other characteristics of plants and systems:

The State Electricity Department produces and distributes power in Bahrain, mainly at the Manama A and B power stations. Large quantities of power are also produced by the petroleum industry in Bahrain. Domestic generating facilities depend upon domestically-produced natural gas and oil. A single network serves most of the island.

SUPPLY AND USE (million kwh)	1958	1959	1960	1961	1962	1963	1964	1965
PRODUCTION (Utilities & industries)								
Total (Gross)	28	33	38	43	47	53	60	
(Net)	--	--	--	--	--	--	--	
Hydro	—	—	—	—	—	—	—	
Conventional thermal	28	33	38	43	47	53	60	
Nuclear	—	—	—	—	—	—	—	
Geothermal	—	—	—	—	—	—	—	
PRODUCTION (Utilities only)								
Total (Gross)	28	33	38	43	47	53	60	
(Net)	--	--	--	--	--	--	--	
Hydro	—	—	—	—	—	—	—	
Conventional thermal	28	33	38	43	47	53	60	
Nuclear	—	—	—	—	—	—	—	
Geothermal	—	—	—	—	—	—	—	
NET IMPORTS	—	—	—	—	—	—	—	
SUPPLY (Gross)	28	33	38	43	47	53	60	
(Net)	--	--	--	--	--	--	--	
CONSUMPTION	23	27	30	34	38	43	49	
Transport	—	—	—	—	—	—	—	
Domestic sector	10	12	13	15	17	19	21	
Industry	13	15	17	19	21	24	28	
LOSS AND USE	5	6	8	9	9	10	11	
PLANT (thousand kw)								
CAPACITY (Utilities & industries)								
Total	7.7	8.5	12	13	13	13	13	
Hydro	—	—	—	—	—	—	—	
Conventional thermal	7.7	8.5	12	13	13	13	13	
Nuclear	—	—	—	—	—	—	—	
Geothermal	—	—	—	—	—	—	—	
CAPACITY (Utilities only)								
Total	7.7	8.5	12	13	13	13	13	
Hydro	—	—	—	—	—	—	—	
Conventional thermal	7.7	8.5	12	13	13	13	13	
Nuclear	—	—	—	—	—	—	—	
Geothermal	—	—	—	—	—	—	—	
FUEL CONSUMPTION (Utilities only)								
Diesel oil (mmt)	9.0	11	13	16	18	20	21	
Total (Tcals)	95	116	137	168	189	210	221	
RESERVOIR STORAGE CAPACITY (million kwh)	—	—	—	—	—	—	—	

SUPPLEMENTARY DATA FOR 1964

Transmission lines, 100 kv+ (km):   —
Households served (thousands):   (1960) 18
Revenues per kwh (U.S. cents) — Total:
  Residential: Railways:
  Industry: Lighting:
Population (thousands):   241

Other characteristics of plants and systems:

    Electricity is provided by the Barbados Light and Power Co., Ltd., a privately-owned utility, which operates an extensive 11 KV network. It is estimated that about one-third of the population is supplied with electricity.

Sources of data:
Benn Bros. *Elec. undertakings.*
UN. *Stat. yrbk.*

BELGIUM

SUPPLY AND USE (million kwh)	1958	1959	1960	1961	1962	1963	1964	1965
PRODUCTION (Utilities & industries)								
Total (Gross)	13435	14141	15152	16029	17545	19043	20800	
(Net)	12518	13179	14118	14968	16410	17800	19478	
Hydro	198	101	172	189	163	144	115	
Conventional thermal	13237	14040	14980	15840	17378	18852	20634	
Nuclear	—	—	—	—	4	47	51	
Geothermal	—	—	—	—	—	—	—	
PRODUCTION (Utilities only)								
Total (Gross)	7577	7993	8853	9222	10308	11138	12299	
(Net)	7048	7440	8248	8610	9633	10408	11526	
Hydro	198	101	172	189	163	144	115	
Conventional thermal	7379	7892	8681	9033	10141	10947	12133	
Nuclear	—	—	—	—	4	47	51	
Geothermal	—	—	—	—	—	—	—	
NET IMPORTS	62	−106	37	−236	−473	−520	−349	
SUPPLY (Gross)	13497	14035	15189	15793	17072	18523	20451	
(Net)	12580	13073	14155	14732	15937	17280	19129	
CONSUMPTION	11865	12376	13395	13886	15030	16230	18024	
Transport	638	627	613	625	649	687	700	
Domestic sector	2268	2421	2707	3010	3425	3757	4305	
Industry	8959	9328	10075	10251	10956	11786	13019	
LOSS AND USE	715	697	760	846	907	1050	1105	

PLANT (thousand kw)

	1958	1959	1960	1961	1962	1963	1964	1965
CAPACITY (Utilities & industries)								
Total	4022	4302	4520	4646	4778	4872	5135	
Hydro	56	54	54	52	52	54	63	
Conventional thermal	3966	4248	4466	4594	4716	4807	5061	
Nuclear	—	—	—	—	10	11	11	
Geothermal	—	—	—	—	—	—	—	
CAPACITY (Utilities only)								
Total	2502	2648	2668	2798	2923	2892	3153	
Hydro	56	54	54	52	52	54	63	
Conventional thermal	2446	2594	2614	2746	2861	2827	3079	
Nuclear	—	—	—	—	10	11	11	
Geothermal	—	—	—	—	—	—	—	

FUEL CONSUMPTION (Utilities only)

	1958	1959	1960	1961	1962	1963	1964	1965
Coal (mmt)	4179	4243	4098	3839	4204	4355	4263	
Fuel oils (mmt)	454	318	404	505	582	846	1121	
Refinery gas (Tcals)	493	288	440	660	561	573	475	
Manufactured gas (Tcals)	202	275	886	987	958	853	1047	
Total (Tcals)	22743	23523	24120	24564	26548	28300	31540	
RESERVOIR STORAGE CAPACITY (million kwh)	7	7	7	7	7	7	7	

SUPPLEMENTARY DATA FOR 1964

Transmission lines, 100 kv+ (km): 1624
Households served (thousands): 3150
Revenues per kwh (U.S. cents) — Total: 2.5
  Residential: 4.7   Railways: 1.7
  Industry: 1.7   Lighting: 7.3
Population (thousands): 9378

Other characteristics of plants and systems:

Most of the population of Belgium is supplied with electricity from an integrated network that covers the entire country. Generating facilities are almost all privately owned, by such companies as the Société Intercommunale Belge d'Electricité, the Société Réunie d'Energie de Bassin de l'Escaut, and Union Intercommunale des Controles Electriques de Brabant. Power is distributed mainly through local systems, most of which are publicly or jointly owned. Substantial quantities of power are generated in industrial establishments - - particularly in the coal industry and the iron and steel industry.

Sources of data:
EEC. Energy stat., 1950-1965 UCPTE. Réseau.
UN. Stat. yrbk. UN. ECE. Elec. power situation.
——. Org. of elec. power services.
UNIPEDE. L'écon. élec.
——. Statistiques.
Fédération Professionnelle des Producteurs et Distributeurs d'Electricité de Belgique (FPE). Annuaire statistique.

BERMUDA

SUPPLY AND USE (million kwh)	1958	1959	1960	1961	1962	1963	1964	1965
PRODUCTION (Utilities & industries)								
Total (Gross)	76	80	92	103	118	124	133	
(Net)	--	--	--	--	--	--	--	
Hydro	—	—	—	—	—	—	—	
Conventional thermal	76	80	92	103	118	124	133	
Nuclear	—	—	—	—	—	—	—	
Geothermal	—	—	—	—	—	—	—	
PRODUCTION (Utilities only)								
Total (Gross)	76	80	92	103	118	124	133	
(Net)	--	--	--	--	--	--	--	
Hydro	—	—	—	—	—	—	—	
Conventional thermal	76	80	92	103	118	124	133	
Nuclear	—	—	—	—	—	—	—	
Geothermal	—	—	—	—	—	—	—	
NET IMPORTS	—	—	—	—	—	—	—	
SUPPLY (Gross)	76	80	92	103	118	124	133	
(Net)	--	--	--	--	--	--	--	
CONSUMPTION	--	69	79	90	--	--	--	
Transport	—	—	—	—	—	—	—	
Domestic sector	--	--	79	--	--	--	--	
Industry	—	—	—	—	—	—	—	
LOSS AND USE	--	11	13	13	--	--	--	

PLANT (thousand kw)

	1958	1959	1960	1961	1962	1963	1964	1965
CAPACITY (Utilities & industries)								
Total	22	24	24	24	30	36	42	
Hydro	—	—	—	—	—	—	—	
Conventional thermal	22	24	24	24	30	36	42	
Nuclear	—	—	—	—	—	—	—	
Geothermal	—	—	—	—	—	—	—	
CAPACITY (Utilities only)								
Total	22	24	24	24	30	36	42	
Hydro	—	—	—	—	—	—	—	
Conventional thermal	22	24	24	24	30	36	42	
Nuclear	—	—	—	—	—	—	—	
Geothermal	—	—	—	—	—	—	—	

FUEL CONSUMPTION (Utilities only)

	1958	1959	1960	1961	1962	1963	1964	1965
Total (Tcals)	--	--	--	--	--	--	--	
RESERVOIR STORAGE CAPACITY (million kwh)	—	—	—	—	—	—	—	

SUPPLEMENTARY DATA FOR 1964

Transmission lines, 100 kv+ (km):
Households served (thousands):   --
Revenues per kwh (U.S. cents) — Total:
  Residential: Railways:
  Industry: Lighting:
Population (thousands):   48

Other characteristics of plants and systems:

A privately-owned utility, the Bermuda Electric Light Co., Ltd., generates and distributes the island's electricity. The extraordinarily high level of consumption per capita is presumably associated with the tourist industry.

Sources of data:
Benn Bros. *Elec. undertakings.*
UN. *Non-self-gov. terr.; summaries.*
———. *Stat. yrbk.*
Bermuda Electric Light Company. *Annual report.*
United Kingdom. Colonial Office. *Bermuda* (Annual report).

BOLIVIA

SUPPLY AND USE (million kwh)	1958	1959	1960	1961	1962	1963	1964	1965
PRODUCTION (Utilities & industries)								
Total (Gross)	444	433	446	463	495	531	534	
(Net)	--	--	--	--	--	--	--	
Hydro	342	375	385	410	377	409	421	
Conventional thermal	102	58	61	53	118	122	113	
Nuclear	—	—	—	—	—	—	—	
Geothermal	—	—	—	—	—	—	—	
PRODUCTION (Utilities only)								
Total (Gross)	250	286	319	325	329	348	352	
(Net)	--	--	--	--	--	--	--	
Hydro	238	267	--	--	305	324	327	
Conventional thermal	12	19	--	--	24	24	25	
Nuclear	—	—	—	—	—	—	—	
Geothermal	—	—	—	—	—	—	—	
NET IMPORTS								
SUPPLY (Gross)	444	433	446	463	495	531	534	
(Net)	--	--	--	--	--	--	--	
CONSUMPTION	356	385	377	393	--	--	--	
Transport	—	—	—	—	—	—	—	
Domestic sector	112	126	135e	147e	--	--	--	
Industry	244	259e	242	246	267	287	277	
LOSS AND USE	88	48	69	70	73e	84e	94e	
PLANT (thousand kw)								
CAPACITY (Utilities & industries)								
Total	143	146	147	148	152	158	160	
Hydro	96	--	--	--	90	92	93	
Conventional thermal	47	--	--	--	62	66	67	
Nuclear	—	—	—	—	—	—	—	
Geothermal	—	—	—	—	—	—	—	
CAPACITY (Utilities only)								
Total	76	75	75	80e	84	86	88	
Hydro	70	--	--	--	71	70	71	
Conventional thermal	6	--	--	--	13	16	17	
Nuclear	—	—	—	—	—	—	—	
Geothermal	—	—	—	—	—	—	—	
FUEL CONSUMPTION (Utilities only)								
Total (Tcals)	--	--	--	--	--	--	--	
RESERVOIR STORAGE CAPACITY (million kwh)	--	--	--	--	--	--	--	

SUPPLEMENTARY DATA FOR 1964

Transmission lines, 100 kv+ (km): --
Households served (thousands):   --
Revenues per kwh (U.S. cents) — Total: 1.6
   Residential: 1.2   Railways:
   Industry: Lighting:
Population (thousands): 3647

Sources of data:
  UN. *Stat. yrbk.* UN. ECLA. *Estud. econ.*
  ———. *Estud. sobre la elec.* ———. *Stat. bull.*
  US. *Foreign serv. desp.*
  UN. ECLA. Data communicated to N. B. Guyol, by letter
    dated August 27, 1965.

Other characteristics of plants and systems:

The principal source of electricity in Bolivia is the Bolivian Power Company, privately owned, which controls about two-thirds of Bolivia's total utility capacity. The largest plant in Bolivia appears to be the Kilpani hydro plant, which has a capacity of 32 MW. Regional networks in the vicinities of La Paz, Oruro, Cochabamba and Potosí distribute much of Bolivia's power, but there are also many isolated stations serving only their own localities. It is estimated that no more than a tenth of Bolivia's population receives electricity.

SUPPLY AND USE (million kwh)	1958	1959	1960	1961	1962	1963	1964	1965
PRODUCTION (Utilities & industries)								
Total (Gross)	19766	21108	22865	24405	27158	27869	29094	
(Net)	--	--	--	--	25861	26702	27950	
Hydro	17485	17869	18384	18946	20662	20728	22097	
Conventional thermal	2281	3239	4481	5459	6496	7141	6997	
Nuclear	—	—	—	—	—	—	—	
Geothermal	—	—	—	—	—	—	—	
PRODUCTION (Utilities only)								
Total (Gross)	15396	16619	18514	20318	22625	23684	25043	
(Net)	--	--	--	--	--	--	--	
Hydro	13696	14237	14831	16099	17719	18651	20413	
Conventional thermal	1700	2382	3683	4219	4906	5033	4630	
Nuclear	—	—	—	—	—	—	—	
Geothermal	—	—	—	—	—	—	—	
NET IMPORTS	—	—	—	—	—	—	—	
SUPPLY (Gross)	19766	21108	22865	24405	27158	27869	29094	
(Net)	--	--	--	--	25861	26702	27950	
CONSUMPTION	16077	17162	18602	19314	22110	22804	23710	
Transport	920	899	925	887	830	849	783	
Domestic sector	7375	7850	8503	8558	10011	10400	10969	
Industry	7782	8413	9174	9869	11269	11555	11958	
LOSS AND USE	3689	3946	4263	5091	3751	3898	4240	

PLANT (thousand kw)	1958	1959	1960	1961	1962	1963	1964	1965
CAPACITY (Utilities & industries)								
Total	3993	4115	4800	5205	5729	6355	6840	
Hydro	3224	3316	3642	3809	4126	4480	4894	
Conventional thermal	769	799	1158	1396	1603	1875	1946	
Nuclear	—	—	—	—	—	—	—	
Geothermal	—	—	—	—	—	—	—	
CAPACITY (Utilities only)								
Total	3076	3215	3783	4164	4535	5060	5626	
Hydro	2505	2611	2920	3202	3504	3971	4486	
Conventional thermal	571	604	863	962	1031	1089	1140	
Nuclear	—	—	—	—	—	—	—	
Geothermal	—	—	—	—	—	—	—	

FUEL CONSUMPTION (Utilities only)	1958	1959	1960	1961	1962	1963	1964	1965
Coal (mmt)	385	417	439	485	776	790	915	
Diesel oil (mmt)	--	--	103	113	119	100	--	
Fuel oil (mmt)	--	--	887	1051	1070	1163	--	
Total (Tcals)	--	--	--	--	--	--	--	
RESERVOIR STORAGE CAPACITY (million kwh)	1139	1850	1900e	1900	1900	5758	5759	

SUPPLEMENTARY DATA FOR 1964

Transmission lines, 100 kv+ (km): --
Households served (thousands): --
Revenues per kwh (U.S. cents) — Total: 0.8
  Residential: 2.3   Railways:
  Industry: (1962) 1.5   Lighting:
Population (thousands): 78427

Other characteristics of plants and systems:

Brazil's electricity supply, which until recently was dominated by private interests, appears to fall now in the category of mixed ownership — partly as a result of the expansion of government facilities, and partly as the result of the purchase of American and Foreign Power and Brazilian Electric Power Company facilities. The only large, privately-owned utilities now operating in Brazil are the subsidiaries of the Brazilian Traction Company — namely, São Paulo Light and Rio Light, which together produce about forty per cent of the electricity generated in Brazil. Electricity is distributed through a number of regional networks (particularly in the vicinity of São Paulo and Rio de Janeiro, Belo Horizonte, and Recife) and from numerous isolated plants, but appears to be available to only a small fraction of the total population.

Sources of data:
UN. *Stat. yrbk.* UN. ECLA. *Estud. econ.*
—. *Estud. sobre la elec.* —. *Stat. bull.*
UNIPEDE. *Statistiques.* Brazilian Embassy, Washington, D.C. *Survey of the Brazilian economy.*
Conselho Nacional de Aguas e Energía Elétrica. *Aguas e energía elétrica.* Conselho Nacional de Estatística. *Anuário estatístico do Brasil.* Petroleo Brasileiro, S.A. *Relatório das actividades.*

SUPPLY AND USE (million kwh)	1958	1959	1960	1961	1962	1963	1964	1965
PRODUCTION (Utilities & industries)								
Total (Gross)	--	--	--	--	--	--	--	
(Net)	--	--	--	--	--	--	--	
Hydro	—	—	—	—	—	—	—	
Conventional thermal	--	--	--	--	--	--	--	
Nuclear	—	—	—	—	—	—	—	
Geothermal	—	—	—	—	—	—	—	
PRODUCTION (Utilities only)								
Total (Gross)	4.4	5.2	5.8	6.2	6.8	9.2	11	
(Net)	--	--	--	--	--	--	--	
Hydro	—	—	—	—	—	—	—	
Conventional thermal	4.4	5.2	5.8	6.2	6.8	9.2	11	
Nuclear	—	—	—	—	—	—	—	
Geothermal	—	—	—	—	—	—	—	
NET IMPORTS	—	—	—	—	—	—	—	
SUPPLY (Gross)	4.4	5.2	5.8	6.2	6.8	9.2	11	
(Net)	--	--	--	--	--	--	--	
CONSUMPTION	--	--	--	--	--	--	--	
Transport	—	—	—	—	—	—	—	
Domestic sector	--	--	--	--	--	--	--	
Industry	--	--	--	--	--	--	--	
LOSS AND USE	--	--	--	--	--	--	--	

PLANT (thousand kw)

	1958	1959	1960	1961	1962	1963	1964	1965
CAPACITY (Utilities & industries)								
Total	--	--	--	--	--	--	--	
Hydro	—	—	—	—	—	—	—	
Conventional thermal	--	--	--	--	--	--	--	
Nuclear	—	—	—	—	—	—	—	
Geothermal	—	—	—	—	—	—	—	
CAPACITY (Utilities only)								
Total	3.3	3.3	3.3	3.3	3.3	3.7	4.7	
Hydro	—	—	—	—	—	—	—	
Conventional thermal	3.3	3.3	3.3	3.3	3.3	3.7	4.7	
Nuclear	—	—	—	—	—	—	—	
Geothermal	—	—	—	—	—	—	—	

FUEL CONSUMPTION (Utilities only)

	1958	1959	1960	1961	1962	1963	1964	1965
Total (Tcals)	--	--	--	--	--	--	--	
RESERVOIR STORAGE CAPACITY (million kwh)	—	—	—	—	—	—	—	

SUPPLEMENTARY DATA FOR 1964

Transmission lines, 100 kv+ (km) :   —
Households served (thousands) :   --
Revenues per kwh (U.S. cents) — Total:
  Residential: Railways:
  Industry: Lighting: 9.8
Population (thousands) :   103

Other characteristics of plants and systems:

The Electricity Board, an agency of the government of British Honduras, supplies electricity to Belize. Available data suggest that only a small part of the population is supplied with current.

Sources of data:
Benn Bros. *Elec. undertakings.*
UN. *Stat. yrbk.*
UN. ECLA. *Estud. econ.*
———. *Stat. bull.*

BRUNEI

SUPPLY AND USE (million kwh)	1958	1959	1960	1961	1962	1963	1964	1965
PRODUCTION (Utilities & industries)								
Total (Gross)	55	60	64	62	62	63	70	
(Net)	--	--	--	--	--	--	--	
Hydro	–	–	–	–	–	–	–	
Conventional thermal	55	60	64	62	62	63	70	
Nuclear	–	–	–	–	–	–	–	
Geothermal	–	–	–	–	–	–	–	
PRODUCTION (Utilities only)								
Total (Gross)	6.6	8.1	9.2	10	11	11	12	
(Net)	--	--	--	--	--	--	--	
Hydro	–	–	–	–	–	–	–	
Conventional thermal	6.6	8.1	9.2	10	11	11	12	
Nuclear	–	–	–	–	–	–	–	
Geothermal	–	–	–	–	–	–	–	
NET IMPORTS								
SUPPLY (Gross)	55	60	64	62	62	63	70	
(Net)	--	--	--	--	--	--	--	
CONSUMPTION	55	59	63	61	61	62	68	
Transport	–	–	–	–	–	–	–	
Domestic sector	6	7	8	10	9	12	13	
Industry	49	52	55	51	52	50	55	
LOSS AND USE	–	1	1	1	1	1	2	
PLANT (thousand kw)								
CAPACITY (Utilities & industries)								
Total	16	17	17	21	20	20	22	
Hydro	–	–	–	–	–	–	–	
Conventional thermal	16	17	17	21	20	20	22	
Nuclear	–	–	–	–	–	–	–	
Geothermal	–	–	–	–	–	–	–	
CAPACITY (Utilities only)								
Total	2.2	3.2	3.2	3.2	4.3	4.3	4.5	
Hydro	–	–	–	–	–	–	–	
Conventional thermal	2.2	3.2	3.2	3.2	4.3	4.3	4.5	
Nuclear	–	–	–	–	–	–	–	
Geothermal	–	–	–	–	–	–	–	
FUEL CONSUMPTION (Utilities only)								
Diesel oil (mmt)	1.2	1.4	1.7	1.9	2.1	2.8	3.1	
Total (Tcals)	13	15	18	20	22	29	33	
RESERVOIR STORAGE CAPACITY (million kwh)	–	–	–	–	–	–	–	

SUPPLEMENTARY DATA FOR 1964

Transmission lines, 100 kv+ (km) : –
Households served (thousands) : 9
Revenues per kwh (U.S. cents) — Total: 4.1
   Residential: 4.2   Railways:
   Industry: 2.9   Lighting: 8.1
Population (thousands): 97

Other characteristics of plants and systems:

Electricity is produced and distributed by the government's Electrical Department, entirely through local systems. The number of customers indicates that somewhat less than half the people of Brunei are supplied with electricity.

Sources of data:
Benn Bros. *Elec. undertakings.*
UN. *Stat. yrbk.*
UN. ECAFE. *Elec. power.*
United Kingdom. Colonial Office. *State of Brunei* (Annual Report).

BULGARIA

SUPPLY AND USE (million kwh)	1958	1959	1960	1961	1962	1963	1964	1965
PRODUCTION (Utilities & industries)								
Total (Gross)	3024	3869	4657	5407	6044	7184	8700	
(Net)	2797	3569	4267	4937	5522	6524	7733	
Hydro	960	1104	1886	1796	1695	2086	1471	
Conventional thermal	2064	2765	2771	3611	4349	5098	7229	
Nuclear	—	—	—	—	—	—	—	
Geothermal	—	—	—	—	—	—	—	
PRODUCTION (Utilities only)								
Total (Gross)	2872	3718	4494	5198	5777	6613	7588	
(Net)	2652	- -	- -	- -	5299	6044	6798	
Hydro	960	1104	1886	1796	1695	2086	1471	
Conventional thermal	1912	2614	2608	3402	4082	4527	6117	
Nuclear	—	—	—	—	—	—	—	
Geothermal	—	—	—	—	—	—	—	
NET IMPORTS	16	26	28	39	71	87	−23	
SUPPLY (Gross)	3040	3895	4685	5446	6115	7271	8677	
(Net)	2813	3595e	4295e	4976e	5593	6611	7710	
CONSUMPTION	2379	3332	4035	4711	4955	5900	6980	
Transport	95	- -	- -	- -	85	133	242	
Domestic sector	660	- -	- -	- -	1334	1589	1950	
Industry	1624	- -	- -	- -	3536	4178	4788	
LOSS AND USE	434	263	260	265	638	711	730	

PLANT (thousand kw)

	1958	1959	1960	1961	1962	1963	1964	1965
CAPACITY (Utilities & industries)								
Total	719	872	925	1043	1198	1493	1986	
Hydro	314	460	460	462	494	545	746	
Conventional thermal	405	412	465	581	704	948	1240	
Nuclear	—	—	—	—	—	—	—	
Geothermal	—	—	—	—	—	—	—	
CAPACITY (Utilities only)								
Total	676	824	874	977	1106	1310	1745	
Hydro	314	460	460	462	494	545	746	
Conventional thermal	362	364	414	515	612	765	999	
Nuclear	—	—	—	—	—	—	—	
Geothermal	—	—	—	—	—	—	—	

FUEL CONSUMPTION (Utilities only)

	1958	1959	1960	1961	1962	1963	1964	1965
Low grade coal (mmt)	1830	2453	2566	2739	- -	- -	- -	
Lignite (mmt)	1035	1870	2068	3839	- -	- -	- -	
Fuel oils (mmt)	20	38	41	43	- -	- -	- -	
Manufactured gas (Tcals)	21	—	—	—	—	—	—	
Total (Tcals)	7227	10565	10588	12871	- -	- -	- -	
RESERVOIR STORAGE CAPACITY (million kwh)	303	496	560	180	109	1170	1242	

SUPPLEMENTARY DATA FOR 1964

Transmission lines, 100 kv+ (km): 3836
Households served (thousands): - -
Revenues per kwh (U.S. cents) — Total:
   Residential: Railways:
   Industry: Lighting: 3.4
Population (thousands): 8144

Other characteristics of plants and systems:

   Bulgaria is served by a nation-wide electric power network, owned and operated by the government through the Ministry of Power and Fuel. The system is interconnected with the Mir international power grid of the COMECON nations.

Sources of data:
  UN. *Stat. yrbk.*
  UN. ECE. *Ann. bull. of elec. energy stat.*
  ——— . *Elec. power situation.*
  EEI. *Rept. on elec. power dev. in Bulgaria.*

BURMA

SUPPLY AND USE (million kwh)	1958	1959	1960	1961	1962	1963	1964	1965
PRODUCTION (Utilities & industries)								
Total (Gross)	384	412	432	472	510	539	570	
(Net)	369e	395	416	458	497	520	550	
Hydro	3e	3e	75e	187	212	236	280	
Conventional thermal	381	409	357	285	298	303	290	
Nuclear	—	—	—	—	—	—	—	
Geothermal	—	—	—	—	—	—	—	
PRODUCTION (Utilities only)								
Total (Gross)	221	246	263	298	333	362	393	
(Net)	--	--	--	--	--	--	--	
Hydro	3e	3e	75e	187	212	236	280	
Conventional thermal	218	243	188	111	121	126	113	
Nuclear	—	—	—	—	—	—	—	
Geothermal	—	—	—	—	—	—	—	
NET IMPORTS	—	—	—	—	—	—	—	
SUPPLY (Gross)	384	412	432	472	510	539	570	
(Net)	369	395	416	458	497	520	550e	
CONSUMPTION	299	321	358	381	400	450	--	
Transport	—	—	—	—	—	—	--	
Domestic sector	95	100	122	136	149	166	--	
Industry	204	221	236	245	251	284	--	
LOSS AND USE	70	74	58	77	97	70	--	

PLANT (thousand kw)	1958	1959	1960	1961	1962	1963	1964	1965
CAPACITY (Utilities & industries)								
Total	162	163	250	251	252	252	252	
Hydro	--	--	85	85	85	85	85	
Conventional thermal	162	163	165	166	167	167	167	
Nuclear	—	—	—	—	—	—	—	
Geothermal	—	—	—	—	—	—	—	
CAPACITY (Utilities only)								
Total	94	105	191	191	191	191	191	
Hydro	--	--	85	85	85	85	--	
Conventional thermal	94	105	106	106	106	106	--	
Nuclear	—	—	—	—	—	—	—	
Geothermal	—	—	—	—	—	—	—	

FUEL CONSUMPTION (Utilities only)	1958	1959	1960	1961	1962	1963	1964	1965
Coal (mmt)	82.5	94.9	64.0	26.2	--	--	--	
Petroleum coke (mmt)	--	1	--	--	--	--	--	
Diesel oil (mmt)	17.1	20.3	20.2	20.7	22.2	21.4	--	
Fuel oil (mmt)	10.4	14.3	12.3	9.9	--	7		
Total (Tcals)	861	1043	896	511	581	301	--	
RESERVOIR STORAGE CAPACITY (million kwh)	—	—	--	--	--	--	--	

SUPPLEMENTARY DATA FOR 1964

Transmission lines, 100 kv + (km): 763 (1963)
Households served (thousands) : 160 (1962)
Revenues per kwh (U.S. cents) — Total: 9.0
  Residential: 12.2   Railways:
  Industry: 4.1   Lighting: 8.7
Population (thousands) : 24229

Sources of data:
  UN. *Stat. yrbk.*
  UN. ECAFE. *Elec. power.*
  Ministry of Finance and Revenue. *Selected monthly
    economic indicators.*

Other characteristics of plants and systems:

    The Ministry of Industry administers the electricity supply industry, which is publicly owned and managed by the Electricity Supply Board of the Union of Burma. Power is supplied to the Rangoon, Mandalay and nearby areas from the Balu Chaung hydro plant, but most communities are served by isolated diesel units. Only a very small fraction of the population is supplied with electricity.

CAMBODIA

SUPPLY AND USE (million kwh)	1958	1959	1960	1961	1962	1963	1964	1965
PRODUCTION (Utilities & industries)								
Total (Gross)	46	52	61	75	84	99	--	
(Net)	45	51	60	73	81	96	--	
Hydro	—	—	—	—	—	—	—	
Conventional thermal	46	52	61	75	84	99	--	
Nuclear	—	—	—	—	—	—	—	
Geothermal	—	—	—	—	—	—	—	
PRODUCTION (Utilities only)								
Total (Gross)	46	52	61	74	82	95	--	
(Net)	--	--	--	--	--	--	--	
Hydro	—	—	—	—	—	—	—	
Conventional thermal	46	52	61	74	82	95	--	
Nuclear	—	—	—	—	—	—	—	
Geothermal	—	—	—	—	—	—	—	
NET IMPORTS	—	—	—	—	—	—	—	
SUPPLY (Gross)	46	52	61	75	84	99	--	
(Net)	45	51	60	73	81	96	--	
CONSUMPTION	36	32	37	36	44	61	--	
Transport	—	—	—	—	—	—	—	
Domestic sector	34	29	33	32	40	57	--	
Industry	2	3	4	4e	4e	4	--	
LOSS AND USE	9	19	23	37	37	35	--	

PLANT (thousand kw)

	1958	1959	1960	1961	1962	1963	1964	1965
CAPACITY (Utilities & industries)								
Total	18	21	26	27	34	39	--	
Hydro	—	—	—	—	—	—	—	
Conventional thermal	18	21	26	27	34	39	--	
Nuclear	—	—	—	—	—	—	—	
Geothermal	—	—	—	—	—	—	—	
CAPACITY (Utilities only)								
Total	18	21	26	27	34	37	--	
Hydro	—	—	—	—	—	—	—	
Conventional thermal	18	21	26	27	34	37	--	
Nuclear	—	—	—	—	—	—	—	
Geothermal	—	—	—	—	—	—	—	

FUEL CONSUMPTION (Utilities only)

	1958	1959	1960	1961	1962	1963	1964	1965
Diesel oil (mmt)	13	17	19	22e	25	24	--	
Fuel oil (mmt)	--	--	--	--	9	5	--	
Total (Tcals)	133	175	203	--	322	301	--	
RESERVOIR STORAGE CAPACITY (million kwh)	—	—	—		—	—	—	

SUPPLEMENTARY DATA FOR 1964

Transmission lines, 100 kv+ (km):
Households served (thousands): 26 (1963)
Revenues per kwh (U.S. cents) — Total: 8.9
  Residential: Railways:
  Industry: 5.5   Lighting:
Population (thousands): 6022

Other characteristics of plants and systems:

The principal cities in Cambodia are supplied with electricity by Electricité du Cambodge, a private company in which the government owns the majority of shares. Service to most of the country is provided by isolated diesel plants. It is available to only a very small fraction of the population.

Sources of data:
UN. *Stat. yrbk.*
UN. ECAFE. *Elec. power.*

SUPPLY AND USE (million kwh)	1958	1959	1960	1961	1962	1963	1964	1965
PRODUCTION (Utilities & industries)								
Total (Gross)	680e	850e	917	1017	1127	1128	1070	
(Net)	--	--	--	--	--	--	--	
Hydro	665e	832e	898	955	1059	1042	1039	
Conventional thermal	15e	18e	19	62	68	86	31	
Nuclear	—	—	—	—	—	—	—	
Geothermal	—	—	—	—	—	—	—	
PRODUCTION (Utilities only)								
Total (Gross)	--	--	--	--	--	--	--	
(Net)	--	--	--	--	--	--	--	
Hydro	--	--	--	--	--	--	--	
Conventional thermal	--	--	--	--	--	--	--	
Nuclear	—	—	—	—	—	—	—	
Geothermal	—	—	—	—	—	—	—	
NET IMPORTS								
SUPPLY (Gross)	680	850	917	1017	1127	1128	1070	
(Net)	--	--	--	--	--	--	--	
CONSUMPTION	--	--	894	962	1065	1075	1048e	
Transport	—	--	—	—	—	—	—	
Domestic sector	--	--	30	41	45	52	55e	
Industry	--	--	864	921	1020	1023	993	
LOSS AND USE	--	--	23	55	62	53	22	

PLANT (thousand kw)	1958	1959	1960	1961	1962	1963	1964	1965
CAPACITY (Utilities & industries)								
Total	160	160	160	168	168e	168e	168e	
Hydro	152	152	152	152	152	152	152	
Conventional thermal	8	8	8	16e	16e	16e	16e	
Nuclear	—	—	—	—	—	—	—	
Geothermal	—	—	—	—	—	—	—	
CAPACITY (Utilities only)								
Total	--	--	--	--	--	--	--	
Hydro	--	--	--	--	--	--	--	
Conventional thermal	--	--	--	--	--	--	--	
Nuclear	—	—	—	—	—	—	—	
Geothermal	—	—	—	—	—	—	—	

FUEL CONSUMPTION (Utilities only)

	1958	1959	1960	1961	1962	1963	1964	1965
Total (Tcals)	--	--	--	--	--	--	--	
RESERVOIR STORAGE CAPACITY (million kwh)	--	--	--	--	--	--		

SUPPLEMENTARY DATA FOR 1964

Transmission lines, 100 kv+ (km) :   —
Households served (thousands) :   20
Revenues per kwh (U.S. cents) — Total: 6.9 (1961)
   Residential: Railways: —
   Industry: Lighting: —
Population (thousands):   5108

Other characteristics of plants and systems:

L'Energie Electrique de Cameroon (ENELCAM), and Cie. Centrale de Distribution d'Energie Electrique, both privately owned, provide the public supply of electricity in Cameroon, mainly from isolated diesel stations. Only a very small part of the population has electricity available. The bulk of the country's power is generated and consumed by an international aluminum company.

Sources of data:
EEC. *Yrbk. Overseas Assoc.*
Soc. R. Moreux. *Industries et travaux. No. 122.*
UN. *Stat. yrbk.*
UN. ECA. *Rept. on econ. coop.\ in Central Africa.*
———. *Situation, trends & prospects.*
Service de la Statistique et de la Mécanographie.
   Quarterly economic bulletin for the Federal Republic
   of Cameroon.

CANADA

SUPPLY AND USE (million kwh)	1958	1959	1960	1961	1962	1963	1964	1965
PRODUCTION (Utilities & industries)								
Total (Gross)	--	--	--	--	--	--	--	
(Net)	97525	104671	114457	113713	117468	122238	134987	
Hydro	90509	97040	105883	103919	104050	103832	113344	
Conventional thermal	7016	7631	8574	9794	13396	18319	21502	
Nuclear	–	–	–	–	22	87	141	
Geothermal	–	–	–	–	–	–	–	
PRODUCTION (Utilities only)								
Total (Gross)	--	--	--	--	--	--	--	
(Net)	75953	83049	89157	89389	92096	93588	102889	
Hydro	71171	77768	83203	82326	81343	78113	84871	
Conventional thermal	4782	5281	5954	7063	10731	15388	17877	
Nuclear	–	–	–	–	22	87	141	
Geothermal	–	–	–	–	–	–	–	
NET IMPORTS	–3841	–4081	–5155	–2763	–1333	–729	–1038	
SUPPLY (Gross)	--	--	--	--	--	--	--	
(Net)	93684	100590	109302	110950	116135	121509	133949	
CONSUMPTION	84741	90759	99382	100746	105314	110391	121220	
Transport	–	–	–	–	–	–	–	
Domestic sector	27865	31023	33029	36391	39816	37080	40415	
Industry	56876	59736	66353	64355	65498	73311	80805	
LOSS AND USE	8943	9831	9920	10204	10821	11118	12729	

PLANT (thousand kw)	1958	1959	1960	1961	1962	1963	1964	1965
CAPACITY (Utilities & industries)								
Total	18669	21128	23035	24091	24967	26300	27027	
Hydro	15687	17550	18643	19019	19338	20100	20313	
Conventional thermal	2982	3578	4392	5072	5609	6180	6694	
Nuclear	–	–	–	–	20	20	20	
Geothermal	–	–	–	–	–	–	–	
CAPACITY (Utilities only)								
Total	14758	16937	18419	19492	20383	21200	21891	
Hydro	12582	14067	14772	15180	15502	15885	16085	
Conventional thermal	2176	2870	3647	4312	4861	5295	5786	
Nuclear	–	–	–	–	20	20	20	
Geothermal	–	–	–	–	–	–	–	

FUEL CONSUMPTION (Utilities only)	1958	1959	1960	1961	1962	1963	1964	1965
Coal (mmt)	810	694	741	863	1933	3139	3553	
Subbituminous coal & lignite (mmt)	688	593	933	1181	1445	1533	2130	
Diesel oil (mmt)	25	31	37	39	49	76	72	
Fuel oil (mmt)	121	143	162	203	199	193	306	
Natural gas (Tcals)	7603	10310	10330	11232	11808	12845	12019	
Total (Tcals)	17553	19358	21299	24477	33747	43921	49482	
RESERVOIR STORAGE CAPACITY (million kwh)	--	--	--	--	--	--	--	

SUPPLEMENTARY DATA FOR 1964

Transmission lines, 100 kv + (km): 70592
Households served (thousands): 5151
Revenues per kwh (U.S. cents) — Total: 1.0
Residential: 1.8   Railways:
Industry: 0.6   Lighting:
Population (thousands): 19271

Sources of data:
UN. *Stat. yrbk.*
Department of Northern Affairs and National Resources.
Water Resources Branch. *Electric power in Canada*
Dominion Bureau of Statistics. *Electric power statistics.*
——. Industry Division. *General review of the manufacturing industries of Canada.*

Other characteristics of plants and systems:

Electricity is produced and distributed through a number of very large, publicly-owned, integrated systems, such as the Hydroelectric Power Commission of Ontario, Quebec Hydroelectric Commission, and the British Columbia Hydro and Power Authority, which took over the properties of British Columbia Electric Company. There are also a number of large, private producers in Canada, such as the Shawinigan Water and Power Company, and an important share of Canada's electricity is generated by industrial establishments, especially paper companies. Electricity is supplied to most of Canada's population.

SUPPLY AND USE (million kwh)	1958	1959	1960	1961	1962	1963	1964	1965
PRODUCTION (Utilities & industries)								
Total (Gross)	--	--	--	--	--	--	--	
(Net)	--	--	--	--	--	--	--	
Hydro	--	--	--	--	--	--	--	
Conventional thermal	—	—	—	—	—	—	—	
Nuclear	—	—	—	—	—	—	—	
Geothermal	—	—	—	—	—	—	—	
PRODUCTION (Utilities only)								
Total (Gross)	6	7	8	9	12	17	20	
(Net)	--	--	--	--	--	--	--	
Hydro	6	7	8	9	12	17	20	
Conventional thermal	—	—	—	—	—	—	—	
Nuclear	—	—	—	—	—	—	—	
Geothermal	—	—	—	—	—	—	—	
NET IMPORTS								
SUPPLY (Gross)	6	7	8	9	12	17	20	
(Net)	--	--	--	--	--	--	--	
CONSUMPTION	4	5	6	7	10	--	--	
Transport	—	—	—	—	—	—	—	
Domestic sector	3	3	4	5	7	--	--	
Industry	1	2	2	2	3	--	--	
LOSS AND USE	2	2	2	2	2	--	--	

PLANT (thousand kw)	1958	1959	1960	1961	1962	1963	1964	1965
CAPACITY (Utilities & industries)								
Total	--	--	--	--	--	--	--	
Hydro	--	--	--	--	--	--	--	
Conventional thermal	--	--	--	--	--	--	--	
Nuclear	—	—	—	—	—	—	—	
Geothermal	—	—	—	—	—	—	—	
CAPACITY (Utilities only)								
Total	6.1	6.1	6.1	6.1	8.3e	8.3	8.3	
Hydro	4.4	4.4	4.4	4.4	6.6	6.6	6.6	
Conventional thermal	1.7	1.7	1.7	1.7	1.7e	1.7	1.7	
Nuclear	—	—	—	—	—	—	—	
Geothermal	—	—	—	—	—	—	—	

FUEL CONSUMPTION (Utilities only)

	1958	1959	1960	1961	1962	1963	1964	
Total (Tcals)	--	--	--	--	--	--	--	
RESERVOIR STORAGE CAPACITY (million kwh)	--	--	--	--	--	--	--	

SUPPLEMENTARY DATA FOR 1964

Transmission lines, 100 kv+ (km) :   —
Households served (thousands) :   2.4 (1962)
Revenues per kwh (U.S. cents) — Total: 8.5 (1961)
    Residential: Railways:
    Industry: Lighting: 8.9 – 12.2
Population (thousands) : 1338

Sources of data:
Benn Bros. *Elec. undertakings.*
EEC. *Yrbk. Overseas Assoc.*
Inst. de la Stat. *Données statistiques.*
Soc. R. Moreux. *Industries et travaux. No. 122.*
UN. *Stat. yrbk.* UN. ECA. *Situation, trends & prospects.*
Service de la Statistique Générale. *Bulletin mensuel de statistique générale.*

Other characteristics of plants and systems:

A private company, L'Union Electrique d'Outre-Mer, is the main source of electricity in Central Africa. A very small fraction of the total population is supplied with electricity, from isolated diesel and hydro plants.

CEYLON

SUPPLY AND USE (million kwh)	1958	1959	1960	1961	1962	1963	1964	1965
PRODUCTION (Utilities & industries)								
Total (Gross)	240	274	311	347	376	450	475	
(Net)	232	272	309	344	372	443e	467e	
Hydro	200	238	272	277	320	327	338	
Conventional thermal	40	36	39	70	56	123	137	
Nuclear	—	—	—	—	—	—	—	
Geothermal	—	—	—	—	—	—	—	
PRODUCTION (Utilities only)								
Total (Gross)	226	261	297	332e	360e	432	455e	
(Net)	215	253	289	311	351	378	405	
Hydro	200	238	272	277	320	327	338	
Conventional thermal	26	23	25	55	40	105	117	
Nuclear	—	—	—	—	—	—	—	
Geothermal	—	—	—	—	—	—	—	
NET IMPORTS	—	—	—	—	—	—	—	
SUPPLY (Gross)	240	274	311	347	376	450	475	
(Net)	232	272	309	344	372	443	467	
CONSUMPTION	186	221	261	296	312	383	412	
Transport	5	5	5	5	5	5	3	
Domestic sector	112	137	164	190	180	187	201	
Industry	69	79	92	101	127	191e	208	
LOSS AND USE	46	51	48	48	60	60	55	
PLANT (thousand kw)								
CAPACITY (Utilities & industries)								
Total	94	102	102	102	127	145	170	
Hydro	55	55	55	55	55	63	63	
Conventional thermal	39	47	47	47	72	82	107	
Nuclear	—	—	—	—	—	—	—	
Geothermal	—	—	—	—	—	—	—	
CAPACITY (Utilities only)								
Total	88	94	94	94	118	120	145	
Hydro	55	55	55	55	55	60	60	
Conventional thermal	33	39	39	39	63	60	85	
Nuclear	—	—	—	—	—	—	—	
Geothermal	—	—	—	—	—	—	—	
FUEL CONSUMPTION (Utilities only)								
Diesel oil (mmt)	6	2	2	2	3	4	4	
Fuel oil (mmt)	4	--	--	--	--	15	19	
Total (Tcals)	109	--	--	--	--	200	236	
RESERVOIR STORAGE CAPACITY (million kwh)	42	42	42	42	44	44	44	

SUPPLEMENTARY DATA FOR 1964

Transmission lines, 100 kv+ (km):   322
Households served (thousands):   83
Revenues per kwh (U.S. cents) — Total: 3.4
  Residential: 3.1   Railways:
  Industry: 2.5   Lighting:
Population (thousands):   10971

Other characteristics of plants and systems:

    The chief agency for the generation and distribution of power is the Department of Government Electrical Undertakings, which operates one network in the Colombo area and another in the Jaffna Peninsula. Supply in much of Ceylon is from small, isolated diesel plants operated by local authorities. Only a small fraction of the population is supplied with electricity.

Sources of data:

  UN. *Stat. yrbk.* UN. ECAFE. *Elec. power.*
  UNIPEDE. *Statistiques.*
  Department of Government Electrical Undertakings.
    Administration report of the Acting General Manager.

CHAD

SUPPLY AND USE (million kwh)	1958	1959	1960	1961	1962	1963	1964	1965
PRODUCTION (Utilities & industries)								
Total (Gross)	--	--	--	--	--	--	--	
(Net)	--	--	--	--	--	--	--	
Hydro	—	—	—	—	—	—	—	
Conventional thermal	--	--	--	--	--	--	--	
Nuclear	—	—	—	—	—	—	—	
Geothermal	—	—	—	—	—	—	—	
PRODUCTION (Utilities only)								
Total (Gross)	5	6	8	9	11	13	15	
(Net)	--	--	--	--	--	--	--	
Hydro	—	—	—	—	—	—	—	
Conventional thermal	5	6	8	9	11	13	15	
Nuclear	—	—	—	—	—	—	—	
Geothermal	—	—	—	—	—	—	—	
NET IMPORTS	—	—	—	—	—	—	—	
SUPPLY (Gross)	5	6	8	9	11	13	15	
(Net)	--	--	--	--	--	--	--	
CONSUMPTION	--	5	7	8	10	11	13	
Transport	—	—	—	—	—	—	—	
Domestic sector	--	4	5	6	7	7	8	
Industry	1	1	2	2	3	4	5	
LOSS AND USE	--	1	1	1	1	2	2	

PLANT (thousand kw)

	1958	1959	1960	1961	1962	1963	1964	1965
CAPACITY (Utilities & industries)								
Total	--	--	--	--	--	--	--	
Hydro	—	—	—	—	—	—	—	
Conventional thermal	--	--	--	--	--	--	--	
Nuclear	—	—	—	—	—	—	—	
Geothermal	—	—	—	—	—	—	—	
CAPACITY (Utilities only)								
Total	2.1	2.1	2.8	2.8	2.8	5.3	9.8	
Hydro	—	—	—	—	—	—	—	
Conventional thermal	2.1	2.1	2.8	2.8	2.8	5.3	9.8	
Nuclear	—	—	—	—	—	—	—	
Geothermal	—	—	—	—	—	—	—	

FUEL CONSUMPTION (Utilities only)

	1958	1959	1960	1961	1962	1963	1964	1965
Diesel oil (mmt)	--	1.5	2.0	2.3	2.9	3.3	3.6e	
Total (Tcals)	--	16	21	24	30	35	38	
RESERVOIR STORAGE CAPACITY (million kwh)	—	—	—	—	—	—	—	

SUPPLEMENTARY DATA FOR 1964

Transmission lines, 100 kv+ (km):   --
Households served (thousands):   2.3
Revenues per kwh (U.S. cents) — Total:
  Residential: Railways:
  Industry: Lighting: 9.3
Population (thousands):   3260

Other characteristics of plants and systems:

The Société Equatoriale d'Energie Electrique, privately owned, generates most of the country's power in small, isolated diesel plants. A very small fraction of the total population is supplied with electricity.

Sources of data:
EEC. Yrbk. Overseas Assoc. UN. Mo. bull. of stat.
_____. Stat. yrbk.
UN. ECA. Rept. on econ. coop. in Central Africa.
Service de la Statistique Générale. Bulletin mensuel de statistique de la République du Tchad.

CHILE

SUPPLY AND USE (million kwh)	1958	1959	1960	1961	1962	1963	1964	1965
PRODUCTION (Utilities & industries)								
Total (Gross)	4146	4605	4592	4880	5286	5623	5932	
(Net)	4106	4562	4547	4833	5238	5565	5882	
Hydro	2661	2930	2977	3141	3312	3404	3723	
Conventional thermal	1485	1675	1615	1739	1974	2219	2209	
Nuclear	—	—	—	—	—	—	—	
Geothermal	—	—	—	—	—	—	—	
PRODUCTION (Utilities only)								
Total (Gross)	2054	2258	2342	2551	2804	3164	3400	
(Net)	--	--	--	--	--	--	--	
Hydro	1897	2159	2172	2338	2494	2631	2925	
Conventional thermal	157	99	170	213	310	533	475	
Nuclear	—	—	—	—	—	—	—	
Geothermal	—	—	—	—	—	—	—	
NET IMPORTS	—	—	—	—	—	—	—	
SUPPLY (Gross)	4146	4605	4592	4880	5286	5623	5932	
(Net)	4106	4562	4547	4833	5238	5565	5882	
CONSUMPTION	3767	4204	4276	4483	4838	4977	5295	
Transport	130	128	119	111	115	129	124	
Domestic sector	876	968	1119	1195	1252	1254	1326	
Industry	2761	3108	3038	3177	3471	3594	3845	
LOSS AND USE	339	358	271	350	400	588	587	
PLANT (thousand kw)								
CAPACITY (Utilities & industries)								
Total	1014	1092	1143	1153	1315	1336	1495	
Hydro	522	594	595	598	649	683	711	
Conventional thermal	492	498	548	555	666	653	784	
Nuclear	—	—	—	—	—	—	—	
Geothermal	—	—	—	—	—	—	—	
CAPACITY (Utilities only)								
Total	545	609	618	676	773	776	926	
Hydro	409	471	486	541	541	569	603	
Conventional thermal	136	138	132	135	232	207	323	
Nuclear	—	—	—	—	—	—	—	
Geothermal	--	—	—	—	—	—	—	
FUEL CONSUMPTION (Utilities only)								
Coal (mmt)	121	136	124	164	216	264	216	
Diesel oil (mmt)	--	46	38	48	65	66	80	
Fuel oil (mmt)	--	479	389	413	421	460	499	
Total (Tcals)	--	--	--	--	--	--	--	
RESERVOIR STORAGE CAPACITY (million kwh)	--	--	--	--	--	--	--	

SUPPLEMENTARY DATA FOR 1964

Transmission lines, 100 kv+ (km) :   --

Households served (thousands) :   --

Revenues per kwh (U.S. cents) — Total: 1.9

    Residential: 2.9   Railways:

    Industry: 1.6 (1962)   Lighting:

Population (thousands) : 8391

Other characteristics of plants and systems:

Chile's electric power supply is provided mainly by a national undertaking, the Empresa Nacional de Electricidad (ENDESA), and the Cia. Chilena de Electricidad, Ltda., which is privately owned. Much of the country is served by a single network, extending north and south from Santiago, but part is served by regional and local plants.

Sources of data:

UN. *Growth of world industry.* ——. *Stat. yrbk.*

UN. ECLA. *Estud. econ.* ——. *Estud. sobre la elec.*

——. *Stat. bull.* UNIPEDE. *Statistiques.*

Dirección de Estadística y Censos. *Sinopsis.*

Empresa Nacional de Electricidad, S.A. (ENDESA).

    Memoria de actividades.

    ——. *Producción y consumo de energía en Chile.*

SUPPLY AND USE (million kwh)	1958	1959	1960	1961	1962	1963	1964	1965
PRODUCTION (Utilities & industries)								
Total (Gross)	3088e	3449	3902	4360e	5011e	5337e	6288	
(Net)	3028	3370	3797	4243	4848	5157	6072	
Hydro	1859	2011	2065	2339	2161	1931	2359	
Conventional thermal	1229	1438	1837	2021	2850	3406	3929	
Nuclear	—	—	—	—	—	—	—	
Geothermal	—	—	—	—	—	—	—	
PRODUCTION (Utilities only)								
Total (Gross)	2930e	3287	3721	4189	4847	5198	6131	
(Net)	2874	3208	3616	4072	4684	5018	5915	
Hydro	1859	2011	2065	2339e	2161e	1931	2359	
Conventional thermal	1071	1276	1656	1850	2686	3267	3772	
Nuclear	—	—	—	—	—	—	—	
Geothermal	—	—	—	—	—	—	—	
NET IMPORTS	—	—	—	—	—	—	—	
SUPPLY (Gross)	3088	3449	3902	4360	5011	5337	6288	
(Net)	3028	3370	3797	4243	4848	5157	6072	
CONSUMPTION	2683e	2927	3304	3687	4220	4498	5217	
Transport								
Domestic sector	500	551	611	679	755	1027	1169	
Industry	2183	2376	2693	3008	3465	3471	4048	
LOSS AND USE	345e	443	493	556	628	659	855	

PLANT (thousand kw)	1958	1959	1960	1961	1962	1963	1964	1965
CAPACITY (Utilities & industries)								
Total	651	702	782	1001	999	1118	1208	
Hydro	399	448	448	538	539e	539e	628	
Conventional thermal	252	254	334	463	460	579	580	
Nuclear	—	—	—	—	—	—	—	
Geothermal	—	—	—	—	—	—	—	
CAPACITY (Utilities only)								
Total	582	633	709	923	923	1040	1130	
Hydro	399	448	448	538	538	538	628	
Conventional thermal	183	185	261	385	385	502	502	
Nuclear								
Geothermal								

FUEL CONSUMPTION (Utilities only)	1958	1959	1960	1961	1962	1963	1964	1965
Coal (mmt)	657	720	859	929e	1207e	1408	1603	
Diesel oil (mmt)	1.1	1.4	1.8	2.0	0.7	1.0	1.5	
Fuel oil (mmt)	4.7	5.9	6	--	--	15	14	
Total (Tcals)	4669	5124	6132	6524	8456	10052	11403	
RESERVOIR STORAGE CAPACITY (million kwh)	--	--	--	--	--	--	--	

SUPPLEMENTARY DATA FOR 1964

Transmission lines, 100 kv+ (km): 1084
Households served (thousands): 1285
Revenues per kwh (U.S. cents) — Total: 1.2
　Residential: 1.9　　Railways:
　Industry: 0.9　　Lighting: 2.3
Population (thousands): 12070

Sources of data:
　UN. *Stat. yrbk.*
　UN. ECAFE. *Elec. power.*
　———. *Role & application of elec. power.*
　Directorate-General of Budgets, Accounts and Statistics.
　　Executive Yuan. *Statistical abstract of the Republic of China.*

Other characteristics of plants and systems:

　The sole agency for power development is the Taiwan Power Company, a mixed-ownership undertaking in which most of the stock is owned by central and provincial governments, a small part by private investors. The system is fully integrated and serves the entire island. On the basis of the number of customers, it is estimated that approximately one-third of the population of Taiwan is supplied with electricity.

COLOMBIA

SUPPLY AND USE (million kwh)	1958	1959	1960	1961	1962	1963	1964	1965
PRODUCTION (Utilities & industries)								
Total (Gross)	3034	3413	3750	3776	4280	5268	5916	
(Net)	--	--	--	--	--	--	--	
Hydro	2049	2316	2587	2513	2762	3218	3721	
Conventional thermal	985	1097	1163	1263	1518	2050	2195	
Nuclear	—	—	—	—	—	—	—	
Geothermal	—	—	—	—	—	—	—	
PRODUCTION (Utilities only)								
Total (Gross)	2432	2768	3105	3123	3400	3964	4565	
(Net)	--	--	--	--	--	--	--	
Hydro	1946	2213	2484	2410	2582	2894	3157	
Conventional thermal	486	555	621	713	818	1070	1408	
Nuclear	—	—	—	—	—	—	—	
Geothermal	—	—	—	—	—	—	—	
NET IMPORTS	—	—	—	—	—	—	—	
SUPPLY (Gross)	3034	3413	3750	3776	4280	5268	5916	
(Net)	--	--	--	--	--	--	--	
CONSUMPTION	2469	2706	2926	3110	3540e	--	--	
Transport	—	—	—	—	—	--	--	
Domestic sector	1377	1517	1626e	1778	1900e	--	--	
Industry	1092	1189	1300	1332e	1640e	2166e	2290e	
LOSS AND USE	565	707	824	666	740e	--	--	

PLANT (thousand kw)	1958	1959	1960	1961	1962	1963	1964	1965
CAPACITY (Utilities & industries)								
Total	874	891	911	929	1158	1371	1469	
Hydro	505	507	505	515	636	773	793	
Conventional thermal	369	384	406	414	522	598	676	
Nuclear	—	—	—	—	—	—	—	
Geothermal	—	—	—	—	—	—	—	
CAPACITY (Utilities only)								
Total	630	656	670	684	848	1039	1117	
Hydro	453	460e	460	470	590e	681	750	
Conventional thermal	177	196e	210	214	258e	358	367	
Nuclear	—	—	—	—	—	—	—	
Geothermal	—	—	—	—	—	—	—	

FUEL CONSUMPTION (Utilities only)	1958	1959	1960	1961	1962	1963	1964	1965
Coal (mmt)	--	--	54	--	--	--	--	
Diesel oil (mmt)	--	--	36	--	--	--	--	
Fuel oil (mmt)	--	--	96	-- .	--	--	--	
Total (Tcals)	--	--	--	--	--	--	--	
RESERVOIR STORAGE CAPACITY (million kwh)	--	--	--	--	--	--	--	

SUPPLEMENTARY DATA FOR 1964

Transmission lines, 100 kv+ (km) :   --
Households served (thousands) :   --
Revenues per kwh (U.S. cents) — Total: 1.7
  Residential: 2.2   Railways:
  Industry: Lighting: 1.0
Population (thousands) :   17485

Other characteristics of plants and systems:

The bulk of Colombia's electricity appears to be generated by publicly-owned utilities such as Empresas Públicas de Medellín, Empresa de Energía Eléctrica de Bogotá, and the Cauca Valley Regional Corporation, an agency of the Colombian government. Service appears to be largely local in nature, and available to only a fraction of the total population.

Sources of data:
UN. *Growth of world industry.* _____. *Stat. yrbk.*
UN. ECLA. *Estud. econ.* _____. *Estud. sobre la elec.*
_____. *Stat. bull.* US. *Foreign serv. desp.*
Banco de la República. *Informe anual del gerente a la junta directiva.*
Ministerio de Fomento. *Memoria del Ministerio de Fomento.*

SUPPLY AND USE (million kwh)	1958	1959	1960	1961	1962	1963	1964	1965
PRODUCTION (Utilities & industries)								
Total (Gross)	--	--	--	--	--	--	--	
(Net)	--	--	--	--	--	--	--	
Hydro	--	--	--	--	--	--	--	
Conventional thermal	--	--	--	--	--	--	--	
Nuclear	—	—	—	—	—	—	—	
Geothermal	—	—	—	—	—	—	—	
PRODUCTION (Utilities only)								
Total (Gross)	--	21	29	32	37	41	43	
(Net)	--	21	25	28	33	36	38	
Hydro	--	--	19	21	24	27	28	
Conventional thermal	--	21	10	11	13	14	15	
Nuclear	—	—	—	—	—	—	—	
Geothermal	—	—	—	—	—	—	—	
NET IMPORTS	--	—	—	—	—	—	—	
SUPPLY (Gross)	--	21	29	32	37	41	43	
(Net)	--	21	25	28	33	36	38	
CONSUMPTION	--	21	24	27	31	35	36	
Transport	—	—	—	—	—	—	—	
Domestic sector	--	11	13	15	18	21	22e	
Industry	--	10	11	12	13	14	14e	
LOSS AND USE	--	—	1	1	2	1	2e	
PLANT (thousand kw)								
CAPACITY (Utilities & industries)								
Total	--	--	--	--	--	--	--	
Hydro	--	--	--	--	--	--	--	
Conventional thermal	--	--	--	--	--	--	--	
Nuclear	—	—	—	—	—	—	—	
Geothermal	—	—	—	—	—	—	—	
CAPACITY (Utilities only)								
Total	--	--	--	27	--	--	31	
Hydro	--	--	--	15	--	--	19	
Conventional thermal	--	--	--	12	--	--	12	
Nuclear	—	—	—	—	—	—	—	
Geothermal	—	—	—	—	—	—	—	
FUEL CONSUMPTION (Utilities only)								
Total (Tcals)	--	--	--	--	--	--	--	
RESERVOIR STORAGE CAPACITY (million kwh)	--	--	--	--	--	--	--	

SUPPLEMENTARY DATA FOR 1964

Transmission lines, 100 kv+ (km) :   --
Households served (thousands) :   9.6
Revenues per kwh (U.S. cents) — Total:
   Residential: Railways:
   Industry: Lighting: 13.8
Population (thousands) :   826

Other characteristics of plants and systems:

   Union Electrique d'Outre-Mer and the Société Equatoriale d'Energie Electrique, both privately owned, generate and distribute the bulk of the country's energy. Service is entirely local in nature, and is available to only a very small part of the total population.

Sources of data:

   Benn Bros. *Elec. undertakings.* EEC. *Yrbk. Overseas Assoc.*
   Inst. de la Stat. *Données statistiques.*
   République du Congo. Cabinet du Premier Ministre. Direction
     de la Service Nationale de la Statistique·des Etudes
     Démographiques et Economiques. *Bulletin mensuel*
     rapide des statistiques (and supplement).

SUPPLY AND USE (million kwh)	1958	1959	1960	1961	1962	1963	1964	1965
PRODUCTION (Utilities & industries)								
Total (Gross)	2519	--	--	--	2692	2407	2435	
(Net)	--	--	--	--	--	--	--	
Hydro	2419	--	--	--	2542e	2231	2265e	
Conventional thermal	100	--	--	--	(150)	176e	170e	
Nuclear	—	—	—	—	—	—	—	
Geothermal	—	—	—	—	—	—	—	
PRODUCTION (Utilities only)								
Total (Gross)	--	--	--	--	--	--	--	
(Net)	--	--	--	--	--	--	--	
Hydro	--	--	--	--	--	--	--	
Conventional thermal	--	--	--	--	--	--	--	
Nuclear	--	--	--	--	--	--	--	
Geothermal	—	—	—	—	—	—	—	
NET IMPORTS	−308	−744	−522	−463	−468	−293	−198e	
SUPPLY (Gross)	2211	--	--	--	2224	2114	2237	
(Net)	--	--	--	--	--	--	--	
CONSUMPTION	--	--	--	--	1835	1762	1894	
Transport	33	44	--	35	31	34	46	
Domestic sector	--	--	--	--	83	97	104	
Industry	--	--	--	--	1721	1631	1744	
LOSS AND USE	--	--	--	--	389	352	343	

PLANT (thousand kw)

	1958	1959	1960	1961	1962	1963	1964	1965
CAPACITY (Utilities & industries)								
Total	659	--	873	900	900	900	900	
Hydro	576	--	767	810	810	810	810	
Conventional thermal	83	--	106	90	90	90	90	
Nuclear	—	—	—	—	—	—	—	
Geothermal	—	—	—	—	—	—	—	
CAPACITY (Utilities only)								
Total	--	--	--	--	--	--	--	
Hydro	--	--	--	--	--	--	--	
Conventional thermal	--	--	--	--	--	--	--	
Nuclear	—	—	—	—	—	—	—	
Geothermal	—	—	—	—	—	—	—	

FUEL CONSUMPTION (Utilities only)

	1958	1959	1960	1961	1962	1963	1964	1965
Total (Tcals)	--	--	--	--	--	--	--	
RESERVOIR STORAGE CAPACITY (million kwh)	--	--	--	--	--	--	--	

SUPPLEMENTARY DATA FOR 1964

Transmission lines, 100 kv+ (km): (1961) 285
Households served (thousands): 22
Revenues per kwh (U.S. cents) — Total:
  Residential: Railways:
  Industry: Lighting:
Population (thousands): 15300

Other characteristics of plants and systems:
    Most of the Congo's power is produced in Katanga Province by mining companies, mainly for their own use. The chief producer is SOGEFOR, a subsidiary of Union Minière du Haut Katanga. Part of SOGEFOR's output is distributed to consuming centers in Katanga by SOGELEC, another subsidiary of UMHK. Outside Katanga power is produced and distributed mainly by REGIDESO, COLECTRIC, and Forces Hydro-Electriques. Some of the power produced in Katanga is exported, via high-tension line, to Zambia. The Congo's utility capacity is mainly of public or mixed ownership. Power is supplied to only a small fraction of the total population.

Sources of data:

EEC. *Yrbk. Overseas Assoc.* UN. *Stat. yrbk.*
UN. ECA. *Situation, trends & prospects.*
US. FPC. *World power data.*
International Union of Railways. *International railway statistics.*
Ministère du Plan et du Développement. *Bulletin trimestriel des statistiques générales de la République Démocratique du Congo.*
Union Minière du Haut Katanga. *Rapport annuel du Haut Katanga.*
United Nations Conference on the Application of Science and Technology (UNCAST). A. Clerfayt, "L'énergie au Congo Ex-Belge et au Ruanda-Urundi."

COSTA RICA

SUPPLY AND USE (million kwh)	1958	1959	1960	1961	1962	1963	1964	1965
PRODUCTION (Utilities & industries)								
Total (Gross)	365	387	438	471	491	548	594	
(Net)	--	--	--	--	--	--	--	
Hydro	291	347	393	405	417	465e	495e	
Conventional thermal	74	40	45	66	74	83	99	
Nuclear	—	—	—	—	—	—	—	
Geothermal	—	—	—	—	—	—	—	
PRODUCTION (Utilities only)								
Total (Gross)	337	361	412	443	466	515	561	
(Net)	--	--	--	--	--	--	--	
Hydro	274	337	380	390	405	454	484	
Conventional thermal	63	24	32	53	61	61	77	
Nuclear	—	—	—	—	—	—	—	
Geothermal	—	—	—	—	—	—	—	
NET IMPORTS	—	—	—	—	—	—	—	
SUPPLY (Gross)	365	387	438	471	491	548	594	
(Net)	--	--	--	--	--	--	--	
CONSUMPTION	301	331	377	399	416	464	521e	
Transport								
Domestic sector	253	283	319	335e	351e	371e	390	
Industry	48e	48e	58e	64	65	93	131	
LOSS AND USE	64e	56	61	72	75	84	73	
PLANT (thousand kw)								
CAPACITY (Utilities & industries)								
Total	107	107	109	109	114	140	150	
Hydro	78	79	78	78	75	105	107	
Conventional thermal	29	28	31	31	39	35	43	
Nuclear	—	—	—	—	—	—	—	
Geothermal	—	—	—	—	—	—	—	
CAPACITY (Utilities only)								
Total	98	98	100	99	106	130	136	
Hydro	73	73	73	71	72	98	100	
Conventional thermal	25	25	27	28	34	32	36	
Nuclear	—	—	—	—	—	—	—	
Geothermal	—	—	—	—	—	—	—	
FUEL CONSUMPTION (Utilities only)								
Total (Tcals)	--	--	--	--	--	--	--	
RESERVOIR STORAGE CAPACITY (million kwh)	--	--	--	--	--	--	--	

SUPPLEMENTARY DATA FOR 1964

Transmission lines, 100 kv+ (km) :   - -
Households served (thousands) :   117
Revenues per kwh (U.S. cents) — Total: 1.9
  Residential: 1.9   Railways:
  Industry: 2.0   Lighting: 2.2
Population (thousands) :   1387

Sources of data:
UN. *Stat. yrbk.* UN. ECLA. *Estud. econ.*
_____. *Estud. sobre la elec.* _____. *Stat. bull.*
_____. Subcom. Centroamer. de elec. *Estadísticas preliminares.*
_____. _____. *Estadísticas de energía eléctrica.*
_____. _____. *Estudio comparativo de costos.*
US. *Foreign serv. desp.*
Banco Central de Costa Rica. *Memoria anual.*
Servicio Nacional de Electricidad. *Informe del Director.*

Other characteristics of plants and systems:

Costa Rica's electricity is supplied principally by the Instituto Costarricense de Electricidad, owned by the government, and the Cia. Nacional de Fuerza y Luz, which is privately owned. Current is supplied mainly from local generating facilities. Available data indicate that somewhat less than half the population of the country is supplied with electricity.

SUPPLY AND USE (million kwh)	1958	1959	1960	1961	1962	1963	1964	1965
PRODUCTION (Utilities & industries)								
Total (Gross)	2589	2806	2981	3030	2998	3057	3250	
(Net)	--	--	--	--	--	--	--	
Hydro	11	7	20	10	30e	50	100	
Conventional thermal	2578	2799	2961	3020	2968e	3007	3150	
Nuclear	—	—	—	—	—	—	—	
Geothermal	—	—	—	—	—	—	—	
PRODUCTION (Utilities only)								
Total (Gross)	1867	2073	2233	2225	2288	2370	2495	
(Net)	--	--	--	--	--	--	--	
Hydro	11	7	20	10	(30)	50	100	
Conventional thermal	1856	2066	2213	2215	2258e	2320	2395	
Nuclear	—	—	—	—	—	—	—	
Geothermal	—	—	—	—	—	—	—	
NET IMPORTS	—	—	—	—	—	—	—	
SUPPLY (Gross)	2589	2806	2981	3030	2998	3057	3250	
(Net)	--	--	--	--	--	--	--	
CONSUMPTION	2216	2388	--	--	--	--	--	
Transport	156	176	--	--	--	--	--	
Domestic sector	1038	1141	--	1371	--	--	--	
Industry	1022	1071	1100	--	--	--	--	
LOSS AND USE	373	418	--	--	--	--	--	

PLANT (thousand kw)

	1958	1959	1960	1961	1962	1963	1964	1965
CAPACITY (Utilities & industries)								
Total	854	939	944	956	966	976	976	
Hydro	2	2	2	2e	--	--	--	
Conventional thermal	852	937	942	954e	--	--	--	
Nuclear	—	—	—	—	—	—	—	
Geothermal	—	—	—	—	—	—	—	
CAPACITY (Utilities only)								
Total	469	545	547	559e	566e	576	576	
Hydro	2	2	2	2e	--	--	--	
Conventional thermal	467	543	545	557e	--	--	--	
Nuclear	—	—	—	—	—	—	—	
Geothermal	—	—	—	—	—	—	—	

FUEL CONSUMPTION (Utilities only)

	1958	1959	1960	1961	1962	1963	1964	1965
Diesel oil (mmt)	25	--	--	--	--	--	--	
Fuel oil (mmt)	634	--	--	--	--	--	--	
Total (Tcals)	6286	--	--	--	--	--	--	
RESERVOIR STORAGE CAPACITY (million kwh)	—	—	—	—	--	--	--	

SUPPLEMENTARY DATA FOR 1964

Transmission lines, 100 kv+ (km): (1960) 316
Households served (thousands):   --
Revenues per kwh (U.S. cents) — Total:
   Residential: Railways:
   Industry: Lighting: 7.0
Population (thousands):   7434

Sources of data:

UN. *Stat. yrbk.* UN. ECLA. *Estud. econ*
———. *Estud. sobre la elec.*
———. *Stat. bull.*
US. *Foreign serv. desp.*
Dirección General de Estadística. Junta Central de
   Planificación. *Boletín estadística de Cuba.*

Other characteristics of plants and systems:

    Most of Cuba's electricity is generated in the plants which
formerly belonged to the Cia. Cubana de Electricidad, through
which power is supplied to more than three-quarters of a million
customers. Much of the island is served by one extensive high-
tension network, but some areas depend on regional networks,
others on local generating facilities. Something like half the
people of Cuba appear to be supplied with electricity.

CYPRUS

SUPPLY AND USE (million kwh)	1958	1959	1960	1961	1962	1963	1964	1965
PRODUCTION (Utilities & industries)								
Total (Gross)	202	221	236	262	288e	300	306	
(Net)	--	--	--	252	277	288	294	
Hydro	—	—	—	—	—	—	—	
Conventional thermal	202	221	236	262	288e	300	306	
Nuclear	—	—	—	—	—	—	—	
Geothermal	—	—	—	—	—	—	—	
PRODUCTION (Utilities only)								
Total (Gross)	178	195	213	233	248	272	282	
(Net)	--	--	--	221	--	260	269	
Hydro	—	—	—	—	—	—	—	
Conventional thermal	178	195	213	233	248	272	282	
Nuclear	—	—	—	—	—	—	—	
Geothermal	—	—	—	—	—	—	—	
NET IMPORTS	—	—	—	—	—	—	—	
SUPPLY (Gross)	202	221	236	262	288e	300	306	
(Net)	--	--	--	252	277	288	294	
CONSUMPTION	172	188	201	227	247	257	262	
Transport	—	—	—	—	—	—	—	
Domestic sector	101	118	125	165	158	160	188	
Industry	71e	70e	76e	62	89	97	74	
LOSS AND USE	--	--	--	25	30	31	32	

PLANT (thousand kw)								
CAPACITY (Utilities & industries)								
Total	73	73	85	84	84	98	102	
Hydro	—	—	—	—	—	—	—	
Conventional thermal	73	73	85	84	84	98	102	
Nuclear	—	—	—	—	—	—	—	
Geothermal	—	—	—	—	—	—	—	
CAPACITY (Utilities only)								
Total	63	63	75	75	75	88	88	
Hydro	—	—	—	—	—	—	—	
Conventional thermal	63	63	75	75	75	88	88	
Nuclear	—	—	—	—	—	—	—	
Geothermal	—	—	—	—	—	—	—	

FUEL CONSUMPTION (Utilities only)								
Fuel oil (mmt)	--	--	--	85	91	100	104	
Total (Tcals)	--	--	--	874	942	1035	1091	
RESERVOIR STORAGE CAPACITY (million kwh)	—	—	—	—	—	—	—	

SUPPLEMENTARY DATA FOR 1964

Transmission lines, 100 kv + (km) :   (1961) 525
Households served (thousands) :   77
Revenues per kwh (U.S. cents) — Total: 2.9
  Residential: 3.7   Railways:
  Industry: 1.9   Lighting:
Population (thousands) : 587

Other characteristics of plants and systems:

Electricity in Cyprus is produced and distributed by the Electricity Authority of Cyprus, which operates a 66 KV network supplying power to most of the island from the steam power plant at Dekhelia. Power is generated entirely from imported fuel oil.

Sources of data:
  UN. *Stat. yrbk.*
  UN. ECE. *Ann. bull. of elec. energy stat.*
  Electricity Authority of Cyprus. *Annual report and accounts.*
  Ministry of Finance. Statistics and Research Department.
    Statistical abstract.

CZECHOSLOVAKIA

SUPPLY AND USE (million kwh)	1958	1959	1960	1961	1962	1963	1964	1965
PRODUCTION (Utilities & industries)								
Total (Gross)	19620	21884	24450	26962	28732	29861	31983	
(Net)	18245	20457	22826	25130	26826	27741	29612	
Hydro	2616	2063	2495	2524	3007	2289	2727	
Conventional thermal	17004	19821	21955	24438	25725	27572	29256	
Nuclear	–	–	–	–	–	–	–	
Geothermal	–	–	–	–	–	–	–	
PRODUCTION (Utilities only)								
Total (Gross)	13777	15780	18168	20377	21936	22564	24235	
(Net)	--	--	--	--	--	--	--	
Hydro	2314	1847	2267	2306	2808	2096	2546	
Conventional thermal	11463	13933	15901	18071	19128	20468	21689	
Nuclear	–	–	–	–	–	–	–	
Geothermal	–	–	–	–	–	–	–	
NET IMPORTS	–224	–248	–263	–322	66	142	702	
SUPPLY (Gross)	19396	21636	24187	26640	28798	30003	32685	
(Net)	18021	20209	22563	24808	26892	27883	30314	
CONSUMPTION	16441	18592	20655	22684	24612	25511	27654	
Transport	363	657	865	1058	1272	1380	1567	
Domestic sector	2430	3554	4381	4389	4575	4257	4820	
Industry	13648	14381	15409	17237	18765	19874	21267	
LOSS AND USE	1580	1617	1908	2124	2280	2372	2660	
PLANT (thousand kw)								
CAPACITY (Utilities & industries)								
Total	4667	5363	5662	6372	6785	7287	8093	
Hydro	772	872	929	1263	1377	1472	1513	
Conventional thermal	3895	4491	4733	5109	5408	5815	6580	
Nuclear	–	–	–	–	–	–	–	
Geothermal	–	–	–	–	–	–	–	
CAPACITY (Utilities only)								
Total	3024	3707	3940	4587	4885	5269	6027	
Hydro	696	813	872	1211	1325	1422	1458	
Conventional thermal	2328	2894	3068	3376	3560	3847	4569	
Nuclear	–	–	–	–	–	–	–	
Geothermal	–	–	–	–	–	–	–	
FUEL CONSUMPTION (Utilities only)								
Coal (mmt)	996	1114	1200	2327	1619	1778	1646	
Low grade coal (mmt)	2460	2792	2964	1982	2471	2315	2179	
Lignite (mmt)	7723	8700	12603	13388	15300	16694	17927	
Peat & fuelwood (mmt)	1776	1788	--	2345	2832	2942	3044	
Fuel oil (mmt)	6	5	8	12	15	17	22	
Natural gas (Tcals)	5547	5824	4690	3075	1129	983	455	
Manufactured gas (Tcals)	--	427	497	526	311	364	383	
Total (Tcals)	45580	52850	57967	63957	66022	70056	71501	
RESERVOIR STORAGE CAPACITY (million kwh)	--	--	499	499	499	499	499	

SUPPLEMENTARY DATA FOR 1964

Transmission lines, 100 kv+ (km) : 10599
Households served (thousands) :   --
Revenues per kwh (U.S. cents) — Total:
   Residential: Railways: 2.1
   Industry: Lighting: 9.7
Population (thousands) :   14058

Sources of data:
   UN. *Stat. yrbk.*   UN. ECE. *Ann. bull. of elec. energy stat.*
   ———. *Org. of elec. power services.*
   UNIPEDE. *Statistique.*
   EEI. *Rept. on elec. power dev. in Czechoslovakia.*
   Státní úřad statistiky. *Statistická ročenka, C.S.S.R.*

Other characteristics of plants and systems:

    All public-supply electric power stations and distribution undertakings in Czechoslovakia are the property of the state. About a quarter of the country's power is supplied by industrial establishments generating mainly for their own use. Service is almost universally available through a network which covers the entire country and which also is interconnected with the Mir international power grid.

DAHOMEY

SUPPLY AND USE (million kwh)	1958	1959	1960	1961	1962	1963	1964	1965
PRODUCTION (Utilities & industries)								
Total (Gross)	--	--	--	--	--	--	--	
(Net)	--	--	--	--	--	--	--	
Hydro	—	—	—	—	—	—	—	
Conventional thermal	--	--	--	--	--	--	--	
Nuclear	—	—	—	—	—	—	—	
Geothermal	—	—	—	—	—	—	—	
PRODUCTION (Utilities only)								
Total (Gross)	6e	8	10	11	14	18	--	
(Net)	--	--	--	--	--	--	--	
Hydro	—	—	—	—	—	—	—	
Conventional thermal	6	8	10	11	14	18	--	
Nuclear	—	—	—	—	—	—	—	
Geothermal	—	—	—	—	—	—	—	
NET IMPORTS	—	—	—	—	—	—	—	
SUPPLY (Gross)	6	8	10	11	14	18	--	
(Net)	--	--	--	--	--	--	--	
CONSUMPTION	5	7	9	10	12	16	--	
Transport	—	—	—	—	—	—	—	
Domestic sector	4	6	7	8	9	11	--	
Industry	1	1	2	2	3	5	--	
LOSS AND USE	1	1	1	1	2	2	--	

PLANT (thousand kw)	1958	1959	1960	1961	1962	1963	1964	1965
CAPACITY (Utilities & industries)								
Total	3.2	5.4	5.9	6.0	6.3	8.2	--	
Hydro	—	—	—	—	—	—	—	
Conventional thermal	3.2	5.4	5.9	6.0	6.3	8.2	--	
Nuclear	—	—	—	—	—	—	—	
Geothermal	—	—	—	—	—	—	—	
CAPACITY (Utilities only)								
Total	--	--	--	--	--	--	--	
Hydro	—	—	—	—	—	—	—	
Conventional thermal	--	--	--	--	--	--	--	
Nuclear	—	—	—	—	—	—	—	
Geothermal	—	—	—	—	—	—	—	

FUEL CONSUMPTION (Utilities only)

	1958	1959	1960	1961	1962	1963	1964	1965
Total (Tcals)	--	--	--	--	--	--	--	
RESERVOIR STORAGE CAPACITY (million kwh)	—	—	—	—	—	—	—	

SUPPLEMENTARY DATA FOR 1964

Transmission lines, 100 kv+ (km) :   —
Households served (thousands) :   6.6
Revenues per kwh (U.S. cents) — Total:
    Residential: Railways:
    Industry: Lighting: 13.4
Population (thousands) :   2300

Other characteristics of plants and systems:

    Cie. Centrale de Distribution d'Energie Electrique, privately owned, is the principal source of electricity in Dahomey. All service is local in nature, and only a small fraction of the population is supplied with electricity.

Sources of data:
EEC. *Yrbk. Overseas Assoc.*
UN. *Stat. yrbk.*
UN. ECA. *Situation, trends & prospects.*
US. FPC. *World power data.*
Electricité de France. *Survey of the future electricity demand in Togo and Dahomey.*

DENMARK

SUPPLY AND USE (million kwh)	1958	1959	1960	1961	1962	1963	1964	1965
PRODUCTION (Utilities & industries)								
Total (Gross)	3860e	5346e	5256e	5401e	6512e	7423e	7900e	
(Net)	3643	5038	4955	5090	6130	6985	7435	
Hydro	29e	23e	26e	26e	26e	25e	25e	
Conventional thermal	3831	5323	5230	5375	6486	7398	7875	
Nuclear	—	—	—	—	—	—	—	
Geothermal	—	—	—	—	—	—	—	
PRODUCTION (Utilities only)								
Total (Gross)	--	--	--	--	--	--	--	
(Net)	3513	4005	4814	4590	5411	6636	7007	
Hydro	29	25	25	26	26	25	25	
Conventional thermal	3484	3980	4789	4564	5385	6611	6982	
Nuclear	—	—	—	—	—	—	—	
Geothermal	—	—	—	—	—	—	—	
NET IMPORTS	786	−142	386	997	744	552	819	
SUPPLY (Gross)	4646e	5204e	5642e	6398e	7256e	7975e	8719e	
(Net)	4429	4896	5341	6087	6874	7537	8254	
CONSUMPTION	3809	4151	4629	5149	5900	6530	7160	
Transport	93	91	95	97	100	102	103	
Domestic sector	2494	2740	3170	3503	4064	4515	5022	
Industry	1222	1320	1364	1549	1736	1913	2035	
LOSS AND USE	620	745	712	938	974	1007	1094	

PLANT (thousand kw)

	1958	1959	1960	1961	1962	1963	1964	1965
CAPACITY (Utilities & industries)								
Total	1705	1844	1953	2160	2225	2255	2355	
Hydro	11	11	10	10	10	10	10	
Conventional thermal	1694	1833	1943	2150	2215	2245	2345	
Nuclear	—	—	—	—	—	—	—	
Geothermal	—	—	—	—	—	—	—	
CAPACITY (Utilities only)								
Total	1605	1744	1853	2060	2125	2105	2205	
Hydro	11	11	10	10	10	10	10	
Conventional thermal	1594	1733	1843	2050	2115	2095	2195	
Nuclear	—	—	—	—	—	—	—	
Geothermal	—	—	—	—	—	—	—	

FUEL CONSUMPTION (Utilities only)

	1958	1959	1960	1961	1962	1963	1964	1965
Coal (mmt)	810	994	1405	1262	1547	1810	1795	
Lignite (mmt)	1840	1792	1660	1596	1610	1600	1366	
Peat & fuelwood (mmt)	54	50	22	8	5	6	8	
Fuel oils (mmt)	384	355	322	335	361	547	645	
Total (Tcals)	12020	12905	14585	14104	16096	19345	19996	
RESERVOIR STORAGE CAPACITY (million kwh)	—	—	—	—	—	—	—	

SUPPLEMENTARY DATA FOR 1964

Transmission lines, 100 kv+ (km): 1664
Households served (thousands): 1580
Revenues per kwh (U.S. cents) — Total: 2.2
  Residential: 2.2   Railways: 1.0
  Industry: 1.1   Lighting: 1.7
Population (thousands): 4720

Sources of data:
UCPTE. *Réseau*. UN. *Stat. yrbk.*
UN. ECE. *Ann. bull. of elec. energy stat.*
———. *Org. of elec. power services.*
UNIPEDE. *L'écon. élec.* ———. *Statistiques.*
Elektricitetsrådet Danske Elvaerkers Forening. *Dansk Elvaerksstatistik.*
Statistiske Departement. *Tiars — oversigt.*

Other characteristics of plants and systems:

There are eleven companies which generate power in Denmark, including two municipal undertakings, eight companies affiliated with cooperative groups, and one independent company. Small quantities of electricity are also generated in industrial establishments. Power is distributed through 176 different undertakings, of which 68 are municipal undertakings and 74 are cooperative societies. Service is available throughout the country via two separate networks - - one on the mainland, and the other serving Copenhagen and associated islands east of the Great Belt. Both systems are connected, by submarine cable, to the Swedish network. Much of Denmark's power is produced in combined heat and power stations which also provide heat to Denmark's cities.

SUPPLY AND USE (million kwh)	1958	1959	1960	1961	1962	1963	1964	1965
PRODUCTION (Utilities & industries)								
Total (Gross)	284	316	350	372	439	452	560e	
(Net)	--	--	--	--	--	--	--	
Hydro	51	43	58	59	52	50	50e	
Conventional thermal	233	273	292	313	387	402	510e	
Nuclear	—	—	—	—	—	—	—	
Geothermal	—	—	—	—	—	—	—	
PRODUCTION (Utilities only)								
Total (Gross)	220	236	255	275	316	340	450e	
(Net)	--	--	--	--	--	--	--	
Hydro	51	43	58	59	52	50	50e	
Conventional thermal	169	193	197	216	264	290	400	
Nuclear	—	—	—	—	—	—	—	
Geothermal	—	—	—	—	—	—	—	
NET IMPORTS	—	—	—	—	—	—	—	
SUPPLY (Gross)	284	316	350	372	439	452	560e	
(Net)	--	--	--	--	--	--	--	
CONSUMPTION	--	--	--	--	--	--	476	
Transport	—	—	—	—	—	—	—	
Domestic sector	--	120	--	--	--	--	235	
Industry	148	157	199	170	226	224e	241e	
LOSS AND USE	--	--	--	--	--	--	84e	

PLANT (thousand kw)								
CAPACITY (Utilities & industries)								
Total	67	90	98	98	112	134	164	
Hydro	8	8	8	8	8	8	8	
Conventional thermal	59	82	90	90	104	126	156	
Nuclear	—	—	—	—	—	—	—	
Geothermal	—	—	—	—	—	—	—	
CAPACITY (Utilities only)								
Total	62	68	68	68	72	73	101	
Hydro	8	8	8	8	8	8	8	
Conventional thermal	54	60	60	60	64	65	93	
Nuclear	—	—	—	—	—	—	—	
Geothermal	—	—	—	—	—	—	—	

FUEL CONSUMPTION (Utilities only)								
Wood (mmt)	--	--	1	3	--	--	--	
Distillate fuel oil (mmt)	3	3	3	4	--	--	6	
Residual fuel oil (mmt)	92	109	94	80	--	--	136	
Total (Tcals)	--	--	--	--	--	--	--	
RESERVOIR STORAGE CAPACITY (million kwh)	--	--	--	--	--	--	--	

SUPPLEMENTARY DATA FOR 1964

Transmission lines, 100 kv+ (km):   —
Households served (thousands):   155
Revenues per kwh (U.S. cents) — Total: 3.3
   Residential: 4.3   Railways:
   Industry: 2.0   Lighting: 24.0
Population (thousands):   3498

Other characteristics of plants and systems:

The Corporación Dominicana de Electricidad, privately owned, provides the island's power through a network which appears to reach most of the country. It is estimated that no more than a quarter of the island's population receives electricity. Current is generated almost entirely from imported fuel oils.

Sources of data:

UN. *Growth of world industry.* _____. *Stat. yrbk.*
UN. ECLA. *Estud. econ.* _____. *Estud. sobre la elec.*
Corporación Dominicana de Electricidad. *Memoria.*
Dirección General de Estadística y Censos. *Estadística industrial de la República Dominicana.*

ECUADOR

SUPPLY AND USE (million kwh)	1958	1959	1960	1961	1962	1963	1964	1965
PRODUCTION (Utilities & industries)								
Total (Gross)	324	349	387	411	451	495	551	
(Net)	--	--	--	--	--	--	--	
Hydro	154	161	175	200	222	239	248	
Conventional thermal	170	188	212	211	229	256	303	
Nuclear	—	—	—	—	—	—	—	
Geothermal	—	—	—	—	—	—	—	
PRODUCTION (Utilities only)								
Total (Gross)	254	256	289	350	385	442	470	
(Net)	--	--	--	--	--	--	--	
Hydro	140e	147e	160e	186	209	224	233	
Conventional thermal	114e	109e	129e	164	176	218	237	
Nuclear	—	—	—	—	—	—	—	
Geothermal	—	—	—	—	—	—	—	
NET IMPORTS	—	—	—	—	—	—	—	
SUPPLY (Gross)	324	349	387	411	451	495	551	
(Net)	--	--	--	--	--	--	--	
CONSUMPTION	283	307	337	373	--	--	--	
Transport	—	—	—	—	—	—	—	
Domestic sector	176	197	210	227	--	--	--	
Industry	107	110	127	146	--	--	120	
LOSS AND USE	41	42	50	38	--	--	--	

PLANT (thousand kw)

	1958	1959	1960	1961	1962	1963	1964	1965
CAPACITY (Utilities & industries)								
Total	101	106	118	145	160	166	186	
Hydro	34	35	40	62	65	67	70	
Conventional thermal	67	71	78	83	95	99	116	
Nuclear	—	—	—	—	—	—	—	
Geothermal	—	—	—	—	—	—	—	
CAPACITY (Utilities only)								
Total	85	87e	90	114	128	132	148	
Hydro	31	32e	35	57	60	62	64	
Conventional thermal	54	55e	55	57	68	70	84	
Nuclear	—	—	—	—	—	—	—	
Geothermal	—	—	—	—	—	—	—	

FUEL CONSUMPTION (Utilities only)

	1958	1959	1960	1961	1962	1963	1964	1965
Diesel oil (mmt)	--	--	--	44	--	--	--	
Total (Tcals)	--	--	--	--	--	--	--	
RESERVOIR STORAGE CAPACITY (million kwh)	--	--	--	--	--	--	--	

SUPPLEMENTARY DATA FOR 1964

Transmission lines, 100 kv+ (km): --
Households served (thousands): --
Revenues per kwh (U.S. cents) — Total: 2.2
  Residential: 2.5   Railways:
  Industry: (1961) 2.0   Lighting:
Population (thousands): 4979

Other characteristics of plants and systems:

    Empresa Eléctrica del Ecuador, privately owned, and Empresa Eléctrica del Quito, which is publicly owned, are the principal sources of electricity in Ecuador. All services are local, and electricity is provided to a relatively small share of the total population — probably less than a quarter.

Sources of data:
  UN. *Growth of world industry.* ——. *Stat. yrbk.*
  UN. ECLA. *Estud. econ.* ——. *Estud. sobre la elec.*
  US. *Foreign serv. desp.*
  Banco Central del Ecuador. *Síntesis estadística del Banco Central.*
  Ministerio de Fomento. Dirección General de Recursos Hidráulicos y Electrificación. *Primer censo nacional de electrificación.*

EL SALVADOR

SUPPLY AND USE (million kwh)	1958	1959	1960	1961	1962	1963	1964	1965
PRODUCTION (Utilities & industries)								
Total (Gross)	212	235	255	274	300	340	377	
(Net)	--	--	--	--	--	--	--	
Hydro	203	227	236	265	297	313	336	
Conventional thermal	9	8	19	9	3	27	41	
Nuclear	—	—	—	—	—	—	—	
Geothermal	—	—	—	—	—	—	—	
PRODUCTION (Utilities only)								
Total (Gross)	205	228	248	267	298	322	356	
(Net)	--	--	--	--	--	--	--	
Hydro	203	227	236	265	297	313	336	
Conventional thermal	2	1	12	2	1	9	20	
Nuclear	—	—	—	—	—	—	—	
Geothermal	—	—	—	—	—	—	—	
NET IMPORTS	—	—	—	—	—	—	—	
SUPPLY (Gross)	212	235	255	274	300	340	377	
(Net)	--	--	--	--	--	--	--	
CONSUMPTION	173	194	209	231	265	301	332	
Transport	—	—	—	—	—	—	—	
Domestic sector	107	122	133	142	175	175	187	
Industry	66	72	76	89	90e	126	145e	
LOSS AND USE	39	41	46	43	35	39	45	

PLANT (thousand kw)

	1958	1959	1960	1961	1962	1963	1964	1965
CAPACITY (Utilities & industries)								
Total	74	74	74	89	89	106	107	
Hydro	56	56	56	71	71	87	87	
Conventional thermal	18	18	18	18	18	19	20	
Nuclear	—	—	—	—	—	—	—	
Geothermal	—	—	—	—	—	—	—	
CAPACITY (Utilities only)								
Total	65	65	65	80	80	96	97	
Hydro	56	56	56	71	71	87	87	
Conventional thermal	9	9	9	9	9	9	10	
Nuclear	—	—	—	—	—	—	—	
Geothermal	—	—	—	—	—	—	—	

FUEL CONSUMPTION (Utilities only)

	1958	1959	1960	1961	1962	1963	1964	1965
Distillate fuel oil (mmt)	0.9	0.4	0.6	0.6	0.3	1.4	1.9	
Residual fuel oil (mmt)	—	—	3.1	—	—	1.1	2.4	
Total (Tcals)	9	4	35	6	3	25	43	
RESERVOIR STORAGE CAPACITY (million kwh)	--	--	--	--	--	--	--	

SUPPLEMENTARY DATA FOR 1964

Transmission lines, 100 kv+ (km):   --
Households served (thousands):   115
Revenues per kwh (U.S. cents) — Total: 3.0
   Residential: 3.1   Railways:
   Industry: 2.6   Lighting:
Population (thousands):   2824

Sources of data:
  UN. *Stat. yrbk.* UN. ECLA. *Estud. econ.*
  ———. *Estud. sobre la elec.*
  ———. Subcom. Centroamer. de elec. *Estadísticas*
    preliminares.
  ———. ———. *Estadísticas de energía eléctrica.*
  Ministerio de Economia. Dirección General de Estadística
    y Censos. *Anuario estadístico. Vol. II.*

Other characteristics of plants and systems:

    Generating facilities in El Salvador are mainly publicly owned, by the Comisión Ejecutiva del Río Lempa. Electricity is supplied to perhaps a quarter of the population through a high-tension network (115 KV and 69 KV) which extends to much of the country. The country's largest plant, the hydro-electric plant 5 de Noviembre, has a capacity of 61 megawatts. The largest steam plant has a capacity of only 5 megawatts.

ETHIOPIA

SUPPLY AND USE (million kwh)	1958	1959	1960	1961	1962	1963	1964	1965
PRODUCTION (Utilities & industries)								
Total (Gross)	79	89	102	124	152	177	208	
(Net)	--	--	--	--	--	--	--	
Hydro	26	28	47	68	92	109	120	
Conventional thermal	53	61	55	56	60	68	88	
Nuclear	—	—	—	—	—	—	—	
Geothermal	—	—	—	—	—	—	—	
PRODUCTION (Utilities only)								
Total (Gross)	63	71	83	106	133	155	186	
(Net)	--	--	--	--	--	--	--	
Hydro	26	28	47	68	92	109	120	
Conventional thermal	37	43	36	38	41	46	66	
Nuclear	—	—	—	—	—	—	—	
Geothermal	—	—	—	—	—	—	—	
NET IMPORTS	—	—	—	—	—	—	—	
SUPPLY (Gross)	79	89	102	124	152	177	208	
(Net)	--	--	--	--	--	--	--	
CONSUMPTION	50	52	60	--	--	--	--	
Transport	—	—	—	—	—	—	—	
Domestic sector	--	--	--	--	--	--	--	
Industry	--	--	--	--	--	--	--	
LOSS AND USE	--	--	42	--	--	--	--	

PLANT (thousand kw)	1958	1959	1960	1961	1962	1963	1964	1965
CAPACITY (Utilities & industries)								
Total	43	44	95	97	105	111	119	
Hydro	10	10	64	64	64	64	73	
Conventional thermal	33	34	31	33	41	47	46	
Nuclear	—	—	—	—	—	—	—	
Geothermal	—	—	—	—	—	—	—	
CAPACITY (Utilities only)								
Total	33	34	84	85	90	96	103	
Hydro	10	10	64	64	64	64	73	
Conventional thermal	23	24	20	21	26	32	30	
Nuclear	—	—	—	—	—	—	—	
Geothermal	—	—	—	—	—	—	—	

FUEL CONSUMPTION (Utilities only)

	1958	1959	1960	1961	1962	1963	1964	1965
Total (Tcals)	--	--	--	--	--	--	--	
RESERVOIR STORAGE CAPACITY (million kwh)	--	--	--	--	--	--	--	

SUPPLEMENTARY DATA FOR 1964

Transmission lines, 100 kv+ (km): (1961) 418
Households served (thousands): --
Revenues per kwh (U.S. cents) — Total: (1961) 3.6
   Residential: Railways:
   Industry: Lighting: 6.0
Population (thousands):   22200

Other characteristics of plants and systems:

A government-owned corporation, the Ethiopian Electric Light and Power Authority, is responsible for generating, transmitting and distributing electrical energy in Ethiopia. It supplies service to most of the important principal towns. A privately-owned company, SEDAO, provides power to Asmara and Massawa. Only a small fraction of the population is supplied with electricity.

Sources of data:
   UN. *Stat. yrbk.*   UN. ECA. *Situation, trends & prospects.*
   US. *Foreign serv. desp.*   US. FPC. *World power data.*
   Central Statistical Office. *Statistical abstract.*

SUPPLY AND USE (million kwh)	1958	1959	1960	1961	1962	1963	1964	1965
PRODUCTION (Utilities & industries)								
Total (Gross)	19	21	23	28	33	38	45	
(Net)	--	--	--	--	--	--	--	
Hydro	18	20	21	26	31	36	41	
Conventional thermal	1	1	2	2	2	2	4	
Nuclear	—	—	—	—	—	—	—	
Geothermal	—	—	—	—	—	—	—	
PRODUCTION (Utilities only)								
Total (Gross)	19	21	23	28	33	38	45	
(Net)	--	--	--	--	--	--	--	
Hydro	18	20	21	26	31	36	41	
Conventional thermal	1	1	2	2	2	2	4	
Nuclear	—	—	—	—	—	—	—	
Geothermal	—	—	—	—	—	—	—	
NET IMPORTS	—	—	—	—	—	—	—	
SUPPLY (Gross)	19	21	23	28	33	38	45	
(Net)	--	--	--	--	--	--	--	
CONSUMPTION	--	--	--	--	--	34	--	
Transport	—	—	—	—	—	—	—	
Domestic sector	--	--	--	--	--	30	--	
Industry	--	--	--	--	--	4	--	
LOSS AND USE	--	--	--	--	--	4	--	

PLANT (thousand kw)

CAPACITY (Utilities & industries)								
Total	11	11	11	14	14	19	19	
Hydro	8	8	8	11	11	16	16	
Conventional thermal	3	3	3	3	3	3	3	
Nuclear	—	—	—	—	—	—	—	
Geothermal	—	—	—	—	—	—	—	
CAPACITY (Utilities only)								
Total	11	11	11	14	14	19	19	
Hydro	8	8	8	11	11	16	16	
Conventional thermal	3	3	3	3	3	3	3	
Nuclear	—	—	—	—	—	—	—	
Geothermal	—	—	—	—	—	—	—	

FUEL CONSUMPTION (Utilities only)

	1958	1959	1960	1961	1962	1963	1964	
Total (Tcals)	--	--	--	--	--	--	--	
RESERVOIR STORAGE CAPACITY (million kwh)	--	--	--	--	--	--	--	

SUPPLEMENTARY DATA FOR 1964

Transmission lines, 100 kv + (km) :   --
Households served (thousands) :   --
Revenues per kwh (U.S. cents) — Total:
  Residential: 2.5   Railways:
  Industry: 0.8   Lighting:
Population (thousands) : 36

Other characteristics of plants and systems:

    Power is supplied to the Faeroe Islands by a number of small hydro and diesel plants.

Sources of data:
UN. *Stat. yrbk.*
Elektricitetsrådet Danske Elvaerkers Forening. *Dansk elvaerksstatistik.*

FIJI ISLANDS

SUPPLY AND USE (million kwh)	1958	1959	1960	1961	1962	1963	1964	1965
PRODUCTION (Utilities & industries)								
Total (Gross)	41	44	55	57	70	84	93	
(Net)	--	--	--	--	--	--	--	
Hydro	—	—	—	—	—	—	—	
Conventional thermal	41	44	55	57	70	84	93	
Nuclear	—	—	—	—	—	—	—	
Geothermal	—	—	—	—	—	—	—	
PRODUCTION (Utilities only)								
Total (Gross)	18	21	22	23	26	35	41	
(Net)	--	--	--	--	--	--	--	
Hydro	—	—	—	—	—	—	—	
Conventional thermal	18	21	22	23	26	35	41	
Nuclear	—	—	—	—	—	—	—	
Geothermal	—	—	—	—	—	—	—	
NET IMPORTS	—	—	—	—	—	—	—	
SUPPLY (Gross)	41	44	55	57	70	84	93	
(Net)	--	--	--	--	--	--	--	
CONSUMPTION	--	--	--	--	--	--	--	
Transport	—	—	—	—	—	—	—	
Domestic sector	--	--	--	--	--	--	--	
Industry	--	--	--	--	--	--	--	
LOSS AND USE	--	--	--	--	--	--	--	

PLANT (thousand kw)	1958	1959	1960	1961	1962	1963	1964	1965
CAPACITY (Utilities & industries)								
Total	16	15	19	22	26	32	43	
Hydro	—	—	—	—	—	—	—	
Conventional thermal	16	15	19	22	26	32	43	
Nuclear	—	—	—	—	—	—	—	
Geothermal	—	—	—	—	—	—	—	
CAPACITY (Utilities only)								
Total	7.7	7.3	7.3	9.6	12	16	19	
Hydro	—	—	—	—	—	—	—	
Conventional thermal	7.7	7.3	7.3	9.6	12	16	19	
Nuclear	—	—	—	—	—	—	—	
Geothermal	—	—	—	—	—	—	—	

FUEL CONSUMPTION (Utilities only)

	1958	1959	1960	1961	1962	1963	1964	1965
Total (Tcals)	--	--	--	--	--	--	--	
RESERVOIR STORAGE CAPACITY (million kwh)	—	—	—	—	—	—	—	

SUPPLEMENTARY DATA FOR 1964

Transmission lines, 100 kv+ (km): —
Households served (thousands): --
Revenues per kwh (U.S. cents) — Total:
  Residential: 3.1   Railways:
  Industry: Lighting: 6.3
Population (thousands): 449

Other characteristics of plants and systems:

Electricity in Fiji is supplied at Lautoka by the Fiji government, and at Suva by the Suva City Council, from diesel engines. About 5,000 customers were supplied by the two agencies in 1960. The diesel fuel required for power generation is imported.

Sources of data:
Benn Bros. *Elec. undertakings.*
UN. *Stat. yrbk.*
United Kingdom. Colonial Office. *Fiji Islands* (Annual report).

FINLAND

SUPPLY AND USE (million kwh)	1958	1959	1960	1961	1962	1963	1964	1965
PRODUCTION (Utilities & industries)								
Total (Gross)	7974	7922	8628	10430	11590	11831	13636	
(Net)	7790	7701	8332	10176	11333	11457	12380	
Hydro	6960	5563	5269	8023	9770	8374	8501	
Conventional thermal	1014	2359	3359	2407	1820	3457	5135	
Nuclear	—	—	—	—	—	—	—	
Geothermal	—	—	—	—	—	—	—	
PRODUCTION (Utilities only)								
Total (Gross)	5425	4683	4917	6540	7627	7042	7440	
(Net)	5050	4500	4810	6056	6782	6551	7150	
Hydro	5325	4142	3912	6069	7443	6594	6784	
Conventional thermal	100	541	1005	471	184	448	656	
Nuclear	—	—	—	—	—	—	—	
Geothermal	—	—	—	—	—	—	—	
NET IMPORTS	5	124	415	180	82	337	696	
SUPPLY (Gross)	7979	8046	9043	10610	11672	12168	14332	
(Net)	7795	7825	8747	10356	11415	11794	13076	
CONSUMPTION	7037	7150	8019	9469	10447	10856	11964	
Transport	29	30	33	32	33	30	32	
Domestic sector	1436	1578	1771	1924	2211	2428	2694	
Industry	5572	5542	6215	7513	8203	8398	9238	
LOSS AND USE	758	675	728	887	968	938	1112	

PLANT (thousand kw)

CAPACITY (Utilities & industries)	1958	1959	1960	1961	1962	1963	1964	1965
Total	2202	2383	2834	3152	3361	3596	3879	
Hydro	1340	1419	1559	1682	1702	1851	1857	
Conventional thermal	862	964	1275	1470	1659	1745	2022	
Nuclear	—	—	—	—	—	—	—	
Geothermal	—	—	—	—	—	—	—	
CAPACITY (Utilities only)								
Total	1279	1361	1685	1831	1881	2031	- -	
Hydro	- -	- -	- -	- -	- -	- -	- -	
Conventional thermal	- -	- -	- -	- -	- -	- -	- -	
Nuclear	—	—	—	—	—	—	—	
Geothermal	—	—	—	—	—	—	—	

FUEL CONSUMPTION (Utilities only)

	1958	1959	1960	1961	1962	1963	1964	1965
Coal (mmt)	- -	- -	- -	- -	- -	82	151	
Fuel oils (mmt)	- -	- -	- -	- -	- -	133	199	
Total (Tcals)	- -	- -	- -	- -	790	1090	905	
RESERVOIR STORAGE CAPACITY (million kwh)	1500	1700	1700	1800	1900	2000	2000	

SUPPLEMENTARY DATA FOR 1964

Transmission lines, 100 kv + (km) :   7711
Households served (thousands) :   1230
Revenues per kwh (U.S. cents) — Total:
   Residential: (1962) 3.7   Railways:
   Industry: 1.0   Lighting: 3.1
Population (thousands) :   4580

Other characteristics of plants and systems:

   Electricity is available throughout Finland via a network which covers the entire country. The generating capacity of public utilities is about equally divided between public and private ownership, but very large quantities of power are also generated by industrial establishments for their own use - - the pulp and paper industry in particular. The fuel required for generating power for the public supply is all imported.

Sources of data:

Benn. Bros. *Elec. undertakings.*   UN. *Stat. yrbk.*
UN. ECE. *Ann. bull. of elec. energy stat.*
UNIPEDE. *Réseaux de transport.* ———. *Statistiques.*
US. *Foreign serv. desp.*
US. Bur. of Mines. *Int'l coal trade.*

FRANCE

SUPPLY AND USE (million kwh)	1958	1959	1960	1961	1962	1963	1964	1965
PRODUCTION (Utilities & industries)								
Total (Gross)	64308	67425	75105	79910	87175	92287	98759	
(Net)	61771	64691	72304	76641	83251	88471	93930	
Hydro	32735	33098	40939	38754	36300	44053	35218	
Conventional thermal	31569	34283	34026	40895	50420	47784	62886	
Nuclear	4	44	140	261	455	450	655	
Geothermal	—	—	—	—	—	—	—	
PRODUCTION (Utilities only)								
Total (Gross)	43581	46525	53816	56330	61817	68128	70581	
(Net)	42307	45067	52329	54552	59553	65869	67607	
Hydro	30150	30339	37930	35890	33713	41232	32951	
Conventional thermal	13427	16142	15746	20179	27649	26446	36975	
Nuclear	4	44	140	261	455	450	655	
Geothermal	—	—	—	—	—	—	—	
NET IMPORTS	445	38	−98	93	−752	570	2228	
SUPPLY (Gross)	64753	67463	75007	80003	86423	92857	100987	
(Net)	62216	64729	72206	76734	82499	89041	96158	
CONSUMPTION	55867	58343	65171	69782	75121	80991	88361	
Transport	3067	3229	3533	3720	4124	4456	4616	
Domestic sector	13178	14082	15434	16799	19107	21870	23906	
Industry	39622	41032	46204	49263	51890	54665	59839	
LOSS AND USE	6349	6386	7035	6952	7378	8050	7797	

PLANT (thousand kw)

CAPACITY (Utilities & industries)								
Total	18966	20727	21851	23170	24053	25602	26729	
Hydro	9070	9503	10231	11037	11284	11868	12407	
Conventional thermal	9895	11172	11523	12036	12672	13588	14156	
Nuclear	1	52	97	97	97	146	166	
Geothermal	—	—	—	—	—	—	—	
CAPACITY (Utilities only)								
Total	13428	14856	15695	17017	17851	19095	20028	
Hydro	8377	8810	9538	10347	10545	11131	11608	
Conventional thermal	5050	5994	6060	6573	7209	7818	8254	
Nuclear	1	52	97	97	97	146	166	
Geothermal	—	—	—	—	—	—	—	

FUEL CONSUMPTION (Utilities only)								
Coal & coke (mmt)	4825	5161	4119	4271	6800	5713	7844	
Lignite (mmt)	742	669	856	1454	1297	842	572	
Fuel oils (mmt)	594	552	462	639	1004	1399	2908	
Natural gas (Tcals)	214	3841	9519	12602	13662	11982	9445	
Other gas (Tcals)	—	—	—	—	—	303	755	
Total (Tcals)	36858	41335	38901	47905	64888	60800	85142	
RESERVOIR STORAGE CAPACITY (million kwh)	3450	4114	5038	5219	5399	5957	6016	

SUPPLEMENTARY DATA FOR 1964

Transmission lines, 100 kv+ (km): 27585
Households served (thousands): 15300
Revenues per kwh (U.S. cents) — Total:
　　Residential: 4.3　　　Railways: 1.2
　　Industry: 1.3　　　　Lighting:
Population (thousands): 48434

Sources of data:
EEC. *Energy stat., 1950-1965.* UCPTE. *Réseau.*
UN. *Stat. yrbk.*　UN. ECE. *Elec. power situation.*
————. *Org. of elec. power services.*
UNIPEDE. *L'écon. élec.* ————. *Statistiques.*

Other characteristics of plants and systems:

Electricité de France, a governmental agency, is the principal producer and distributor of electricity, but does not have an absolute monopoly. Substantial quantities of electricity are generated by industrial establishments, especially coal mines and the iron and steel plants. A single, integrated network provides power to practically the entire population. The French network is connected with the networks of adjoining countries and, by submarine cable, with the British network.

FRENCH GUIANA

SUPPLY AND USE (million kwh)	1958	1959	1960	1961	1962	1963	1964	1965
PRODUCTION (Utilities & industries)								
Total (Gross)	--	--	--	--	--	--	--	
(Net)	--	--	--	--	--	--	--	
Hydro	—	—	—	—	—	—	—	
Conventional thermal	--	--	--	--	--	--	--	
Nuclear	—	—	—	—	—	—	—	
Geothermal	—	—	—	—	—	—	—	
PRODUCTION (Utilities only)								
Total (Gross)	3.2	3.8	4.4	4.7	5.8	7.4	8.7	
(Net)	--	--	--	--	--	--	--	
Hydro	—	—	—	—	—	—	—	
Conventional thermal	3.2	3.8	4.4	4.7	5.8	7.4	8.7	
Nuclear	—	—	—	—	—	—	—	
Geothermal	—	—	—	—	—	—	—	
NET IMPORTS	—	—	—	—	—	—	—	
SUPPLY (Gross)	3.2	3.8	4.4	4.7	5.8	7.4	8.7	
(Net)	--	--	--	--	--	--	--	
CONSUMPTION	--	3.0	3.2	3.5	--	--	--	
Transport	—	—	—	—	—	—	—	
Domestic sector	--	2.8	2.9	3.2	--	--	--	
Industry	--	0.2	0.3	0.3	--	--	--	
LOSS AND USE	--	0.8	1.2	1.2	--	--	--	
PLANT (thousand kw)								
CAPACITY (Utilities & industries)								
Total	--	--	--	--	--	--	--	
Hydro	—	—	—	—	—	—	—	
Conventional thermal	--	--	--	--	--	--	--	
Nuclear	—	—	—	—	—	—	—	
Geothermal	—	—	—	—	—	—	—	
CAPACITY (Utilities only)								
Total	1.5	1.8	2.9	2.9	3.1	4.2	5.8	
Hydro	—	—	—	—	—	—	—	
Conventional thermal	1.5	1.8	2.9	2.9	·3.1	4.2	5.8	
Nuclear	—	—	—	—	—	—	—	
Geothermal	—	—	—	—	—	—	—	
FUEL CONSUMPTION (Utilities only)								
Total (Tcals)	--	--	--	--	--	--	--	
RESERVOIR STORAGE CAPACITY (million kwh)	—	—	—	—	—	—	—	

SUPPLEMENTARY DATA FOR 1964

Transmission lines, 100 kv+ (km): --
Households served (thousands): --
Revenues per kwh (U.S. cents) — Total:
   Residential: Railways:
   Industry: Lighting:
Population (thousands): 36

Other characteristics of plants and systems:

French Guiana's electricity is generated mainly by the Cie. Centrale de Distribution d'Energie Electrique, which is publicly owned but privately managed. Most of the country is served by small, isolated plants.

Sources of data:

Benn Bros. *Elec. undertakings.* EEC. *Yrbk. Overseas Assoc.*
UN. *Stat. yrbk.* US. *Foreign serv. desp.*
Inst. de la Stat. *Ann. stat. de la Guyane.*

FRENCH POLYNESIA

SUPPLY AND USE (million kwh)	1958	1959	1960	1961	1962	1963	1964	1965
PRODUCTION (Utilities & industries)								
Total (Gross)	5.7	6.3	6.7	8.4	10	12	16	
(Net)	--	--	--	--	--	--	--	
Hydro	—	—	—	—	—	—	—	
Conventional thermal	5.7	6.3	6.7	8.4	10	12	16	
Nuclear	—	—	—	—	—	—	—	
Geothermal	—	—	—	—	—	—	—	
PRODUCTION (Utilities only)								
Total (Gross)	5.7	6.3	6.7	8.4	10	12	16	
(Net)	--	--	--	--	--	--	--	
Hydro	—	—	—	—	—	—	—	
Conventional thermal	5.7	6.3	6.7	8.4	10	12	16	
Nuclear	—	—	—	—	—	—	—	
Geothermal	—	—	—	—	—	—	—	
NET IMPORTS	—	—	—	—	—	—	—	
SUPPLY (Gross)	5.7	6.3	6.7	8.4	10	12	16	
(Net)	--	--	--	--	--	--	--	
CONSUMPTION	--	--	--	7.4	9	11	13	
Transport	—	—	—	—	—	—	—	
Domestic sector	--	--	--	5.4	6	7	8	
Industry	--	--	--	2.0	3	4	5	
LOSS AND USE	--	--	--	1.0	1	1	3	

PLANT (thousand kw)

CAPACITY (Utilities & industries)								
Total	--	2.0	2.0	3.1	5.2	7.3	7.3	
Hydro	—	—	—	—	—	—	—	
Conventional thermal	--	2.0	2.0	3.1	5.2	7.3	7.3	
Nuclear	—	—	—	—	—	—	—	
Geothermal	—	—	—	—	—	—	—	
CAPACITY (Utilities only)								
Total	--	2.0	2.0	3.1	5.2	7.3	7.3	
Hydro	—	—	—	—	—	—	—	
Conventional thermal	--	2.0	2.0	3.1	5.2	7.3	7.3	
Nuclear	—	—	—	—	—	—	—	
Geothermal	—	—	—	—	—	—	—	

FUEL CONSUMPTION (Utilities only)

Total (Tcals)	--	--	--	--	--	--	--	
RESERVOIR STORAGE CAPACITY (million kwh)	—	—	—	—	—	—	—	

SUPPLEMENTARY DATA FOR 1964

Transmission lines, 100 kv+ (km):　　—
Households served (thousands):　　6
Revenues per kwh (U.S. cents) — Total:
　Residential:　　Railways:
　Industry:　　Lighting:　11.1
Population (thousands):　82

Other characteristics of plants and systems:

The principal supplier of electricity is the Etablissement Emil Martin, which is privately owned.

Sources of data:
EEC. *Yrbk. Overseas Assoc.*
UN. *Stat. yrbk.*
Inst. de la Stat. *Ann. stat. des territoires d'outre-mer.*

FRENCH SOMALILAND

SUPPLY AND USE (million kwh)	1958	1959	1960	1961	1962	1963	1964	1965
PRODUCTION (Utilities & industries)								
Total (Gross)	--	--	--	--	--	--	--	
(Net)	--	--	--	--	--	--	--	
Hydro	—	—	—	—	—	—	—	
Conventional thermal	--	--	--	--	--	--	--	
Nuclear	—	—	—	—	—	—	—	
Geothermal	—	—	—	—	—	—	—	
PRODUCTION (Utilities only)								
Total (Gross)	8	9	10	11	13	16	20	
(Net)	--	--	--	--	--	--	--	
Hydro	—	—	—	—	—	—	—	
Conventional thermal	8	9	10	11	13	16	20	
Nuclear	—	—	—	—	—	—	—	
Geothermal	—	—	—	—	—	—	—	
NET IMPORTS	—	—	—	—	—	—	—	
SUPPLY (Gross)	--	--	--	--	--	--	20	
(Net)	--	--	--	--	--	--	--	
CONSUMPTION	7	8	8	10	11	14	16	
Transport	—	—	—	—	—	—	—	
Domestic sector	--	--	--	7	8	10	11	
Industry	--	--	--	3	3	4	5	
LOSS AND USE	1	1	1	1	2	2	4	

PLANT (thousand kw)

	1958	1959	1960	1961	1962	1963	1964	1965
CAPACITY (Utilities & industries)								
Total	--	--	--	--	--	--	--	
Hydro	—	—	—	—	—	—	—	
Conventional thermal	--	--	--	--	--	--	--	
Nuclear	—	—	—	—	—	—	—	
Geothermal	—	—	—	—	—	—	—	
CAPACITY (Utilities only)								
Total	3.0	3.0	3.0	5.1	5.1	6.2	6.2	
Hydro	—	—	—	—	—	—	—	
Conventional thermal	3.0	3.0	3.0	5.1	5.1	6.2	6.2	
Nuclear	—	—	—	—	—	—	—	
Geothermal	—	—	—	—	—	—	—	

FUEL CONSUMPTION (Utilities only)

	1958	1959	1960	1961	1962	1963	1964	1965
Total (Tcals)	--	--	--	--	--	--	--	
RESERVOIR STORAGE CAPACITY (million kwh)	—	—	—	—	—	—	—	

SUPPLEMENTARY DATA FOR 1964

Transmission lines, 100 kv+ (km):   —
Households served (thousands):   3.9
Revenues per kwh (U.S. cents) — Total:
  Residential: Railways:
  Industry: Lighting:
Population (thousands):   81

Other characteristics of plants and systems:

Electricité de Djibouti, publicly owned, is responsible for production and distribution of electricity in Djibouti and Arta. The principal power plant is a diesel facility at Djibouti.

Sources of data:
EEC. *Yrbk. Overseas Assoc.*
Inst. de la Stat. *Ann. stat. des territoires d'outre-mer.*
Soc. R. Moreux. *Industries et travaux. No. 122.*
UN. *Stat. yrbk.* ———. *Water desalination.*
UN. ECA. *Situation, trends & prospects.*
US. FPC. *Spec. comm.* ———. *World power data.*

GABON

SUPPLY AND USE (million kwh)	1958	1959	1960	1961	1962	1963	1964	1965
PRODUCTION (Utilities & industries)								
Total (Gross)	14	16	20	22	27	32	36	
(Net)	--	--	--	19	25	30	34	
Hydro	—	—	—	—	—	—	—	
Conventional thermal	14	16	20	22	27	32	36	
Nuclear	—	—	—	—	—	—	—	
Geothermal	—	—	—	—	—	—	—	
PRODUCTION (Utilities only)								
Total (Gross)	14	16	20	22	27	32	36	
(Net)	--	--	--	--	--	--	--	
Hydro	—	—	—	—	—	—	—	
Conventional thermal	14	16	20	22	27	32	36	
Nuclear	—	—	—	—	—	—	—	
Geothermal	—	—	—	—	—	—	—	
NET IMPORTS								
SUPPLY (Gross)	14	16	20	22	27	32	36	
(Net)	--	--	--	19	25	30	34	
CONSUMPTION	--	--	--	13	15	18	21	
Transport	—	—	—	—	—	—	—	
Domestic sector	--	--	--	10	11	14	16	
Industry	--	--	--	3	4	4	5	
LOSS AND USE	--	--	--	6	10	12	13	
PLANT (thousand kw)								
CAPACITY (Utilities & industries)								
Total	8.2	8.2	8.2	9.5	9.6	11	13	
Hydro	—	—	—	—	—	—	—	
Conventional thermal	8.2	8.2	8.2	9.5	9.6	11	13	
Nuclear	—	—	—	—	—	—	—	
Geothermal	—	—	—	—	—	—	—	
CAPACITY (Utilities only)								
Total	8.2	8.2	8.2	9.5	9.6	11	13	
Hydro	—	—	—	—	—	—	—	
Conventional thermal	8.2	8.2	8.2	9.5	9.6	11	13	
Nuclear	—	—	—	—	—	—	—	
Geothermal	—	—	—	—	—	—	—	
FUEL CONSUMPTION (Utilities only)								
Total (Tcals)	--	--	--	--	--	--	--	
RESERVOIR STORAGE CAPACITY (million kwh)	—	—	—	—	—	—	—	

SUPPLEMENTARY DATA FOR 1964

Transmission lines, 100 kv+ (km) : --
Households served (thousands) : 5.6
Revenues per kwh (U.S. cents) — Total: (1961) 6.7
   Residential: Railways:
   Industry: Lighting: 14.6
Population (thousands) : 459

Sources of data:
EEC. *Yrbk. Overseas Assoc.*
Inst. de la Stat. *Données statistiques.*
UN. *Stat. yrbk.*
UN. ECA. *Situation, trends & prospects.*

Other characteristics of plants and systems:

Cie. Centrale de Distribution d'Energie Electrique, and Société d'Energie et d'Eau du Gabon, both privately owned, are the main suppliers of Gabon's electricity. Outside of Port Gentil, service is provided by small, isolated diesel plants. A very small fraction of the total population is supplied with electricity.

SUPPLY AND USE (million kwh)	1958	1959	1960	1961	1962	1963	1964	1965
PRODUCTION (Utilities & industries)								
Total (Gross)	--	4.5	5.0	5.6	6.0	7.4	7.4	
(Net)	--	--	--	--	--	--	--	
Hydro	—	—	—	—	—	—	—	
Conventional thermal	--	4.5	5.0	5.6	6.0	7.4	7.4	
Nuclear	—	—	—	—	—	—	—	
Geothermal	—	—	—	—	—	—	—	
PRODUCTION (Utilities only)								
Total (Gross)	4.0	4.2	4.5	5.1	5.5	6.4	6.1	
(Net)	--	--	--	--	--	--	--	
Hydro	—	—	—	—	—	—	—	
Conventional thermal	4.0	4.2	4.5	5.1	5.5	6.4	6.1	
Nuclear	—	—	—	—	—	—	—	
Geothermal	—	—	—	—	—	—	—	
NET IMPORTS	—	—	—	—	—	—	—	
SUPPLY (Gross)	--	4.5	5.0	5.6	6.0	7.4	7.4	
(Net)	--	--	--	--	--	--	--	
CONSUMPTION	--	--	--	--	--	--	--	
Transport	—	—	—	—	—	—	—	
Domestic sector	--	--	--	--	--	--	--	
Industry	--	--	--	--	--	--	--	
LOSS AND USE	--	--	--	--	--	--	--	
PLANT (thousand kw)								
CAPACITY (Utilities & industries)								
Total	4.0	4.0	4.0	4.0	4.0	4.8	4.8	
Hydro	—	—	—	—	—	—	—	
Conventional thermal	4.0	4.0	4.0	4.0	4.0	4.8	4.8	
Nuclear	—	—	—	—	—	—	—	
Geothermal	—	—	—	—	—	—	—	
CAPACITY (Utilities only)								
Total	2.3	3.0	3.0	3.0	3.0	3.0	3.0	
Hydro	—	—	—	—	—	—	—	
Conventional thermal	2.3	3.0	3.0	3.0	3.0	3.0	3.0	
Nuclear	—	—	—	—	—	—	—	
Geothermal	—	—	—	—	—	—	—	
FUEL CONSUMPTION (Utilities only)								
Total (Tcals)	--	--	--	--	--	--	--	
RESERVOIR STORAGE CAPACITY (million kwh)	—	—	—	—	—	—	—	

SUPPLEMENTARY DATA FOR 1964

Transmission lines, 100 kv+ (km) :   –
Households served (thousands) : (1961) 2.2
Revenues per kwh (U.S. cents) — Total: 4.7+
  Residential: 4.6+   Railways:
  Industry: 4.6+   Lighting:
Population (thousands) : 323

Other characteristics of plants and systems:

Electricity is supplied to Gambia by the Electricity Department of the government of Gambia, principally from a diesel plant at Bathurst. A very small fraction of the population is supplied with electricity.

Sources of data:
Benn Bros. *Elec. undertakings*.
UN. *Stat. yrbk*.
UN. ECA. *Situation, trends & prospects*.
United Kingdom. Colonial Office. *Gambia* (Biennial report).

SUPPLY AND USE (million kwh)	1958	1959	1960	1961	1962	1963	1964	1965
PRODUCTION (Utilities & industries)								
Total (Gross)	34874	37248	40305	42515	45063	47450	51032	
(Net)	33214	35303	38069	40085	42456	44375	47618	
Hydro	635	536	617	676	611	547	536	
Conventional thermal	34239	36712	39688	41839	44452	46903	50496	
Nuclear	—	—	—	—	—	—	—	
Geothermal	—	—	—	—	—	—	—	
PRODUCTION (Utilities only)								
Total (Gross)	15685	18134	20751	22007	23810	25805	28461	
(Net)	--	--	--	--	--	--	--	
Hydro	--	--	--	--	--	--	--	
Conventional thermal	--	--	--	--	--	--	--	
Nuclear	—	—	—	—	—	—	—	
Geothermal	—	—	—	—	—	—	—	
NET IMPORTS	−297	−339	−378	−359	−179	−2	+147	
SUPPLY (Gross)	34577	36909	39927	42156	44884	47448	51179	
(Net)	32917	34964	37691	39726	42277	44373	47765	
CONSUMPTION	30747	32654	35138	36946	39287	41193	44385	
Transport	662	621	772	840	830	841	976	
Domestic sector	5800	6356	7303	7924	8574	9380	10008	
Industry	24285	25677	27063	28182	29883	30972	33401	
LOSS AND USE	2170	2310	2553	2780	2990	3180	3380	

PLANT (thousand kw)

	1958	1959	1960	1961	1962	1963	1964	1965
CAPACITY (Utilities & industries)								
Total	6832	7298	7905	8329	8427	8894	9604	
Hydro	248	287	326	326	323	320	314	
Conventional thermal	6584	7011	7579	8003	8104	8574	9290	
Nuclear	—	—	—	—	—	—	—	
Geothermal	—	—	—	—	—	—	—	
CAPACITY (Utilities only)								
Total	3133	3551	3989	4312	4388	4887	5424	
Hydro	--	--	--	--	--	--	--	
Conventional thermal	--	--	--	--	--	--	--	
Nuclear	—	—	—	—	—	—	—	
Geothermal	—	—	—	—	—	—	—	

FUEL CONSUMPTION (Utilities only)

	1958	1959	1960	1961	1962	1963	1964	1965
Coal (mmt)	--	--	--	--	--	--	--	913
Lignite (mmt)	--	--	--	--	--	--	--•	48614
Fuel oils (mmt)	--	--	--	--	--	--	--	213
Natural gas (Tcals)	--	--	--	--	--	--	--	397
Other fuels (Tcals)	--	--	--	--	--	--	--	39
Total (Tcals)	--	--	--	--	--	--	--	110608
RESERVOIR STORAGE CAPACITY (million kwh)	--	--	--	--	--	--	--	

SUPPLEMENTARY DATA FOR 1964

Transmission lines, 100 kv+ (km): 14850
Households served (thousands): --
Revenues per kwh (U.S. cents) — Total:
  Residential: Railways:
  Industry: Lighting:
Population (thousands): 16991

Sources of data:
  Benn Bros. *Elec. undertakings* UCPTE. *Réseau.*
  UN. *Stat yrbk.* UN. ECE. *Ann. bull. of elec. energy stat.*
  UNIPEDE. *Réseaux de transport.*
  ——. *Statistiques.*
  Piens, Dr. Heinz. "Die Energiewirtschaft Mitteldeutschlands
    im Jahre 1964." *Glückauf.*

Other characteristics of plants and systems:

East Germany is served by a nationwide network which provides electricity to most of the people. Generation, transmission and public distribution are presumably the responsibilities of government, but much electricity is generated by industrial establishments for their own use.

SUPPLY AND USE (million kwh)	1958	1959	1960	1961	1962	1963	1964	1965
PRODUCTION (Utilities & industries)								
Total (Gross)	100393	108558	119028	127332	138411	150438	164436	
(Net)	94313	101750	111381	119073	129364	140374	153071	
Hydro	13189	11094	12993	12919	12546	12378	12102	
Conventional thermal	87204	97464	106035	114389	125765	138004	152230	
Nuclear	—	—	—	24	100	56	104	
Geothermal	—	—	—	—	—	—	—	
PRODUCTION (Utilities only)								
Total (Gross)	60398	65783	72960	77941	84652	92685	103149	
(Net)	56827	61669	68375	72966	79192	86477	96143	
Hydro	11330	9471	11166	11150	10814	10726	10504	
Conventional thermal	49068	56312	61794	66767	73738	81903	92541	
Nuclear	—	—	—	24	100	56	104	
Geothermal	—	—	—	—	—	—	—	
NET IMPORTS	2151	2649	4165	4324	3058	2466	960	
SUPPLY (Gross)	102544	111207	123193	131656	141469	152904	165396	
(Net)	96464	104399	115546	123397	132422	142840	154031	
CONSUMPTION	87881	95763	106522	113842	121883	131466	142360	
Transport	3197	3559	3859	3988	4424	4891	5272	
Domestic sector	21602	23839	26933	30175	34193	38463	41951	
Industry	63082	68365	75730	79679	83266	88112	95137	
LOSS AND USE	8583	8636	9024	9555	10539	11374	11671	

PLANT (thousand kw)	1958	1959	1960	1961	1962	1963	1964	1965
CAPACITY (Utilities & industries)								
Total	23526	25477	27665	29102	31207	33977	36160	
Hydro	3188	3259	3349	3475	3511	3566	3693	
Conventional thermal	20338	22218	24316	25612	27681	30396	32452	
Nuclear	—	—	—	15	15	15	15	
Geothermal	—	—	—	—	—	—	—	
CAPACITY (Utilities only)								
Total	14431	15868	17203	17799	19161	21071	23644	
Hydro	2786	2849	2956	3081	3109	3164	3289	
Conventional thermal	11645	13019	14247	14703	16037	17892	20340	
Nuclear	—	—	—	15	15	15	15	
Geothermal	—	—	—	—	—	—	—	
FUEL CONSUMPTION (Utilities only)								
Coal (mmt)	11652	12662	13771	14771	15873	16725	17496	
Pech coal (mmt)	662	736	792	843	858	895	865	
Lignite (mmt)	35940	40224	42714	43128	46622	50388	56623	
Fuel oils (mmt)	120	188	229	400	515	939	1306	
Natural gas (Tcals)	75	187	238	470	576	1694	3616	
Other gas (Tcals)	614	397	508	401	309	230	286	
Total (Tcals)	148235	164075	177401	187530	203413	220660	242456	
RESERVOIR STORAGE CAPACITY (million kwh)	351	358	326	326	337	337	337	

SUPPLEMENTARY DATA FOR 1964

Transmission lines, 100 kv+ (km) :   39210
Households served (thousands) :   16960
Revenues per kwh (U.S. cents) — Total: - -
  Residential: 3.6   Railways: 1.3
  Industry: 1.8   Lighting: 6.3
Population (thousands) :   58290

Sources of data:
EEC. *Energy stat., 1950-1965.*
UCPTE. *Réseau.*
UN. *Stat. yrbk.*
UN. ECE. *Ann. bull. of elec. energy stat.*
  ————. *Elec. power situation.*
  ————. *Org. of elec. power services.*
UNIPEDE. *L'écon. élec.*
  ————. *Statistiques.*

Other characteristics of plants and systems:

    Electricity is available throughout Western Germany via a national network which covers the entire country and is interconnected with the systems of adjoining countries. Production is largely in the hands of private companies, much of whose stock is owned by the government. Electricity generated by the public network is supplemented extensively by power generated in industry, especially the coal and chemical industries. Much of Germany's electricity is distributed through undertakings concerned exclusively with distribution, many of which are associated in the Vereinigung Deutscher Elektrizitätswerke.

GHANA

SUPPLY AND USE (million kwh)	1958	1959	1960	1961	1962	1963	1964	1965
PRODUCTION (Utilities & industries)								
Total (Gross)	312	339	374	390	433	470	485	
(Net)	--	--	--	--	--	--	--	
Hydro	—	—	—	—	—	—	—	
Conventional thermal	312	339	374	390	433	470	485	
Nuclear	—	—	—	—	—	—	—	
Geothermal	—	—	—	—	—	—	—	
PRODUCTION (Utilities only)								
Total (Gross)	106	122	149	175	203	237	275	
(Net)	--	--	--	--	--	--	--	
Hydro	—	—	—	—	—	—	—	
Conventional thermal	106	122	149	175	203	237	275	
Nuclear	—	—	—	—	—	—	—	
Geothermal	—	—	—	—	—	—	—	
NET IMPORTS	—	—	—	—	—	—	—	
SUPPLY (Gross)	312	339	374	390	433	470	485	
(Net)	--	--	--	--	--	--	--	
CONSUMPTION	296	321	344	350	--	--	--	
Transport	—	—	—	—	—	—	—	
Domestic sector	64	86	91	105e	--	--	--	
Industry	232	235	253	245	--	--	--	
LOSS AND USE	16	18	30	40	--	--	--	

PLANT (thousand kw)

	1958	1959	1960	1961	1962	1963	1964	1965
CAPACITY (Utilities & industries)								
Total	89	95	103	122	126	143	147	
Hydro	—	—	—	—	—	—	—	
Conventional thermal	89	95	103	122	126	143	147	
Nuclear	—	—	—	—	—	—	—	
Geothermal	—	—	—	—	—	—	—	
CAPACITY (Utilities only)								
Total	34	38	42	57	59	75	80	
Hydro	—	—	—	—	—	—	—	
Conventional thermal	34	38	42	57	59	75	80	
Nuclear	—	—	—	—	—	—	—	
Geothermal	—	—	—	—	—	—	—	

FUEL CONSUMPTION (Utilities only)

	1958	1959	1960	1961	1962	1963	1964	1965
Diesel oil (mmt)	27	--	--	--	54	--	--	
Total (Tcals)	284	--	--	--	567	--	--	
RESERVOIR STORAGE CAPACITY (million kwh)	—	—	—	—	—	—	—	

SUPPLEMENTARY DATA FOR 1964

Transmission lines, 100 kv+ (km):   —
Households served (thousands):   (1963) 64
Revenues per kwh (U.S. cents) — Total: 5.1
  Residential:(1962/63) 3.7 Railways:
  Industry: 3.7   Lighting: 2.3
Population (thousands):   7537

Sources of data:

Benn Bros. *Elec. undertakings.* UN. *Stat. yrbk.*
UN. ECA. *Situation, trends & prospects.*
Central Bureau of Statistics. *Statistical yearbook.*
——. *Quarterly digest of statistics.*
——. *Economic survey.*
Electricity Department. *Annual report on Electricity Department.*

Other characteristics of plants and systems:

The Electricity Division, Ministry of Construction and Communication, Government of Ghana, is responsible for electricity supply. Isolated diesel plants provided much of the country's electricity until very recently, but the bulk is now generated at the Akosombo Dam on the Volta River. Large quantities of electricity are privately generated and consumed by the gold mining industry. A very small fraction of the country's population is supplied with electricity.

GIBRALTAR

SUPPLY AND USE (million kwh)	1958	1959	1960	1961	1962	1963	1964	1965
PRODUCTION (Utilities & industries)								
Total (Gross)	--	--	--	--	--	--	--	
(Net)	--	--	--	--	--	--	--	
Hydro	—	—	—	—	--	--	—	
Conventional thermal	--	--	--	--	--	--	--	
Nuclear	—	—	—	—	—	—	—	
Geothermal	—	—	—	—	—	—	—	
PRODUCTION (Utilities only)								
Total (Gross)	20	21	23	24	32	38	39	
(Net)	--	--	--	--	--	--	--	
Hydro	—	—	—	—	—	—	—	
Conventional thermal	20	21	23	24	32	38	39	
Nuclear	—	—	—	—	—	—	—	
Geothermal	—	—	—	—	—	—	—	
NET IMPORTS	—	—	—	—	—	—	—	
SUPPLY (Gross)	20	21	23	24	32	38	39	
(Net)	--	--	--	--	--	--	--	
CONSUMPTION	--	--	--	--	--	--	--	
Transport	—	—	—	—	—	—	—	
Domestic sector	--	--	--	--	--	--	--	
Industry	--	--	--	--	--	--	--	
LOSS AND USE	--	--	--	--	--	--	--	

PLANT (thousand kw)

	1958	1959	1960	1961	1962	1963	1964	1965
CAPACITY (Utilities & industries)								
Total	--	--	--	--	--	--	--	
Hydro	—	—	—	—	—	—	—	
Conventional thermal	--	--	--	--	--	--	--	
Nuclear	—	—	—	—	—	—	—	
Geothermal	—	—	—	—	—	—	—	
CAPACITY (Utilities only)								
Total	6.2	6.2	6.2	8.7	11	11	11	
Hydro	—	—	—	—	—	—	—	
Conventional thermal	6.2	6.2	6.2	8.7	11	11	11	
Nuclear	—	—	—	—	—	—	—	
Geothermal	—	—	—	—	—	—	—	

FUEL CONSUMPTION (Utilities only)

	1958	1959	1960	1961	1962	1963	1964	1965
Total (Tcals)	--	--	--	--	--	--	--	
RESERVOIR STORAGE CAPACITY (million kwh)	—	—	—	—	—	—	—	

SUPPLEMENTARY DATA FOR 1964

Transmission lines, 100 kv+ (km):   —
Households served (thousands):   (1960) 8
Revenues per kwh (U.S. cents) — Total:
   Residential: Railways:
   Industry: Lighting: 11.6
Population (thousands):   24

Other characteristics of plants and systems:

   Gibraltar's electricity supply is provided by the Electricity Department of the City Council. All of the colony's electricity is generated from imported oil.

Sources of data:
Benn Bros. *Elec. undertakings*.
UN. *Stat. yrbk*.
United Kingdom. Colonial Office. *Gibraltar* (Annual Report).

GREECE

SUPPLY AND USE (million kwh)	1958	1959	1960	1961	1962	1963	1964	1965
PRODUCTION (Utilities & industries)								
Total (Gross)	1802	2095	2290	2521	2794	3168	3780	
(Net)	--	--	--	--	--	--	--	
Hydro	449	431	465	552	613	805	749	
Conventional thermal	1353	1664	1825	1969	2181	2363	3031	
Nuclear	—	—	—	—	—	—	—	
Geothermal	—	—	—	—	—	—	—	
PRODUCTION (Utilities only)								
Total (Gross)	1770	2013	2230	2478	2742	3111	3715	
(Net)	--	--	--	--	--	--	--	
Hydro	437	419	455	552	613	805	749	
Conventional thermal	1333	1594	1775	1926	2129	2306	2966	
Nuclear	—	—	—	—	—	—	—	
Geothermal	—	—	—	—	—	—	—	
NET IMPORTS	—	—	8	−14	−1	−6	−15	
SUPPLY (Gross)	1802	2095	2298	2507	2793	3162	3765	
(Net)	--	--	--	--	--	--	--	
CONSUMPTION	1530	1704	1887	2156	2421	2738	3267	
Transport	40	39	38	41	42	42	42	
Domestic sector	673	956	982	978	1132	1301	1558	
Industry	817	709	867	1137	1247	1395	1667	
LOSS AND USE	272	391	411	351	372	424	498	

PLANT (thousand kw)								
CAPACITY (Utilities & industries)								
Total	499	590e	611	658	832e	827e	866	
Hydro	116	140e	178e	226	261	260	268	
Conventional thermal	383	450e	433	432	571	567	598	
Nuclear	—	—	—	—	—	—	—	
Geothermal	—	—	—	—	—	—	—	
CAPACITY (Utilities only)								
Total	476	571	605	645	817	812	851	
Hydro	113	134	174	222	261	260	268	
Conventional thermal	363	437	431	423	556	552	583	
Nuclear	—	—	—	—	—	—	—	
Geothermal	—	—	—	—	—	—	—	

FUEL CONSUMPTION (Utilities only)								
Lignite (mmt)	766	1000	1717	1815	1794	2357	2933	
Diesel oil (mmt)	--	--	--	--	--	--	57	
Fuel oil (mmt)	202e	225e	213e	--	--	340e	353	
Total (Tcals)	4756	5671	6370	6976	7934	8493	10660	
RESERVOIR STORAGE CAPACITY (million kwh)	28	403	748	748	709	709	709	

SUPPLEMENTARY DATA FOR 1964

Transmission lines, 100 kv + (km): 2363
Households served (thousands):   - -
Revenues per kwh (U.S. cents) — Total:
    Residential: Railways:
    Industry: Lighting: 6.1
Population (thousands):   8510

More characteristics of plants and systems:

Most of Greece's electricity is produced by the Public Power Corporation, owned by the government of Greece. As of 1964, much of Greece remained to be electrified. Most of mainland Greece is interconnected via a 150 KV integrated network, the island of Crete by a separate, 66 KV network.

Sources of data:

OECD. *Elec. ind. survey.* UN. *Stat. yrbk.*
UN. ECE. *Ann. bull. of elec. energy stat.*
—————. *Org. of elec. power services.*
UNIPEDE. *Statistiques.*
US. *Foreign serv. desp.*
Public Power Corporation. *Activities report and balance sheet.*

GREENLAND

SUPPLY AND USE (million kwh)	1958	1959	1960	1961	1962	1963	1964	1965
PRODUCTION (Utilities & industries)								
Total (Gross)	21	23	26	29	31	35	38	
(Net)	--	--	--	--	--	--	--	
Hydro	—	—	—	—	—	—	—	
Conventional thermal	21	23	26	29	31	35	38	
Nuclear	—	—	—	—	—	—	—	
Geothermal	—	—	—	—	—	—	—	
PRODUCTION (Utilities only)								
Total (Gross)	11	12	13	16	19	23	26	
(Net)	--	--	--	--	--	--	--	
Hydro	—	—	—	—	—	—	—	
Conventional thermal	11	12	13	16	19	23	26	
Nuclear	—	—	—	—	—	—	—	
Geothermal	—	—	—	—	—	—	—	
NET IMPORTS	—	—	—	—	—	—	—	
SUPPLY (Gross)	21	23	26	29	31	35	38	
(Net)	--	--	--	--	--	--	--	
CONSUMPTION	--	--	--	--	--	--	--	
Transport	—	—	—	—	—	—	—	
Domestic sector	--	--	--	--	--	--	--	
Industry	--	--	--	--	--	--	--	
LOSS AND USE	--	--	--	--	--	--	--	

PLANT (thousand kw)

	1958	1959	1960	1961	1962	1963	1964	1965
CAPACITY (Utilities & industries)								
Total	12	14	15	16	19	21	24	
Hydro	—	—	—	—	—	—	—	
Conventional thermal	12	14	15	16	19	21	24	
Nuclear	—	—	—	—	—	—	—	
Geothermal	—	—	—	—	—	—	—	
CAPACITY (Utilities only)								
Total	6.5	7.8	8.7	9.6	9.9	11	14	
Hydro	—	—	—	—	—	—	—	
Conventional thermal	6.5	7.8	8.7	9.6	9.9	11	14	
Nuclear	—	—	—	—	—	—	—	
Geothermal	—	—	—	—	—	—	—	

FUEL CONSUMPTION (Utilities only)

	1958	1959	1960	1961	1962	1963	1964	1965
Total (Tcals)	--	--	--	--	--	--	--	
RESERVOIR STORAGE CAPACITY (million kwh)	—	—	—	—	—	—	—	

SUPPLEMENTARY DATA FOR 1964

Transmission lines, 100 kv+ (km) : —
Households served (thousands) :   --
Revenues per kwh (U.S. cents) — Total: 4.6
   Residential: Railways:
   Industry: Lighting:
Population (thousands) : 37

Other characteristics of plants and systems:

   Greenland's electricity supply is provided by sixteen state-operated, isolated diesel plants. Fuel for the generation of electric power is all imported.

Sources of data:
UN. *Stat. yrbk.*
Elektricitetsrådet Danske Elvaerkers Forening. *Dansk elvaerksstatistik.*

GUADELOUPE

SUPPLY AND USE (million kwh)	1958	1959	1960	1961	1962	1963	1964	1965
PRODUCTION (Utilities & industries)								
Total (Gross)	14	17	21	24	29	34	40	
(Net)	--	--	--	--	--	--	--	
Hydro	1	—	1	1	1	1	1	
Conventional thermal	13	17	20	23	28	33	39	
Nuclear	—	—	—	—	—	—	—	
Geothermal	—	—	—	—	—	—	—	
PRODUCTION (Utilities only)								
Total (Gross)	14	17	21	24	29	34	40	
(Net)	--	--	--	--	--	--	--	
Hydro	1	—	1	1	1	1	1	
Conventional thermal	13	17	20	23	28	33	39	
Nuclear	—	—	—	—	—	—	—	
Geothermal	—	—	—	—	—	—	—	
NET IMPORTS	—	—	—	—	—	—	—	
SUPPLY (Gross)	14	17	21	24	29	34	40	
(Net)	--	--	--	--	--	--	--	
CONSUMPTION	12	13	17	20	24	28	33	
Transport	—	—	—	—	—	—	—	
Domestic sector	8	9	12	14	16	18	21	
Industry	4	4	5	6	8	10	12	
LOSS AND USE	2	4	4	4	5	6	7	

PLANT (thousand kw)

CAPACITY (Utilities & industries)								
Total	--	--	--	--	--	--	--	
Hydro	--	--	--	--	--	--	--	
Conventional thermal	--	--	--	--	--	--	--	
Nuclear	—	—	—	—	—	—	—	
Geothermal	—	—	—	—	—	—	—	
CAPACITY (Utilities only)								
Total	6.3	6.3	8.6	8.6	8.6	11	14e	
Hydro	--	--	--	0.2	0.2	--	--	
Conventional thermal	--	--	--	8.4	8.4	11	14	
Nuclear	—	—	—	—	—	—	—	
Geothermal	—	—	—	—	—	—	—	

FUEL CONSUMPTION (Utilities only)

Total (Tcals)	--	--	--	--	--	--	--	
RESERVOIR STORAGE CAPACITY (million kwh)	—	—	—	—	—	—	—	

SUPPLEMENTARY DATA FOR 1964

Transmission lines, 100 kv+ (km): --
Households served (thousands): 28
Revenues per kwh (U.S. cents) — Total:
  Residential: Railways:
  Industry: Lighting:
Population (thousands): 308

Other characteristics of plants and systems:

Electricity is supplied to Guadeloupe by the Société de Production et de Distribution d'Electricité de la Guadeloupe, of mixed ownership, which operates a 30 KV network on the main island and isolated plants on other islands in the group. Power is generated in small diesel plants, and distributed to an estimated one-third of the island's population.

Sources of data:
EEC. *Yrbk. Overseas Assoc.*
Soc. R. Moreux. *Industries et travaux.* No. 122.
UN. *Stat. yrbk.* UN. ECLA. *Estud. econ.*
——. *Stat. bull.* US. *Foreign serv. desp.*
Inst. de la Stat. *Ann. stat. de la Guadeloupe.*

SUPPLY AND USE (million kwh)	1958	1959	1960	1961	1962	1963	1964	1965
PRODUCTION (Utilities & industries)								
Total (Gross)	244	262	275	296	295	310	335	
(Net)	--	--	--	--	--	--	--	
Hydro	—	—	—	—	—	—	—	
Conventional thermal	244	262	275	296	295	310	335	
Nuclear	—	—	—	—	—	—	—	
Geothermal	—	—	—	—	—	—	—	
PRODUCTION (Utilities only)								
Total (Gross)	244	262	275	296	295	310	335	
(Net)	--	--	--	--	--	--	--	
Hydro	—	—	—	—	—	—	—	
Conventional thermal	244	262	275	296	295	310	335	
Nuclear	—	—	—	—	—	—	—	
Geothermal	—	—	—	—	—	—	—	
NET IMPORTS	—	—	—	—	—	—	—	
SUPPLY (Gross)	244	262	275	296	295	310	335	
(Net)	--	--	--	--	--	--	--	
CONSUMPTION	--	--	--	--	--	--	--	
Transport	—	—	—	—	—	—	—	
Domestic sector	--	--	--	--	--	--	--	
Industry	--	--	--	--	--	--	--	
LOSS AND USE	--	--	--	--	--	--	--	

PLANT (thousand kw)

CAPACITY (Utilities & industries)								
Total	58	59	70	70	70	70	90	
Hydro	—	—	—	—	—	—	—	
Conventional thermal	58	59	70	70	70	70	90	
Nuclear	—	—	—	—	—	—	—	
Geothermal	—	—	—	—	—	—	—	
CAPACITY (Utilities only)								
Total	58	59	70	70	70	70	90	
Hydro	—	—	—	—	—	—	—	
Conventional thermal	58	59	70	70	70	70	90	
Nuclear	—	—	—	—	—	—	—	
Geothermal	—	—	—	—	—	—	—	

FUEL CONSUMPTION (Utilities only)

Total (Tcals)	--	--	--	--	--	--	--	
RESERVOIR STORAGE CAPACITY (million kwh)	—	—	—	—	—	—	—	

SUPPLEMENTARY DATA FOR 1964

Transmission lines, 100 kv+ (km) : —
Households served (thousands) :   - -
Revenues per kwh (U.S. cents) — Total:
  Residential: Railways:
  Industry: Lighting:
Population (thousands) :   72

Other characteristics of plants and systems:

    Power in Guam is generated and distributed by the government.

Sources of data:
  UN. *Stat. yrbk.*

GUATEMALA

SUPPLY AND USE (million kwh)	1958	1959	1960	1961	1962	1963	1964	1965
PRODUCTION (Utilities & industries)								
Total (Gross)	228	256	310	328	371	423	470	
(Net)	--	--	--	--	--	--	--	
Hydro	106	106	126	112	118	117	120	
Conventional thermal	122	150	184	216	253	306	350	
Nuclear	—	—	—	—	—	—	—	
Geothermal	—	—	—	—	—	—	—	
PRODUCTION (Utilities only)								
Total (Gross)	178	201	246	262	297	341	382	
(Net)	--	--	--	--	--	--	--	
Hydro	106	106	126	112	118	117	120	
Conventional thermal	72	95	120	150	179	224	262	
Nuclear	—	—	—	—	—	—	—	
Geothermal	—	—	—	—	—	—	—	
NET IMPORTS	—	—	—	—	—	—	—	
SUPPLY (Gross)	228	256	310	328	371	423	470	
(Net)	--	--	--	--	--	--	--	
CONSUMPTION	189	204	189	205	230	263	312	
Transport	—	—	—	—	—	—	—	
Domestic sector	101	109	103	116	132	142	160	
Industry	88	95	86	89	98	121	152	
LOSS AND USE	39	52	121e	123e	141e	160e	158e	

PLANT (thousand kw)

	1958	1959	1960	1961	1962	1963	1964	1965
CAPACITY (Utilities & industries)								
Total	57	72	73	85	87	88	103	
Hydro	30	30	31	31e	31e	31e	31e	
Conventional thermal	27	42	42	54e	56e	57e	72e	
Nuclear	—	—	—	—	—	—	—	
Geothermal	—	—	—	—	—	—	—	
CAPACITY (Utilities only)								
Total	44	59	60	71	72	72	86	
Hydro	25	27	27	27	27	27	27	
Conventional thermal	19	32	33	44	45	45	59	
Nuclear	—	—	—	—	—	—	—	
Geothermal	—	—	—	—	—	—	—	

FUEL CONSUMPTION (Utilities only)

	1958	1959	1960	1961	1962	1963	1964	1965
Total (Tcals)	--	--	--	--	--	--	--	
RESERVOIR STORAGE CAPACITY (million kwh)	--	--	--	--	--	--	--	

SUPPLEMENTARY DATA FOR 1964

Transmission lines, 100 kv+ (km):   —
Households served (thousands):   81
Revenues per kwh (U.S. cents) — Total: 3.6
  Residential: 4.5   Railways:
  Industry: 2.4   Lighting: 3.0
Population (thousands):   4305

Other characteristics of plants and systems:

The principal supplier of electricity in Guatemala is Empresa Eléctrica de Guatemala, privately-owned, which generates three-quarters of the public supply of electricity. The largest generating plant, La Laguna, includes 30 MW of steam capacity and 12.5 MW of gas turbine capacity. A very small part of Guatemala's population, perhaps ten per cent, is supplied with electricity.

Sources of data:

UN. *Stat. yrbk.* UN. ECLA. *Estud. econ.*
————. *Estud. sobre la elec.*
————. Subcom. Centroamer. de elec. *Estadísticas de energía eléctrica.*
————. ————. *Estadísticas preliminares.*
————. ————. *Estudio comparativo de costos.*

GUINEA

SUPPLY AND USE (million kwh)	1958	1959	1960	1961	1962	1963	1964	1965
PRODUCTION (Utilities & industries)								
Total (Gross)	21	31	102	135	147	156	168	
(Net)	--	--	--	--	--	--	--	
Hydro	10	10	10	10	10	10	14	
Conventional thermal	11	21	92	125	137	146	154	
Nuclear	—	—	—	—	—	—	—	
Geothermal	—	—	—	—	—	—	—	
PRODUCTION (Utilities only)								
Total (Gross)	17	22	26	--	30	--	--	
(Net)	--	--	--	--	--	--	--	
Hydro	10	10	10	10	10	10	14	
Conventional thermal	7	12	16	--	20	--	--	
Nuclear	—	—	—	—	—	—	—	
Geothermal	—	—	—	—	—	—	—	
NET IMPORTS	—	—	—	—	—	—	—	
SUPPLY (Gross)	21	31	102	135	147	156	168	
(Net)	--	--	--	--	--	--	--	
CONSUMPTION	--	29	100	129	140	148e	--	
Transport	—	—	—	—	—	—	—	
Domestic sector	--	15	20	19	22	--	--	
Industry	--	14	80	110	118	125e	--	
LOSS AND USE	--	2	2	6	7	--	--	
PLANT (thousand kw)								
CAPACITY (Utilities & industries)								
Total	--	--	58	58	58	68	68	
Hydro	10	10	10	10	10	20	20	
Conventional thermal	--	--	48	48	48	48	48	
Nuclear	—	—	—	—	—	—	—	
Geothermal	—	—	—	—	—	—	—	
CAPACITY (Utilities only)								
Total	--	--	16	16	16	26	26	
Hydro	10	10	10	10	10	20	20	
Conventional thermal	--	--	6	6	6	6	6	
Nuclear	—	—	—	—	—	—	—	
Geothermal	—	—	—	—	—	—	—	
FUEL CONSUMPTION (Utilities only)								
Total (Tcals)	--	--	--	--	--	--	--	
RESERVOIR STORAGE CAPACITY (million kwh)	--	--	--	--	--	--	--	

SUPPLEMENTARY DATA FOR 1964

Transmission lines, 100 kv+ (km): —
Households served (thousands): 16
Revenues per kwh (U.S. cents) — Total:
  Residential: Railways:
  Industry: Lighting:
Population (thousands): 3420

Other characteristics of plants and systems:

    Société Nationale d'Electricité, owned by the government of Guinea, operates interconnected plants at Grandes Chutes and Conakry. Localities in the interior are served mainly by small diesel and hydro plants. A diesel plant of 41 MW at Fria generates power privately for use in the processing of bauxite. Electrical service is available to only a small part of Guinea's population.

Sources of data:
  Soc. R. Moreux. *Industries et travaux.* No. 122.
  UN. *Stat. yrbk.*
  US. FPC. *World power data.*

SUPPLY AND USE (million kwh)	1958	1959	1960	1961	1962	1963	1964	1965
PRODUCTION (Utilities & industries)								
Total (Gross)	67	73	88	96	105	101	171	
(Net)	--	--	--	--	--	--	--	
Hydro	—	—	—	—	—	—	—	
Conventional thermal	67	73	88	96	105	101	171	
Nuclear	—		—	—	—	—	—	
Geothermal	—	—	—	—	—	—	—	
PRODUCTION (Utilities only)								
Total (Gross)	40	43	50	55	58	59	64	
(Net)	--	--	--	--	--	--	--	
Hydro	—	—	—	—	—	—	—	
Conventional thermal	40	43	50	55	58	59	64	
Nuclear	—	—	—	—	—	—	—	
Geothermal	—	—	—	—	—	—	—	
NET IMPORTS	—	—	—	—	—	—	—	
SUPPLY (Gross)	67	73	88	96	105	101	171	
(Net)	--	--	--	--	--	--	--	
CONSUMPTION	59	65	78	87	96	92	159	
Transport	—	—	—	—	—	—	—	
Domestic sector	22	23	25	28	30	31	29	
Industry	37	42	53	59	66	61	130	
LOSS AND USE	8	8	10	9	9	9	12	

PLANT (thousand kw)

	1958	1959	1960	1961	1962	1963	1964	1965
CAPACITY (Utilities & industries)								
Total	39	40	52	52	53	74	98	
Hydro	—	—	—	—	—	—	—	
Conventional thermal	39	40	52	52	53	74	98	
Nuclear	—	—	—	—	—	—	—	
Geothermal	—	—	—	—	—	—	—	
CAPACITY (Utilities only)								
Total	14	15	17	18	18	38	38	
Hydro	—	—	—	—	—	—	—	
Conventional thermal	14	15	17	18	18	38	38	
Nuclear	—	—	—	—	—	—	—	
Geothermal	—	—	—	—	—	—	—	

FUEL CONSUMPTION (Utilities only)

	1958	1959	1960	1961	1962	1963	1964	1965
Total (Tcals)	--	--	--	--	--	--	--	
RESERVOIR STORAGE CAPACITY (million kwh)	—	—	—	—	—	—	—	

SUPPLEMENTARY DATA FOR 1964

Transmission lines, 100 kv+ (km):   —
Households served (thousands):   --
Revenues per kwh (U.S. cents) — Total:
  Residential: Railways:
  Industry: Lighting: 8.8
Population (thousands):   629

Other characteristics of plants and systems:

A steam plant at Georgetown provides most of the public supply of electricity for Guyana through a publicly-owned system which, until independence at least, was known as the British Guiana Electricity Corporation. Large additional quantities of power are generated privately for the use of the Demerara Bauxite Company, an industrial establishment.

Sources of data:
EEC. *Yrbk. Overseas Assoc.* UN. *Stat. yrbk.*
UN. ECLA. *Estud. econ.* US. *Foreign serv. desp.*
Ministry of Economic Affairs. The Statistical Bureau.
  Quarterly statistical digest.
United Kingdom. Colonial Office. *British Guiana*
  (Annual report).

SUPPLY AND USE (million kwh)	1958	1959	1960	1961	1962	1963	1964	1965
PRODUCTION (Utilities & industries)								
Total (Gross)	80	90	90	95	100e	100e	110	
(Net)	--	--	--	--	--	--	--	
Hydro	—	—	—	—	—	—	—	
Conventional thermal	80	90	90e	95	100	100	110	
Nuclear	—	—	—	—	—	—	—	
Geothermal	—	—	—	—	—	—	—	
PRODUCTION (Utilities only)								
Total (Gross)	47	53	60	65	73	74	71	
(Net)	--	--	--	--	--	--	--	
Hydro	←	—	—	—	—	—	—	
Conventional thermal	47	53	60	65	73	74	71	
Nuclear	—	—	—	—	—	—	—	
Geothermal	—	—	—	—	—	—	—	
NET IMPORTS	—	—	—	—	—	—	—	
SUPPLY (Gross)	80	90	90	95	100	100	110	
(Net)	--	--	--	--	--	--	--	
CONSUMPTION	--	--	--	--	--	--	--	
Transport	—	—	—	—	--	--	--	
Domestic sector	--	--	--	--	--	--	--	
Industry	--	--	--	--	--	--	--	
LOSS AND USE	--	--	--	--	--	--	--	

PLANT (thousand kw)	1958	1959	1960	1961	1962	1963	1964	1965
CAPACITY (Utilities & industries)								
Total	22	23	25	27	27	27	27	
Hydro	—	—	—	—	—	—	—	
Conventional thermal	22	23	25	27	27	27	27	
Nuclear	—	—	—	—	—	—	—	
Geothermal	—	—	—	—	—	—	—	
CAPACITY (Utilities only)								
Total	--	17	17	--	--	--	--	
Hydro	—	—	—	—	—	—	—	
Conventional thermal	--	17	17	--	--	--	--	
Nuclear	—	—	—	—	—	—	—	
Geothermal	—	—	—	—	—	—	—	

FUEL CONSUMPTION (Utilities only)

	1958	1959	1960	1961	1962	1963	1964	1965
Total (Tcals)	--	--	--	--	--	--	--	
RESERVOIR STORAGE CAPACITY (million kwh)	—	—	—	—	—	—	—	

SUPPLEMENTARY DATA FOR 1964

Transmission lines, 100 kv+ (km) :   —
Households served (thousands) :   --
Revenues per kwh (U.S. cents) — Total:
    Residential: Railways:
    Industry: Lighting:
Population (thousands) :   4310

Other characteristics of plants and systems:

The principal source of electric power in Haiti is the Cie. d'Eclairage Electrique des Villes de Port-au-Prince et du Cap Haïtien, which is privately owned. Power is generated mainly in small, isolated diesel plants, and is supplied to a very small fraction of the total population — probably less than ten per cent.

Sources of data:
    Benn Bros. *Elec. undertakings.* UN. *Stat. yrbk.*
    UN. ECLA. *Estud. econ.* US. *Foreign serv. desp.*
    US. FPC. *World power data.*
    Institut Haïtien de Statistique. *Bulletin trimestriel de statistique.*

HONDURAS

SUPPLY AND USE (million kwh)	1958	1959	1960	1961	1962	1963	1964	1965
PRODUCTION (Utilities & industries)								
Total (Gross)	80	87	97	102	109	116	131	
(Net)	--	--	--	--	--	--	--	
Hydro	13	16	20	20	20e	20e	74e	
Conventional thermal	67	71	77	82	89e	96e	57e	
Nuclear	—	—	—	—	—	—	—	
Geothermal	—	—	—	—	—	—	—	
PRODUCTION (Utilities only)								
Total (Gross)	39	43	66	71	76	83	119	
(Net)	--	--	--	--	--	--	--	
Hydro	11	12	16	15	16	15	70	
Conventional thermal	28	31	50	56	60	68	49	
Nuclear	—	—	—	—	—	—	—	
Geothermal	—	—	—	—	—	—	—	
NET IMPORTS	—	—	—	—	—	—	—	
SUPPLY (Gross)	80	87	97	102	109	116	131	
(Net)	--	--	--	--	--	--	--	
CONSUMPTION	68	76	85e	88e	92	99	109	
Transport	2	2	--	--	--	--	--	
Domestic sector	19	23	35e	38e	47	50	59	
Industry	47	51	50e	50e	45	49	50	
LOSS AND USE	12	11	12e	14e	17	17	22	

PLANT (thousand kw)	1958	1959	1960	1961	1962	1963	1964	1965
CAPACITY (Utilities & industries)								
Total	30	31	33	35	37	37	70	
Hydro	4	4	5	5	5	5e	33e	
Conventional thermal	26	27	28	30	32	32e	37	
Nuclear	—	—	—	—	—	—	—	
Geothermal	—	—	—	—	—	—	—	
CAPACITY (Utilities only)								
Total	15	16	24	26	28	28	58	
Hydro	3	3	3	3	4	4	32	
Conventional thermal	12	13	21	23	24	24	26	
Nuclear	—	—	—	—	—	—	—	
Geothermal	—	—	—	—	—	—	—	

FUEL CONSUMPTION (Utilities only)

	1958	1959	1960	1961	1962	1963	1964	1965
Total (Tcals)	--	--	--	--	--	--	--	
RESERVOIR STORAGE CAPACITY (million kwh)	--	--	--	--	--	--	--	

SUPPLEMENTARY DATA FOR 1964

Transmission lines, 100 kv+ (km): —
Households served (thousands): 33
Revenues per kwh (U.S. cents) — Total: 3.7
  Residential: 5.9   Railways:
  Industry: 2.6   Lighting: 6.0
Population (thousands): 2209

Sources of data:
UN. *Stat. yrbk.* UN. ECLA. *Estud. econ.*
——. *Estud. sobre la elec.*
——. Subcom. Centroamer. de elec. *Estadísticas de energía eléctrica.*
——. ——. *Estadísticas preliminares.*
Dirección General de Estadística y Censos. Secretaria de Economia y Hacienda. *Anuario estadístico.*
——. Consejo Superior de Planiticación Economica. *Compendio estadístico.*

Other characteristics of plants and systems:

More than three-quarters of the public electricity supply of Honduras is generated by the Empresa Nacional de Energía Eléctrica, publicly owned. Most of the country's power is generated in one large hydro plant at Canaveral, the remainder at isolated diesel and hydro plants scattered throughout the country. Service is provided to an estimated ten per cent of the people.

HONG KONG

SUPPLY AND USE (million kwh)	1958	1959	1960	1961	1962	1963	1964	1965
PRODUCTION (Utilities & industries)								
Total (Gross)	929	1099	1301	1542	1787	2060	2385	
(Net)	881e	1044e	1232	1456	1688	1953	2254	
Hydro	—	—	—	—	—	—	—	
Conventional thermal	929	1099	1301	1542	1787	2060	2385	
Nuclear	—	—	—	—	—	—	—	
Geothermal	—	—	—	—	—	—	—	
PRODUCTION (Utilities only)								
Total (Gross)	929	1099	1301	1542	1787	2060	2385	
(Net)	881e	1044e	1232	1456	1688	1953	2254	
Hydro	—	—	—	—	—	—	—	
Conventional thermal	929	1099	1301	1542	1787	2060	2385	
Nuclear	—	—	—	—	—	—	—	
Geothermal	—	—	—	—	—	—	—	
NET IMPORTS	—	—	—	—	—	—	—	
SUPPLY (Gross)	929	1099	1301	1542	1787	2060	2385	
(Net)	881	1044	1232	1456	1688	1953	2254	
CONSUMPTION	758e	912	1116	1330	1540	1785	2075	
Transport	- -	- -	- -	18	18	18	18e	
Domestic sector	510	587	722	847	989	1012	1311	
Industry	248	325	394	465	533	755	746	
LOSS AND USE	123e	132	116	126	148	168	179	
PLANT (thousand kw)								
CAPACITY (Utilities & industries)								
Total	245	335	365	365	485	499	592	
Hydro	—	—	—	—	—	—	—	
Conventional thermal	245	335	365	365	485	499	592	
Nuclear	—	—	—	—	—	—	—	
Geothermal	—	—	—	—	—	—	—	
CAPACITY (Utilities only)								
Total	245	335	365	365	485	499	592	
Hydro	—	—	—	—	—	—	—	
Conventional thermal	245	335	365	365	485	499	592	
Nuclear	—	—	—	—	—	—	—	
Geothermal	—	—	—	—	—	—	—	
FUEL CONSUMPTION (Utilities only)								
Coal (mmt)	- -	- -	- -	27	- -	11	- -	
Fuel oils (mmt)	- -	- -	- -	481	- -	617	- -	
Total (Tcals)	1715	1890	3850	6048	6755	7217	- -	
RESERVOIR STORAGE CAPACITY (million kwh)	—	—	—	—	—	—	—	

SUPPLEMENTARY DATA FOR 1964

Transmission lines, 100 kv+ (km): 8
Households served (thousands): 426
Revenues per kwh (U.S. cents) — Total: 2.7
  Residential: Railways:
  Industry: (1962) 2.0   Lighting: 13.8
Population (thousands): 3594

Sources of data:
UN. *Stat. yrbk.*
UN. ECAFE. *Elec. power.*
Department of Commerce and Industry. *Hong Kong Government Gazette.*
United Kingdom. Colonial Office. *Hong Kong* (Annual Report).

Other characteristics of plants and systems:

The island is served by the Hong Kong Electric Company, Ltd., Kowloon City and the New Territories by the China Light and Power Company, Ltd. A new firm, the Peninsula Electric Power Company, was formed recently to provide additional generating facilities for the system operated by China Light and Power. The number of customers indicates that power is supplied to perhaps half the people of the colony. The fuel oil required for power generation is entirely imported.

HUNGARY

SUPPLY AND USE (million kwh)	1958	1959	1960	1961	1962	1963	1964	1965
PRODUCTION (Utilities & industries)								
Total (Gross)	6479	7093	7617	8382	9119	9665	10580	
(Net)	5877	6441	6904	7566	8216	8676	9535	
Hydro	48	79	94	82	82	81	74	
Conventional thermal	6431	7014	7523	8300	9037	9584	10506	
Nuclear	—	—	—	—	—	—	—	
Geothermal	—	—	—	—	—	—	—	
PRODUCTION (Utilities only)								
Total (Gross)	5386	5958	6511	7207	7904	8486	9379	
(Net)	4898	5423	5916	6529	7146	7660	8487	
Hydro	48	79	94	82	82	81	74	
Conventional thermal	5338	5879	6417	7125	7822	8405	9305	
Nuclear	—	—	—	—	—	—	—	
Geothermal	—	—	—	—	—	—	—	
NET IMPORTS	333	360	536	498	562	930	1081	
SUPPLY (Gross)	6812	7453	8153	8880	9681	10595	11661	
(Net)	6210	6801	7440	8064	8778	9606	10616	
CONSUMPTION	5538	6096	6686	7314	7979	8725	9639	
Transport	246	267	275	292	324	371	415e	
Domestic sector	1022	1133	1296	1445	1637	1967	2332e	
Industry	4270	4696	5115	5577	6018	6387	6892e	
LOSS AND USE	672	705	754	750	799	881	977	

PLANT (thousand kw)

	1958	1959	1960	1961	1962	1963	1964	1965
CAPACITY (Utilities & industries)								
Total	1337	1428	1465	1575	1647	1785	1908	
Hydro	12	17	19	19	19	20	21	
Conventional thermal	1325	1411	1446	1556	1628	1765	1887	
Nuclear	—	—	—	—	—	—	—	
Geothermal	—	—	—	—	—	—	—	
CAPACITY (Utilities only)								
Total	1056	1043	1164	1260	1325	1472	1576	
Hydro	12	17	19	19	19	20	21	
Conventional thermal	1044	1026	1145	1241	1306	1452	1555	
Nuclear	—	—	—	—	—	—	—	
Geothermal	—	—	—	—	—	—	—	

FUEL CONSUMPTION (Utilities only)	1958	1959	1960	1961	1962	1963	1964	1965
Coal (mmt)	--	624	662	737	850	1003	1173	
Low grade coal (mmt)	4852	5337	5793	6359	7205	7598	7892	
Lignite (mmt)	2718	2798	2938	3077	3091	2877	2930	
Fuel oils (mmt)	52	53	98	177	174	205	427	
Natural gas (Tcals)	—	699	532	245	178	1386	1503	
Manufactured gas (Tcals)	—	—	3	2	2	—	—	
Total (Tcals)	22401	23876	25549	27417	29817	31979	35366	
RESERVOIR STORAGE CAPACITY (million kwh)	—	—	—	—	—	—	—	

SUPPLEMENTARY DATA FOR 1964

Transmission lines, 100 kv+ (km): 3737
Households served (thousands): 2420
Revenues per kwh (U.S. cents) — Total:
  Residential: Railways:
  Industry: Lighting: 4.3
Population (thousands): 10120

Other characteristics of plants and systems:

    All undertakings engaged in the production and public distribution of electricity belong to the government of Hungary and fall within the jurisdiction of the Nehezipari Miniszterium. The entire country is served by an integrated network which is interconnected with the networks of Yugoslavia, Czechoslovakia, and the Soviet Union.

Sources of data:
  UCPTE. *Réseau.* UN. *Stat. yrbk.*
  UN. ECE. *Ann. bull. of elec. energy stat.*
  ———. *Org. of elec. power services.*
  UNIPEDE. *L'écon. élec.* ———. *Réseaux de transport.*
  ———. *Statistiques.*
  Central Statistical Office. *Statistical yearbook.*

ICELAND

SUPPLY AND USE (million kwh)	1958	1959	1960	1961	1962	1963	1964	1965
PRODUCTION (Utilities & industries)								
Total (Gross)	460	499	551	604	621	656	681	
(Net)	--	--	--	--	--	--	--	
Hydro	437	473	526	579	596	632	656	
Conventional thermal	23	26	25	25	25	24	25	
Nuclear	—	—	—	—	—	—	—	
Geothermal	—	—	—	—	—	—	—	
PRODUCTION (Utilities only)								
Total (Gross)	445	484	536	589	606	641	666	
(Net)	--	--	--	--	--	--	--	
Hydro	431	470	523	576	593	629	653	
Conventional thermal	14	14	13	13	13	12	13	
Nuclear	—	—	—	—	—	—	—	
Geothermal	—	—	—	—	—	—	—	
NET IMPORTS	—	—	—	—	—	—	—	
SUPPLY (Gross)	460	499	551	604	621	656	681	
(Net)	--	--	--	--	--	--	--	
CONSUMPTION	376	410	452	507	520	545	573	
Transport	—	—	—	—	—	—	—	
Domestic sector	210	228	237	284	304	322	326	
Industry	166	182	215	223	216	223	247	
LOSS AND USE	84	89	99	97	101	111	108	

PLANT (thousand kw)

	1958	1959	1960	1961	1962	1963	1964	1965
CAPACITY (Utilities & industries)								
Total	108	140	142	147	148	166	170	
Hydro	83	109	109	109	109	126	127	
Conventional thermal	25	31	33	38	39	40	43	
Nuclear	—	—	—	—	—	—	—	
Geothermal	—	—	—	—	—	—	—	
CAPACITY (Utilities only)								
Total	95	121	122	128	128	147	149	
Hydro	79	105	105	105	105	122	123	
Conventional thermal	16	16	17	23	23	25	26	
Nuclear	—	—	—	—	—	—	—	
Geothermal	—	—	—	—	—	—	—	

FUEL CONSUMPTION (Utilities only)

	1958	1959	1960	1961	1962	1963	1964	1965
Diesel oil (mmt)	4	4	5	5	4	4	4	
Total (Tcals)	46	44	50	45	48	36	38	
RESERVOIR STORAGE CAPACITY (million kwh)	4	25	25	25	25	25	25	

SUPPLEMENTARY DATA FOR 1964

Transmission lines, 100 kv + (km): 51
Households served (thousands): - -
Revenues per kwh (U.S. cents) — Total:
  Residential: (1965) 2.8 Railways:
  Industry: (1965) 2.0 Lighting: 2.1
Population (thousands): 189

Sources of data:
Benn Bros. *Elec. undertakings.* UN. *Stat. yrbk.*
UN. ECE. *Ann. bull. of elec. energy stat.*
UNIPEDE. *Statistiques.*
The State Electricity Authority. *Orkumál frá rafortumálastjóra.*

Other characteristics of plants and systems:

The Sog Hydro-Electric Development is the principal producer of electric power. Most of its output is wholesaled to the State, to municipal distribution systems, and to the fertilizer plant. Service is provided to most of the people of Iceland through a number of independent regional networks distributed along the country's coast.

INDIA

SUPPLY AND USE (million kwh)	1958	1959	1960	1961	1962	1963	1964	1965
PRODUCTION (Utilities & industries)								
Total (Gross)	15415	17794	20041	22951	26227	30305	33129	
(Net)	14885e	17193	19348	22137	25314	29357	31827	
Hydro	5861	7040	7847	9824	11814	13973	14807	
Conventional thermal	9554	10754	12194	13127	14413	16332	18322	
Nuclear	—	—	—	—	—	—	—	
Geothermal	—	—	—	—	—	—	—	
PRODUCTION (Utilities only)								
Total (Gross)	12994	15032	16937	19670	22365	25498	29543	
(Net)	--	--	--	--	--	--	--	
Hydro	5848	7027	7837	9814	11804	13957	13593	
Conventional thermal	7146	8005	9100	9856	10561	11541	15950	
Nuclear	—	—	—	—	—	—	—	
Geothermal	—	—	—	—	—	—	—	
NET IMPORTS	—	—	—	—	—	—	—	
SUPPLY (Gross)	15415	17794	20041	22951	26227	30305	33129	
(Net)	14885e	17193	19348	22137	25314	29357	31827	
CONSUMPTION	13104	15123	16811	19362	22069	25494	27700	
Transport	674	756	849	1000e	1150e	1296	1440	
Domestic sector	3054	3501	3802	4318	4845	5392	5802	
Industry	9376	10866	12160	14044	16074	18806	20458e	
LOSS AND USE	1781	2070	2537	2775	3245	3863	4127	

PLANT (thousand kw)

	1958	1959	1960	1961	1962	1963	1964	1965
CAPACITY (Utilities & industries)								
Total	4324	4790	5579	6046	6906	7623	8371	
Hydro	1365	1486	1855	2243	2919	3170	3331	
Conventional thermal	2959	3304	3724	3803	3987	4453	5040	
Nuclear	—	—	—	—	—	—	—	
Geothermal	—	—	—	—	—	—	—	
CAPACITY (Utilities only)								
Total	3512	3873	4563	5034	5779	6201	7336	
Hydro	1362	1530	1852	2240	2916	3148	3328	
Conventional thermal	2150	2343	2711	2794	2863	3053	4008	
Nuclear	—	—	—	—	—	—	—	
Geothermal	—	—	—	—	—	—	—	

FUEL CONSUMPTION (Utilities only)

	1958	1959	1960	1961	1962	1963	1964	1965
Coal (mmt)	4960	5524	6424	6936	7696	8457	8987	
Lignite (mmt)	—	—	—	—	166	1000	1580	
Diesel oil (mmt)	91	100	112	118	119	113	118	
Fuel oil (mmt)	160	235	276	300	300	302	291	
Natural gas (Tcals)	—	—	—	—	—	--	580	
Total (Tcals)	36792	41363	48076	51891	57225	--	80717	
RESERVOIR STORAGE CAPACITY (million kwh)	--	--	--	--	--	--	--	

SUPPLEMENTARY DATA FOR 1964

Transmission lines, 100 kv+ (km): 22757
Households served (thousands): 5600
Revenues per kwh (U.S. cents) — Total: 1.6
  Residential: 3.6 Railways:
  Industry: 1.1 Lighting: 4.0
Population (thousands): 471624

Sources of data:
UN. *Stat. yrbk.* UN. ECAFE. *Elec. power.*
UNIPEDE. *Statistiques.*
Central Water and Power Commission. *Public electricity supply, all India statistics.*

Other characteristics of plants and systems:
Responsibility for the electric power industry rests jointly with the Central Government and the State Governments. About 20% of the industry is in the hands of private licensees. Service is provided mainly through regional networks and local systems, but is available to only a very small part of India's population. On the basis of the number of customers served, it appears that only about five per cent of the people of India are supplied with electricity. At the end of the Third Plan period, only 54,000 of the country's 561,000 cities, towns and villages were electrified. Significant quantities of electricity are privately generated, primarily for their own use, by the iron and steel, cement, textile and sugar industries, and by the Indian railways.

INDONESIA

SUPPLY AND USE (million kwh)	1958	1959	1960	1961	1962	1963	1964	1965
PRODUCTION (Utilities & industries)								
Total (Gross)	1127	1212	1260	1353	1588	--	--	
(Net)	--	--	--	--	--	--	--	
Hydro	--	--	--	--	--	--	--	
Conventional thermal	--	--	--	--	--	--	--	
Nuclear	—	—	—	—	—	—	—	
Geothermal	—	—	—	—	—	—	—	
PRODUCTION (Utilities only)								
Total (Gross)	1005	1080	1161	1205	1335	1548	--	
(Net)	--	--	--	--	--	--	--	
Hydro	751	785	770e	774	777	--	--	
Conventional thermal	254	295	391	431	558	--	--	
Nuclear	—	—	—	—	—	—	—	
Geothermal	—	—	—	—	—	—	—	
NET IMPORTS	—	—	—	—	—	—	—	
SUPPLY (Gross)	1127	1212	1260	1353	1588	--	--	
(Net)	--	--	--	--	--	--	--	
CONSUMPTION	894	875	935	959	--	--	--	
Transport	—	—	—	—	—	—	—	
Domestic sector	671	643	695	708	772	--	--	
Industry	223	232	240	251	--	--	--	
LOSS AND USE	233	337	325	394	--	--	--	

PLANT (thousand kw)

	1958	1959	1960	1961	1962	1963	1964	1965
CAPACITY (Utilities & industries)								
Total	351	363	391	404	--	--	--	
Hydro	--	--	--	--	--	--	--	
Conventional thermal	--	--	--	--	--	--	--	
Nuclear	—	—	—	—	—	—	—	
Geothermal	—	—	—	—	—	—	—	
CAPACITY (Utilities only)								
Total	266	276	308	311	358	391	--	
Hydro	132	143	169	166	174	188	--	
Conventional thermal	134	133	139	145	184	203	--	
Nuclear	—	—	—	—	—	—	—	
Geothermal	—	—	—	—	—	—	—	

FUEL CONSUMPTION (Utilities only)

	1958	1959	1960	1961	1962	1963	1964	1965
Coal (mmt)	11	9	--	12	--	--	--	
Diesel oil (mmt)	--	101	--	131	--	--	--	
Fuel oil (mmt)	35	34	--	33	--	--	--	
Total (Tcals)	--	1498	--	--	2982	--	--	
RESERVOIR STORAGE CAPACITY (million kwh)	--	--	--	--	--	--	--	

SUPPLEMENTARY DATA FOR 1964

Transmission lines, 100 kv+ (km) :   —
Households served (thousands) : (1962)   755
Revenues per kwh (U.S. cents) — Total:
  Residential: Railways:
  Industry: (1961) 3.4   Lighting:
Population (thousands) :   102200

Sources of data:
  UN. *Stat. yrbk.* UN. ECAFE. *Elec. power.*
  Biro Pusat Statistik. *Statistical pocketbook of Indonesia.*
  Service de l'Expansion Economique en Indonesie. "Le
    développement de l'énergie en Indonesie."

Other characteristics of plants and systems:

    The State Electricity Enterprise of the Indonesian government owns and operates regional systems in 13 different areas in Indonesia. Most of the country's electricity is thus generated in publicly owned plants, but industrial establishments also generate electricity, mainly for their own use. Data on average use per domestic consumer and on number of customers indicate that less than 10% of the people of Indonesia are supplied with electricity.

IRAN

SUPPLY AND USE (million kwh)	1958	1959	1960	1961	1962	1963	1964	1965
PRODUCTION (Utilities & industries)								
Total (Gross)	720	907	1461	1855	1925	2150	2250	
(Net)	--	--	--	--	--	--	--	
Hydro	5e	5	5	8	130	250	270	
Conventional thermal	715e	902e	1456	1847	1795	1900	1980	
Nuclear	—	—	—	—	—	—	—	
Geothermal	—	—	—	—	—	—	—	
PRODUCTION (Utilities only)								
Total (Gross)	362	442	860	1164	1235	--	--	
(Net)	--	--	--	--	--	--	--	
Hydro	5e	5	5	8	130	250	270	
Conventional thermal	357e	437	855	1156	1105	--	--	
Nuclear	—	—	—	—	—	—	—	
Geothermal	—	—	—	—	—	—	—	
NET IMPORTS	—	—	—	—	—	—	—	
SUPPLY (Gross)	720	907	1461	1855	1925	2150	2250	
(Net)	--	--	--	--	--	--	--	
CONSUMPTION	--	--	--	--	--	--	--	
Transport	—	—	—	—	—	—	—	
Domestic sector	--	--	--	--	--	--	--	
Industry	--	--	--	--	--	--	--	
LOSS AND USE	--	--	--	--	--	--	--	

PLANT (thousand kw)

CAPACITY (Utilities & industries)	1958	1959	1960	1961	1962	1963	1964	1965
Total	--	445	595	670	810	845	979	
Hydro	2	2	2	77	207	233e	233	
Conventional thermal	--	443	593	593	603	612	746	
Nuclear	—	—	—	—	—	—	—	
Geothermal	—	—	—	—	—	—	—	
CAPACITY (Utilities only)								
Total	156	171	275	543	727	773	790	
Hydro	2e	2	2	77	207	233e	233	
Conventional thermal	154	169	273	466	520	540	557	
Nuclear	—	—	—	—	—	—	—	
Geothermal	—	—	—	—	—	—	—	

FUEL CONSUMPTION (Utilities only)

	1958	1959	1960	1961	1962	1963	1964	1965
Total (Tcals)	--	--	--	--	--	--	--	
RESERVOIR STORAGE CAPACITY (million kwh)	—	—	—	—	—	—	—	

SUPPLEMENTARY DATA FOR 1964

Transmission lines, 100 kv+ (km): (1962) 326
Households served (thousands): --
Revenues per kwh (U.S. cents) — Total:
  Residential: Railways:
  Industry: Lighting: 5.6
Population (thousands): 23900

Sources of data:
Benn Bros. *Elec. undertakings.* UN. *Stat. yrbk.*
UN. ECAFE. *Elec. power.* US. FPC. *World power data.*
Ministry of Industry and Mines. *Industry and mines statistical yearbook.*
US. Bureau of Mines. *The petroleum industry of Iran.*
Miller-Freeman Publications. *Energy international.*

Other characteristics of plants and systems:

In March 1964, the Government of Iran established the Ministry of Water and Power to take over all functions and responsibilities of the Iran Electric Authority. The principal generators of power are the Khuzestan Water and Power Authority and the Teheran Electricity Department.

208

IRAQ

SUPPLY AND USE (million kwh)	1958	1959	1960	1961	1962	1963	1964	1965
PRODUCTION (Utilities & industries)								
Total (Gross)	--	--	--	--	--	--	--	
(Net)	--	--	--	--	--	--	--	
Hydro	—	—	—	—	—	—	—	
Conventional thermal	--	--	--	--	--	--	--	
Nuclear	—	—	—	—	—	—	—	
Geothermal	—	—	—	—	—	—	—	
PRODUCTION (Utilities only)								
Total (Gross)	700e	830e	960	1050	1120	1200e	1300e	
(Net)	--	--	--	--	--	--	--	
Hydro	—	—	—	—	—	—	—	
Conventional thermal	700e	830e	960e	1050e	1120e	1200e	1300e	
Nuclear	—	—	—	—	—	—	—	
Geothermal	—	—	—	—	—	—	—	
NET IMPORTS	—	—	—	—	—	—	—	
SUPPLY (Gross)	700e	830e	960	1050	1120	1200e	1300e	
(Net)	--	--	--	--	--	--	--	
CONSUMPTION	626	736	852	934	995	1063	1166	
Transport	—	—	—	—	—	—	—	
Domestic sector	--	--	327	353	430	365	439	
Industry	--	--	525	581	565	698	727	
LOSS AND USE	74e	94e	108e	116e	125e	137e	134e	

PLANT (thousand kw)

CAPACITY (Utilities & industries)								
Total	--	--	--	--	--	--	--	
Hydro	—	—	—	—	—	—	—	
Conventional thermal	--	--	--	--	--	--	--	
Nuclear	—	—	—	—	—	—	—	
Geothermal	—	—	—	—	—	—	—	
CAPACITY (Utilities only)								
Total	--	275	275	430	430	430	457	
Hydro	—	—	—	—	—	—	—	
Conventional thermal	--	275	275	430	430	430	457	
Nuclear	—	—	—	—	—	—	—	
Geothermal	—	—	—	—	—	—	—	

FUEL CONSUMPTION (Utilities only)

	1958	1959	1960	1961	1962	1963	1964	
Fuel oil (mmt)	--	--	--	86	--	--	--	
Diesel oil (mmt)	--	--	--	76	--	--	--	
Natural gas (Tcals)	--	--	--	371	--	--	--	
Total (Tcals)	--	--	--	--	--	--	--	
RESERVOIR STORAGE CAPACITY (million kwh)	—	—	—	—	—	—	—	

SUPPLEMENTARY DATA FOR 1964

Transmission lines, 100 kv+ (km): —
Households served (thousands): --
Revenues per kwh (U.S. cents) — Total:
    Residential: Railways:
    Industry: 16.4   Lighting:
Population (thousands): 7910

Other characteristics of plants and systems:

The principal producer of electricity in Iraq appears to be the National Electricity Administration (NEA), established in October 1958. NEA supplies power in bulk to Baghdad Electricity Services and to Mosul Electricity and Water Board.

Sources of data:
Benn Bros. *Elec. undertakings.* UN. *Stat. yrbk.*
US. *Foreign serv. desp.* US. FPC. *World power data.*
US. Department of Commerce. Overseas Business Reports
    Series. *Basic data on the economy of Iraq.*
Ministry of Planning. Central Bureau of Statistics.
    The monthly industrial survey.
——. *Quarterly bulletin of statistics.*
——. *Statistical abstract of Iraq.*

IRELAND

SUPPLY AND USE (million kwh)	1958	1959	1960	1961	1962	1963	1964	1965
PRODUCTION (Utilities & industries)								
Total (Gross)	1897	2096	2262	2453	2715	2900	3368	
(Net)	1816	1997	2162	2337	2583	2758	3082	
Hydro	782	747	932	737	660	656	784	
Conventional thermal	1115	1349	1330	1716	2055	2244	2584	
Nuclear	—	—	—	—	—	—	—	
Geothermal	—	—	—	—	—	—	—	
PRODUCTION (Utilities only)								
Total (Gross)	1895	2094	2260	2450	2709	2894	3231	
(Net)	—	1995	2160	2334	2577	2751	3072	
Hydro	782	747	932	737	660	656	783	
Conventional thermal	1113	1347	1328	1713	2049	2238	2448	
Nuclear	—	—	—	—	—	—	—	
Geothermal	—	—	—	—	—	—	—	
NET IMPORTS	4	1	—	—	—	—	—	
SUPPLY (Gross)	1901	2097	2262	2453	2715	2900	3368	
(Net)	1820	1998	2162	2337	2583	2758	3082	
CONSUMPTION	1549	1692	1864	2005	2239	2376	2683	
Transport	—	—	—	—	—	—	—	
Domestic sector	1089	1141	1247	1344	1529	1616	1836	
Industry	460	551	617	661	710	760	847	
LOSS AND USE	271	306	298	332	344	382	399	

PLANT (thousand kw)

	1958	1959	1960	1961	1962	1963	1964	1965
CAPACITY (Utilities & industries)								
Total	688	688	724	725	766	852	--	
Hydro	219	219	219	219	219	219	--	
Conventional thermal	469	469	505	506e	547e	633e	--	
Nuclear	—	—	—	—	—	—	—	
Geothermal	—	—	—	—	—	—	—	
CAPACITY (Utilities only)								
Total	688	688	724	724	764	850	890	
Hydro	219	219	219	219	219	219	219	
Conventional thermal	469	469	505	505	545	631	671	
Nuclear	—	—	—	—	—	—	—	
Geothermal	—	—	—	—	—	—	—	

FUEL CONSUMPTION (Utilities only)

	1958	1959	1960	1961	1962	1963	1964	1965
Coal (mmt)	154	237	247	141	73	65	55	
Peat (mmt)	728	875	1092	1354	1630	1573	1551	
Fuel oils (mmt)	--	78	44	175	272	350	405	
Total (Tcals)	--	4101	5232	6548	7792	8347	8981	
RESERVOIR STORAGE CAPACITY (million kwh)	56	56	56	61	61	61	61	

SUPPLEMENTARY DATA FOR 1964

Transmission lines, 100 kv+ (km) : 3277
Households served (thousands) : 620
Revenues per kwh (U.S. cents) — Total: 2.4
  Residential: Railways:
  Industry: 1.6   Lighting: 2.3
Population (thousands) : 2864

Other characteristics of plants and systems:

The generation, transmission, distribution and sale of electricity in Ireland have been nationalized since 1927, and are under the control of the Electricity Supply Board. A national network carries electricity to all parts of the country, but the number of consumers, related to Ireland's population, indicates that the country is still less than fully electrified. Ireland is the only country except the Soviet Union that makes extensive use of peat in the generation of electric power.

Sources of data:
Benn Bros. *Elec. undertakings.* UN. *Stat. yrbk.*
UN. ECE. *Ann. bull. of elec. energy stat.*
_____. *Org. of elec. power services.*
UNIPEDE. *L'écon. élec.* _____. *Réseaux de transport.*
_____. *Statistiques.* Electricity Supply Board, *Annual report.*
The Economic Research Institute. J. L. Booth, *Fuel and power in Ireland. Part II: Electricity and turf.*

ISRAEL

SUPPLY AND USE (million kwh)	1958	1959	1960	1961	1962	1963	1964	1965
PRODUCTION (Utilities & industries)								
Total (Gross)	1766	1968	2313	2546	2936	3160	3625	
(Net)	--	--	--	--	--	--	--	
Hydro	—	—	—	—	—	—	—	
Conventional thermal	1766	1968	2313	2546	2936	3160	3625	
Nuclear	—	—	—	—	—	—	—	
Geothermal	—	—	—	—	—	—	—	
PRODUCTION (Utilities only)								
Total (Gross)	--	--	--	2433	2807	3042	3543	
(Net)	--	--	--	--	--	--	--	
Hydro	—	—	—	—	—	—	—	
Conventional thermal	--	--	--	2433	2807	3042	3543	
Nuclear	—	—	—	—	—	—	—	
Geothermal	—	—	—	—	—	—	—	
NET IMPORTS								
SUPPLY (Gross)	1766	1968	2313	2546	2936	3160	3625	
(Net)	--	--	--	--	--	--	--	
CONSUMPTION	1496	1665	1970	2157	2498	2692	3098	
Transport	—	—	—	—	—	—	—	
Domestic sector	964	1035	1200	1287	1504	1655	1890	
Industry	532	630	770	870	994	1037	1208	
LOSS AND USE	270	303	343	389	438	468	527	
PLANT (thousand kw)								
CAPACITY (Utilities & industries)								
Total	380e	430e	430e	505e	580e	665e	740e	
Hydro	—	—	—	—	—	—	—	
Conventional thermal	380e	430e	430e	505e	580e	665e	740e	
Nuclear	—	—	—	—	—	—	—	
Geothermal	—	—	—	—	—	—	—	
CAPACITY (Utilities only)								
Total	360	410	410	485	560	645	720	
Hydro	—	—	—	—	—	—	—	
Conventional thermal	360	410	410	485	560	645	720	
Nuclear	—	—	—	—	—	—	—	
Geothermal	—	—	—	—	—	—	—	
FUEL CONSUMPTION (Utilities only)								
Fuel oils (mmt)	502	546	636	685	772	834	961	
Total (Tcals)	4769	5187	6042	6508	7334	7923	9130	
RESERVOIR STORAGE CAPACITY (million kwh)	—	—	—	—	—	—	—	

SUPPLEMENTARY DATA FOR 1964

Transmission lines, 100 kv+ (km) :   - -
Households served (thousands) :   745
Revenues per kwh (U.S. cents) — Total:
  Residential: Railways:
  Industry: Lighting:
Population (thousands) :   2477

Other characteristics of plants and systems:

Israel Electric Corporation, which is ninety-eight per cent government-owned, produces the country's entire supply of electricity. Fuel oil, imported or derived from imported crude, is the source of the country's electricity. Power is available to most of the population of Israel.

Sources of data:

UN. *Stat. yrbk.* US. *Foreign serv. desp.*
Central Bureau of Statistics. *Statistical abstract of Israel.*
Electricity Corporation, Ltd. *Annual report.*
Israel National Committee of the World Power Conference.
    Energy resources and power development in Israel.
Miller-Freeman Publications. *Energy international.*

ITALY

SUPPLY AND USE (million kwh)	1958	1959	1960	1961	1962	1963	1964	1965
PRODUCTION (Utilities & industries)								
Total (Gross)	45492	49350	56240	60565	64859	71344	76738	
(Net)	44684	48421	55282	59360	63054	69723	74618	
Hydro	35953	38398	46106	41982	39264	46107	39328	
Conventional thermal	7609	8873	8030	16291	23249	22487	32482	
Nuclear	—	—	—	—	—	323	2401	
Geothermal	1930	2079	2104	2292	2346	2427	2527	
PRODUCTION (Utilities only)								
Total (Gross)	37576	40104	43880	47292	50636	54217	57955	
(Net)	36928	39439	43230	46335	49202	53075	56399	
Hydro	30010	32232	37552	33076	30684	37578	31860	
Conventional thermal	5636	5793	4224	11924	17606	13889	21167	
Nuclear	—	—	—	—	—	323	2401	
Geothermal	1930	2079	2104	2292	2346	2427	2527	
NET IMPORTS	137	189	−128	168	1269	1300	1002	
SUPPLY (Gross)	45629	49539	56112	60733	66128	72644	77740	
(Net)	44821	48610	55154	59528	64323	71023	75620	
CONSUMPTION	38384	42090	47584	51275	56281	61781	66894	
Transport	2769	2964	3197	3279	3467	3533	3357	
Domestic sector	9663	10520	11737	13153	15016	16830	19157	
Industry	25952	28606	32650	34843	37798	41418	44380	
LOSS AND USE	6437	6520	7570	8253	8042	9242	8726	
PLANT (thousand kw)								
CAPACITY (Utilities & industries)								
Total	15079	16511	17686	18441	19586	21193	23297	
Hydro	11607	11940	12612	12833	13282	13737	13955	
Conventional thermal	3179	4278	4787	5298	5992	6922	8455	
Nuclear	—	—	—	—	—	210	556	
Geothermal	293	293	287	310	312	324	331	
CAPACITY (Utilities only)								
Total	12586	13703	14689	14858	15396	16583	18300	
Hydro	10136	10440	11076	10876	11077	11528	11723	
Conventional thermal	2157	2970	3326	3672	4007	4521	5690	
Nuclear	—	—	—	—	—	210	556	
Geothermal	293	293	287	310	312	324	331	
FUEL CONSUMPTION (Utilities only)								
Coal (mmt)	884	694	494	1040	1136	642	670	
Lignite (mmt)	544	1028	713	1563	1726	1365	1191	
Fuel oils (mmt)	689	685	555	1795	2855	2722	4464	
Natural gas (Tcals)	2657	2421	1362	2795	4098	770	600	
Total (Tcals)	15573	15607	11223	29780	43174	34338	50535	
RESERVOIR STORAGE CAPACITY (million kwh)	5566	5586	5953	6008	6076	6216	6382	

SUPPLEMENTARY DATA FOR 1964

Transmission lines, 100 kv+ (km): 39465
Households served (thousands): 13870
Revenues per kwh (U.S. cents) — Total:
Residential: 3.7   Railways: 0.7
Industry: 1.5   Lighting: 6.4
Population (thousands): 51137

Other characteristics of plants and systems:

L'Ente Nazionale per l'Energia Elettrica (Enel), a public enterprise, now supplies the great bulk of Italy's electricity. Most of Italy is served by an integrated network that is being extended to Sicily, Sardinia and Corsica, and also is interconnected with the systems of each of the neighboring countries. In addition to ordinary facilities for power generation, Italy boasts the world's first geothermal plant, and, as of 1964, was still the leader in output of geothermal electricity. Although the national network does not reach all parts of Italy, the number of meters in use indicates that most of the people of Italy are supplied with electricity. In the generation of conventional thermal power, Italy depends mainly upon imported fuel oils.

Sources of data:

EEC. Energy stat., 1950-1965. UCPTE. Réseau.
UN. Stat. yrbk.
UN. ECE. Ann. bull. of elec. energy stat.
———. Elec. power situation
———. Org. of elec. power services.
UNIPEDE. L'écon. élec. ———. Statistiques.

SUPPLY AND USE (million kwh)	1958	1959	1960	1961	1962	1963	1964	1965
PRODUCTION (Utilities & industries)								
Total (Gross)	41	52	67	93	118	155	183	
(Net)	--	--	--	--	--	--	--	
Hydro	–	5	59	73	90	107	96	
Conventional thermal	41	47	8	20	28	48	87	
Nuclear	–	–	–	–	–	–	–	
Geothermal	–	–	–	–	–	–	–	
PRODUCTION (Utilities only)								
Total (Gross)	41	52	67	93	118	155	183	
(Net)	--	--	--	--	--	--	--	
Hydro	–	5	59	73	90	107	96	
Conventional thermal	41	47	8	20	28	48	87	
Nuclear	–	–	–	–	–	–	–	
Geothermal	–	–	–	–	–	–	–	
NET IMPORTS	–	–	–	–	–	–	–	
SUPPLY (Gross)	41	52	67	93	118	155	183	
(Net)	--	--	--	--	--	--	--	
CONSUMPTION	--	--	50	79	102	131	158	
Transport	--	–	–	–	–	–	–	
Domestic sector	--	--	30	42	57	72	83	
Industry	--	--	20	37	45	59	75	
LOSS AND USE	--	--	17	14	16	24	25	

PLANT (thousand kw)

	1958	1959	1960	1961	1962	1963	1964	1965
CAPACITY (Utilities & industries)								
Total	--	--	38	43	43	52	67	
Hydro	–	--	19	19	19	19	19	
Conventional thermal	--	--	19	24	24	33	48	
Nuclear	–	–	–	–	–	–	–	
Geothermal	–	–	–	–	–	–	–	
CAPACITY (Utilities only)								
Total	--	--	38	43	43	52	67	
Hydro	–	--	19	19	19	19	19	
Conventional thermal	--	--	19	24	24	33	48	
Nuclear	–	–	–	–	–	–	–	
Geothermal	–	–	–	–	–	–	–	

FUEL CONSUMPTION (Utilities only)

	1958	1959	1960	1961	1962	1963	1964	1965
Total (Tcals)	--	--	--	--	--	--	--	
RESERVOIR STORAGE CAPACITY (million kwh)	--	--	--	--	--	--	--	

SUPPLEMENTARY DATA FOR 1964

Transmission lines, 100 kv+ (km): –
Households served (thousands): 34
Revenues per kwh (U.S. cents) — Total:
 Residential: Railways:
 Industry: Lighting: 10.1
Population (thousands): 3750

Other characteristics of plants and systems:

The Société d'Energie Electrique de la Côte d'Ivoire, of mixed ownership, serves most of the Ivory Coast. Outside of Abidjan, service is provided mainly by small, isolated diesel plants. A very small fraction of the country's population has electricity available.

Sources of data:
EEC. *Yrbk. Overseas Assoc.*
Inst. de la Stat. *Données statistiques.*
UN. *Stat. yrbk.*

JAMAICA

SUPPLY AND USE (million kwh)	1958	1959	1960	1961	1962	1963	1964	1965
PRODUCTION (Utilities & industries)								
Total (Gross)	383	454	514	592	627	652	715	
(Net)	--	--	--	--	--	--	--	
Hydro	85	93	126	112	121	138	153	
Conventional thermal	298	361	388	480	506	514	562	
Nuclear	—	—	—	—	—	—	—	
Geothermal	—	—	—	—	—	—	—	
PRODUCTION (Utilities only)								
Total (Gross)	208	245	262	305	332	375	423	
(Net)	--	--	--	--	--	--	--	
Hydro	85	93	126	112	121	138	153	
Conventional thermal	123	152	136	193	211	237	270	
Nuclear	—	—	—	—	—	—	—	
Geothermal	—	—	—	—	—	—	—	
NET IMPORTS	—	—	—	—	—	—	—	
SUPPLY (Gross)	383	454	514	592	627	652	715	
(Net)	--	--	--	--	--	--	--	
CONSUMPTION	348	417	468	547	581	608	664	
Transport	—	—	—	—	—	—	—	
Domestic sector	130	159	166	207	240	262	300	
Industry	218	258	302	340	341	346e	364e	
LOSS AND USE	35e	37e	46e	45e	46	44	51	

PLANT (thousand kw)

	1958	1959	1960	1961	1962	1963	1964	1965
CAPACITY (Utilities & industries)								
Total	110	146	150	168	183	186	--	
Hydro	13e	13	22	20	21	21	19e	
Conventional thermal	97	133	128	148	162	165	--	
Nuclear	—	—	—	—	—	—	—	
Geothermal	—	—	—	—	—	—	—	
CAPACITY (Utilities only)								
Total	64	64	68	86	105	105	112	
Hydro	13	13	22	20	21	21	19	
Conventional thermal	51	51	46	66	84	84	93	
Nuclear	—	—	—	—	—	—	—	
Geothermal	—	—	—	—	—	—	—	

FUEL CONSUMPTION (Utilities only)

	1958	1959	1960	1961	1962	1963	1964	1965
Total (Tcals)	--	--	--	--	--	--	--	
RESERVOIR STORAGE CAPACITY (million kwh)	--	--	--	--	--	--	--	

SUPPLEMENTARY DATA FOR 1964

Transmission lines, 100 kv+ (km): —
Households served (thousands) : (1963) 60
Revenues per kwh (U.S. cents) — Total: 2.7
  Residential: 3.7   Railways:
  Industry: 2.6   Lighting:
Population (thousands) : 1742

Other characteristics of plants and systems:

The Jamaica Public Service Co., Ltd., privately owned, operates a network which supplies power to much of the island, mainly at 69 KV and 34.5 KV. Its principal plant, at Kingston, is an oil-burning steam plant, with a capacity of 41 MW. Service appears to be provided to no more than a quarter of Jamaica's population.

Sources of data:
Benn Bros. *Elec. undertakings.* UN. *Stat. yrbk.*
UN. ECLA. *Estud. econ.*
Department of Statistics. *Annual statistical abstract.*
Electricity Authority. *Electricity in Jamaica.*

SUPPLY AND USE (million kwh)	1958	1959	1960	1961	1962	1963	1964	1965
PRODUCTION (Utilities & industries)								
Total (Gross)	85423	99105	115472	132037	140369	160212	179592	
(Net)	83923	96818	112173	128567	135669	154155	172103	
Hydro	60772	61706	58471	67956	62373	69167	68957	
Conventional thermal	24651	37399	57001	64081	77996	91042	110633	
Nuclear	—	—	—	—	—	3	2	
Geothermal	—	—	—	—	—	—	—	
PRODUCTION (Utilities only)								
Total (Gross)	74603	86752	101683	116821	124005	141288	158160	
(Net)	--	--	--	--	--	--	--	
Hydro	55194	55949	53095	62425	57120	63568	63173	
Conventional thermal	19409	30803	48588	54396	66885	77720	94987	
Nuclear	—	—	—	—	—	—	—	
Geothermal	—	—	—	—	—	—	—	
NET IMPORTS	—	—	—	—	—	—	—	
SUPPLY (Gross)	85423	99105	115472	132037	140369	160212	179592	
(Net)	83923	96818	112173	128567	135669	154155	172103	
CONSUMPTION	72759	84485	99382	114613	121716	140387	158014	
Transport	4262	4543	4976	5431	5833	6435	7139	
Domestic sector	25807	29401	30651	37153	42157	48348	55130	
Industry	42690	50541	63755	72029	73726	85604	95745	
LOSS AND USE	11164	12333	12791	13954	13953	13768	14089	

PLANT (thousand kw)	1958	1959	1960	1961	1962	1963	1964	1965
CAPACITY (Utilities & industries)								
Total	18366	21243	23657	25954	29153	34295	38072	
Hydro	10797	11408	12678	13506	14137	15106	15629	
Conventional thermal	7569	9835	10979	12448	15016	19177	22431	
Nuclear	—	—	—	—	—	12	12	
Geothermal	—	—	—	—	—	—	—	
CAPACITY (Utilities only)								
Total	15777	18424	20649	22756	25506	30211	33729	
Hydro	9905	10513	11770	12576	13187	14109	14614	
Conventional thermal	5872	7911	8879	10180	12319	16102	19115	
Nuclear	—	—	—	—	—	—	—	
Geothermal	—	—	—	—	—	—	—	
FUEL CONSUMPTION (Utilities only)								
Coal, wet (mmt)	9581	13708	16600	17152	19056	20851	21557	
Diesel & light fuel oils (mmt)	20	32	32	34	43	66	57	
Crude & heavy fuel oils (mmt)	997	1495	4708	5688	7211	7593	11281	
Total (Tcals)	61258	69901	123476	163673	175651	204478	234739	
RESERVOIR STORAGE CAPACITY (million kwh)	--	--	--	--	--	--	--	

SUPPLEMENTARY DATA FOR 1964

Transmission lines, 100 kv+ (km): 35767
Households served (thousands): 21370
Revenues per kwh (U.S. cents) — Total: 1.7
  Residential: 3.4   Railways:
  Industry: 1.2   Lighting: 2.8
Population (thousands): 96906

Other characteristics of plants and systems:

Most of the electric power industry in Japan is under the control of nine private companies and the Electric Power Development Company, established jointly by the government and the nine companies for undertaking the construction and operation of large, remote and expensive hydroelectric projects. Integrated service is available throughout the country. The number of customers indicates that electricity is supplied to better than eighty per cent of the population. Substantial quantities of power are privately generated, especially by the iron and steel, pulp and paper, chemical and cement industries, and by the Japanese railways. Domestic coal still provides much of Japan's thermal electric power, but imported crude oil, and residual fuel oil obtained from imported crude, now provide about as much electricity as does Japanese coal.

Sources of data:

OECD. *Elec. ind. survey.*   UN. *Stat. yrbk.*
UN. ECAFE. *Elec. power.*   UNIPEDE. *Statistiques.*
Editions Techniques et Economiques. *Revue française de l'énergie.*
Belgium. Fédération Professionnelle des Producteurs et Distributeurs d'Electricité de Belgique. (FPE). *Annuaire statistique.*
Office of the Prime Minister. Bureau of Statistics. *Japan statistical yearbook.*
Overseas Electrical Industry Survey Institute, Inc. *Electric power industry in Japan.*
Miller Freeman Publications. *Energy international.*

SUPPLY AND USE (million kwh)	1958	1959	1960	1961	1962	1963	1964	1965
PRODUCTION (Utilities & industries)								
Total (Gross)	--	48	68	87	104	114	136	
(Net)	--	--	--	--	--	--	--	
Hydro	—	—	—	—	—	—	—	
Conventional thermal	--	48	68	87	104	114	136	
Nuclear	—	—	—	—	—	—	—	
Geothermal	—	—	—	—	—	—	—	
PRODUCTION (Utilities only)								
Total (Gross)	--	30	48	63	79	81	102	
(Net)	--	--	--	--	--	--	--	
Hydro	—	—	—	—	—	—	—	
Conventional thermal	--	30	48	63	79	81	102	
Nuclear	—	—	—	—	—	—	—	
Geothermal	—	—	—	—	—	—	—	
NET IMPORTS	—	—	—	—	—	—	—	
SUPPLY (Gross)	--	48	68	87	104	114	136	
(Net)	--	--	--	--	--	--	--	
CONSUMPTION	--	--	--	--	--	--	--	
Transport	—	—	—	—	—	—	—	
Domestic sector	--	--	--	--	--	--	--	
Industry	--	--	--	--	--	--	--	
LOSS AND USE	--	--	--	--	--	--	--	

PLANT (thousand kw)

CAPACITY (Utilities & industries)								
Total	--	--	--	--	--	41	41	
Hydro	—	—	—	—	—	—	—	
Conventional thermal	--	--	--	--	--	41	41	
Nuclear	—	—	—	—	—	—	—	
Geothermal	—	—	—	—	—	—	—	
CAPACITY (Utilities only)								
Total	--	--	--	--	--	--	--	
Hydro	—	—	—	—	—	—	—	
Conventional thermal	--	--	--	--	--	--	--	
Nuclear	—	—	—	—	—	—	—	
Geothermal	—	—	—	—	—	—	—	

FUEL CONSUMPTION (Utilities only)

	1958	1959	1960	1961	1962	1963	1964	
Total (Tcals)	--	--	--	--	--	--	--	
RESERVOIR STORAGE CAPACITY (million kwh)	—	—	—	—	—	—	—	

SUPPLEMENTARY DATA FOR 1964

Transmission lines, 100 kv+ (km):   --
Households served (thousands):   --
Revenues per kwh (U.S. cents) — Total:
    Residential: Railways:
    Industry: Lighting: 7.8
Population (thousands):   1898

Other characteristics of plants and systems:

Electricity is generated by the Jordan Electric Power Company and various municipalities and manufacturing industries, mainly if not entirely in diesel electric plants.

Sources of data:
UN. *Stat. yrbk.*
US. Dept. of Commerce. *Overseas business reports.*
US. FPC. *World power data.*
Ministry of National Economy. Department of Statistics.
   Statistical yearbook of Jordan.

KENYA

SUPPLY AND USE (million kwh)	1958	1959	1960	1961	1962	1963	1964	1965
PRODUCTION (Utilities & industries)								
Total (Gross)	--	--	--	--	--	--	--	
(Net)	--	--	--	--	--	--	--	
Hydro	--	--	--	--	--	--	--	
Conventional thermal	--	--	--	--	--	--	--	
Nuclear	—	—	—	—	—	—	—	
Geothermal	—	—	—	—	—	—	—	
PRODUCTION (Utilities only)								
Total (Gross)	214	212	222	215	239	263	323	
(Net)	--	--	--	--	--	--	--	
Hydro	147	138	147	132	162	171	205	
Conventional thermal	67	74	75	83	77	92	118	
Nuclear	—	—	—	—	—	—	—	
Geothermal	—	—	—	—	—	—	—	
NET IMPORTS	114	151	181	211	208	205	180	
SUPPLY (Gross)	328	363	403	426	447	468	503	
(Net)	--	--	--	--	--	--	--	
CONSUMPTION	267	301	336	357	373	393	426	
Transport	—	—	—	—	—	—	—	
Domestic sector	163	177	197	207	227	237	--	
Industry	104	124	139	150	146	156	--	
LOSS AND USE	61	62	67	69	74	75	77	

PLANT (thousand kw)

CAPACITY (Utilities & industries)	1958	1959	1960	1961	1962	1963	1964	1965
Total	--	--	--	--	--	--	--	
Hydro	--	--	--	--	--	--	--	
Conventional thermal	--	--	--	--	--	--	--	
Nuclear	—	—	—	—	—	—	—	
Geothermal	—	—	—	—	—	—	—	
CAPACITY (Utilities only)								
Total	82	81	82	82	100	102	101	
Hydro	26	26	26	26	26	28	28	
Conventional thermal	56	55	56	56	74	74	73	
Nuclear	—	—	—	—	—	—	—	
Geothermal	—	—	—	—	—	—	—	

FUEL CONSUMPTION (Utilities only)

	1958	1959	1960	1961	1962	1963	1964	1965
Total (Tcals)	--	--	--	--	--	--	--	
RESERVOIR STORAGE CAPACITY (million kwh)	--	--	--	--	--	--	--	

SUPPLEMENTARY DATA FOR 1964

Transmission lines, 100 kv+ (km) : (1961) 400
Households served (thousands) :   --
Revenues per kwh (U.S. cents) — Total: (1961) 2.9
  Residential: Railways:
  Industry: Lighting: 1.7
Population (thousands) : 9104

Other characteristics of plants and systems:

Kenya's power is generated by the East African Power and Lighting Company and the Kenya Power Company. It is also imported from Uganda. Partial integration is provided by high-tension lines delivering power from KPC and Uganda to the East African Power and Light Company.

Sources of data:
UN. *Stat. yrbk.*
East African Common Services Organization. *Economic and statistical review.*
Office of the Minister of Finance and Economic Planning. Economic and Statistics Division. *Statistical abstract of Kenya.*

KOREA—SOUTH

SUPPLY AND USE (million kwh)	1958	1959	1960	1961	1962	1963	1964	1965
PRODUCTION (Utilities & industries)								
Total (Gross)	1521	1743	1760	1817	2172	2514	2966	
(Net)	1421e	1620	1672	1728	2084	2411	2818	
Hydro	614	779	580	652	702	727	750	
Conventional thermal	907	964	1180	1165	1470	1787	2216	
Nuclear	—	—	—	—	—	—	—	
Geothermal	—	—	—	—	—	—	—	
PRODUCTION (Utilities only)								
Total (Gross)	1514	1688	1699	1773	1978	2209	2700	
(Net)	--	1565	1611	1684	1890	2106	2552	
Hydro	614	779	580	652	702	727	750	
Conventional thermal	900	909	1119	1121	1276	1482	1950	
Nuclear	—	—	—	—	—	—	—	
Geothermal	—	—	—	—	—	—	—	
NET IMPORTS	—	—	—	—	—	—	—	
SUPPLY (Gross)	1521	1743	1760	1817	2172	2514	2966	
(Net)	1421e	1620	1672	1728	2084	2411	2818	
CONSUMPTION	961	1177	1216	1234	1663	1974	2309	
Transport	13	--	--	--	--	--	--	
Domestic sector	577	452	493	544	435	491	511	
Industry	371	725	723	690	1228	1483	1798	
LOSS AND USE	460	443	456	494	421	437	509	

PLANT (thousand kw)

	1958	1959	1960	1961	1962	1963	1964	1965
CAPACITY (Utilities & industries)								
Total	387	430	439	478	591	622	754	
Hydro	143	143	143	143	143	143	146	
Conventional thermal	244	287	296	335	448	479	608	
Nuclear	—	—	—	—	—	—	—	
Geothermal	—	—	—	—	—	—	—	
CAPACITY (Utilities only)								
Total	367	367	367	367	434	465	597	
Hydro	143	143	143	143	143	143	146	
Conventional thermal	224	224	224	224	291	322	451	
Nuclear	—	—	—	—	—	—	—	
Geothermal	—	—	—	—	—	—	—	

FUEL CONSUMPTION (Utilities only)

	1958	1959	1960	1961	1962	1963	1964	1965
Coal (mmt)	599	585	787	804	722	892	1173	
Diesel oil (mmt)	1	1	1	1e	20	18	19	
Fuel oil (mmt)	38	66	52	33	114e	117	137	
Total (Tcals)	3123	3354	4090	3999	4678	5459	6952	
RESERVOIR STORAGE CAPACITY (million kwh)	--	--	--	--	--	--	--	

SUPPLEMENTARY DATA FOR 1964

Transmission lines, 100 kv+ (km): 725
Households served (thousands): 895
Revenues per kwh (U.S. cents) — Total: 1.4
  Residential: 3.0   Railways:
  Industry: 1.3   Lighting: 5.0
Population (thousands): 27631

Other characteristics of plants and systems:

The Korea Electric Company, the shares of which are largely owned by the government, is in charge of the electricity supply for the whole country. It operates an integrated system covering most of the country, but supplies power to only a fraction of the total population, probably no more than twenty-five per cent. In the generation of thermal electric power, it depends mainly on domestic coal.

Sources of data:
UN. *Stat. yrbk.* UN. ECAFE. *Elec. power.*
Bank of Korea. *Economic statistics yearbook.*
———. *Monthly statistical review.*
Economic Planning Board. *Economic survey.*

SUPPLY AND USE (million kwh)	1958	1959	1960	1961	1962	1963	1964	1965
PRODUCTION (Utilities & industries)								
Total (Gross)	--	--	--	--	--	--	--	
(Net)	--	--	--	--	--	--	--	
Hydro	—	—	—	—	—	—	—	
Conventional thermal	--	--	--	--	--	--	--	
Nuclear	—	—	—	—	—	—	—	
Geothermal	—	—	—	—	—	—	—	
PRODUCTION (Utilities only)								
Total (Gross)	166	204	249	313	414	453	647	
(Net)	--	--	--	--	--	--	--	
Hydro	—	—	—	—	—	—	—	
Conventional thermal	166	204	249	313	414	453	647	
Nuclear	—	—	—	—	—	—	—	
Geothermal	—	—	—	—	—	—	—	
NET IMPORTS	—	—	—	—	—	—	—	
SUPPLY (Gross)	--	--	--	--	--	--	--	
(Net)	--	--	--	--	--	--	--	
CONSUMPTION	--	--	--	--	--	--	--	
Transport	—	—	—	—	—	—	—	
Domestic sector	--	--	--	--	--	--	--	
Industry	--	--	--	--	--	--	--	
LOSS AND USE	--	--	--	--	--	--	--	

PLANT (thousand kw)

CAPACITY (Utilities & industries)								
Total	--	--	--	--	--	--	--	
Hydro	—	—	—	—	—	—	—	
Conventional thermal	--	--	--	--	--	--	--	
Nuclear	—	—	—	—	—	—	—	
Geothermal	—	—	—	—	—	—	—	
CAPACITY (Utilities only)								
Total	70	70	73	73	160	163	163	
Hydro	—	—	—	—	—	—	—	
Conventional thermal	70	70	73	73	160	163	163	
Nuclear	—	—	—	—	—	—	—	
Geothermal	—	—	—	—	—	—	—	

FUEL CONSUMPTION (Utilities only)

Total (Tcals)	--	--	--	--	--	--	--	
RESERVOIR STORAGE CAPACITY (million kwh)	—	—	—	—	—	—	—	

SUPPLEMENTARY DATA FOR 1964

Transmission lines, 100 kv+ (km) : —
Households served (thousands) : (1962) 71
Revenues per kwh (U.S. cents) — Total:
Residential: 1.7   Railways:
Industry: 1.3   Lighting: 1.7
Population (thousands) :   426

Other characteristics of plants and systems:

Kuwait's electricity supply is provided by the Ministry of Electricity and Water, Government of Kuwait.

Sources of data:
Miller Freeman Publications. *Energy international.*
UN. *Water desalination.* _____. *Stat. yrbk.*
Kuwait Oil Company. *Annual report.*
The Planning Board. Central Statistical Office.
   Statistical abstract.

LAOS

SUPPLY AND USE (million kwh)	1958	1959	1960	1961	1962	1963	1964	1965
PRODUCTION (Utilities & industries)								
Total (Gross)	10	12	13	14	15	19	22	
(Net)	--	--	--	--	--	--	--	
Hydro	—	—	—	—	—	—	—	
Conventional thermal	10	12	13	14	15	19	22	
Nuclear	—	—	—	—	—	—	—	
Geothermal	—	—	—	—	—	—	—	
PRODUCTION (Utilities only)								
Total (Gross)	3.4	5.6	6.8	8.0	9.4	10	13	
(Net)	--	--	--	--	--	--	--	
Hydro	—	—	—	—	—	—	—	
Conventional thermal	3.4	5.6	6.8	8.0	9.4	10	13	
Nuclear	—	—	—	—	—	—	—	
Geothermal	—	—	—	—	—	—	—	
NET IMPORTS	—	—	—	—	—	—	—	
SUPPLY (Gross)	10	12	13	14	15	19	22	
(Net)	--	--	--	--	--	--	--	
CONSUMPTION	9e	10e	11e	12e	13e	17e	19e	
Transport	—	—	—	—	—	—	—	
Domestic sector	3	4	5e	6	7e	--	--	
Industry	6e	6e	6	6	6	--	--	
LOSS AND USE	1e	2e	2e	2	2	2	3	

PLANT (thousand kw)

	1958	1959	1960	1961	1962	1963	1964	1965
CAPACITY (Utilities & industries)								
Total	7.2	6.6	6.8	--	--	--	11	
Hydro	—	—	—	—	—	—	—	
Conventional thermal	7.2	6.6	6.8	--	--	--	11	
Nuclear	—	—	—	—	—	—	—	
Geothermal	—	—	—	—	—	—	—	
CAPACITY (Utilities only)								
Total	3.6	3.6	3.8	4.6	4.6	5.8	--	
Hydro	—	—	—	—	—	—	—	
Conventional thermal	3.6	3.6	3.8	4.6	4.6	5.8	--	
Nuclear	—	—	—	—	—	—	—	
Geothermal	—	—	—	—	—	—	—	

FUEL CONSUMPTION (Utilities only)

	1958	1959	1960	1961	1962	1963	1964	1965
Diesel oil (mmt)	1.3	1.8	2.4e	3.1	3.6	4e	4.5	
Total (Tcals)	14	19	25	33	38	42	47	
RESERVOIR STORAGE CAPACITY (million kwh)	—	—	—	—	—	—	—	

SUPPLEMENTARY DATA FOR 1964

Transmission lines, 100 kv+ (km): —
Households served (thousands): 13
Revenues per kwh (U.S. cents) — Total: 13.2
  Residential: 13.2   Railways:
  Industry: Lighting:
Population (thousands): 2570

Other characteristics of plants and systems:

Public electricity supply in Laos is the responsibility of the Société Electricité du Laos, a public sector agency, which owns and operates diesel power plants in six separate urban centers. Power is supplied through local distribution systems to a very small fraction of the total population — apparently less than 10%. It is generated entirely from imported diesel oil.

Sources of data:
  UN. *Stat. yrbk.*
  UN. ECAFE. *Elec. power.*
  US. FPC. *World power data.*

LEBANON

SUPPLY AND USE (million kwh)	1958	1959	1960	1961	1962	1963	1964	1965
PRODUCTION (Utilities & industries)								
Total (Gross)	290	367	422	475	551	624	692	
(Net)	--	--	--	--	--	--	--	
Hydro	141	123	109	174	251	350	375	
Conventional thermal	149	244	313	301	300	274	317	
Nuclear	—	—	—	—	—	—	—	
Geothermal	—	—	—	—	—	—	—	
PRODUCTION (Utilities only)								
Total (Gross)	--	--	--	--	--	--	--	
(Net)	--	--	--	--	--	--	--	
Hydro	--	--	--	--	--	--	--	
Conventional thermal	--	--	--	--	--	--	--	
Nuclear	—	—	—	—	—	—	—	
Geothermal	—	—	—	—	—	—	—	
NET IMPORTS	—	—	—	—	—	—	—	
SUPPLY (Gross)	290	367	422	475	551	624	692	
(Net)	--	--	--	--	--	--	--	
CONSUMPTION	--	--	--	--	--	--	463	
Transport	—	—	—	—	—	—	—	
Domestic sector	--	--	--	--	--	--	256	
Industry	--	--	--	--	--	--	207	
LOSS AND USE	--	--	--	--	--	--	229	

PLANT (thousand kw)

CAPACITY (Utilities & industries)								
Total	144	144	146	219	283	285	285	
Hydro	63	63	65	73	126	126	126	
Conventional thermal	81	81	81	146	157	159	159	
Nuclear	—	—	—	—	—	—	—	
Geothermal	—	—	—	—	—	—	—	
CAPACITY (Utilities only)								
Total	--	--	--	--	--	--	--	
Hydro	--	--	--	--	--	--	--	
Conventional thermal	--	--	--	--	--	--	--	
Nuclear	—	—	—	—	—	—	—	
Geothermal	—	—	—	—	—	—	—	

FUEL CONSUMPTION (Utilities only)

	1958	1959	1960	1961	1962	1963	1964	
Diesel oil (mmt)	--	--	24	--	--	--	--	
Fuel oil (mmt)	--	--	87	--	--	--	--	
Total (Tcals)	--	--	730	--	--	--	--	
RESERVOIR STORAGE CAPACITY (million kwh)	--	--	--	--	--	--	--	

SUPPLEMENTARY DATA FOR 1964

Transmission lines, 100 kv+ (km) :   –
Households served (thousands) :   228
Revenues per kwh (U.S. cents) — Total:
  Residential: Railways:
  Industry: Lighting: 12.8 – 13.7
Population (thousands) :   2345

Other characteristics of plants and systems:

The Office de l'Electricité et de Transport en Commun, Government of Lebanon, is the principal supplier of electricity.

Sources of data:
UN. *Stat. yrbk.*
Office de l'Electricité du Liban. *Statistiques Libanaise.*
Société de la Presse Economique. "La production et la consommation d'électricité au Liban." *Le commerce du Levant.*

LIBERIA

SUPPLY AND USE (million kwh)	1958	1959	1960	1961	1962	1963	1964	1965
PRODUCTION (Utilities & industries)								
Total (Gross)	66	84	95e	115	134	182	212	
(Net)	--	--	--	--	--	--	--	
Hydro	15	16	14	17	17	17	17	
Conventional thermal	51	68	81	98	117	165	195	
Nuclear	—	—	—	—	—	—	—	
Geothermal	—	—	—	—	—	—	—	
PRODUCTION (Utilities only)								
Total (Gross)	20	27	35	47	60	73	92	
(Net)	--	--	--	--	--	--	--	
Hydro	—	—	—	—	—	—	—	
Conventional thermal	20	27	35	47	60	73	92	
Nuclear	—	—	—	—	—	—	—	
Geothermal	—	—	—	—	—	—	—	
NET IMPORTS				—	—		—	
SUPPLY (Gross)	66	84	95e	115	134	182	212	
(Net)	--	--	--	--	--	--	--	
CONSUMPTION	--	--	--	102	--	--	--	
Transport	—	—	—	—	—	—	—	
Domestic sector	--	--	--	36e	--	--	--	
Industry	--	--	--	66e	--	--	--	
LOSS AND USE	--	--	--	13e	--	--	--	

PLANT (thousand kw)

CAPACITY (Utilities & industries)								
Total	13	19	--	24	33	63	118	
Hydro	3	3	--	4	4	4	4	
Conventional thermal	10	16	--	20	29	59	114	
Nuclear	—	—	—	—	—	—	—	
Geothermal	—	—	—	—	—	—	—	
CAPACITY (Utilities only)								
Total	6	8	--	7	15	22	22	
Hydro	—	—	—	—	—	—	—	
Conventional thermal	6	8	--	7	15	22	22	
Nuclear	—	—	—	—	—	—	—	
Geothermal	—	—	—	—	—	—	—	

FUEL CONSUMPTION (Utilities only)

Total (Tcals)	--	--	--	--	--	--	--	
RESERVOIR STORAGE CAPACITY (million kwh)	--	--	--	--	--	--	--	

SUPPLEMENTARY DATA FOR 1964

Transmission lines, 100 kv+ (km) :   --
Households served (thousands) :   --
Revenues per kwh (U.S. cents) — Total:
  Residential: Railways:
  Industry: Lighting:
Population (thousands) :   1041

Other characteristics of plants and systems:

The principal source of electricity in Liberia is in the Monrovia Power Authority, owned and operated by the government of Liberia. A very small fraction of the population has electricity available. Substantial quantities of electricity are privately generated — mainly by the Liberian Mining Company and the Firestone Rubber Company.

Sources of data:
UN. *Stat. yrbk.*
UN. ECA. *Situation, trends & prospects.*
International Labour Office. *Bulletin of labour statistics.*

SUPPLY AND USE (million kwh)	1958	1959	1960	1961	1962	1963	1964	1965
PRODUCTION (Utilities & industries)								
Total (Gross)	--	--	--	--	--	--	--	
(Net)	--	--	--	--	--	--	--	
Hydro	—	—	—	—	—	—	—	
Conventional thermal	--	--	--	--	--	--	--	
Nuclear	—	—	—	—	—	—	—	
Geothermal	—	—	—	—	—	—	—	
PRODUCTION (Utilities only)								
Total (Gross)	78	86	105	110	133	149	157	
(Net)	--	--	--	--	--	--	--	
Hydro	—	—	—	—	—	—	—	
Conventional thermal	78	86	105	110	133	149	157	
Nuclear	—	—	—	—	—	—	—	
Geothermal	—	—	—	—	—	—	—	
NET IMPORTS	—	—	—	—	—	—	—	
SUPPLY (Gross)	78	86	105	110	133	149	157	
(Net)	--	--	--	--	--	--	--	
CONSUMPTION	--	--	--	--	--	--	--	
Transport	—	—	—	—	—	—	—	
Domestic sector	--	--	--	--	--	--	--	
Industry	--	--	--	--	--	--	--	
LOSS AND USE	--	--	--	--	--	--	--	

PLANT (thousand kw)	1958	1959	1960	1961	1962	1963	1964	1965
CAPACITY (Utilities & industries)								
Total	--	--	--	--	--	--	--	
Hydro	—	—	—	—	—	—	—	
Conventional thermal	--	--	--	--	--	--	--	
Nuclear	—	—	—	—	—	—	—	
Geothermal	—	—	—	—	—	—	—	
CAPACITY (Utilities only)								
Total	29	31	33	34	56	62	69	
Hydro	—	—	—	—	—	—	—	
Conventional thermal	29	31	33	34	56	62	69	
Nuclear	—	—	—	—	—	—	—	
Geothermal	—	—	—	—	—	—	—	

FUEL CONSUMPTION (Utilities only)

	1958	1959	1960	1961	1962	1963	1964	1965
Total (Tcals)	--	--	--	--	--	--	--	
RESERVOIR STORAGE CAPACITY (million kwh)	—	—	—	—	—	—	—	

SUPPLEMENTARY DATA FOR 1964

Transmission lines, 100 kv+ (km):   —
Households served (thousands):   --
Revenues per kwh (U.S. cents) — Total:
  Residential: (1961) 7.0   Railways:
  Industry: 5.6   Lighting: 3.5
Population (thousands):   1559

Other characteristics of plants and systems:

The principal sources of electricity in Libya appear to be the Electricity Corporation of Libya and the Public Works Department, Government of Cyrenaica. Electricity is supplied to a relatively small fraction of the Libyan population through a number of small regional networks and local facilities.

Sources of data:
Benn Bros. *Elec. undertakings.*
UN. *Stat. yrbk.*
Ministry of Economy and Trade. Department of Census and
  Statistics. *Statistical abstract of Libya.*

LUXEMBOURG

SUPPLY AND USE (million kwh)	1958	1959	1960	1961	1962	1963	1964	1965
PRODUCTION (Utilities & industries)								
Total (Gross)	1298	1378	1464	1528	1525	1845	2216	
(Net)	1229	1309	1388	1451	1450	1765	2128	
Hydro	4	3	20	57	110	492	805	
Conventional thermal	1294	1375	1444	1471	1415	1353	1411	
Nuclear	—	—	—	—	—	—	—	
Geothermal	—	—	—	—	—	—	—	
PRODUCTION (Utilities only)								
Total (Gross)	4	3	20	57	110	492	805	
(Net)	4	3	20	57	110e	486	793	
Hydro	4	3	20	57	110	492	805	
Conventional thermal	—	—	—	—	—	—	—	
Nuclear	—	—	—	—	—	—	—	
Geothermal	—	—	—	—	—	—	—	
NET IMPORTS	7	21	9	−23	154	478	693	
SUPPLY (Gross)	1305	1399	1473	1505	1679	2323	2909	
(Net)	1236	1330	1397	1428	1604	2243	2821	
CONSUMPTION	1199	1289	1352	1390	1470	1570	1721	
Transport	7	12	18	30	33	34	32	
Domestic sector	94	99	115	130	150	162	176	
Industry	1098	1178	1219	1230	1287	1374	1513	
LOSS AND USE	37	41	45	38	134	673	1100	

PLANT (thousand kw)

	1958	1959	1960	1961	1962	1963	1964	1965
CAPACITY (Utilities & industries)								
Total	260	260	275	276	485	886	1189	
Hydro	1	1	16	16	223	623	929	
Conventional thermal	259	259	259	260	262	263	260	
Nuclear	—	—	—	—	—	—	—	
Geothermal	—	—	—	—	—	—	—	
CAPACITY (Utilities only)								
Total	1	1	16	16	223	623	929	
Hydro	1	1	16	16	223	623	929	
Conventional thermal	—	—	—	—	—	—	—	
Nuclear	—	—	—	—	—	—	—	
Geothermal	—	—	—	—	—	—	—	

FUEL CONSUMPTION (Utilities only)

	1958	1959	1960	1961	1962	1963	1964	1965
Total (Tcals)	—	—	—	—	—	—	—	
RESERVOIR STORAGE CAPACITY (million kwh)	—	—	5	5	5	5	5	

SUPPLEMENTARY DATA FOR 1964

Transmission lines, 100 kv + (km): 18
Households served (thousands): 85
Revenues per kwh (U.S. cents) — Total:
   Residential: 4.9   Railways: 1.7
   Industry: 1.8   Lighting:
Population (thousands): 328

Sources of data:
EEC. *Energy stat., 1950-1965.* UCPTE. *Réseau.*
UN. ECE. *Org. of elec. power services.*
UNIPEDE. *Statistiques.*
Ministère des Transports et de l'Energie. Conseil
   Supérieur de l'Electricité. *Rapport sur la production
   et la consommation de l'énergie électrique dans le
   Grand-Duché de Luxembourg.*

Other characteristics of plants and systems:

Most of Luxembourg's power is generated in the iron and steel industry and sold to the Cie. Grand-Ducale d'Electricité du Luxembourg for distribution to the public. Generation of power by utilities is confined to small hydroelectric plants owned by the government of Luxembourg. The very substantial quantities of hydroelectric power shown as generated in Luxembourg are in fact derived from the pump-storage plant at Vianden, which obtains its energy from Germany and returns most of its output to Germany. Power is supplied to the entire country by a nationwide network.

SUPPLY AND USE (million kwh)	1958	1959	1960	1961	1962	1963	1964	1965
PRODUCTION (Utilities & industries)								
Total (Gross)	13	14	15	16	18	22	26	
(Net)	--	--	--	--	--	--	--	
Hydro	—	—	—	—	—	—	—	
Conventional thermal	13	14	15	16	18	22	26	
Nuclear	—	—	—	—	—	—	—	
Geothermal	—	—	—	—	—	—	—	
PRODUCTION (Utilities only)								
Total (Gross)	13	14	15	16	18	22	26	
(Net)	--	--	--	--	--	--	--	
Hydro	—	—	—	—	—	—	—	
Conventional thermal	13	14	15	16	18	22	26	
Nuclear	—	—	—	—	—	—	—	
Geothermal	—	—	—	—	—	—	—	
NET IMPORTS	—	—	—	—	—	—	—	
SUPPLY (Gross)	13	14	15	16	18	22	26	
(Net)	--	--	--	--	--	--	--	
CONSUMPTION	--	--	--	16	18	22	26	
Transport	—	—	—	—	—	—	—	
Domestic sector	--	--	--	11	12	15	19	
Industry	--	--	--	5	6	7	7	
LOSS AND USE	--	--	--	--	--	--	--	

PLANT (thousand kw)	1958	1959	1960	1961	1962	1963	1964	1965
CAPACITY (Utilities & industries)								
Total	5.5	7.1	7.2	7.2	8.8	8.9	11	
Hydro	—	—	—	—	—	—	—	
Conventional thermal	5.5	7.1	7.2	7.2	8.8	8.9	11	
Nuclear	—	—	—	—	—	—	—	
Geothermal	—	—	—	—	—	—	—	
CAPACITY (Utilities only)								
Total	5.5	7.1	7.2	7.2	8.8	8.9	11	
Hydro	—	—	—	—	—	—	—	
Conventional thermal	5.5	7.1	7.2	7.2	8.8	8.9	11	
Nuclear	—	—	—	—	—	—	—	
Geothermal	—	—	—	—	—	—	—	

FUEL CONSUMPTION (Utilities only)

	1958	1959	1960	1961	1962	1963	1964	1965
Total (Tcals)	--	--	--	--	--	--	--	
RESERVOIR STORAGE CAPACITY (million kwh)	—	—	—	—	—	—	—	

SUPPLEMENTARY DATA FOR 1964

Transmission lines, 100 kv + (km) : —
Households served (thousands) : (1960) 22
Revenues per kwh (U.S. cents) — Total:
   Residential: Railways:
   Industry: Lighting:
Population (thousands) : 282

Other characteristics of plants and systems:

   Macao Electric Lighting Company, privately owned, provides the colony's electricity supply.

Sources of data:
  UN. *Stat. yrbk.*
  Inst. de Est. *Anuário estatístico do ultramar.*

MALAGASY

SUPPLY AND USE (million kwh)	1958	1959	1960	1961	1962	1963	1964	1965
PRODUCTION (Utilities & industries)								
Total (Gross)	94	100	107	113	120	128	139	
(Net)	--	--	--	--	--	--	--	
Hydro	52	54	61	66	70	74	81	
Conventional thermal	42	46	46	47	50	54	58	
Nuclear	—	—	—	—	—	—	—	
Geothermal	—	—	—	—	—	—	—	
PRODUCTION (Utilities only)								
Total (Gross)	70	75	77	82	87	93	102	
(Net)	--	--	--	--	--	--	--	
Hydro	52	54	61	66	70	74	81	
Conventional thermal	18	21	16	16	17	19	21	
Nuclear	—	—	—	—	—	—	—	
Geothermal	—	—	—	—	—	—	—	
NET IMPORTS	—	—	—	—	—	—	—	
SUPPLY (Gross)	94	100	107	113	120	128	139	
(Net)	--	--	--	--	--	--	--	
CONSUMPTION	80	86	94	93	101	107	116	
Transport	2	2	3	--	--	--	--	
Domestic sector	30	33	35	46	50	54	59	
Industry	48e	51e	56e	47	51	53	57	
LOSS AND USE	14	14	13	20	19	21	23	

PLANT (thousand kw)

	1958	1959	1960	1961	1962	1963	1964	1965
CAPACITY (Utilities & industries)								
Total	53	62	66	69	70	74	73	
Hydro	19	24	24	28	28	28	28	
Conventional thermal	34	38	42	41	42	46	45	
Nuclear	—	—	—	—	—	—	—	
Geothermal	—	—	—	—	—	—	—	
CAPACITY (Utilities only)								
Total	34	39	42	45	45	49	47	
Hydro	19	24	24	28	28	28	28	
Conventional thermal	15	15	18	17	17	21	19	
Nuclear	—	—	—	—	—	—	—	
Geothermal	—	—	—	—	—	—	—	

FUEL CONSUMPTION (Utilities only)

	1958	1959	1960	1961	1962	1963	1964
Total (Tcals)	--	--	--	--	--	--	--
RESERVOIR STORAGE CAPACITY (million kwh)	--	--	--	--	--	--	--

SUPPLEMENTARY DATA FOR 1964

Transmission lines, 100 kv+ (km) : —
Households served (thousands) : 50
Revenues per kwh (U.S. cents) — Total:
  Residential: (1961) 6.0   Railways:
  Industry: Lighting: 10.5
Population (thousands) :   6180

Other characteristics of plants and systems:

La Société Electricité et Eaux de Madagascar and La Société d'Energie de Madagascar, both privately owned, are the principal suppliers of electricity in Malagasy. Most of the country is served by isolated diesel plants. Only a small fraction of the population has electricity available.

Sources of data:
  EEC. *Yrbk. Overseas Assoc.*
  Inst. de la Stat. *Données statistiques.* UN. *Stat. yrbk.*
  UN. ECA. *Situation, trends & prospects.*
  Service de la Statistique et des Etudes Socio-Economiques.
    Bulletin mensuel de statistique.
  ——— . *Economie Malagache.*

MALAWI

SUPPLY AND USE (million kwh)	1958	1959	1960	1961	1962	1963	1964	1965
PRODUCTION (Utilities & industries)								
Total (Gross)	--	--	--	--	--	--	--	
(Net)	22	26	28	35	38	39	43	
Hydro	3	3	3	2	--	--	4	
Conventional thermal	19	23	25	33	--	--	39	
Nuclear	—	—	—	—	—	—	—	
Geothermal	—	—	—	—	—	—	—	
PRODUCTION (Utilities only)								
Total (Gross)	--	--	--	--	--	--	--	
(Net)	22	26	28	35	38	39	43	
Hydro	3	3	3	2	--	--	4	
Conventional thermal	19	23	25	33	--	--	39	
Nuclear	—	—	—	—	—	—	—	
Geothermal	—	—	—	—	—	—	—	
NET IMPORTS	—	—	—	—	—	—	—	
SUPPLY (Gross)	--	--	--	--	--	--	--	
(Net)	22	26	28	35	38	39	43	
CONSUMPTION	20	22	25	32	35	35	39	
Transport	—	—	—	—	—	—	—	
Domestic sector	11	12	13	15	16	17	18	
Industry	9	10	12	17	19	18	21	
LOSS AND USE	2	4	3	3	3	4	4	
PLANT (thousand kw)								
CAPACITY (Utilities & industries)								
Total	8.8	10	10	12	13	13	14	
Hydro	0.7	0.7	0.6	0.6	0.6	0.6	0.6	
Conventional thermal	8.1	9.3	9.4	11	12	12	13	
Nuclear	—	—	—	—	—	—	—	
Geothermal	—	—	—	—	—	—	—	
CAPACITY (Utilities only)								
Total	8.8	10	10	12	13	13	14	
Hydro	0.7	0.7	0.6	0.6	0.6	0.6	0.6	
Conventional thermal	8.1	9.3	9.4	11	12	12	13	
Nuclear	—	—	—	—	—	—	—	
Geothermal	—	—	—	—	—	—	—	
FUEL CONSUMPTION (Utilities only)								
Coal (mmt)	--	25	27	33	--	--	--	
Diesel oil (mmt)	--	0.2	0.2	0.3	--	--	--	
Total (Tcals)	--	--	--	--	--	--	--	
RESERVOIR STORAGE CAPACITY (million kwh)	--	--	--	--	--	--	--	

SUPPLEMENTARY DATA FOR 1964

Transmission lines, 100 kv+ (km):   --
Households served (thousands):   --
Revenues per kwh (U.S. cents) — Total:
  Residential: Railways:
  Industry: Lighting:
Population (thousands): 3845

Other characteristics of plants and systems:

A governmental agency, the Electricity Supply Commission, produces and distributes Malawi's power. Only a small fraction of the population is supplied with electricity, mainly from a single steam plant at Blantyre.

Sources of data:

UN. *Stat. yrbk.*
UN. ECA. *Situation, trends & prospects.*
Central Statistical Office. *Annual abstract of statistics.*
Ministry of Finance. *Economic report.*
——. *Quarterly digest of statistics.*

MALAYA

SUPPLY AND USE (million kwh)	1958	1959	1960	1961	1962	1963	1964	1965
PRODUCTION (Utilities & industries)								
Total (Gross)	893	918	1190	1344	1474	1622	1851	
(Net)	848e	872e	1130e	1284	1406	1549	1776	
Hydro	200	191	195	216	235	317	544	
Conventional thermal	693	727	995	1128	1239	1305	1307	
Nuclear	–	–	–	–	–	–	–	
Geothermal	–	–	–	–	–	–	–	
PRODUCTION (Utilities only)								
Total (Gross)	828	859	1121	1268	1400	1545	1762	
(Net)	- -	- -	- -	- -	- -	- -	- -	
Hydro	171	165	166	185	209	299	531	
Conventional thermal	657	694	955	1083	1191	1246	1231	
Nuclear	–	–	–	–	–	–	–	
Geothermal	–	–	–	–	–	–	–	
NET IMPORTS	–	–	–	–	–	–	–	
SUPPLY (Gross)	893	918	1190	1344	1474	1622	1851	
(Net)	848e	872e	1130e	1284	1406	1549	1776	
CONSUMPTION	792	820	1067	1209	1323	1462	1634	
Transport	–	–	–	–	–	–	–	
Domestic sector	387	436	497	557	627	700	802	
Industry	405	384	570	652	696	762	832	
LOSS AND USE	56	52	63	75	83	87	142	

PLANT (thousand kw)	1958	1959	1960	1961	1962	1963	1964	1965
CAPACITY (Utilities & industries)								
Total	280	281	308	319	315	387	501	
Hydro	40	41	38	38	38e	81	138	
Conventional thermal	240	240	270	281	277e	306	363	
Nuclear	–	–	–	–	–	–	–	
Geothermal	–	–	–	–	–	–	–	
CAPACITY (Utilities only)								
Total	257	270	276	276	305	377	- -	
Hydro	29	30	30	30	30	73e	- -	
Conventional thermal	228	240	246	246	275	304e	- -	
Nuclear	–	–	–	–	–	–	–	
Geothermal	–	–	–	–	–	–	–	

FUEL CONSUMPTION (Utilities only)	1958	1959	1960	1961	1962	1963	1964	1965
Coal (mmt)	12	1	3	11	- -	13	2	
Diesel oil (mmt)	21	22	23	24	- -	34	35	
Fuel oil (mmt)	217	202	286	331	- -	404	378	
Total (Tcals)	3444	3164	3696	5117	5390	4760	4473	
RESERVOIR STORAGE CAPACITY (million kwh)	- -	- -	- -	- -	- -	- -	- -	

SUPPLEMENTARY DATA FOR 1964

Transmission lines, 100 kv+ (km): 385
Households served (thousands): 332
Revenues per kwh (U.S. cents) — Total: 3.0
  Residential: 4.7   Railways:
  Industry: 1.9   Lighting: 8.8
Population (thousands): 7814

Sources of data:
  UN. *Stat. yrbk.* UN. ECAFE. *Elec. power.*
  Federation of Malaya. Central Electricity Board.
    Annual report.
  ——. Department of Statistics. *Annual bulletin of statistics.*
  ——. ——. *Monthly statistical bulletin of the States of*
  Malaya.

Other characteristics of plants and systems:
    The principal source of electricity in Malaya is the National Electricity Board, which distributes something more than half the total electricity supply. Other important producers are the Perak River Hydro Electric Power Company, the Kinta Electric Distribution Company, and the Penang Municipal Council. Service to much of the country is provided by a network which extends from Chenderoh, in the north, to and beyond Malacca, in the south, but service in the eastern and northern portions of the country is mainly through local systems. Public supply is augmented by supplies from the tin and iron mining industries. Data on number of customers indicate that less than one-quarter of the population is supplied with electricity. Thermal electric power is generated entirely from imported fuel oil.

SUPPLY AND USE (million kwh)	1958	1959	1960	1961	1962	1963	1964	1965
PRODUCTION (Utilities & industries)								
Total (Gross)	--	--	--	--	--	--	--	
(Net)	--	--	--	--	--	--	--	
Hydro	--	--	--	--	--	--	--	
Conventional thermal	--	--	--	--	--	--	--	
Nuclear	—	—	—	—	—	—	—	
Geothermal	—	—	—	—	—	—	—	
PRODUCTION (Utilities only)								
Total (Gross)	12e	13	15	16	19	21	25	
(Net)	--	--	--	--	--	--	--	
Hydro	—	—	—	1	—	1	1	
Conventional thermal	12e	13e	15e	15	19	20	24	
Nuclear	—	—	—	—	—	—	—	
Geothermal	—	—	—	—	—	—	—	
NET IMPORTS	—	—	—	—	—	—	—	
SUPPLY (Gross)	12e	13	15	16	19	21	25	
(Net)	--	--	--	--	--	--	--	
CONSUMPTION	11e	12	12	13	15	16	19	
Transport	—	—	—	—	—	—	—	
Domestic sector	6e	6	6	6	8	9	12	
Industry	5e	6	6	7	7	7e	7	
LOSS AND USE	1e	1	3	3	4	5e	6	

PLANT (thousand kw)

	1958	1959	1960	1961	1962	1963	1964	1965
CAPACITY (Utilities & industries)								
Total	--	--	--	10	10	--	--	
Hydro	--	--	--	1	1	--	--	
Conventional thermal	--	--	--	9	9	--	--	
Nuclear	—	—	—	—	—	—	—	
Geothermal	—	—	—	—	—	—	—	
CAPACITY (Utilities only)								
Total	--	--	--	10	10	--	--	
Hydro	--	--	--	1	1	--	--	
Conventional thermal	--	--	--	9	9	--	--	
Nuclear	—	—	—	—	—	—	—	
Geothermal	—	—	—	—	—	—	—	

FUEL CONSUMPTION (Utilities only)

	1958	1959	1960	1961	1962	1963	1964	1965
Total (Tcals)	--	--	--	--	--	--	--	
RESERVOIR STORAGE CAPACITY (million kwh)	--	--	--	--	--	--	--	

SUPPLEMENTARY DATA FOR 1964

Transmission lines, 100 kv+ (km) :   —
Households served (thousands) : (1962) 9.3
Revenues per kwh (U.S. cents) — Total: 12.0
  Residential: Railways:
  Industry: Lighting: 16.2
Population (thousands):   4485

Other characteristics of plants and systems:

La Société Energie du Mali, of mixed ownership, is the principal source of electricity in Mali. Service originates mainly in small, isolated diesel plants; it is available to only a small fraction of Mali's population.

Sources of data:
  EEC. *Yrbk. Overseas Assoc.* UN. *Stat. yrbk.*
  UN. ECA. *Situation, trends & prospects.*
  Chambre de Commerce, d'Agriculture et d'Industrie de
    Bomako. *Annuaire statistique de la République du Mali.*

MALTA

SUPPLY AND USE (million kwh)	1958	1959	1960	1961	1962	1963	1964	1965
PRODUCTION (Utilities & industries)								
Total (Gross)	49	62	68	76	90	99	135	
(Net)	44	57	62	69	83	91	126	
Hydro	—	—	—	—	—	—	—	
Conventional thermal	49	62	68	76	90	99	135	
Nuclear	—	—	—	—	—	—	—	
Geothermal	—	—	—	—	—	—	—	
PRODUCTION (Utilities only)								
Total (Gross)	49	62	68	76	90	99	135	
(Net)	44	57	62	69	83	91	126	
Hydro	—	—	—	—	—	—	—	
Conventional thermal	49	62	68	76	90	99	135	
Nuclear	—	—	—	—	—	—	—	
Geothermal	—	—	—	—	—	—	—	
NET IMPORTS	—	—	—	—	—	—	—	
SUPPLY (Gross)	49	62	68	76	90	99	135	
(Net)	44	57	62	69	83	91	126	
CONSUMPTION	31	42	53	52	71	78	112	
Transport	—	—	—	—	—	—	—	
Domestic sector	18	21	35	38	45	52	60	
Industry	13	21	18	14	26	26	52	
LOSS AND USE	13	15	9	17	12	13	14	

PLANT (thousand kw)								
CAPACITY (Utilities & industries)								
Total	30	20	25	25	25	25	30	
Hydro	—	—	—	—	—	—	—	
Conventional thermal	30	20	25	25	25	25	30	
Nuclear	—	—	—	—	—	—	—	
Geothermal	—	—	—	—	—	—	—	
CAPACITY (Utilities only)								
Total	30	20	25	25	25	25	30	
Hydro	—	—	—	—	—	—	—	
Conventional thermal	30	20	25	25	25	25	30	
Nuclear	—	—	—	—	—	—	—	
Geothermal	—	—	—	—	—	—	—	

FUEL CONSUMPTION (Utilities only)								
Fuel Oil (mmt)	21	26	28	31	37	43	55	
Total (Tcals)	221	273	294	326	389	452	578	
RESERVOIR STORAGE CAPACITY (million kwh)	—	—	—	—	—	—	—	

SUPPLEMENTARY DATA FOR 1964

Transmission lines, 100 kv+ (km): —
Households served (thousands): 65
Revenues per kwh (U.S. cents) — Total:
  Residential: Railways:
  Industry: Lighting: 7.0
Population (thousands): 324

Other characteristics of plants and systems:

Power is generated and distributed throughout Malta and Gozo by the government. Imported fuel oil is used to generate all the power produced.

Sources of data:
Benn Bros. *Elec. undertakings.*
UN. *Stat. yrbk.*
Central Office of Statistics. *Annual abstract of statistics.*
——. *Malta statistical handbook.*

MARTINIQUE

SUPPLY AND USE (million kwh)	1958	1959	1960	1961	1962	1963	1964	1965
PRODUCTION (Utilities & industries)								
Total (Gross)	20	21	23	25	28	32	37	
(Net)	--	--	--	--	--	--	--	
Hydro	—	—	—	—	—	—	—	
Conventional thermal	20	21	23	25	28	32	37	
Nuclear	—	—	—	—	—	—	—	
Geothermal	—	—	—	—	—	—	—	
PRODUCTION (Utilities only)								
Total (Gross)	20	21	23	25	28	32	37	
(Net)	--	--	--	--	--	--	--	
Hydro	—	—	—	—	—	—	—	
Conventional thermal	20	21	23	25	28	32	37	
Nuclear	—	—	—	—	—	—	—	
Geothermal	—	—	—	—	—	—	—	
NET IMPORTS	—	—	—		—		—	
SUPPLY (Gross)	20	21	23	25	28	32	37	
(Net)	--	--	--	--	--	--	--	
CONSUMPTION	16	17	18	20e	23e	26	31	
Transport	—	—	—	—	—	—	—	
Domestic sector	11	11	12	14	16	17	19	
Industry	5	6	6	6	7	9	12	
LOSS AND USE	4	4	5	5e	5e	6	6	

PLANT (thousand kw)	1958	1959	1960	1961	1962	1963	1964	1965
CAPACITY (Utilities & industries)								
Total	9.6	9.6	9.6	9.8	9.8	9.8	13	
Hydro	—	—	—	—	—	—	—	
Conventional thermal	9.6	9.6	9.6	9.8	9.8	9.8	13	
Nuclear	—	—	—	—	—	—	—	
Geothermal	—	—	—	—	—	—	—	
CAPACITY (Utilities only)								
Total	9.6	9.6	9.6	9.8	9.8	9.8	13	
Hydro	—	—	—	—	—	—	—	
Conventional thermal	9.6	9.6	9.6	9.8	9.8	9.8	13	
Nuclear	—	—	—	—	—	—	—	
Geothermal	—	—	—	—	—	—	—	

FUEL CONSUMPTION (Utilities only)	1958	1959	1960	1961	1962	1963	1964	1965
Diesel oil (mmt)					19	11	23	
Fuel oil (mmt)	20	21	23	26	13	14	18	
Total (Tcals)	200e	210e	230e	260e	324	249	413	
RESERVOIR STORAGE CAPACITY (million kwh)	—	—	—	—	—	—	—	

SUPPLEMENTARY DATA FOR 1964

Transmission lines, 100 kv+ (km):   —
Households served (thousands):   22
Revenues per kwh (U.S. cents) — Total:
    Residential: Railways:
    Industry: Lighting:
Population (thousands):   314

Sources of data:

EEC. *Yrbk. Overseas Assoc.*
Soc. R. Moreux. *Industries et travaux. No. 122.*
UN. *Stat. yrbk.* US. *Foreign serv. desp.*
Inst. de la Stat. *Ann. stat. de la Martinique.*

Other characteristics of plants and systems:

The Société de Production et de Distribution de l'Electricité de la Martinique, of mixed ownership, provides service to Martinique via a 20 KV network which reaches most of the island. About a quarter of the population appears to be supplied with electricity.

SUPPLY AND USE (million kwh)	1958	1959	1960	1961	1962	1963	1964	1965
PRODUCTION (Utilities & industries)								
Total (Gross)	49	56	55	63	77	87	93	
(Net)	--	--	--	--	--	--	--	
Hydro	31	30	29	20	45	56	56	
Conventional thermal	18	26	26	43	32	31	37	
Nuclear	—	—	—	—	—	—	—	
Geothermal	—	—	—	—	—	—	—	
PRODUCTION (Utilities only)								
Total (Gross)	47	46	48	52	63	--	--	
(Net)	--	--	--	--	--	--	--	
Hydro	31	30	29	20	45	56	56	
Conventional thermal	16	16	19	32	18	--	--	
Nuclear	—	—	—	—	—	—	—	
Geothermal	—	—	—	—	—	—	—	
NET IMPORTS	—	—	—	—	—	—	—	
SUPPLY (Gross)	49	56	55	63	77	87	93	
(Net)	--	--	--	--	--	--	--	
CONSUMPTION	--	46	38	44	58	66	75	
Transport	—	—	—	—	—	—	—	
Domestic sector	--	--	--	34	40	45	49	
Industry	--	--	--	10	18	21	26	
LOSS AND USE	--	10	17	19	19	21	18	

PLANT (thousand kw)

	1958	1959	1960	1961	1962	1963	1964	1965
CAPACITY (Utilities & industries)								
Total	40	57	68	73	79	81	96	
Hydro	9.4	11	12	15	15	16	16	
Conventional thermal	31	46	56	58	64	65	80	
Nuclear	—	—	—	—	—	—	—	
Geothermal	—	—	—	—	—	—	—	
CAPACITY (Utilities only)								
Total	16	17	24	26	31	32	44	
Hydro	9.4	11	12	15	15	16	16	
Conventional thermal	6.6	6	12	11	16	16	28	
Nuclear	—	—	—	—	—	—	—	
Geothermal	—	—	—	—	—	—	—	

FUEL CONSUMPTION (Utilities only)

	1958	1959	1960	1961	1962	1963	1964
Total (Tcals)	--	--	--	--	--	--	--
RESERVOIR STORAGE CAPACITY (million kwh)	--	--	--	--	--	--	--

SUPPLEMENTARY DATA FOR 1964

Transmission lines, 100 kv+ (km):   –
Households served (thousands): 69
Revenues per kwh (U.S. cents) — Total: 4.0
  Residential: 4.6   Railways:
  Industry: 3.5   Lighting: 14.3
Population (thousands): 722

Other characteristics of plants and systems:

    The Central Electricity Board of the Government of Mauritius supplies most of the country's power from its own facilities or with power purchased from the sugar estates. Power is distributed through an extensive network of 22 KV transmission lines.

Sources of data:
UN. *Stat. yrbk.*
Central Electricity Board. *Annual report and accounts.*
Central Statistical Office. *Yearbook of statistics.*
United Kingdom. Colonial Office. *Mauritius.*

SUPPLY AND USE (million kwh)	1958	1959	1960	1961	1962	1963	1964	1965
PRODUCTION (Utilities & industries)								
Total (Gross)	9098	9775	10728	11747	12507	13707	15748	
(Net)	--	--	--	--	--	--	--	
Hydro	4458	4563	5149	5032	5345	5803	6866	
Conventional thermal	4640	5212	5579	6715	7162	7904	8882	
Nuclear	–	–	–	–	–	–	–	
Geothermal	–	–	–	–	–	–	–	
PRODUCTION (Utilities only)								
Total (Gross)	7374	7841	8589	9448	10112	11111	13400	
(Net)	--	--	--	--	--	--	--	
Hydro	4289	4370	4965	4849	5150e	5615e	6742	
Conventional thermal	3085	3471	3624	4599	4962	5496	6658	
Nuclear	–	–	–	–	–	–	–	
Geothermal	–	–	–	–	–	–	–	
NET IMPORTS	389	462	604	532	536	605	121	
SUPPLY (Gross)	9487	10237	11332	12279	13043	14312	15869	
(Net)	--	--	--	--	--	--	--	
CONSUMPTION	7955	8660	9636	10502	10925e	12040	13743	
Transport	–	–	–	–	–	–	–	
Domestic sector	3517	3770	3969	4477	4680e	5097	5358	
Industry	4438	4890	5667	6025	6245	6943	8385	
LOSS AND USE	1532	1577	1696	1777	2118e	2272	2126	
PLANT (thousand kw)								
CAPACITY (Utilities & industries)								
Total	2560	2739	3021	3275	3564	4243	4892	
Hydro	1159	1197	1328	1333	1564	1573	1920	
Conventional thermal	1401	1542	1693	1942	2000	2670	2972	
Nuclear	–	–	–	–	–	–	–	
Geothermal	–	–	–	–	–	–	–	
CAPACITY (Utilities only)								
Total	1999	2093	2308	2435	2724	3369	4019	
Hydro	1090	1128	1257	1261	1495	1500e	1850e	
Conventional thermal	909	965	1051	1174	1229	1869e	2069e	
Nuclear	–	–	–	–	–	–	–	
Geothermal	–	–	–	–	–	–	–	
FUEL CONSUMPTION (Utilities only)								
Coal (mmt)	–	–	–	–	–	39	17	
Fuel oil (mmt)	--	--	--	--	--	918	856	
Diesel oil (mmt)	--	--	--	--	--	67	87	
Natural gas (Tcals)	--	--	--	--	--	9972	12879	
Total (Tcals)	--	--	--	--	--	20340	22180	
RESERVOIR STORAGE CAPACITY (million kwh)	--	--	--	--	--	--	--	

SUPPLEMENTARY DATA FOR 1964

Transmission lines, 100 kv+ (km): --
Households served (thousands): 2954
Revenues per kwh (U.S. cents) — Total: 2.1
Residential: 3.4 Railways:
Industry: 1.4 Lighting: 3.8
Population (thousands): 41253

Other characteristics of plants and systems:

Mexico's electric power supply is completely under the control of the Comisión Federal de Electricidad. Some of the more important parts of Mexico are served by regional networks, but many localities are still wholly dependent on local facilities. The number of customers, considered in conjunction with the level of consumption in the domestic sector, indicates that perhaps a third of Mexico's people are supplied with electricity.

Sources of data:

UN. *Growth of world industry.* ———. *Stat. yrbk.* UN. ECLA. *Estud. sobre la elec.* ———. *Rev. Latinoamer. de elec.* ———. *Stat. bull.* UNIPEDE. *Statistiques* US. *Foreign serv. desp.* Comisión Federal de Electricidad (CFE). *Estadísticas de explotación divisiones CFE.* ———. *Estadísticas de explotación total federal.* Comité de Estudios para la Restructuración de la Industria Republicana. *Informe anual.* Dirección General de Estadística. *Anuário estadístico.* ———. Secretaría de Industria y Comercio. *Censo industrial.* ———. ———. *Estadística industrial anual.* Nacional Financiera, S. A. *Informe anual.* ———. *Statistics on the Mexican economy.* Comisión Federal de Electricidad. Subdirección General. Data communicated to N. B. Guyol.

SUPPLY AND USE (million kwh)	1958	1959	1960	1961	1962	1963	1964	1965
PRODUCTION (Utilities & industries)								
Total (Gross)	948	960	1012	1053	1097	1160	1356e	
(Net)	928e	936	991	1029	1067	1138	1326	
Hydro	873	914	931	951	1020	1080	1171	
Conventional thermal	75	46	81	102	77	80	185	
Nuclear	—	—	—	—	—	—	—	
Geothermal	—	—	—	—	—	—	—	
PRODUCTION (Utilities only)								
Total (Gross)	948	960	1012	1053	1097	1160	1336e	
(Net)	--	--	--	--	1067	1138	1306	
Hydro	873	914	931	951	1020	1080	1171	
Conventional thermal	75	46	81	102	77	80	165	
Nuclear	—	—	—	—	—	—	—	
Geothermal	—	—	—	—	—	—	—	
NET IMPORTS	—	—	—	—	—	—	—	
SUPPLY (Gross)	948	960	1012	1053	1097	1160	1356e	
(Net)	928e	936	991	1029	1067	1138	1326	
CONSUMPTION	805	785	839	873	892	949	1129	
Transport	67	62	66	66	62	59	59	
Domestic sector	261	255	269	278	275	301	405	
Industry	477	468	504	529	555	589	665	
LOSS AND USE	123	151	152	156	175	189	197	

PLANT (thousand kw)	1958	1959	1960	1961	1962	1963	1964	1965
CAPACITY (Utilities & industries)								
Total	424	398	398	399	399	409	448	
Hydro	319	319	319	319	319	331	344	
Conventional thermal	105	79	79	80	80	78	104	
Nuclear	—	—	—	—	—	—	—	
Geothermal	—	—	—	—	—	—	—	
CAPACITY (Utilities only)								
Total	424	398	398	399	399	409	440	
Hydro	319	319	319	319	319	331	344	
Conventional thermal	105	79	79	80	80	78	96	
Nuclear	—	—	—	—	—	—	—	
Geothermal	—	—	—	—	—	—	—	

FUEL CONSUMPTION (Utilities only)	1958	1959	1960	1961	1962	1963	1964	1965
Coal (mmt)	59	50	51	61	44	60	75	
Fuel oil (mmt)	6	6	4	--	--	--	--	
Diesel oil (mmt)	22	21	19	--	--	--	--	
Total (Tcals)	--	--	--	--	--	--	--	
RESERVOIR STORAGE CAPACITY (million kwh)	1003	1003	1003	1003	1003	1003	1003	

SUPPLEMENTARY DATA FOR 1964

Transmission lines, 100 kv+ (km): (1961) 1194
Households served (thousands):
Revenues per kwh (U.S. cents) — Total: (1961) 1.9
  Residential: Railways: 1.8
  Industry: Lighting: 6.9
Population (thousands):   12959

Other characteristics of plants and systems:

L'Energie Electrique du Maroc, an agency of government, operates an integrated system which supplies current to most of Morocco. The available data indicate that a relatively large share of the population is supplied with electricity.

Sources of data:
UN. *Stat. yrbk.* UNIPEDE. *Statistiques.*
US. *Foreign serv. desp.*
Delegation Générale à la Promotion Nationale et au Plan.
  Division du Plan et des Statistiques. *La situation*
  économique du Maroc.
Ministère des Travaux Publics. *L'électricité au Maroc.*
Société d'Etudes Economiques Sociales et Statistiques.
  Bulletin économique et sociale du Maroc, revue
  trimestrielle.

SUPPLY AND USE (million kwh)	1958	1959	1960	1961	1962	1963	1964	1965
PRODUCTION (Utilities & industries)								
Total (Gross)	--	194e	227e	269e	287e	325e	368e	
(Net)	--	--	--	--	--	--	--	
Hydro	--	102e	128e	138e	150e	158e	160e	
Conventional thermal	--	92e	99e	131e	137e	167e	208e	
Nuclear	—	—	—	—	—	—	—	
Geothermal	—	—	—	—	—	—	—	
PRODUCTION (Utilities only)								
Total (Gross)	--	140	172	200	221	260	305	
(Net)	--	--	--	--	--	--	--	
Hydro	--	102	128	138	150	158	160	
Conventional thermal	--	38	44	62	71	102	145	
Nuclear	—	—	—	—	—	—	—	
Geothermal	—	—	—	—	—	—	—	
NET IMPORTS	—	−54	−59	−61	−70	−88	−102	
SUPPLY (Gross)	--	140e	168e	208e	217e	237e	266e	
(Net)	--	--	--	--	--	--	--	
CONSUMPTION	83	127	153	189	197	215e	242	
Transport	—	—	—	—	—	—	—	
Domestic sector	--	--	40	48	53	59	68	
Industry	--	--	113	141	144	156	174	
LOSS AND USE	--	--	15e	19e	20e	22e	24e	

PLANT (thousand kw)	1958	1959	1960	1961	1962	1963	1964	1965
CAPACITY (Utilities & industries)								
Total	63	105	122	159	182	211	209	
Hydro	12	47	47	65	66	66	66	
Conventional thermal	51	58	75	94	116	145	143	
Nuclear	—	—	—	—	—	—	—	
Geothermal	—	—	—	—	—	—	—	
CAPACITY (Utilities only)								
Total	28	69	85	122	141	145	143	
Hydro	12	47	47	65	66	66	66	
Conventional thermal	16	22	38	57	75	79	77	
Nuclear	—	—	—	—	—	—	—	
Geothermal	—	—	—	—	—	—	—	

FUEL CONSUMPTION (Utilities only)	1958	1959	1960	1961	1962	1963	1964	1965
Coal (mmt)	--	--	45	49	60	61	--	
Wood (mmt)	--	--	8	5	—	—	--	
Fuel oils (mmt)	--	--	6	8	7	7	--	
Total (Tcals)	--	--	--	--	--	--	--	
RESERVOIR STORAGE CAPACITY (million kwh)	--	--	--	--	--	--	--	

SUPPLEMENTARY DATA FOR 1964

Transmission lines, 100 kv+ (km) :   - -
Households served (thousands) :   39
Revenues per kwh (U.S. cents) — Total:
  Residential: Railways:
  Industry: Lighting:
Population (thousands) :   6872

Sources of data:
Soc. R. Moreux. *Industries et travaux. No. 122.*
UN. *Stat. yrbk.* US. *Foreign serv. desp.*
Direccão dos Serviços de Economia e Estatística Geral.
    Provinçia de Moçambique. *Estatística industrial.*

Other characteristics of plants and systems:

    The principal producer of electricity in Mozambique is the Sociedade Hidro-Electrica do Revué (SHER) and the Sociedade Nacional de Estudo e Financiamentos de Empreendimentos Ultramarinos. Most of Revué's power is sold to the Electricity Supply Commission of Southern Rhodesia. Some is sold to the Beira Municipal Power Services for redistribution, and some direct to various industrial consumers.

NAURU

SUPPLY AND USE (million kwh)	1958	1959	1960	1961	1962	1963	1964	1965
PRODUCTION (Utilities & industries)								
Total (Gross)	7.2	7.2	8	10	10	10	11	
(Net)	--	--	--	--	--	--	--	
Hydro	—	—	—	—	—	—	—	
Conventional thermal	7.2	7.2	8	10	10	10	11	
Nuclear	—	—	—	—	—	—	—	
Geothermal	—	—	—	—	—	—	—	
PRODUCTION (Utilities only)								
Total (Gross)	7.2	7.2	8	10	10	10	11	
(Net)	--	--	--	--	--	--	--	
Hydro	—	—	—	—	—	—	—	
Conventional thermal	7.2	7.2	8	10	10	10	11	
Nuclear	—	—	—	—	—	—	—	
Geothermal	—	—	—	—	—	—	—	
NET IMPORTS	—	—	—	—	—	—	—	
SUPPLY (Gross)	7.2	7.2	8	10	10	10	11	
(Net)	--	--	--	--	--	--	--	
CONSUMPTION	--	--	--	--	--	--	--	
Transport	—	—	—	—	—	—	—	
Domestic sector	--	--	--	--	--	--	--	
Industry	--	--	--	--	--	--	--	
LOSS AND USE	--	--	--	--	--	--	--	

PLANT (thousand kw)

	1958	1959	1960	1961	1962	1963	1964	1965
CAPACITY (Utilities & industries)								
Total	3.7	3.7	3.7	3.7	3.7	6.1	6.8	
Hydro	—	—	—	—	—	—	—	
Conventional thermal	3.7	3.7	3.7	3.7	3.7	6.1	6.8	
Nuclear	—	—	—	—	—	—	—	
Geothermal	—	—	—	—	—	—	—	
CAPACITY (Utilities only)								
Total	3.7	3.7	3.7	3.7	3.7	6.1	6.8	
Hydro	—	—	—	—	—	—	—	
Conventional thermal	3.7	3.7	3.7	3.7	3.7	6.1	6.8	
Nuclear	—	—	—	—	—	—	—	
Geothermal	—	—	—	—	—	—	—	

FUEL CONSUMPTION (Utilities only)

	1958	1959	1960	1961	1962	1963	1964	1965
Total (Tcals)	--	--	--	--	--	--	--	
RESERVOIR STORAGE CAPACITY (million kwh)	—	—	—	—	—	—	—	

SUPPLEMENTARY DATA FOR 1964

Transmission lines, 100 kv+ (km): —
Households served (thousands): --
Revenues per kwh (U.S. cents) — Total:
  Residential: Railways:
  Industry: Lighting:
Population (thousands): 5

Other characteristics of plants and systems:

    Power in Nauru is generated and distributed by the British Phosphate Commission.

Sources of data:
Benn Bros. *Elec. undertakings.*
UN. *Stat. yrbk.*

SUPPLY AND USE (million kwh)	1958	1959	1960	1961	1962	1963	1964	1965
PRODUCTION (Utilities & industries)								
Total (Gross)	13	10	11	11	13	13	15	
(Net)	--	--	10	10	12	12	14	
Hydro	6	7	7	7	7	--	6	
Conventional thermal	7	3	4	4	6	--	9	
Nuclear	—	—	—	—	—	—	—	
Geothermal	—	—	—	—	—	—	—	
PRODUCTION (Utilities only)								
Total (Gross)	13	10	11	11	13	13	15	
(Net)	--	--	10	10	12	12	14	
Hydro	6	7	7e	7	7	--	6	
Conventional thermal	7	3	4	4	6	--	9	
Nuclear	—	—	—	—	—	—	—	
Geothermal	—	—	—	—	—	—	—	
NET IMPORTS	—	—	—	—	—	—	—	
SUPPLY (Gross)	13	10	11	11	13	13	15	
(Net)	--	--	10	10	12	12	14	
CONSUMPTION	8	9	8	8	9	--	--	
Transport	—	—	—	—	—	—	—	
Domestic sector	8	9	8	8	9	--	--	
Industry	—	—	—	—	—	--	1	
LOSS AND USE	--	1e	2	2	3	--	--	
PLANT (thousand kw)								
CAPACITY (Utilities & industries)								
Total	7.0	5.6	6.4	6	7	7	8	
Hydro	3.4	3.4	3.4	3	3	3	3	
Conventional thermal	3.6	2.2	3.0	3	4	4	5	
Nuclear	—	—	—	—	—	—	—	
Geothermal	—	—	—	—	—	—	—	
CAPACITY (Utilities only)								
Total	7.0	5.6	6.4	6	7	7	8	
Hydro	3.4	3.4	3.4	3	3	3	3	
Conventional thermal	3.6	2.2	3.0	3	4	4	5	
Nuclear	—	—	—	—	—	—	—	
Geothermal	—	—	—	—	—	—	—	
FUEL CONSUMPTION (Utilities only)								
Diesel oil (mmt)	--	--	--	1.3	1.8	2e	2.5	
Total (Tcals)	--	--	--	14	21	--	28	
RESERVOIR STORAGE CAPACITY (million kwh)	--	--	--	--	--	--	--	

SUPPLEMENTARY DATA FOR 1964

Transmission lines, 100 kv + (km) : —
Households served (thousands) : 19
Revenues per kwh (U.S. cents) — Total: 4.1
  Residential: 4.9   Railways:
  Industry: 2.0   Lighting:
Population (thousands): 9920

Other characteristics of plants and systems:

The electricity supply industry of Nepal is owned by the government and operated by the Government Electricity Department. Service is strictly local, and reaches only a small fraction of the total population –– probably less than five per cent.

Sources of data:
UN. *Stat. yrbk.*
UN. ECAFE. *Elec. power.*

NETHERLANDS

SUPPLY AND USE (million kwh)	1958	1959	1960	1961	1962	1963	1964	1965
PRODUCTION (Utilities & industries)								
Total (Gross)	13854	14971	16516	17624	19255	20984	22975	
(Net)	13118	14178	15633	16656	18214	19839	21739	
Hydro	–	–	–	–	–	–	–	
Conventional thermal	13854	14971	16516	17624	19255	20984	22975	
Nuclear	–	–	–	–	–	–	–	
Geothermal	–	–	–	–	–	–	–	
PRODUCTION (Utilities only)								
Total (Gross)	10737	11505	12756	13716	15207	16818	18405	
(Net)	10134	10859	12029	12915	14340	15852	17364	
Hydro	–	–	–	–	–	–	–	
Conventional thermal	10737	11505	12756	13716	15207	16818	18405	
Nuclear	–	–	–	–	–	–	–	
Geothermal	–	–	–	–	–	–	–	
NET IMPORTS	191	75	118	43	–20	47	18	
SUPPLY (Gross)	14045	15046	16634	17667	19235	21031	22993	
(Net)	13309	14253	15751	16699	18194	19886	21757	
CONSUMPTION	12337	13234	14663	15571	17004	18569	20335	
Transport	720	702	731	755	735	738	734	
Domestic sector	4838	5128	5799	6356	7231	8104	8982	
Industry	6779	7404	8133	8460	9038	9727	10619	
LOSS AND USE	972	1019	1088	1128	1190	1317	1422	
PLANT (thousand kw)								
CAPACITY (Utilities & industries)								
Total	4518	4702	5262	5598	5647	6332	6752	
Hydro	–	–	–	–	–	–	–	
Conventional thermal	4518	4702	5262	5598	5647	6332	6752	
Nuclear	–	–	–	–	–	–	–	
Geothermal	–	–	–	–	–	–	–	
CAPACITY (Utilities only)								
Total	3485	3650	4165	4504	4464	5046	5450	
Hydro	–	–	–	–	–	–	–	
Conventional thermal	3485	3650	4165	4504	4464	5046	5450	
Nuclear	–	–	–	–	–	–	–	
Geothermal	–	–	–	–	–	–	–	
FUEL CONSUMPTION (Utilities only)								
Coal & coke (mmt)	4234	3983	4183	4482	4715	4542	4032	
Fuel oils (mmt)	269	500	596	615	784	1252	1866	
Natural gas (Tcals)	–	88	412	412	403	389	408	
Blast furnace gas (Tcals)	293	638	868	736	672	708	1036	
Total (Tcals)	32707	33959	36591	38353	41386	45149	48122	
RESERVOIR STORAGE CAPACITY (million kwh)	–	–	–	–	–	–	–	

SUPPLEMENTARY DATA FOR 1964

Transmission lines, 100 kv+ (km): 1939
Households served (thousands): (1963) 3030
Revenues per kwh (U.S. cents) — Total:
  Residential: 2.6   Railways: 1.9
  Industry: 1.4   Lighting: 3.9
Population (thousands): 12127

Sources of data:
EEC. *Energy stat., 1950-1965.* UCPTE. *Réseau.*
UN. *Stat. yrbk.* UN. ECE. *Org. of elec. power services.*
UNIPEDE. *L'écon. élec.* _____. *Statistiques.*
Centraal Bureau voor de Statistiek. *Statistiek van de
elektriciteitsvoorziening in Nederland.* Vol. I
Produktie and Vol. II *Distributie.*

Other characteristics of plants and systems:

Virtually all the people in the Netherlands receive power from an integrated network which serves the entire country. Power is produced, transmitted and distributed by municipal and regional undertakings, most of which are owned, directly or indirectly, by public authorities. An important part of the total supply of electricity is generated by the coal and chemical industries, primarily for their own use.

NETHERLANDS ANTILLES

SUPPLY AND USE (million kwh)	1958	1959	1960	1961	1962	1963	1964	1965
PRODUCTION (Utilities & industries)								
Total (Gross)	784	813	827	826	859	869	1025	
(Net)	--	--	--	--	--	--	--	
Hydro	—	—	—	—	—	—	—	
Conventional thermal	784	813	827	826	859	869	1025	
Nuclear	—	—	—	—	—	—	—	
Geothermal	—	—	—	—	—	—	—	
PRODUCTION (Utilities only)								
Total (Gross)	89	99	110	117	128	134	328	
(Net)	--	--	--	--	--	--	--	
Hydro	—	—	—	—	—	—	—	
Conventional thermal	89	99	110	117	128	134	328	
Nuclear	—	—	—	—	—	—	—	
Geothermal	—	—	—	—	—	—	—	
NET IMPORTS	—	—	—	—	—	—	—	
SUPPLY (Gross)	784	813	827	826	859	869	1025	
(Net)	--	--	--	--	--	--	--	
CONSUMPTION	--	--	--	--	--	--	--	
Transport	—	—	—	—	—	—	—	
Domestic sector	--	--	--	--	--	--	--	
Industry	705e	732e	741e	735	759e	--	--	
LOSS AND USE	--	--	--	--	--	--	--	

PLANT (thousand kw)	1958	1959	1960	1961	1962	1963	1964	1965
CAPACITY (Utilities & industries)								
Total	148	157	164	178	186	243	276	
Hydro	—	—	—	—	—	—	—	
Conventional thermal	148	157	164	178	186	243	276	
Nuclear	—	—	—	—	—	—	—	
Geothermal	—	—	—	—	—	—	—	
CAPACITY (Utilities only)								
Total	24	34	34	36	49	130	163	
Hydro	—	—	—	—	—	—	—	
Conventional thermal	24	34	34	36	49	130	163	
Nuclear	—	—	—	—	—	—	—	
Geothermal	—	—	—	—	—	—	—	

FUEL CONSUMPTION (Utilities only)	1958	1959	1960	1961	1962	1963	1964	1965
Fuel oils (mmt)	--	32	--	--	--	--	--	
Total (Tcals)	--	336	--	--	--	--	--	
RESERVOIR STORAGE CAPACITY (million kwh)	—	—	—	—	—	—	—	

SUPPLEMENTARY DATA FOR 1964

Transmission lines, 100 kv+ (km) :   —
Households served (thousands) :   --
Revenues per kwh (U.S. cents) — Total:
  Residential: Railways:
  Industry: Lighting: 5.8
Population (thousands): 205

Other characteristics of plants and systems:

N. V. Overzeese Gas- en Electriciteit Maatschappij is responsible for the public supply of electricity in Curaçao, Aruba and Bonaire. Substantial quantities of electricity are also produced by the government, in connection with the operation of sea-water distillation plants on Curaçao and Aruba, and by the petroleum refineries on Curaçao and Aruba, which generate mainly for their own use.

Sources of data:

Benn Bros. *Elec. undertakings.* EEC. *Yrbk. Overseas Assoc.*
UN. *Stat. yrbk.* ————. *Water desalination.*
US. *Foreign serv. desp.*
Statistiek- en Planbureau. *Statistisch Jaarboek.*
N.V. Overzeese Gas- en Electriciteit Maatschappij. Data communicated to N. B. Guyol, by letter dated Sept. 26, 1967.

239

SUPPLY AND USE (million kwh)	1958	1959	1960	1961	1962	1963	1964	1965
PRODUCTION (Utilities & industries)								
Total (Gross)	--	232	383	425	429	504	498	
(Net)	--	--	--	--	--	--	--	
Hydro	--	210	259	366	381	382	315	
Conventional thermal	--	22	124	59	48	122	183	
Nuclear	—	—	—	—	—	—	—	
Geothermal	—	—	—	—	—	—	—	
PRODUCTION (Utilities only)								
Total (Gross)	--	210	259	366	381	382	320	
(Net)	--	--	--	--	--	--	--	
Hydro	--	210	259	366	381	382	315	
Conventional thermal	—	—	--	—	—	—	5	
Nuclear	—	—	—	—	—	—	—	
Geothermal	—	—	—	—	—	—	—	
NET IMPORTS	—	—	—	—	—	—	—	
SUPPLY (Gross)	--	232	383	425	429	504	498	
(Net)	--	--	--	--	--	--	--	
CONSUMPTION	--	--	--	419	420	498	494	
Transport	—	—	—	—	—	—	—	
Domestic sector	--	--	--	22	24	27	31	
Industry	--	210	358	397	396	471	463	
LOSS AND USE	--	--	--	6	9	6	4	
PLANT (thousand kw)								
CAPACITY (Utilities & industries)								
Total	--	--	--	101	101	101	105	
Hydro	--	--	--	68	68	68	68	
Conventional thermal	--	--	--	33	33	33	37	
Nuclear	—	—	—	—	—	—	—	
Geothermal	—	—	—	—	—	—	—	
CAPACITY (Utilities only)								
Total	--	--	71	71	71	71	75	
Hydro	--	--	68	68	68	68	68	
Conventional thermal	—	—	3e	3	3	3	7	
Nuclear	—	—	—	—	—	—	—	
Geothermal	—	—	—	—	—	—	—	
FUEL CONSUMPTION (Utilities only)								
Total (Tcals)	--	--	--	--	--	--	--	
RESERVOIR STORAGE CAPACITY (million kwh)	--	--	--	--	--	--	--	

SUPPLEMENTARY DATA FOR 1964

Transmission lines, 100 kv+ (km) :   - -
Households served (thousands) :   7
Revenues per kwh (U.S. cents) — Total:
  Residential: Railways:
  Industry: Lighting: 8.9
Population (thousands) :   89

Other characteristics of plants and systems:

The principal generator of power in New Caledonia is the Société Néo-Calédonienne d'Energie, which produces power at the Yaté hydro plant and sells it to the nickel company and to UNELCO, a privately-owned distribution system. Power is also produced by the nickel company for its own use.

Sources of data:
EEC. *Yrbk. Overseas Assoc.*
Soc. R. Moreux. *Industries et travaux.* No. 122.
UN. *Stat. yrbk.*
Inst. de la Stat. *Ann. stat. des territoires d'outre-mer.*
Service des Mines. *L'activité minière.*

SUPPLY AND USE (million kwh)	1958	1959	1960	1961	1962	1963	1964	1965
PRODUCTION (Utilities & industries)								
Total (Gross)	35	35	36	38	37	39	40	
(Net)	--	--	--	--	--	--	--	
Hydro	26	24	24	24	22	21	19	
Conventional thermal	9	11	12	14	15	18	21	
Nuclear	—	—	—	—	—	—	—	
Geothermal	—	—	—	—	—	—	—	
PRODUCTION (Utilities only)								
Total (Gross)	9	11	13	15	16	19	--	
(Net)	--	--	--	--	--	--	--	
Hydro	—	—	1	1	1	1	1	
Conventional thermal	9	11	12	14	15	18	--	
Nuclear	—	—	—	—	—	—	—	
Geothermal	—	—	—	—	—	—	—	
NET IMPORTS	—	—	—	—	—	—	—	
SUPPLY (Gross)	35	35	36	38	37	39	40	
(Net)	--	--	--	--	--	--	--	
CONSUMPTION	--	--	--	--	--	--	--	
Transport	—	—	—	—	—	—	—	
Domestic sector	--	--	--	--	--	--	--	
Industry	--	--	--	--	--	--	--	
LOSS AND USE	--	--	--	--	--	--	--	
PLANT (thousand kw)								
CAPACITY (Utilities & industries)								
Total	8.8	9.2	10	13	13	13	15	
Hydro	5.6	5.7	5.7	5.9	5.9	5.9	5.9	
Conventional thermal	3.2	3.5	4.3	7.1	7.1	7.1	9.1	
Nuclear	—	—	—	—	—	—	—	
Geothermal	—	—	—	—	—	—	—	
CAPACITY (Utilities only)								
Total	3.3	3.7	4.5	7.6	7.5	7.8	9.1	
Hydro	0.1	0.2	0.2	0.4	0.3	0.4	0.4	
Conventional thermal	3.2	3.5	4.3	7.2	7.2	7.4	8.7	
Nuclear	—	—	—	—	—	—	—	
Geothermal	—	—	—	—	—	—	—	
FUEL CONSUMPTION (Utilities only)								
Total (Tcals)	--	--	--	--	--	--	--	
RESERVOIR STORAGE CAPACITY (million kwh)	--	--	--	--	--	--	--	

SUPPLEMENTARY DATA FOR 1964

Transmission lines, 100 kv+ (km) :   —
Households served (thousands) :   --
Revenues per kwh (U.S. cents) — Total:
    Residential: Railways:
    Industry: Lighting:
Population (thousands) :   1539

Other characteristics of plants and systems:

New Guinea's electricity supply is produced by the Administration of Papua and New Guinea in isolated diesel plants. Some hydroelectricity is generated privately for use by the mining industry.

Sources of data:
  Benn Bros. *Elec. undertakings.*
  UN. *Stat. yrbk.*
  Commonwealth of Australia. *Territory of New Guinea:*
    Report to the General Assembly of the United Nations.

NEW ZEALAND

SUPPLY AND USE (million kwh)	1958	1959	1960	1961	1962	1963	1964	1965
PRODUCTION (Utilities & industries)								
Total (Gross)	5677	6361	6835	7399	7951	8963	9718	
(Net)	--	--	--	--	--	--	--	
Hydro	5275	5483	5512	5946	6779	6852	7753	
Conventional thermal	396	709	939	962	411	1107	771	
Nuclear	—	—	—	—	—	—	—	
Geothermal	6	169	384	491	761	1004	1194	
PRODUCTION (Utilities only)								
Total (Gross)	5677	6361	6835	7399	7951	8963	9718	
(Net)	--	--	--	--	--	--	--	
Hydro	5275	5483	5512	5946	6779	6852	7753	
Conventional thermal	396	709	939	962	411	1107	771	
Nuclear	—	—	—	—	—	—	—	
Geothermal	6	169	384	491	761	1004	1194	
NET IMPORTS	—	—	—	—	—	—	—	
SUPPLY (Gross)	5677	6361	6835	7399	7951	8963	9718	
(Net)	--	--	--	--	--	--	--	
CONSUMPTION	4702	5274	5684	6169	6684	7577	8189	
Transport	44	46	46	46	45	44	45	
Domestic sector	3484	3947	4224	4587	4867	5425	5821	
Industry	1174	1281	1414	1536	1772	2108	2323	
LOSS AND USE	975	1087	1151	1230	1267	1386	1529	

PLANT (thousand kw)	1958	1959	1960	1961	1962	1963	1964	1965
CAPACITY (Utilities & industries)								
Total	1360	1509	1566	1815	1944	2006	2336	
Hydro	1176	1197	1254	1481	1547	1580	1910	
Conventional thermal	184	243	232	243	235	234	234	
Nuclear	—	—	—	—	—	—	—	
Geothermal	--	69	80	91	162	192	192	
CAPACITY (Utilities only)								
Total	1360	1509	1566	1815	1944	2006	2336	
Hydro	1176	1197	1254	1481	1547	1580	1910	
Conventional thermal	184	243	232	243	235	234	234	
Nuclear	—	—	—	—	—	—	—	
Geothermal	--	69	80	91	162	192	192	

FUEL CONSUMPTION (Utilities only)	1958	1959	1960	1961	1962	1963	1964	1965
Coal (mmt)	251	363	610	612	347	606	595	
Fuel oils (mmt)	—	—	—	—	—	1	2	
Total (Tcals)	--	--	--	--	--	4844	3248	
RESERVOIR STORAGE CAPACITY (million kwh)	1649	1649	1649	1751	1752	1841	1963	

SUPPLEMENTARY DATA FOR 1964

Transmission lines, 100 kv+ (km): 8650
Households served (thousands): 812
Revenues per kwh (U.S. cents) — Total: 1.5
  Residential: 1.3   Railways:
  Industry: 1.5   Lighting: 1.1
Population (thousands): 2594

Other characteristics of plants and systems:

Electricity is produced mainly by the New Zealand Electricity Department and distributed through local power boards. Both North and South Island are served by extensive networks which are interconnected by submarine cable. Electricity is supplied to practically all of the people of New Zealand.

Sources of data:
UN. *Stat. yrbk.* UN. ECAFE. *Elec. power.*
UNIPEDE. *Statistiques.*
Department of Statistics. *New Zealand official yearbook.*
Public Works Department. *Electric power development and operation.*
The Electrical Supply Authorities Association of New Zealand. N. M. Speer, *The electrical supply industry in New Zealand.*

242

SUPPLY AND USE (million kwh)	1958	1959	1960	1961	1962	1963	1964	1965
PRODUCTION (Utilities & industries)								
Total (Gross)	143	165	183	195	212	251	281	
(Net)	140	158	176	186	204	240	268	
Hydro	41	41	--	43	39	46	43	
Conventional thermal	102	124	--	152	173	205	238	
Nuclear	—	—	—	—	—	—	—	
Geothermal	—	—	—	—	—	—	—	
PRODUCTION (Utilities only)								
Total (Gross)	74	96	109	122	145	173	208	
(Net)	71	89	102	114	136	163	195	
Hydro	3	1	1	1	1	2	2	
Conventional thermal	71	95	108	121	144	171	206	
Nuclear	—	—	—	—	—	—	—	
Geothermal	—	—	—	—	—	—	—	
NET IMPORTS	—	—	—	—	—	—	—	
SUPPLY (Gross)	143	165	183	195	212	251	281	
(Net)	140	158	176	186	204	240	268	
CONSUMPTION	125	142	158	159	173	205	230	
Transport	--	--	--	--	--	--	--	
Domestic sector	39	53	61	63	72	84	98	
Industry	86	89	97	96	101	121	132	
LOSS AND USE	15	16	18	27	31	35	38	
PLANT (thousand kw)								
CAPACITY (Utilities & industries)								
Total	75	74	75	77	77	84	84	
Hydro	9	9	9	9	9	9	9	
Conventional thermal	66	65	66	68	68	75	75	
Nuclear	—	—	—	—	—	—	—	
Geothermal	—	—	—	—	—	—	—	
CAPACITY (Utilities only)								
Total	46	47	48	46	50	52	57	
Hydro	1	1	1	1	1	1	1	
Conventional thermal	45	46	47	45	49	51	56	
Nuclear	—	—	—	—	—	—	—	
Geothermal	—	—	—	—	—	—	—	
FUEL CONSUMPTION (Utilities only)								
Total (Tcals)	--	--	--	--	--	--	--	
RESERVOIR STORAGE CAPACITY (million kwh)	--	--	--	--	--	--	--	

SUPPLEMENTARY DATA FOR 1964

Transmission lines, 100 kv + (km): —
Households served (thousands): 63
Revenues per kwh (U.S. cents) — Total: 4.5
  Residential: 6.3   Railways:
  Industry: 3.0   Lighting:
Population (thousands): 1597

Other characteristics of plants and systems:

Nicaragua's power is generated mainly by the Empresa Nacional de Luz y Fuerza, which is publicly owned. Service is provided by ENALUF through a limited 69 KV network in the western part of the country and isolated stations elsewhere. Its principal facilities are a 30 MW steam plant and a 19 MW diesel plant at Managua.

Sources of data:
UN. *Stat. yrbk.* UN. ECLA. *Estud. econ.*
———. *Estud. sobre la elec.* ———. *Stat. bull.*
———. Subcom. Centroamer. de elec. *Estadísticas de energía eléctrica.*
———. ———. *Estadísticas preliminares.*
———. ———. *Estudio comparativo de costos.*
US. *Foreign serv. desp.*

NIGER

SUPPLY AND USE (million kwh)	1958	1959	1960	1961	1962	1963	1964	1965
PRODUCTION (Utilities & industries)								
Total (Gross)	4.8	6.0	7.9	9.2	13	14	15	
(Net)	--	--	--	--	--	--	--	
Hydro	—	—	—	—	—	—	—	
Conventional thermal	4.8	6.0	7.9	9.2	13	14	15	
Nuclear	—	—	—	—	—	—	—	
Geothermal	—	—	—	—	—	—	—	
PRODUCTION (Utilities only)								
Total (Gross)	4.8	6.0	7.9	9.2	13	14	15	
(Net)	--	--	--	--	--	--	--	
Hydro	—	—	—	—	—	—	—	
Conventional thermal	4.8	6.0	7.9	9.2	13	14	15	
Nuclear	—	—	—	—	—	—	—	
Geothermal	—	—	—	—	—	—	—	
NET IMPORTS	—	—	—	—	—	—	—	
SUPPLY (Gross)	5	6	8	9	13	14	15	
(Net)	--	--	--	--	--	--	--	
CONSUMPTION	--	--	6	8	11	12	13	
Transport	—	—	—	—	—	—	—	
Domestic sector	--	--	4	5	7	--	--	
Industry	--	--	2	3	4	--	--	
LOSS AND USE	--	--	2	1	2	2	2	

PLANT (thousand kw)

	1958	1959	1960	1961	1962	1963	1964	1965
CAPACITY (Utilities & industries)								
Total	1.9	2.1	2.9	3	3	7	8	
Hydro	—	—	—	—	—	—	—	
Conventional thermal	1.9	2.1	2.9	3	3	7	8	
Nuclear	—	—	—	—	—	—	—	
Geothermal	—	—	—	—	—	—	—	
CAPACITY (Utilities only)								
Total	1.9	2.1	2.9	3	3	7	8	
Hydro	—	—	—	—	—	—	—	
Conventional thermal	1.9	2.1	2.9	3	3	7	8	
Nuclear	—	—	—	—	—	—	—	
Geothermal	—	—	—	—	—	—	—	

FUEL CONSUMPTION (Utilities only)

	1958	1959	1960	1961	1962	1963	1964	1965
Total (Tcals)	--	--	--	--	--	--	--	
RESERVOIR STORAGE CAPACITY (million kwh)	—	—	—	—	—	—	—	

SUPPLEMENTARY DATA FOR 1964

Transmission lines, 100 kv+ (km) : - -
Households served (thousands) : 4.2
Revenues per kwh (U.S. cents) — Total:
  Residential: Railways:
  Industry: Lighting: 19.0
Population (thousands) : 3237

Other characteristics of plants and systems:

Société Africaine d'Electricité, privately owned, is the principal generator of electricity in Niger. Service is provided by isolated plants, the largest of which has a capacity of 2.5 MW. Electricity is supplied to a very small fraction of the total population.

Sources of data:
EEC. *Yrbk. Overseas Assoc.*
Inst. de la Stat. *Données statistiques.*
Soc. R. Moreux. *Industries et travaux.* No. 122.
UN. *Stat. yrbk.*   US. FPC. *World power data.*

NIGERIA

SUPPLY AND USE (million kwh)	1958	1959	1960	1961	1962	1963	1964	1965
PRODUCTION (Utilities & industries)								
Total (Gross)	344	403	528	642	750	893	1024	
(Net)	--	--	--	--	--	--	--	
Hydro	52	55	91	101	108	113	126	
Conventional thermal	292	348	437	541	642	780	898	
Nuclear	—	—	—	—	—	—	—	
Geothermal	—	—	—	—	—	—	—	
PRODUCTION (Utilities only)								
Total (Gross)	328	387	512	626	736	879	1008	
(Net)	--	--	--	--	--	--	--	
Hydro	52	55	91	101	108	113	126	
Conventional thermal	276	332	421	525	628	766	882	
Nuclear	—	—	—	—	—	—	—	
Geothermal	—	—	—	—	—	—	—	
NET IMPORTS	—	—	—	—	—	—	—	
SUPPLY (Gross)	344	403	528	642	750	893	1024	
(Net)	--	--	--	--	--	--	--	
CONSUMPTION	309e	361e	472e	555	649	778	895	
Transport	—	—	—	—	—	—	—	
Domestic sector	--	--	157e	186	212	244	266	
Industry	--	--	315	369	437	534	629	
LOSS AND USE	35e	42e	56	87	101	115	129	

PLANT (thousand kw)								
CAPACITY (Utilities & industries)								
Total	121	127	173	207	238	256	272	
Hydro	20	20	20	18	18	21	21	
Conventional thermal	101	107	153	189	220	235	251	
Nuclear	—	—	—	—	—	—	—	
Geothermal	—	—	—	—	—	—	—	
CAPACITY (Utilities only)								
Total	117	123	170	203	233	252	268	
Hydro	20	20	20	18	18	21	21	
Conventional thermal	97	103	150	185	215	231	247	
Nuclear	—	—	—	—	—	—	—	
Geothermal	—	—	—	—	—	—	—	

FUEL CONSUMPTION (Utilities only)								
Coal (mmt)	206	170	130	138	188	151	164	
Diesel oil (mmt)	17	23	28	32	36	31	--	
Fuel oil (mmt)	—	27	65	84	—	—	—	
Total (Tcals)	--	--	--	--	--	--	--	
RESERVOIR STORAGE CAPACITY (million kwh)	--	--	--	--	--	--	--	

SUPPLEMENTARY DATA FOR 1964

Transmission lines, 100 kv+ (km): (1961) 404
Households served (thousands): (1965) 205
Revenues per kwh (U.S. cents) — Total: 4.1
    Residential: 4.4   Railways:
    Industry: 4.3   Lighting: 4.7
Population (thousands): 56,400

Sources of data:
UN. *Stat. yrbk.*
Electricity Corporation of Nigeria. *Annual report.*
Federal Office of Statistics. *Annual abstract of statistics.*
———. *Quarterly digest of statistics.*

Other characteristics of plants and systems:
    Nigeria's electricity is generated mainly by the publicly-owned Electricity Corporation of Nigeria, which operates a high-tension network covering much of southern Nigeria, from Lagos to Port Harcourt, and isolated stations scattered throughout the country. Another undertaking, the Nigerian Electricity Supply Corporation, also produces substantial quantities of hydroelectricity for the use of the mining industry. Only a very small fraction of the country's 56 million people is supplied with electricity.

NORWAY

SUPPLY AND USE (million kwh)	1958	1959	1960	1961	1962	1963	1964	1965
PRODUCTION (Utilities & industries)								
Total (Gross)								
(Net)	27500	28635	31121	33594	37743	39561	44028	
Hydro	27280	28395	30915	33386	37624	39365	43864	
Conventional thermal	220	240	206	208	119	196	164	
Nuclear	–	–	–	–	–	–	–	
Geothermal	–	–	–	–	–	–	–	
PRODUCTION (Utilities only)								
Total (Gross)								
(Net)	17389	17738	19747	21730	24388	28317	32097	
Hydro	17359	17708	19724	21717	24387	28237	32042	
Conventional thermal	30	30	23	13	1	80	55	
Nuclear	–	–	–	–	–	–	–	
Geothermal	–	–	–	–	–	–	–	
NET IMPORTS	–	–	–162	–101	–334	–945	–1391	
SUPPLY (Gross)	– –	– –	– –	– –	– –	– –	– –	
(Net)	27500	28635	30959	33493	37409	38616	42637	
CONSUMPTION	23925	25315	27509	29989	33789	35006	38539	
Transport	310	322	337	343	361	431	433	
Domestic sector	8400	8700	9033	9675	11078	12308	13054	
Industry	15215	16293	18139	19971	22350	22267	25052	
LOSS AND USE	3575	3320	3450	3504	3620	3610	4098	
PLANT (thousand kw)								
CAPACITY (Utilities & industries)								
Total	5641	6094	6607	7132	7686	8351	9166	
Hydro	5491	5938	6443	6965	7521	8210	9033	
Conventional thermal	150	156	164	167	165	141	133	
Nuclear	–	–	–	–	–	–	–	
Geothermal	–	–	–	–	–	–	–	
CAPACITY (Utilities only)								
Total	3818	4292	4750	5215	5716	6239	7090	
Hydro	3774	4248	4705	5171	5672	6182	7034	
Conventional thermal	44	44	45	44	44	57	56	
Nuclear	–	–	–	–	–	–	–	
Geothermal	–	–	–	–	–	–	–	
FUEL CONSUMPTION (Utilities only)								
Fuel oils (mmt)	11	10	9	4	–	2	2	
Total (Tcals)	116	105	94	42	–	21	21	
RESERVOIR STORAGE CAPACITY (million kwh)	15180	15750	17160	17910	20329	22650	24514	

SUPPLEMENTARY DATA FOR 1964

Transmission lines, 100 kv+ (km): 5941
Households served (thousands): (1961) 1080
Revenues per kwh (U.S. cents) — Total: 0.6
  Residential: (1962) 0.7 Railways: 0.6
  Industry: 0.4 Lighting:
Population (thousands): 3694

Sources of data:
UN. *Stat. yrbk.*
UN. ECE. *Ann. bull. of elec. energy stat.*
UNIPEDE. *L'écon élec.*
———. *Réseaux de transport.* ———. *Statistiques.*
Central Bureau of Statistics. *Elektrisitetsstatistikk.*

Other characteristics of plants and systems:
The more densely populated portions of Norway are supplied by a single network which covers most of the nation. Other areas are supplied by regional networks or local installations. The bulk of the supply for public use is generated by municipal or state authorities. An important share of Norway's electricity is produced by the electrochemical and electrometallurgical industries, principally for their own use. The Norwegian network is connected with the Swedish network, to which it provides well over a billion kwh of electricity annually. Virtually the entire population of Norway is supplied with electricity.

PAKISTAN

SUPPLY AND USE (million kwh)	1958	1959	1960	1961	1962	1963	1964	1965
PRODUCTION (Utilities & industries)								
Total (Gross)	--	--	--	--	--	--	--	
(Net)	--	--	--	--	--	--	--	
Hydro	--	--	--	--	--	--	--	
Conventional thermal	--	--	--	--	--	--	--	
Nuclear	—	—	—	—	—	—	—	
Geothermal	—	—	—	—	, —	—	—	
PRODUCTION (Utilities only)								
Total (Gross)	1225	1302	1450	1819	2307	2584	3220	
(Net)	--	--	--	1745	2212	2467	3100e	
Hydro	457	511	539	801	1267	1396	1635	
Conventional thermal	768	791	911	1018	1040	1188	1585	
Nuclear	—	—	—	—	—	—	—	
Geothermal	—	—	—	—	—	—	—	
NET IMPORTS	—	—	—	—	—	—	—	
SUPPLY (Gross)	1225	1302	1450	1819	2307	2584	3220	
(Net)	--	--	--	1745	2212	2467	3100e	
CONSUMPTION	--	1045	1154	1286	1715	1961	--	
Transport	—	—	—	—	—	—	—	
Domestic sector	--	399	460	439	725	857	--	
Industry	--	646	694	847	990	1104	--	
LOSS AND USE	--	--	--	459	497	506	--	
PLANT (thousand kw)								
CAPACITY (Utilities & industries)								
Total	--	--	--	--	--	--	--	
Hydro	--	--	--	--	--	--	--	
Conventional thermal	--	--	--	--	--	--	--	
Nuclear	—	—	—	—	—	—	—	
Geothermal	—	—	—	—	—	—	—	
CAPACITY (Utilities only)								
Total	277	335	658	688	839	859	971	
Hydro	67	76	253	254	333	347	348	
Conventional thermal	210	259	405	434	506	512	623	
Nuclear	—	—	—	—	—	—	—	
Geothermal	—	—	—	—	—	—	—	
FUEL CONSUMPTION (Utilities only)								
Coal (mmt)	106	89	54	41	56	68	--	
Diesel oil (mmt)	42	59	39	56	30	29	--	
Fuel oil (mmt)	45	93	75	73	47	42	--	
Natural gas (mil m^3)	102	169	245	287	330	356	--	
Total (Tcals)	3654	4179	4333	4431	4368	4683	--	
RESERVOIR STORAGE CAPACITY (million kwh)	--	--	--	--	--	--	--	

SUPPLEMENTARY DATA FOR 1964

Transmission lines, 100 kv+ (km) : (1963) 3877
Households served (thousands) :   --
Revenues per kwh (U.S. cents) — Total: (1963) 3.0
    Residential: Railways:
    Industry: Lighting: 4.6
Population (thousands) : 100753

Other characteristics of plants and systems:

There are three major agencies responsible for power development in Pakistan: the Karachi Electric Supply Corporation (50% government owned), the West Pakistan Water and Power Development Authority (which covers West Pakistan outside of Karachi) and the East Pakistan Water and Power Development Authority. The two development authorities are publicly owned. Partial networks cover portions of both West and East Pakistan. There appear to be somewhat less than one million customers in the entire country, indicating that electricity is supplied to less than ten per cent of Pakistan's people. Domestically produced natural gas and coal are the principal fuels used in generating thermal electric power.

Sources of data:

UN. *Stat. yrbk.* UN. ECAFE. *Elec. power.*
UN. ECAFE. *Proceedings of the regional seminar on energy resources and electric power development.*
US. *Foreign serv. desp.*
Central Statistical Office. *Electric power statistics.*
West Pakistan Water and Power Development Authority. *WAPDA annual report.*

PANAMA

SUPPLY AND USE (million kwh)	1958	1959	1960	1961	1962	1963	1964	1965
PRODUCTION (Utilities & industries)								
Total (Gross)	197	217	234	263	325	368	400	
(Net)	--	--	--	--	--	--	--	
Hydro	14	17	18	19	21	28	31	
Conventional thermal	183	200	216	244	304	340	369	
Nuclear	–	–	–	–	–	–	–	
Geothermal	–	–	–	–	–	–	–	
PRODUCTION (Utilities only)								
Total (Gross)	172	191	203	229	256	295	326	
(Net)	--	--	--	--	--	--	--	
Hydro	14	17	18	19	21	28	31	
Conventional thermal	158	174	185	210	235	267	295	
Nuclear	–	–	–	–	–	–	–	
Geothermal	–	–	–	–	–	–	–	
NET IMPORTS	–	–	–	–	–	–	–8	
SUPPLY (Gross)	197	217	234	263	325	368	392	
(Net)	--	--	--	--	--	--	--	
CONSUMPTION	--	--	--	231	292	328	347	
Transport	–	–	–	–	–	–	–	
Domestic sector	--	--	--	163	187	214	229	
Industry	--	--	--	68	105	114	118	
LOSS AND USE	--	--	--	32	33	40e	45	
PLANT (thousand kw)								
CAPACITY (Utilities & industries)								
Total	62	62	72	79	93	94	108	
Hydro	5	5	7	7	7	7	7	
Conventional thermal	57	57	65	72	86	87	101	
Nuclear	–	–	–	–	–	–	–	
Geothermal	–	–	–	–	–	–	–	
CAPACITY (Utilities only)								
Total	53	52	62	67	71	72	86	
Hydro	5	5	7	7	7	7	7	
Conventional thermal	48	47	55	60	64	65	79	
Nuclear	–	–	–	–	–	–	–	
Geothermal	–	–	–	–	–	–	–	
FUEL CONSUMPTION (Utilities only)								
Fuel oil (mmt)	50	53	57	65	72	78	89	
Total (Tcals)	475	504	542	618	684	741	846	
RESERVOIR STORAGE CAPACITY (million kwh)	–	–	–	–	–	–	–	

SUPPLEMENTARY DATA FOR 1964

Transmission lines, 100 kv+ (km): –
Households served (thousands): 99
Revenues per kwh (U.S. cents) — Total: 4.0
 Residential: 4.9   Railways:
 Industry: 2.5   Lighting: 8.7
Population (thousands): 1205

Sources of data:
UN. *Stat. yrbk.* UN. ECLA. *Estud. econ.*
——. *Estud. sobre la elec.*
——. Subcom. Centroamer. de elec. *Estadísticas de energía eléctrica.*
—. ——. *Estadísticas preliminares.*
Dirección de Estadística y Censo. *Estadística panameña.*

Other characteristics of plants and systems:
Cia. Panameña de Fuerza y Luz, privately owned, is the principal producer and distributor of electricity. Its 63 MW of capacity represents more than three-quarters of the total available in the public service. Most of the country's power is generated in steam plants in Panama and Colon, the largest of which has a capacity of 37.5 MW; but away from the vicinity of the Canal, power is made available through small, regional networks and local facilities. About a quarter of the country's population appears to be supplied with electricity.

PANAMA CANAL ZONE

SUPPLY AND USE (million kwh)	1958	1959	1960	1961	1962	1963	1964	1965
PRODUCTION (Utilities & industries)								
Total (Gross)	250	246	269	319	330	368	418	
(Net)	--	--	--	316	--	--	--	
Hydro	209	207	245	269	259	293	263	
Conventional thermal	41	39	24	50	71	75	155	
Nuclear	—	—	—	—	—	—	—	
Geothermal	—	—	—	—	—	—	—	
PRODUCTION (Utilities only)								
Total (Gross)	250	246	269	319	330	368	418	
(Net)	--	--	--	--	--	--	--	
Hydro	209	207	245	269	259	293	263	
Conventional thermal	41	39	24	50	71	75	155	
Nuclear	—	—	—	—	—	—	—	
Geothermal	—	—	—	—	—	—	8	
NET IMPORTS	—	—	—	—	—	—	8	
SUPPLY (Gross)	250	246	269	319	330	368	426	
(Net)	--	--	--	316	--	--	--	
CONSUMPTION	220	234	257	290	291	354	401	
Transport	72	76	82	86	89	93	112	
Domestic sector	38	45	50	59	64	80	85	
Industry (Government)	110	113	125	145	138	181	204	
LOSS AND USE	30	12	12	26	39	14	25	

PLANT (thousand kw)

	1958	1959	1960	1961	1962	1963	1964	1965
CAPACITY (Utilities & industries)								
Total	60	64	64	64	64	86	86	
Hydro	37	44	46	46	46	46	46	
Conventional thermal	23	20	18	18	18	40	40	
Nuclear	—	—	—	—	—	—	—	
Geothermal	—	—	—	—	—	—	—	
CAPACITY (Utilities only)								
Total	60	64	64	64	64	86	86	
Hydro	37	44	46	46	46	46	46	
Conventional thermal	23	20	18	18	18	40	40	
Nuclear	—	—	—	—	—	—	—	
Geothermal	—	—	—	—	—	—	—	

FUEL CONSUMPTION (Utilities only)

	1958	1959	1960	1961	1962	1963	1964	1965
Total (Tcals)	--	--	--	--	--	--	--	
RESERVOIR STORAGE CAPACITY (million kwh)	--	--	--	--	--	--	--	

SUPPLEMENTARY DATA FOR 1964

Transmission lines, 100 kv+ (km):   –
Households served (thousands):   7
Revenues per kwh (U.S. cents) — Total:
  Residential: Railways:
  Industry: Lighting:
Population (thousands):   54

Other characteristics of plants and systems:

The electricity supply of the Canal Zone is provided almost entirely by the Panama Canal Company, which is publicly owned. The principal sources of power are the Madden and Gatun hydro plants, with capacities of 24 MW and 22.5 MW respectively, and the gas turbine plant at Miraflores. The Company's plants are interconnected, and provide power to perhaps half the Canal Zone's population.

Sources of data:
UN. *Stat. yrbk.*
UN. ECLA. *Estud. sobre la elec.*
———. Subcom. Centroamer. de elec. *Estadísticas preliminares.*
US. FPC. *Power system statement.*

PAPUA

SUPPLY AND USE (million kwh)	1958	1959	1960	1961	1962	1963	1964	1965
PRODUCTION (Utilities & industries)								
Total (Gross)	17	19	21	24	25	29	34	
(Net)	--	--	--	--	--	--	--	
Hydro	16	18	19	21	24	27	28	
Conventional thermal	1	1	2	3	1	2	6	
Nuclear	—	—	—	—	—	—	—	
Geothermal	—	—	—	—	—	—	—	
PRODUCTION (Utilities only)								
Total (Gross)	17	19	21	24	25	29	34	
(Net)	--	--	--	--	--	--	--	
Hydro	16	18	19	21	24	27	28	
Conventional thermal	1	1	2	3	1	2	6	
Nuclear	—	—	—	—	—	—	—	
Geothermal	—	—	—	—	—	—	—	
NET IMPORTS	—	—	—	—	—	—	—	
SUPPLY (Gross)	17	19	21	24	25	29	34	
(Net)	--	--	--	--	--	--	--	
CONSUMPTION	--	--	--	--	--	--	--	
Transport	—	—	—	—	—	—	—	
Domestic sector	--	--	--	--	--	--	--	
Industry	--	--	--	--	--	--	--	
LOSS AND USE	--	--	--	--	--	--	--	

PLANT (thousand kw)

	1958	1959	1960	1961	1962	1963	1964	1965
CAPACITY (Utilities & industries)								
Total	5.6	5.5	8.0	8.0	8.0	8.0	8.2	
Hydro	3.0	3.0	5.5	5.5	5.5	5.5	5.5	
Conventional thermal	2.6	2.5	2.5	2.5	2.5	2.5	2.7	
Nuclear	—	—	—	—	—	—	—	
Geothermal	—	—	—	—	—	—	—	
CAPACITY (Utilities only)								
Total	5.6	5.5	8.0	8.0	8.0	8.0	8.2	
Hydro	3.0	3.0	5.5	5.5	5.5	5.5	5.5	
Conventional thermal	2.6	2.5	2.5	2.5	2.5	2.5	2.7	
Nuclear	—	—	—	—	—	—	—	
Geothermal	—	—	—	—	—	—	—	

FUEL CONSUMPTION (Utilities only)

	1958	1959	1960	1961	1962	1963	1964
Total (Tcals)	--	--	--	--	--	--	--
RESERVOIR STORAGE CAPACITY (million kwh)	--	--	--	--	--	--	--

SUPPLEMENTARY DATA FOR 1964

Transmission lines, 100 kv+ (km) : —
Households served (thousands) : - -
Revenues per kwh (U.S. cents) — Total:
  Residential: Railways:
  Industry: Lighting:
Population (thousands) : 562

Other characteristics of plants and systems:

  Papua's electricity supply is produced by the Administration of Papua and New Guinea at a number of small hydro and diesel plants scattered throughout the country.

Sources of data:
  Benn Bros. *Elec. undertakings.*
  UN. *Stat. yrbk.*
  Commonwealth of Australia. *Territory of Papua: Report to the General Assembly of the United Nations.*

PARAGUAY

SUPPLY AND USE (million kwh)	1958	1959	1960	1961	1962	1963	1964	1965
PRODUCTION (Utilities & industries)								
Total (Gross)	82	87	96	100	106	125	129	
(Net)	--	--	--	--	--	--	--	
Hydro	—	—	—	—	—	—	—	
Conventional thermal	82	87	96	100	106	125	129	
Nuclear	—	—	—	—	—	—	—	
Geothermal	—	—	—	—	—	—	—	
PRODUCTION (Utilities only)								
Total (Gross)	66	71	80	85	90	105	116	
(Net)	--	--	--	--	--	--	--	
Hydro	—	—	—	—	—	—	—	
Conventional thermal	66	71	80	85	90	105	116	
Nuclear	—	—	—	—	—	—	—	
Geothermal	—	—	—	—	—	—	—	
NET IMPORTS	—	—	—	—	—	—	—	
SUPPLY (Gross)	82	87	96	100	106	125	129	
(Net)	--	--	--	--	--	--	--	
CONSUMPTION	65	71	79	85	--	96	102	
Transport	2	2	1e	1	2	2	1	
Domestic sector	32	36	36e	37	--	--	--	
Industry	31	33	42	47	52	54	59	
LOSS AND USE	17	16	17	15e	--	--	--	
PLANT (thousand kw)								
CAPACITY (Utilities & industries)								
Total	29	29	30	--	--	50	--	
Hydro	—	—	—	—	—	—	—	
Conventional thermal	29	29	30	--	--	50	--	
Nuclear	—	—	—	—	—	—	—	
Geothermal	—	—	—	—	—	—	—	
CAPACITY (Utilities only)								
Total	28	28	28	24	24	--	--	
Hydro	—	—	—	—	—	—	—	
Conventional thermal	28	28	28	24	24	--	--	
Nuclear	—	—	—	—	—	—	—	
Geothermal	—	—	—	—	—	—	—	
FUEL CONSUMPTION (Utilities only)								
Fuelwood (mmt)	--	--	--	59	--	--	--	
Fuel oil (mmt)	--	--	--	26	--	--	--	
Total (Tcals)	--	--	--	--	--	--	--	
RESERVOIR STORAGE CAPACITY (million kwh)	—	—	—	—	—	—	—	

SUPPLEMENTARY DATA FOR 1964

Transmission lines, 100 kv+ (km):   --
Households served (thousands):   --
Revenues per kwh (U.S. cents) — Total: 6.0
  Residential: 6.6   Railways:
  Industry: (1961) 5.1   Lighting: 7.1
Population (thousands):   1968

Sources of data:
UN. *Stat. yrbk.*   UN. ECLA. *Estud. econ.*
———. *Estud. sobre la elec.*   US. *Foreign serv. desp.*
Ministerio de Industria y Comercio. *Censos economicos.*
UN. ECLA. *Data communicated to N. B. Guyol.*

Other characteristics of plants and systems:
    The Administracion Nacional de Electricidad *(ANDE)*, owned by the Government of Paraguay, generates most of the country's electricity in the Puerto Sajonia thermal plant at Asunción, which has a capacity of 24 MW. Supplies to other towns and cities are provided entirely by small, local facilities. It is estimated that no more than a tenth of the population of Paraguay is supplied with electricity.

PERU

SUPPLY AND USE (million kwh)	1958	1959	1960	1961	1962	1963	1964	1965
PRODUCTION (Utilities & industries)								
Total (Gross)	1990	2219	2656	2945	3067	3419	3689	
(Net)	--	--	--	--	--	--	--	
Hydro	1433	1595	1730	1878	1946	2159	2448	
Conventional thermal	557	624	926	1067	1121	1260	1241	
Nuclear	—	—	—	—	—	—	—	
Geothermal	—	—	—	—	—	—	—	
PRODUCTION (Utilities only)								
Total (Gross)	899	1082	1209	1330	1408	1499	1634	
(Net)	--	--	--	--	--	--	--	
Hydro	796	968	1071	1170	1200	1271	1345	
Conventional thermal	103	114	138	160	208	228	289	
Nuclear	—	—	—	—	—	—	—	
Geothermal	—	—	—	—	—	—	—	
NET IMPORTS								
SUPPLY (Gross)	1990	2219	2656	2945	3067	3419	3689	
(Net)	--	--	--	--	--	--	--	
CONSUMPTION	1754	1747	2144	2404	2530	2867	3095	
Transport	25	22	23	21	20	18	16	
Domestic sector	309	340	380	425	508	586	647	
Industry	1420	1385	1741	1958	2002	2263	2432	
LOSS AND USE	236	472	512	541	537	552	594	
PLANT (thousand kw)								
CAPACITY (Utilities & industries)								
Total	653	746	841	863	917	999	1123	
Hydro	401	441	515	463	504	551	663	
Conventional thermal	252	305	326	400	413	448	460	
Nuclear	—	—	—	—	—	—	—	
Geothermal	—	—	—	—	—	—	—	
CAPACITY (Utilities only)								
Total	291	320	348	385	410	448	522	
Hydro	213	222e	222	248	272	299	369	
Conventional thermal	78	98	126	137	138	149	153	
Nuclear	—	—	—	—	—	—	—	
Geothermal	—	—	—	—	—	—	—	
FUEL CONSUMPTION (Utilities only)								
Total (Tcals)	--	--	--	--	--	--	--	
RESERVOIR STORAGE CAPACITY (million kwh)	--	--	--	--	--	--	--	

SUPPLEMENTARY DATA FOR 1964

Transmission lines, 100 kv + (km) :   —
Households served (thousands) :   262*
Revenues per kwh (U.S. cents) — Total: 2.2
   Residential: 2.2*   Railways:
   Industry: 1.7*   Lighting: 3.2
Population (thousands) :   11298
* Lima Light & Power Co. only
Sources of data:
UN. *Stat. yrbk.*   UN. ECLA. *Estud. econ.*
———. *Estud. sobre la elec.*
Empresas Eléctricas Asociadas. *Memoria del Directorio.*
———. *Datos estadísticos.*
Instituto Nacional de Investigación y Fomento Mineros. Dirección de Minería. *Anuario de la industria minera del Perú.*
Instituto Nacional de Planificación. Dirección Nacional de Estadística y Censos. *Boletín de estadística Peruana.*
Ministerio de Fomento. Dirección de Industrias y Electricidad. *Estadística de los servicios eléctricos del Perú.*

Other characteristics of plants and systems:

     The public supply of electricity in Peru is generated mainly by Lima Light and Power Company and Hidrandina - - both privately owned - - and Corporacion Peruana del Santa, which is publicly owned. Except for a regional network centering in Lima, the country is served mainly by isolated plants. More than half the total supply of electricity is privately generated for the use of industry, the copper industry in particular.

PHILIPPINES

SUPPLY AND USE (million kwh)	1958	1959	1960	1961	1962	1963	1964	1965
PRODUCTION (Utilities & industries)								
Total (Gross)	1955	2287	2761	3095	3680	4217	4678	
(Net)	--	--	--	--	--	--	--	
Hydro	744	688	1224	1187	1246	1444	1554	
Conventional thermal	1211	1599	1537	1908	2434	2773	3124	
Nuclear	—	—	—	—	—	—	—	
Geothermal	—	—	—	—	—	—	—	
PRODUCTION (Utilities only)								
Total (Gross)	1756	2032	2259	2555	3010	3406	3828	
(Net)	--	--	--	--	--	--	--	
Hydro	744	688	1224	1187	1246	1444	1554	
Conventional thermal	1012	1344	1035	1368	1764	1962	2274	
Nuclear	—	—	—	—	—	—	—	
Geothermal	—	—	—	—	—	—	—	
NET IMPORTS	—	—	—	—	—	—	—	
SUPPLY (Gross)	1955	2287	2761	3095	3680	4217	4678	
(Net)	--	--	--	--	--	--	--	
CONSUMPTION	1481	1938	2389	2740	3200	3666	--	
Transport	—	—	—	—	—	—	—	
Domestic sector	953	970e	1149	1298	1472	1498	--	
Industry	528	968	1240	1442	1728	2168	--	
LOSS AND USE	474	349e	372	355	480	551	--	
PLANT (thousand kw)								
CAPACITY (Utilities & industries)								
Total	495	505	765	857	869	958	992	
Hydro	187	190	290	290	291	291	291	
Conventional thermal	308	315	475	567	578	667	701	
Nuclear	—	—	—	—	—	—	—	
Geothermal	—	—	—	—	—	—	—	
CAPACITY (Utilities only)								
Total	424	435	596	653	661	730	732	
Hydro	187	188	290	290	291	291	291	
Conventional thermal	237	247	306	363	370	439	441	
Nuclear	—	—	—	—	—	—	—	
Geothermal	—	—	—	—	—	—	—	
FUEL CONSUMPTION (Utilities only)								
Coal (mmt)	—	7	19	24	28	22e	--	
Diesel oil (mmt)	53.3	46.7	61.5	59.5	65.7	69e	--	
Fuel oil (mmt)	276	373	267	318	--	428	--	
Total (Tcals)	3654	4676	3731	4389	4991	--	--	
RESERVOIR STORAGE CAPACITY (million kwh)	--	--	--	--	--	--	--	

SUPPLEMENTARY DATA FOR 1964

Transmission lines, 100 kv+ (km): 698
Households served (thousands) : (1963) 814
Revenues per kwh (U.S. cents) — Total: 1.2
    Residential: 1.7   Railways:
    Industry: 0.9   Lighting: 3.1
Population (thousands) : 31270

Sources of data:
  UN. *Stat. yrbk.* UN. ECAFE. *Elec. power.*
  US. *Foreign serv. desp.*
  International Atomic Energy Agency. *Pre-investment*
    study on power including nuclear power in Luzon,
    Republic of the Philippines; general report.

Other characteristics of plants and systems:
    Electric power service is provided mainly by the National Power Corporation, government-owned, and the Manila Electric Power Company (MERALCO), which is privately owned. Much of the output of the NPC is distributed through municipalities or MERALCO. The bulk of the Philippines' electricity is produced and distributed on the island of Luzon, where the principal plants are interconnected via the Luzon grid. With less than a million customers altogether, it is estimated that considerably less than twenty per cent of the people of the Philippines are supplied with electricity. Imported fuel oil is the principal fuel used in generating thermal electric power in the Philippines.

SUPPLY AND USE (million kwh)	1958	1959	1960	1961	1962	1963	1964	1965
PRODUCTION (Utilities & industries)								
Total (Gross)	23962	26380	29307	32254	35383	36962	40611	
(Net)	21919	24128	26869	29585	32409	33373	36754	
Hydro	761	551	657	618	773	668	726	
Conventional thermal	23201	25829	28650	31636	34610	36294	39885	
Nuclear	—	—	—	—	—	—	—	
Geothermal	—	—	—	—	—	—	—	
PRODUCTION (Utilities only)								
Total (Gross)	18003	20014	22437	25322	28227	30371	34155	
(Net)	--	--	--	--	--	--	--	
Hydro	761	551	657	618	773	668	726	
Conventional thermal	17242	19463	21780	24704	27454	29703	33429	
Nuclear	—	—	—	—	—	—	—	
Geothermal	—	—	—	—	—	—	—	
NET IMPORTS	247	357	302	304	−26	−50	−558	
SUPPLY (Gross)	24209	26737	29609	32558	35357	36912	40053	
(Net)	22166	24485	27171	29889	32383	33323	36196	
CONSUMPTION	19788	21842	24335	26873	29191	29939	32449	
Transport	546	612	684	832	990	1170	1315	
Domestic sector	3716	4197	4712	5086	5557	5511	5697	
Industry	15526	17033	18939	20955	22644	23258	25437	
LOSS AND USE	2378	2643	2836	3016	3192	3384	3747	

PLANT (thousand kw)

	1958	1959	1960	1961	1962	1963	1964	1965
CAPACITY (Utilities & industries)								
Total	5571	5891	6316	6768	7716	8463	9203	
Hydro	248	248	261	311	327	349	350	
Conventional thermal	5323	5643	6055	6457	7389	8114	8853	
Nuclear	—	—	—	—	—	—	—	
Geothermal	—	—	—	—	—	—	—	
CAPACITY (Utilities only)								
Total	3836	4104	4479	4915	5892	6588	7357	
Hydro	248	248	261	311	327	349	350	
Conventional thermal	3588	3856	4218	4604	5565	6239	7007	
Nuclear	—	—	—	—	—	—	—	
Geothermal	—	—	—	—	—	—	—	

FUEL CONSUMPTION (Utilities only)

	1958	1959	1960	1961	1962	1963	1964	1965
Coal (mmt)	12514	13331	14685	15656	16394	16338	16076	
Lignite (mmt)	606	1682	1807	2449	3428	6830	12016	
Peat & fuelwood (mmt)	—	—	18	10	9	5	3	
Fuel oils (mmt)	14	11	8	17	26	44	95	
Natural gas (Tcals)	—	—	180	1060	1680	1597	1508	
Manufactured gas (Tcals)	399	304	390	343	330	347	377	
Total (Tcals)	62717	67585	73720	81217	87801	91518	98136	
RESERVOIR STORAGE CAPACITY (million kwh)	17	17e	17	20	20	20	20	

SUPPLEMENTARY DATA FOR 1964

Transmission lines, 100 kv+ (km): 16107
Households served (thousands): 6570
Revenues per kwh (U.S. cents) — Total:
   Residential: Railways: 1.3
   Industry: Lighting: 22.5
Population (thousands): 31161

Other characteristics of plants and systems:

All utility generating plants are owned by the Polish government. All important plants are interconnected in a national network which provides electricity to an estimated eighty per cent of the Polish population. There is a considerable trade in electricity between Poland and other countries in the COMECON group.

Sources of data:

UN. *Stat. yrbk.* UN. ECE. *Ann. bull. of elec. energy stat.*
_____. *Org. of elec. power services.*
UNIPEDE. *L'écon. élec.* _____. *Réseaux de transport.*
_____. *Statistiques.*
EEI. *Rept. on elec. power dev. in Poland.*
Głowny Urzad Statystyczny. *Rocznik statystyczny.*
Zjednoczenie Energetyki. Statystyka Rozwoju.
   Electroenergetyki Polskiej.

PORTUGAL

SUPPLY AND USE (million kwh)	1958	1959	1960	1961	1962	1963	1964	1965
PRODUCTION (Utilities & industries)								
Total (Gross)	2667	2994	3264	3611	3833	4302	4761	
(Net)	2640	2971	3237	3595	3815	4285	4742	
Hydro	2509	2864	3105	3422	3511	4002	4220	
Conventional thermal	158	130	159	189	322	300	541	
Nuclear	—	—	—	—	—	—	—	
Geothermal	—	—	—	—	—	—	—	
PRODUCTION (Utilities only)								
Total (Gross)	2529	2854	3113	3450	3648	4092	4496	
(Net)	2502	2831	3086	3434	3630	4075	4477	
Hydro	2478	2831	3067	3389	3482	3961	4180	
Conventional thermal	51	23	46	61	166	131	316	
Nuclear	—	—	—	—	—	—	—	
Geothermal	—	—	—	—	—	—	—	
NET IMPORTS	5	1	1	11	27	−55	−12	
SUPPLY (Gross)	2672	2995	3265	3622	3860	4247	4749	
(Net)	2645	2972	3238	3606	3842	4230	4730	
CONSUMPTION	2261	2568	2794	3080	3308	3640	4073	
Transport	113	123	136	136	146	156	176	
Domestic sector	560	632	722	793	955	1041	1144	
Industry	1588	1813	1936	2151	2207	2443	2753	
LOSS AND USE	384	404	444	526	534	590	657	
PLANT (thousand kw)								
CAPACITY (Utilities & industries)								
Total	1146	1299	1335	1471	1470	1495	1607	
Hydro	932	1034	1085	1204	1204	1204	1311	
Conventional thermal	214	265	250	267	266	291	296	
Nuclear	—	—	—	—	—	—	—	
Geothermal	—	—	—	—	—	—	—	
CAPACITY (Utilities only)								
Total	1042	1192	1232	1349	1350	1371	1468	
Hydro	917	1018	1070	1188	1189	1189	1296	
Conventional thermal	125	174	162	161	161	182	172	
Nuclear	—	—	—	—	—	—	—	
Geothermal	—	—	—	—	—	—	—	
FUEL CONSUMPTION (Utilities only)								
Coal (mmt)	—	—	—	—	—	2	11	
Low grade coal (mmt)	28	15	49	46	132	94	203	
Fuel oils (mmt)	9	3	3	3	7	8	14	
Total (Tcals)	205	91	194	187	527	422	923	
RESERVOIR STORAGE CAPACITY (million kwh)	1052	1043	1043	1043	1070	1071	2040	

SUPPLEMENTARY DATA FOR 1964

Transmission lines, 100 kv+ (km): 2232
Households served (thousands): 1040
Revenues per kwh (U.S. cents) — Total:
  Residential: Railways: 0.7
  Industry: Lighting: 6.9
Population (thousands): 9106

Other characteristics of plants and systems:

Portugal's power is generated mainly by private undertakings, organized under State direction and with some State participation. The principal plants are interconnected in a system covering about three-quarters of the country. The number of domestic meters in service indicates that something less than half the people of Portugal are provided with electricity. There is now a considerable volume of trade in electricity between Portugal and Spain.

Sources of data:
UCPTE. *Réseau.* UN. *Stat. yrbk.*
UN. ECE. *Ann. bull. of elec. energy stat.*
  ————. *The future development potential of reservoir storage and firm hydro-electric capacity in Europe.*
  ————. *Elec. power situation.*
  ————. *Org. of elec. power services.*
UNIPEDE. *L'écon. élec.* ————. *Statistiques.*

PORTUGUESE GUINEA

SUPPLY AND USE (million kwh)	1958	1959	1960	1961	1962	1963	1964	1965
PRODUCTION (Utilities & industries)								
Total (Gross)	--	2.4e	3.2e	2.0e	2.8e	3.4e	3.7e	
(Net)	--	--	--	--	--	--	--	
Hydro	—	—	—	—	—	—	—	
Conventional thermal	--	2.4e	3.2e	2.0e	2.8e	3.4e	3.7e	
Nuclear	—	—	—	—	—	—	—	
Geothermal	—	—	—	—	—	—	—	
PRODUCTION (Utilities only)								
Total (Gross)	--	2.4e	3.2e	2.0e	2.8e	3.4e	3.7e	
(Net)	--	--	--	--	--	--	--	
Hydro	—	—	—	—	—	—	—	
Conventional thermal	--	2.4e	3.2e	2.0e	2.8e	3.4e	3.7e	
Nuclear	—	—	—	—	—	—	—	
Geothermal	—	—	—	—	—	—	—	
NET IMPORTS	—	—	—	—	—	—	—	
SUPPLY (Gross)	--	2.4e	3.2e	2.0e	2.8e	3.4e	3.7e	
(Net)	--	--	--	--	--	--	--	
CONSUMPTION	--	2.1	2.9	1.8	2.5	3.1	3.3	
Transport	—	—	—	—	—	—	—	
Domestic sector	--	1.3	2.1	1.4	2.1	2.7	2.4	
Industry	--	0.8	0.8	0.4	0.4	0.4	0.9	
LOSS AND USE	--	0.3	0.3	0.2	0.3	0.3	0.4	

PLANT (thousand kw)

	1958	1959	1960	1961	1962	1963	1964	1965
CAPACITY (Utilities & industries)								
Total	--	3.0	3.0	3.1	--	--	--	
Hydro	—	—	—	—	—	—	—	
Conventional thermal	--	3.0	3.0	3.1	--	--	--	
Nuclear	—	—	—	—	—	—	—	
Geothermal	—	—	—	—	—	—	—	
CAPACITY (Utilities only)								
Total	--	--	--	--	--	--	--	
Hydro	—	—	—	—	—	—	—	
Conventional thermal	--	--	--	--	--	--	--	
Nuclear	—	—	—	—	—	—	—	
Geothermal	—	—	—	—	—	—	—	

FUEL CONSUMPTION (Utilities only)

	1958	1959	1960	1961	1962	1963	1964	1965
Total (Tcals)	--	--	--	--	--	--	--	
RESERVOIR STORAGE CAPACITY (million kwh)	—	—	—	—	—	—	—	

SUPPLEMENTARY DATA FOR 1964

Transmission lines, 100 kv+ (km) :   —
Households served (thousands) :   --
Revenues per kwh (U.S. cents) — Total:
  Residential: Railways:
  Industry: Lighting:
Population (thousands) : 525

Other characteristics of plants and systems:

  Electricity is supplied to only a small fraction of the population.

Sources of data:
  Inst. de Est. *Anuário estatístico do ultramar.*

SUPPLY AND USE (million kwh)	1958	1959	1960	1961	1962	1963	1964	1965
PRODUCTION (Utilities & industries)								
Total (Gross)	1641	1875	2151	2438	2742	3164	3638	
(Net)	--	--	--	--	--	--	--	
Hydro	295	225	243	268	207	277	152	
Conventional thermal	1346	1650	1908	2170	2535	2887	3486	
Nuclear	—	—	—	—	—	—	—	
Geothermal	—	—	—	—	—	—	—	
PRODUCTION (Utilities only)								
Total (Gross)	1623	1860	2042	2393	2656	3059	3632	
(Net)	--	--	--	--	--	--	--	
Hydro	295	225	243	268	207	277	152	
Conventional thermal	1328	1635	1799	2125	2449	2782	3480	
Nuclear	—	—	—	—	—	—	—	
Geothermal	—	—	—	—	—	—	—	
NET IMPORTS	—	—	—	—	—	—	—	
SUPPLY (Gross)	1641	1875	2151	2438	2742	3164	3638	
(Net)	--	--	--	--	--	--	--	
CONSUMPTION	1357	1544	1781	2025	2296	2665	3028	
Transport	—	—	—	—	—	—	—	
Domestic sector	887	1010	1187	1368	1586	1873	2148	
Industry	470	534	594	657	710	792	880	
LOSS AND USE	284	331	370	413	446	499	610	
PLANT (thousand kw)								
CAPACITY (Utilities & industries)								
Total	--	--	--	--	--	--	--	
Hydro	108	108	109	107	107	107	107	
Conventional thermal	--	--	--	--	--	--	--	
Nuclear	—	—	—	—	—	—	—	
Geothermal	—	—	—	—	—	—	—	
CAPACITY (Utilities only)								
Total	368	373	472	585	668	738	750	
Hydro	108	108	109	107	107	107	107	
Conventional thermal	260	265	363	478	561	631	643	
Nuclear	—	—	—	—	—	—	—	
Geothermal	—	—	—	—	—	—	—	
FUEL CONSUMPTION (Utilities only)								
Fuel oils (mmt)	394	--	--	561	690	--	--	
Total (Tcals)	3743	--	--	5330	6555	--	--	
RESERVOIR STORAGE CAPACITY (million kwh)	--	--	--	--	--	--	--	

SUPPLEMENTARY DATA FOR 1964

Transmission lines, 100 kv+ (km): 388
Households served (thousands): 518
Revenues per kwh (U.S. cents) — Total: 2.3
  Residential: 2.6   Railways:
  Industry: 1.5   Lighting: 5.0
Population (thousands): 2578

Other characteristics of plants and systems:

The Puerto Rico Water Resources Authority, a public agency, provides power by HT network to most of Puerto Rico. Its principal plant is the San Juan steam plant, with a capacity of 278 MW. Puerto Rico now has Latin America's first nuclear plant, Bonus, of 16.5 MW. More than eighty per cent of the country's population appears to be supplied with electricity.

Sources of data:
UN. *Stat. yrbk.*   UN. ECLA. *Estud. econ.*
———. *Rev. Latinoamer. de elec.*
Bureau of Economics and Statistics. *Anuario estadístico.*
———. *Monthly bulletin of statistics.*
Government Development Bank for Puerto Rico. *A special report on Puerto Rico Water Resources Authority.*

SUPPLY AND USE (million kwh)	1958	1959	1960	1961	1962	1963	1964	1965
PRODUCTION (Utilities & industries)								
Total (Gross)	--	--	--	--	--	--	--	
(Net)	--	--	--	--	--	--	--	
Hydro	--	--	--	--	--	--	--	
Conventional thermal	--	--	--	--	--	--	--	
Nuclear	—	—	—	—	—	—	—	
Geothermal	—	—	—	—	—	—	—	
PRODUCTION (Utilities only)								
Total (Gross)	10	12	14	17	19	24	32	
(Net)	--	--	--	--	--	--	--	
Hydro	—	—	—	2	13	14	22	
Conventional thermal	10	12	14	15	6	10	10	
Nuclear	—	—	—	—	—	—	—	
Geothermal	—	—	—	—	—	—	—	
NET IMPORTS	—	—	—	—	—	—	—	
SUPPLY (Gross)	10	12	14	17	19	24	32	
(Net)	--	--	--	--	--	--	--	
CONSUMPTION	9	10	12	14	--	--	--	
Transport	—	—	—	—	—	—	—	
Domestic sector	3	4	4	--	--	--	--	
Industry	6	6	8	--	--	--	--	
LOSS AND USE	1	2	2	3	--	--	--	
PLANT (thousand kw)								
CAPACITY (Utilities & industries)								
Total	--	--	--	--	--	--	--	
Hydro	--	--	--	--	--	--	--	
Conventional thermal	--	--	--	--	--	--	--	
Nuclear	—	—	—	—	—	—	—	
Geothermal	—	—	—	—	—	—	—	
CAPACITY (Utilities only)								
Total	3.9	5.1	5.1	8.4	8.4	8.4	12	
Hydro	—	—	—	3.8	3.8	3.8	4	
Conventional thermal	3.9	5.1	5.1	4.6	4.6	4.6	8	
Nuclear	—	—	—	—	—	—	—	
Geothermal	—	—	—	—	—	—	—	
FUEL CONSUMPTION (Utilities only)								
Total (Tcals)	--	--	--	--	--	--	--	
RESERVOIR STORAGE CAPACITY (million kwh)	—	—	—	—	—	—	—	

SUPPLEMENTARY DATA FOR 1964

Transmission lines, 100 kv+ (km):   —
Households served (thousands):   21
Revenues per kwh (U.S. cents) — Total: 6.3
   Residential: Railways:
   Industry: Lighting:
Population (thousands):   384

Sources of data:
Benn. Bros. *Elec. undertakings.*
Soc. R. Moreux. *Industries et travaux. No. 122.*
UN. *Stat. yrbk.*
———. ECA. *Situation, trends & prospects.*
Institut National de la Statistique et des Etudes
   Economiques. *Annuaire statistique de la Réunion.*

Other characteristics of plants and systems:

The Société Anonyme d'Economie is responsible for public supply electricity throughout the island of Reunion and for electricity distribution in all communes but St. Denis. Most of the island is served by a 15 KV network of some 400 kilometers, which obtains its power principally from the Langevin Hydro-Electric plant and a number of small diesel plants.

RHODESIA

SUPPLY AND USE (million kwh)	1958	1959	1960	1961	1962	1963	1964	1965
PRODUCTION (Utilities & industries)								
Total (Gross)	--	--	--	--	--	--	--	
(Net)	1462	1531	2389	2782	2990	3369	3801	
Hydro	2	2	1046	2206	2736	3142	3571	
Conventional thermal	1460	1529	1343	576	254	227	230	
Nuclear	—	—	—	—	—	—	—	
Geothermal	—	—	—	—	—	—	—	
PRODUCTION (Utilities only)								
Total (Gross)								
(Net)	1366	1440	2321	2710	2919	3285	3708	
Hydro	2	2	1046	2206	2736	3142	3571	
Conventional thermal	1364	1438	1275	504	183	143	137	
Nuclear	—	—	—	—	—	—	—	
Geothermal	—	—	—	—	—	—	—	
NET IMPORTS	—	54	−743	−1053	−1215	−1478	−1751	
SUPPLY (Gross)	--	--	--	--	--	--	--	
(Net)	1462	1585	1646	1729	1775	1891	2050	
CONSUMPTION	1365	1453	1515	1602	1632	1709	1868	
Transport	—	—	—	—	—	—	—	
Domestic sector	597	644	688	760	792	792	844	
Industry	768	809	827	842	840	917	1024	
LOSS AND USE	97	132	131	127	143	182	182	

PLANT (thousand kw)	1958	1959	1960	1961	1962	1963	1964	1965
CAPACITY (Utilities & industries)								
Total	512	609	801	1064	1149	1188	1177	
Hydro	1	100	300	562	675	705	705	
Conventional thermal	511	509	501	502	474	483	472	
Nuclear	—	—	—	—	—	—	—	
Geothermal	—	—	—	—	—	—	—	
CAPACITY (Utilities only)								
Total	481	581	781	1043	1127	1157	1140	
Hydro	1	100	300	562	675	705	705	
Conventional thermal	480	481	481	481	452	452	435	
Nuclear	—	—	—	—	—	—	—	
Geothermal	—	—	—	—	—	—	—	

FUEL CONSUMPTION (Utilities only)	1958	1959	1960	1961	1962	1963	1964	1965
Coal (mmt)	--	844	756	368	--	--	--	
Wood (mmt CE)	--	10	10	11	--	--	--	
Diesel oil (mmt)	--	8	1	1	--	--	--	
Fuel oil (mmt)	--	1	1	1	--	--	--	
Total (Tcals)	--	6069	5383	2667	--	--	--	
RESERVOIR STORAGE CAPACITY (million kwh)	--	--	--	--	--	--	--	

SUPPLEMENTARY DATA FOR 1964

Transmission lines, 100 kv+ (km): --
Households served (thousands): (1963) 8.2
Revenues per kwh (U.S. cents) — Total: 1.5
  Residential: 2.5   Railways:
  Industry: 1.2   Lighting: 2.3
Population (thousands): 4140

Other characteristics of plants and systems:
    Most of Rhodesia's power is generated by facilities under the control of the Central African Power Corporation, which distributes power from Kariba and various thermal power plants in Rhodesia. Most of the thermal plants now serve as standby facilities. A 330 KV transmission system distributes power to various municipalities and to Zambia, which absorbs approximately half the output of Kariba. A small part of Rhodesia's electricity is imported from the Revué plant in Mozambique.

Sources of data:
Benn Bros. *Elec. undertakings.*
Central Statistical Office. *Monthly digest of statistics.*
Electricity Supply Commission. *Annual report and accounts.*
Ministry of Economic Affairs. *Economic report.*

ROMANIA

SUPPLY AND USE (million kwh)	1958	1959	1960	1961	1962	1963	1964	1965
PRODUCTION (Utilities & industries)								
Total (Gross)	6184	6824	7650	8657	10087	11682	13851	
(Net)	--	--	--	--	--	--	--	
Hydro	281	298	397	465	652	537	585	
Conventional thermal	5903	6526	7253	8192	9435	11145	13266	
Nuclear	—	—	—	—	—	—	—	
Geothermal	—	—	—	—	—	—	—	
PRODUCTION (Utilities only)								
Total (Gross)	4421	5022	5810	6742	8112	9626	11578	
(Net)	--	--	--	--	--	--	--	
Hydro	183	205	297	392	577	469	507	
Conventional thermal	4238	4817	5513	6350	7535	9157	11071	
Nuclear	—	—	—	—	—	—	—	
Geothermal	—	—	—	—	—	—	—	
NET IMPORTS	−16	−26	−28	−39	−33	−4	4	
SUPPLY (Gross)	6168	6798	7622	8618	10054	11678	13855	
(Net)	--	--	--	--	--	--	--	
CONSUMPTION	5007	5541	6265	7106	8197	9510	11199	
Transport	166	193	211	237	256	281	278	
Domestic sector	963	1069	1186	1402	1695	1964	2234	
Industry	3878	4279	4868	5467	6246	7265	8687	
LOSS AND USE	1161	1257	1357	1512	1857	2168	2656	

PLANT (thousand kw)

	1958	1959	1960	1961	1962	1963	1964	1965
CAPACITY (Utilities & industries)								
Total	1507	1604	1779	1863	2099	2356	2866	
Hydro	100	100	210	209	308	327	416	
Conventional thermal	1407	1504	1569	1654	1791	2029	2450	
Nuclear	—	—	—	—	—	—	—	
Geothermal	—	—	—	—	—	—	—	
CAPACITY (Utilities only)								
Total	958	1036	1221	1319	1525	1780	2266	
Hydro	67	67	178	179	278	299	388	
Conventional thermal	891	969	1043	1140	1247	1481	1878	
Nuclear	—	—	—	—	—	—	—	
Geothermal	—	—	—	—	—	—	—	

FUEL CONSUMPTION (Utilities only)

	1958	1959	1960	1961	1962	1963	1964	1965
Coal (mmt)	57	92	242	51	111	244	158	
Low grade coal (mmt)	1837	1804	1819	2258	2321	2634	2895	
Fuel oils (mmt)	377	249	185	209	162	207	180	
Natural gas (Tcals)	7299	9933	11401	13039	16191	18508	22135	
Manufactured gas (Tcals)	—	—	—	—	119	399	536	
Total (Tcals)	15796	17031	18728	21078	24038	28525	32947	
RESERVOIR STORAGE CAPACITY (million kwh)	8	8	293	297	304	387	547	

SUPPLEMENTARY DATA FOR 1964

Transmission lines, 100 kv+ (km): 5641
Households served (thousands): --
Revenues per kwh (U.S. cents) — Total:
 Residential: 3.3 Railways:
 Industry: 2.5 Lighting:
Population (thousands): 18927

Sources of data:
 UN. *Stat. yrbk.* UN. ECE. *Ann. bull. of elec. energy stat.*
 ———. *Org. of elec. power services.*
 UNIPEDE. *Réseaux de transport.*
 ———. *Statistiques.*
 EEI. *Rept. on elec. power dev. in Romania.*

Other characteristics of plants and systems:

The entire electric power industry in Romania is the property of the State. A significant part of the electricity produced is generated in combination heat and power stations. Romania's major power stations, industrial centers and large communities are tied together by a 110 KV system which covers much of the country. The national grid is interconnected with the systems of the Soviet Union, Czechoslovakia, and Hungary by means of a 400 KV line. The current level of consumption per capita in the domestic sector indicates that only a fraction of the population, probably less than half, is currently receiving electricity.

RWANDA

SUPPLY AND USE (million kwh)	1958	1959	1960	1961	1962	1963	1964	1965
PRODUCTION (Utilities & industries)								
Total (Gross)	8e	8e	10e	13	10	11	12e	
(Net)	--	--	--	--	--	--	--	
Hydro	4	3	6	4	9e	10	11e	
Conventional thermal	4	5	4	9	1	1	1	
Nuclear	—	—	—	—	—	—	—	
Geothermal	—	—	—	—	—	—	—	
PRODUCTION (Utilities only)								
Total (Gross)	--	--	--	--	--	--	--	
(Net)	--	--	--	--	--	--	--	
Hydro	--	--	--	--	--	--	--	
Conventional thermal	--	--	--	--	--	--	--	
Nuclear	—	—	—	—	—	—	—	
Geothermal	—	—	—	—	—	—	—	
NET IMPORTS	—	—	—	—	—	—	—	
SUPPLY (Gross)	8e	8e	10e	13	10	11	12	
(Net)	--	--	--	--	--	--	--	
CONSUMPTION	--	--	--	--	10	11	--	
Transport	—	—	—	—	—	—	—	
Domestic sector	2	2	2	2	2	2	--	
Industry	--	--	--	--	8	9	--	
LOSS AND USE	--	--	--	--	—	—	--	

PLANT (thousand kw)

	1958	1959	1960	1961	1962	1963	1964	1965
CAPACITY (Utilities & industries)								
Total	--	--	--	--	9.0	9.0	22	
Hydro	--	--	--	--	7.4	7.4	21	
Conventional thermal	--	--	--	--	1.6	1.6	1	
Nuclear	—	—	—	—	—	—	—	
Geothermal	—	—	—	—	—	—	—	
CAPACITY (Utilities only)								
Total	--	--	--	--	9.0	9.0	22	
Hydro	--	--	--	--	7.4	7.4	21	
Conventional thermal	--	--	--	--	1.6	1.6	1	
Nuclear	—	—	—	—	—	—	—	
Geothermal	—	—	—	—	—	—	—	

FUEL CONSUMPTION (Utilities only)

	1958	1959	1960	1961	1962	1963	1964
Total (Tcals)	--	--	--	--	--	--	--
RESERVOIR STORAGE CAPACITY (million kwh)	--	--	--	--	--	--	--

SUPPLEMENTARY DATA FOR 1964

Transmission lines, 100 kv+ (km):   —
Households served (thousands): (1963) 0.9
Revenues per kwh (U.S. cents) — Total:
  Residential: Railways:
  Industry: Lighting: 6.0
Population (thousands):   3018

Other characteristics of plants and systems:

  Electricity is supplied to only a small fraction of the population.

Sources of data:
  EEC. *Yrbk. Overseas Assoc.*
  UN. *Stat. yrbk.*
  US. FPC. *World power data.*
  République Rwandaise. *Bulletin de statistique.*

SUPPLY AND USE (million kwh)	1958	1959	1960	1961	1962	1963	1964	1965
PRODUCTION (Utilities & industries)								
Total (Gross)	277	310	390	421	487	556	593	
(Net)	--	--	--	--	--	--	--	
Hydro	—	—	—	—	—	—	—	
Conventional thermal	277	310	390	421	487	556	593	
Nuclear	—	—	—	—	—	—	—	
Geothermal	—	—	—	—	—	—	—	
PRODUCTION (Utilities only)								
Total (Gross)	277	310	390	421	487	556	593	
(Net)	--	--	--	--	--	--	--	
Hydro	—	—	—	—	—	—	—	
Conventional thermal	277	310	390	421	487	556	593	
Nuclear	—	—	—	—	—	—	—	
Geothermal	—	—	—	—	—	—	—	
NET IMPORTS	—	—	—	—	—	—	—	
SUPPLY (Gross)	277	310	390	421	487	556	593	
(Net)	--	--	--	--	--	--	--	
CONSUMPTION	--	--	--	415	482	552	--	
Transport	—	—	—	—	—	—	—	
Domestic sector	66	81	109	120	160	199	--	
Industry (Government)	--	--	--	295	322	353	--	
LOSS AND USE	--	--	--	6	5	4	--	

PLANT (thousand kw)

	1958	1959	1960	1961	1962	1963	1964	1965
CAPACITY (Utilities & industries)								
Total	112	112	112	116	118	142	142	
Hydro	—	—	—	—	—	—	—	
Conventional thermal	112	112	112	116	118	142	142	
Nuclear	—	—	—	—	—	—	—	
Geothermal	—	—	—	—	—	—	—	
CAPACITY (Utilities only)								
Total	112	112	112	116	118	142	142	
Hydro	—	—	—	—	—	—	—	
Conventional thermal	112	112	112	116	118	142	142	
Nuclear	—	—	—	—	—	—	—	
Geothermal	—	—	—	—	—	—	—	

FUEL CONSUMPTION (Utilities only)

	1958	1959	1960	1961	1962	1963	1964	1965
Total (Tcals)	--	--	--	--	--	--	--	
RESERVOIR STORAGE CAPACITY (million kwh)	—	—	—	—	—	—	—	

SUPPLEMENTARY DATA FOR 1964

Transmission lines, 100 kv+ (km) :   —
Households served (thousands) :   - -
Revenues per kwh (U.S. cents) — Total:
   Residential: Railways:
   Industry: Lighting:
Population (thousands) :   923

Other characteristics of plants and systems:

Electricity for the Ryukyu Islands is provided by the Okinawa Integrated Power System, owned by the U. S. government. Approximately 200 million kwh of electricity are provided to the civilian population of the islands. The remainder is presumably required for operation of the military establishment.

Sources of data:
   UN. *Stat. yrbk.*
   High Commissioner of the Ryukyu Islands.
   Civil Administration of the Ryukyu Islands. *Report.*

SUPPLY AND USE (million kwh)	1958	1959	1960	1961	1962	1963	1964	1965
PRODUCTION (Utilities & industries)								
Total (Gross)	11	13	19	21	26	32	41	
(Net)	--	--	--	--	--	--	--	
Hydro	—	—	—	—	—	—	—	
Conventional thermal	11	13	19	21	26	32	41	
Nuclear	—	—	—	—	—	—	—	
Geothermal	—	—	—	—	—	—	—	
PRODUCTION (Utilities only)								
Total (Gross)	8	10	16	19	23	29	39	
(Net)	--	--	--	--	--	--	--	
Hydro	—	—	—	—	—	—	—	
Conventional thermal	8	10	16	19	23	29	39	
Nuclear	—	—	—	—	—	—	—	
Geothermal	—	—	—	—	—	—	—	
NET IMPORTS	—	—	—		—	—	—	
SUPPLY (Gross)	11	13	19	21	26	32	41	
(Net)	--	--	--	--	--	--	--	
CONSUMPTION	10	12	--	19	24	30	36	
Transport	—	—	—	—	—	—	—	
Domestic sector	5e	7e	--	13	16	20	20	
Industry	5	5	5	6	8	10	16	
LOSS AND USE	1e	1	--	2	2	2	5	

PLANT (thousand kw)

	1958	1959	1960	1961	1962	1963	1964	1965
CAPACITY (Utilities & industries)								
Total	8.5	8.8	11	12	12	14	18	
Hydro	—	—	—	—	—	—	—	
Conventional thermal	8.5	8.8	11	12	12	14	18	
Nuclear	—	—	—	—	—	—	—	
Geothermal	—	—	—	—	—	—	—	
CAPACITY (Utilities only)								
Total	5.7	5.7	7.8	9.7	11	13	16	
Hydro	—	—	—	—	—	—	—	
Conventional thermal	5.7	5.7	7.8	9.7	11	13	16	
Nuclear	—	—	—	—	—	—	—	
Geothermal	—	—	—	—	—	—	—	

FUEL CONSUMPTION (Utilities only)

	1958	1959	1960	1961	1962	1963	1964	1965
Diesel oil (mmt)	0.2	2.7	4.0	5.6	6.0	7.8	--	
Fuelwood (mmt)	1.2	6.3	11.2				--	
Total (Tcals)	7	35	56	--	--	--	--	
RESERVOIR STORAGE CAPACITY (million kwh)	—	—	—	—	—	—	—	

SUPPLEMENTARY DATA FOR 1964

Transmission lines, 100 kv+ (km) :   —
Households served (thousands) :   9
Revenues per kwh (U.S. cents) — Total: 6.8
  Residential: 5.8   Railways:
  Industry: 3.4   Lighting: 11.4
Population (thousands) : 507

Other characteristics of plants and systems:

    The distribution of electricity in Sabah is the responsibility of the Sabah Electricity Board, which operates a number of small, isolated diesel stations. Electricity is supplied to less than ten per cent of the population of Sabah. The diesel oil used in generating electric power in Sabah is imported.

Sources of data:
  Benn Bros. *Elec. undertakings.* UN. *Stat. yrbk.*
  UN. ECAFE. *Elec. power.*
  Federation of Malaya. Department of Statistics. *Annual bulletin of statistics.*
  United Kingdom. Colonial Office. *North Borneo (Annual report).*

SUPPLY AND USE (million kwh)	1958	1959	1960	1961	1962	1963	1964	1965
PRODUCTION (Utilities & industries)								
Total (Gross)	--	--	2.4	2.5	--	--	--	
(Net)	--	--	--	--	--	--	--	
Hydro	—	—	—	—	—	—	—	
Conventional thermal	--	--	2.4	2.5	--	--	--	
Nuclear	—	—	—	—	—	—	—	
Geothermal	—	—	—	—	—	—	—	
PRODUCTION (Utilities only)								
Total (Gross)	--	--	2.4	2.5	--	--	--	
(Net)	--	--	--	--	--	--	--	
Hydro	—	—	—	—	—	—	—	
Conventional thermal	--	--	2.4	2.5	--	--	--	
Nuclear	—	—	—	—	—	—	—	
Geothermal	—	—	—	—	—	—	—	
NET IMPORTS	—	—	—	—	—	—	—	
SUPPLY (Gross)	--	--	2.4	2.5	--	--	--	
(Net)	--	--	--	--	--	--	--	
CONSUMPTION	--	2.0	2.2	2.3	--	--	--	
Transport	—	—	—	—	—	—	—	
Domestic sector	--	1.2	1.3	1.3	--	--	--	
Industry	--	0.8	0.9	1.0	--	--	--	
LOSS AND USE	--	--	0.2e	0.2	--	--	--	

PLANT (thousand kw)								
CAPACITY (Utilities & industries)								
Total	1.3	1.3	1.3	1.3	1.3	1.3	--	
Hydro	—	—	—	—	—	—	—	
Conventional thermal	1.3	1.3	1.3	1.3	1.3	1.3	--	
Nuclear	—	—	—	—	—	—	—	
Geothermal	—	—	—	—	—	—	—	
CAPACITY (Utilities only)								
Total	1.3	1.3	1.3	1.3	1.3	1.3	--	
Hydro	—	—	—	—	—	—	—	
Conventional thermal	1.3	1.3	1.3	1.3	1.3	1.3	--	
Nuclear	—	—	—	—	—	—	—	
Geothermal	—	—	—	—	—	—	—	

FUEL CONSUMPTION (Utilities only)

	1958	1959	1960	1961	1962	1963	1964	1965
Total (Tcals)	--	--	--	--	--	--	--	
RESERVOIR STORAGE CAPACITY (million kwh)	—	—	—	—	—	—	—	

SUPPLEMENTARY DATA FOR 1964

Transmission lines, 100 kv+ (km):   —
Households served (thousands): (1961) 1
Revenues per kwh (U.S. cents) — Total:
  Residential: Railways:
  Industry: Lighting: 6.5
Population (thousands): 5

Sources of data:
EEC. *Yrbk. Overseas Assoc.*
UN. *Stat. yrbk.*
Inst. de la Stat. *Ann. stat. des territoires d'outre-mer.*

ST. THOMAS-PRINCE

SUPPLY AND USE (million kwh)	1958	1959	1960	1961	1962	1963	1964	1965
PRODUCTION (Utilities & industries)								
Total (Gross)	--	2.5	4.6	5.5	6.0	5.5	6.0	
(Net)	--	--	--	--	--	--	--	
Hydro	--	--	--	--	--	--	--	
Conventional thermal	--	--	--	--	--	--	--.	
Nuclear	—	—	—	—	—	—	—	
Geothermal	—	—	—	—	—	—	—	
PRODUCTION (Utilities only)								
Total (Gross)	0.5	1.5	2.5	2.3	3.0	3.1	(3.0)	
(Net)	--	--	--	--	--	--	--	
Hydro	--	--	--	--	--	--	--	
Conventional thermal	--	--	--	--	--	--	--	
Nuclear	—	—	—	—	—	—	—	
Geothermal	—	—	—	—	—	—	—	
NET IMPORTS	—	—	—	—	—	—	—	
SUPPLY (Gross)	1.2e	2.5e	4.6e	5.5e	6.0e	5.5e	6.0e	
(Net)	--	--	--	--	--	--	--	
CONSUMPTION	1.1	2.3	4.2	5.1	5.5	5.0	5.5	
Transport	—	—	—	—	—	—	—	
Domestic sector	1.1	1.8	3.1	2.8	3.1	2.8	3.2	
Industry	--	0.5	1.1	2.3	2.3	2.2	2.3	
LOSS AND USE	0.1	0.2	0.4	0.4	0.5	0.5	0.5	
PLANT (thousand kw)								
CAPACITY (Utilities & industries)								
Total	1.0	1.2	1.8	2.3	2.4	2.2	1.9	
Hydro	0.2	0.2	0.6	0.5	0.5	0.5	0.2	
Conventional thermal	0.8	1.0	1.2	1.8	1.9	1.7	1.7	
Nuclear	—	—	—	—	—	—	—	
Geothermal	—	—	—	—	—	—	—	
CAPACITY (Utilities only)								
Total	--	--	--	--	--	--	--	
Hydro	--	--	--	--	--	--	--	
Conventional thermal	--	--	--	--	--	--	--	
Nuclear	—	—	—	—	—	—	—	
Geothermal	—	—	—	—	—	—	—	
FUEL CONSUMPTION (Utilities only)								
Total (Tcals)	--	--	--	--	--	--	--	
RESERVOIR STORAGE CAPACITY (million kwh)	--	--	--	--	--	--	--	

SUPPLEMENTARY DATA FOR 1964

Transmission lines, 100 kv+ (km):   —
Households served (thousands):   --
Revenues per kwh (U.S. cents) — Total:
  Residential: Railways:
  Industry: Lighting:
Population (thousands): 58

Other characteristics of plants and systems:

  Electricity appears to be available to only a small fraction of the population.

Sources of data:
  Inst. de Est. *Anuário estatístico do ultramar.*
  UN. *Stat. yrbk.*

SARAWAK

SUPPLY AND USE (million kwh)	1958	1959	1960	1961	1962	1963	1964	1965
PRODUCTION (Utilities & industries)								
Total (Gross)	--	--	--	43	47	49	58	
(Net)	--	--	--	--	46e	48	57	
Hydro	—	—	—	—	—	—	—	
Conventional thermal	--	--	--	43	47	49	58	
Nuclear	—	—	—	—	—	—	—	
Geothermal	—	—	—	—	—	—	—	
PRODUCTION (Utilities only)								
Total (Gross)	14	16	19	23	27	32	39	
(Net)	--	--	--	--	25	31	--	
Hydro	—	—	—	—	—	—	—	
Conventional thermal	14	16	19	23	27	32	39	
Nuclear	—	—	—	—	—	—	—	
Geothermal	—	—	—	—	—	—	—	
NET IMPORTS	—	—	—	—	—	—	—	
SUPPLY (Gross)	--	--	--	43	47	49	58	
(Net)	--	--	--	--	46	48	57	
CONSUMPTION	--	--	--	39	42	43	51	
Transport	—	—	—	—	—	—	—	
Domestic sector	--	--	--	17	19	22	28	
Industry	--	--	--	22e	23e	21e	23	
LOSS AND USE	2	3	3	4	4e	5	6	

PLANT (thousand kw)

	1958	1959	1960	1961	1962	1963	1964	1965
CAPACITY (Utilities & industries)								
Total	13	12	17	18	18	20	22	
Hydro	—	—	—	—	—	—	—	
Conventional thermal	13	12	17	18	18	20	22	
Nuclear	—	—	—	—	—	—	—	
Geothermal	—	—	—	—	—	—	—	
CAPACITY (Utilities only)								
Total	6.3	8.1	9.8	11	11	13	14	
Hydro	—	—	—	—	—	—	—	
Conventional thermal	6.3	8.1	9.8	11	11	13	14	
Nuclear	—	—	—	—	—	—	—	
Geothermal	—	—	—	—	—	—	—	

FUEL CONSUMPTION (Utilities only)

	1958	1959	1960	1961	1962	1963	1964	1965
Diesel oil (mmt)	3.4	4.4	4.9	6.2	6.9	8.3	10	
Total (Tcals)	35	46	49	63	70	84	105	
RESERVOIR STORAGE CAPACITY (million kwh)	—	—	—	—	—	—	—	

SUPPLEMENTARY DATA FOR 1964

Transmission lines, 100 kv+ (km): —
Households served (thousands): 19
Revenues per kwh (U.S. cents) — Total: 6.1
  Residential: 7.9   Railways:
  Industry: 3.6   Lighting: 9.7
Population (thousands): 818

Other characteristics of plants and systems:

The Sarawak Electricity Supply Corporation, owned by the government of Sarawak, is responsible for electricity supply throughout the country. Electricity is generated in numerous small, isolated diesel plants, and distributed to an estimated ten per cent of the total population. Substantial quantities of power are privately generated by the oil industry for its own use.

Sources of data:
Benn Bros. *Elec. undertakings.* UN. *Stat. yrbk.*
UN. ECAFE. *Elec. power.*
Federation of Malaya. Department of Statistics.
  Annual bulletin of statistics.
Sarawak Electricity Supply Corporation. *Annual report.*

SAUDI ARABIA

SUPPLY AND USE (million kwh)	1958	1959	1960	1961	1962	1963	1964	1965
PRODUCTION (Utilities & industries)								
Total (Gross)	--	--	--	--	--	--	--	
(Net)	--	--	--	--	--	--	--	
Hydro	—	—	—	—	—	—	—	
Conventional thermal	--	--	--	--	--	--	--	
Nuclear	—	—	—	—	—	—	—	
Geothermal	—	—	—	—	—	—	—	
PRODUCTION (Utilities only)								
Total (Gross)	71	89	111	139	174	218	273	
(Net)	--	--	--	--	--	--	--	
Hydro	—	—	—	—	—	—	—	
Conventional thermal	71	89	111	139	174	218	273	
Nuclear	—	—	—	—	—	—	—	
Geothermal	—	—	—	—	—	—	—	
NET IMPORTS	—	—	—	—	—	—	—	
SUPPLY (Gross)	71	89	111	139	174	218	273	
(Net)	--	--	--	--	--	--	--	
CONSUMPTION	--	--	--	--	--	--	--	
Transport	—	—	—	—	—	—	—	
Domestic sector	--	--	--	--	--	--	--	
Industry	--	--	--	--	--	--	--	
LOSS AND USE	--	--	--	--	--	--	--	

PLANT (thousand kw)

	1958	1959	1960	1961	1962	1963	1964	1965
CAPACITY (Utilities & industries)								
Total	--	--	--	--	232	--	--	
Hydro	—	—	—	—	—	—	—	
Conventional thermal	--	--	--	--	232	--	--	
Nuclear	—	—	—	—	—	—	—	
Geothermal	—	—	—	—	—	—	—	
CAPACITY (Utilities only)								
Total	29	36	45	56	70	87	109	
Hydro	—	—	—	—	—	—	—	
Conventional thermal	29	36	45	56	70	87	109	
Nuclear	—	—	—	—	—	—	—	
Geothermal	—	—	—	—	—	—	—	

FUEL CONSUMPTION (Utilities only)

	1958	1959	1960	1961	1962	1963	1964	1965
Diesel oil (mmt)	22	27	34	42	53	67	83	
Total (Tcals)	231	284	357	441	557	704	872	
RESERVOIR STORAGE CAPACITY (million kwh)	—	—	—	—	—	—	—	

SUPPLEMENTARY DATA FOR 1964

Transmission lines, 100 kv+ (km):   —
Households served (thousands) :   --
Revenues per kwh (U.S. cents) — Total:
   Residential: Railways:
   Industry: Lighting:
Population (thousands) :   6630

Other characteristics of plants and systems:

Electricity for public use is generated by the Saudi National Electric Company and the Jiddah Electricity Company. Large quantities of power are also generated by the petroleum industry for its own use. Service is entirely local in nature.

Sources of data:

UN. *Economic developments in the Middle East.*
————. *Stat. yrbk.* US. *Foreign serv. desp.*
Ministry of Finance and National Economy. Central Department of Statistics. *Statistical yearbook of Saudi Arabia.*

SUPPLY AND USE (million kwh)	1958	1959	1960	1961	1962	1963	1964	1965
PRODUCTION (Utilities & industries)								
Total (Gross)	--	--	--	--	--	--	--	
(Net)	--	--	--	--	--	--	--	
Hydro	—	—	—	—	—	—	—	
Conventional thermal	--	--	--	--	--	--	--	
Nuclear	—	—	—	—	—	—	—	
Geothermal	—	—	—	—	—	—	—	
PRODUCTION (Utilities only)								
Total (Gross)	--	--	--	174	197	--	--	
(Net)	--	--	--	--	--	--	--	
Hydro	—	—	—	—	—	—	—	
Conventional thermal	--	--	--	174	197	--	--	
Nuclear	—	—	—	—	—	—	—	
Geothermal	—	—	—	—	—	—	—	
NET IMPORTS	—	—	—	—	—	—	—	
SUPPLY (Gross)	--	--	--	174	197	--	--	
(Net)	--	--	--	--	--	--	--	
CONSUMPTION	95	106	127	152	172	175	197	
Transport	—	—	—	—	—	—	—	
Domestic sector	--	--	46	51	55	61	66	
Industry	--	--	81	101	117	114	131	
LOSS AND USE	--	--	--	22	25	--	--	
PLANT (thousand kw)								
CAPACITY (Utilities & industries)								
Total	--	--	--	--	--	--	--	
Hydro	—	—	—	—	—	—	—	
Conventional thermal	--	--	--	--	--	--	--	
Nuclear	—	—	—	—	—	—	—	
Geothermal	—	—	—	—	—	—	—	
CAPACITY (Utilities only)								
Total	43	56	56	68	70	70	69	
Hydro	—	—	—	—	—	—	—	
Conventional thermal	43	56	56	68	70	70	69	
Nuclear	—	—	—	—	—	—	—	
Geothermal	—	—	—	—	—	—	—	
FUEL CONSUMPTION (Utilities only)								
Diesel oil (mmt)	--	--	--	--	--	--		
Fuel oil (mmt)	--	--	--	--	--	--	75	
Total (Tcals)	--	--	--	--	--	--	788	
RESERVOIR STORAGE CAPACITY (million kwh)	—	—	—	—	—	—	—	

SUPPLEMENTARY DATA FOR 1964

Transmission lines, 100 kv + (km):   —
Households served (thousands):   71.5
Revenues per kwh (U.S. cents) — Total:
   Residential: Railways:
   Industry: (1961) 2.0   Lighting:
Population (thousands):   3400

Sources of data:
EEC. *Yrbk. Overseas Assoc.*
Inst. de la Stat. *Données statistiques.* UN. *Stat. yrbk.*
Ministère du Plan et du Développement. Service de la
   Statistique. *Bulletin statistique et économique mensuel.*
———— . *Situation économique du Sénégal.*

Other characteristics of plants and systems:

   Cie. des Eaux et Electricité de l'Ouest-Africain, privately
owned, serves Dakar and environs via a high-tension network
of 90 and 30 KV. The company operates a steam plant at Dakar,
and numerous isolated diesel plants of small capacity. Service
is supplied to an estimated one-tenth of Senegal's population.

SIERRA LEONE

SUPPLY AND USE (million kwh)	1958	1959	1960	1961	1962	1963	1964	1965
PRODUCTION (Utilities & industries)								
Total (Gross)	39	43	41	53e	61	72	84	
(Net)	--	--	--	--	--	--	--	
Hydro	—	—	—	—	—	—	—	
Conventional thermal	39	43	41	53e	61	72	84	
Nuclear	—	—	—	—	—	—	—	
Geothermal	—	—	—	—	—	—	—	
PRODUCTION (Utilities only)								
Total (Gross)	21	23	24	37	42	51	56	
(Net)	--	--	--	--	--	--	--	
Hydro	—	—	—	—	—	—	—	
Conventional thermal	21	23	24	37	42	51	56	
Nuclear	—	—	—	—	—	—	—	
Geothermal	—	—	—	—	—	—	—	
NET IMPORTS	—		—	—		—	—	
SUPPLY (Gross)	39	43	41	53	61	72	84	
(Net)	--	--	--	--	--	--	--	
CONSUMPTION	--	--	--	--	--	--	--	
Transport	—	—	—	—	—	—	—	
Domestic sector	--	--	--	--	--	--	--	
Industry	--	--	--	--	--	--	--	
LOSS AND USE	--	--	--	--	--	--	--	

PLANT (thousand kw)								
CAPACITY (Utilities & industries)								
Total	18	20	21	21	23	33	41	
Hydro	—	—	—	—	—	—	—	
Conventional thermal	18	20	21	21	23	33	41	
Nuclear	—	—	—	—	—	—	—	
Geothermal	—	—	—	—	—	—	—	
CAPACITY (Utilities only)								
Total	8.8	11	12	--	--	--	--	
Hydro	—	—	—	—	—	—	—	
Conventional thermal	8.8	11	12	--	--	--	--	
Nuclear	—	—	—	—	—	—	—	
Geothermal	—	—	—	—	—	—	—	

FUEL CONSUMPTION (Utilities only)								
Diesel oil (mmt)	--	--	3	--	--	--	--	
Fuel oil (mmt)	--	9	12	--	--	--	--	
Total (Tcals)	--	--	146	--	--	--	--	
RESERVOIR STORAGE CAPACITY (million kwh)	—	—	—	—	—	—	—	

SUPPLEMENTARY DATA FOR 1964

Transmission lines, 100 kv+ (km) :   —
Households served (thousands) : (1960) 16
Revenues per kwh (U.S. cents) — Total:
   Residential: Railways:
   Industry: Lighting: 7.0
Population (thousands) :   2332

Other characteristics of plants and systems:

The Electricity Department, Government of Sierra Leone, is responsible for electricity supply, which is generated mainly in Freetown. Outside of Freetown, service is provided mainly by small, isolated diesel plants to a very small fraction of the country's population.

Sources of data:
UN. *Stat. yrbk.*
Central Statistical Office. *Quarterly statistical bulletin.*

SINGAPORE

SUPPLY AND USE (million kwh)	1958	1959	1960	1961	1962	1963	1964	1965
PRODUCTION (Utilities & industries)								
Total (Gross)	571	615	658	720	776	823	914	
(Net)	546	588	628	688	741	784	872	
Hydro	–	–	–	–	–	–	–	
Conventional thermal	571	615	658	720	776	823	914	
Nuclear	–	–	–	–	–	–	–	
Geothermal	–	–	–	–	–	–	–	
PRODUCTION (Utilities only)								
Total (Gross)	571	615	658	720	776	823	914	
(Net)	546	588	628	688	741	784	872	
Hydro	–	–	–	–	–	–	–	
Conventional thermal	571	615	658	720	776	823	914	
Nuclear	–	–	–	–	–	–	–	
Geothermal	–	–	–	–	–	–	–	
NET IMPORTS	–	–	–	–	–	–	–	
SUPPLY (Gross)	571	615	658	720	776	823	914	
(Net)	546	588	628	688	741	784	872	
CONSUMPTION	493	524	577	637	689	724	831	
Transport	–	–	–	–	–	–	–	
Domestic sector	239	261	293	331	358	396	454	
Industry	254	263	284	306	331	328	377	
LOSS AND USE	53	64	51	51	52	60	41	
PLANT (thousand kw)								
CAPACITY (Utilities & industries)								
Total	152	152	188	188	213	224	224	
Hydro	–	–	–	–	–	–	–	
Conventional thermal	152	152	188	188	213	224	224	
Nuclear	–	–	–	–	–	–	–	
Geothermal	–	–	–	–	–	–	–	
CAPACITY (Utilities only)								
Total	152	152	188	188	213	224	224	
Hydro	–	–	–	–	–	–	–	
Conventional thermal	152	152	188	188	213	224	224	
Nuclear	–	–	–	–	–	–	–	
Geothermal	–	–	–	–	–	–	–	
FUEL CONSUMPTION (Utilities only)								
Diesel oil (mmt)	- -	- -	3	3	1	2	7	
Fuel oil (mmt)	176	187	198	215	238	254	278	
Total (Tcals)	1946	2086	2254	2436	2688	2624	2996	
RESERVOIR STORAGE CAPACITY (million kwh)	–	–	–	–	–	–	–	

SUPPLEMENTARY DATA FOR 1964

Transmission lines, 100 kv+ (km) :   –
Households served (thousands) :   147
Revenues per kwh (U.S. cents) — Total: 2.4
   Residential: 4.9   Railways:
   Industry: 1.5   Lighting: 5.8
Population (thousands) :   1820

Sources of data:
  UN. *Stat. yrbk.*   UN. ECAFE. *Elec. power.*
  ——— . *Role & application of elec. power.*
  City Council. *Annual report of the Electricity Department.*
  Department of Statistics. *Monthly digest of statistics.*
  Federation of Malaya. Department of Statistics. *Annual bulletin of statistics.*
  Public Utilities Board. Electricity Department. *Annual report.*

Other characteristics of plants and systems:

The principal source of electricity in Singapore is the Electricity Department of the Public Utilities Board, which operates both steam and gas turbine installations. Imported fuel oil is used to generate practically all of Singapore's electricity. The number of customers served – close to 150,000 – suggests that perhaps a third of Singapore's population is supplied with electricity.

SOMALIA

SUPPLY AND USE (million kwh)	1958	1959	1960	1961	1962	1963	1964	1965
PRODUCTION (Utilities & industries)								
Total (Gross)	--	--	--	--	--	--	--	
(Net)	--	--	--	--	--	--	--	
Hydro	—	—	—	—	—	—	—	
Conventional thermal	--	--	--	--	--	--	--	
Nuclear	—	—	—	—	—	—	—	
Geothermal	—	—	—	—	—	—	—	
PRODUCTION (Utilities only)								
Total (Gross)	--	4.1	5.1	6.4	7.4	9.3	10.6	
(Net)	--	--	--	--	--	--	--	
Hydro	—	—	—	—	—	—	—	
Conventional thermal	--	4.1	5.1	6.4	7.4	9.3	10.6	
Nuclear	—	—	—	—	—	—	—	
Geothermal	—	—	—	—	—	—	—	
NET IMPORTS	—	—	—	—	—	—	—	
SUPPLY (Gross)	--	4.1	5.1	6.4	7.4	9.3	10.6	
(Net)	--	--	--	--	--	--	--	
CONSUMPTION	--	3.6	4.2	5.3	6.4	7.8	8.8	
Transport	—	—	—	—	—	—	—	
Domestic sector	--	2.4	2.8	3.6	4.7	6.0	6.7	
Industry	--	1.2	1.4	1.7	1.7	1.8	2.1	
LOSS AND USE	--	0.5	0.9	1.1	1.0	1.5	1.8	
PLANT (thousand kw)								
CAPACITY (Utilities & industries)								
Total	--	--	--	--	--	--	--	
Hydro	—	—	—	—	—	—	—	
Conventional thermal	--	--	--	--	--	--	--	
Nuclear	—	—	—	—	—	—	—	
Geothermal	—	—	—	—	—	—	—	
CAPACITY (Utilities only)								
Total	--	--	2.3	2.3	2.3	3.2	3.2	
Hydro	—	—	—	—	—	—	—	
Conventional thermal	--	--	2.3	2.3	2.3	3.2	3.2	
Nuclear	—	—	—	—	—	—	—	
Geothermal	—	—	—	—	—	—	—	
FUEL CONSUMPTION (Utilities only)								
Diesel oil (mmt)	1	1	2	2	2	3	3	
Total (Tcals)	11	11	21	21	21	32	32	
RESERVOIR STORAGE CAPACITY (million kwh)	—	—	—	—	—	—	—	

SUPPLEMENTARY DATA FOR 1964

Transmission lines, 100 kv+ (km) :   —
Households served (thousands) :   --
Revenues per kwh (U.S. cents) — Total: (1961) 15+
  Residential: Railways:
  Industry: Lighting:
Population (thousands) :   2420

Other characteristics of plants and systems:

    Somalia's electricity is supplied by the Ministry of Communications and Works, Government of Somalia, and the Società Elettro Industriali Italo-Somala, privately owned. All service is provided by small, isolated plants.

Sources of data:
  EEC. *Yrbk. Overseas Assoc.*
  Soc. R. Moreux. *Industries et travaux.* No. 122.
  UN. *Situation, trends & prospects.*
  ———. *Stat yrbk.* US. *Foreign serv. desp.*

SOUTH AFRICA

SUPPLY AND USE (million kwh)	1958	1959	1960	1961	1962	1963	1964	1965
PRODUCTION (Utilities & industries)								
Total (Gross)	21164	22561	24365	25700	26969	29399	32000e	
(Net)	19838	21088	22783	23761	25111	27400e	30000e	
Hydro	(12)	8	13	29	40	40e	40e	
Conventional thermal	21152e	22553	24352	25671	26929	29359	31960	
Nuclear	—	—	—	—	—	—	—	
Geothermal	—	—	—	—	—	—	—	
PRODUCTION (Utilities only)								
Total (Gross)	19658	21128	23002	24259	25381	26800	30422	
(Net)	--	--	--	--	--	--	--	
Hydro	9	2	8	8	9	(10)	(10)	
Conventional thermal	19649	21126	22994	24251	25372	26790e	30412e	
Nuclear	—	—	—	—	—	—	—	
Geothermal	—	—	—	—	—	—	—	
NET IMPORTS	—	—	—	—	—	—	—	
SUPPLY (Gross)	21164	22561	24365	25700	26969	29399	32000e	
(Net)	19838	21088	22783	23761	25111	27400e	30000e	
CONSUMPTION	18132	19334	20968	22066	23706	25213	27500e	
Transport	975	1151	1291	1447	1586	1697	1860e	
Domestic sector	3556	3793	4051	3951	4152	4654	5140e	
Industry	13601	14390	15626	16668	17968	18862	20500e	
LOSS AND USE	1706	1754	1815	1695	1405	2187	2500e	

PLANT (thousand kw)

	1958	1959	1960	1961	1962	1963	1964	1965
CAPACITY (Utilities & industries)								
Total	4800e	5135	5371	5552	5970	6300e	6500e	
Hydro	(10)	10	11	12	14	14	--	
Conventional thermal	4790e	5125	5360	5540	5956	6286e	--	
Nuclear	—	—	—	—	—	—	—	
Geothermal	—	—	—	—	—	—	—	
CAPACITY (Utilities only)								
Total	4381	4713	4946	5115	5495	5800e	6000e	
Hydro	5	6	8	8	8	--	--	
Conventional thermal	4376	4707	4938	5107	5487	--	--	
Nuclear								
Geothermal								

FUEL CONSUMPTION (Utilities only)

	1958	1959	1960	1961	1962	1963	1964	1965
Coal (mmt)	13503	14267	15413	16095	16836	17638	18554	
Total (Tcals)	74267	78469	84772	88523	92598	97009	102047	
RESERVOIR STORAGE CAPACITY (million kwh)	--	--	--	--	--	--	--	

SUPPLEMENTARY DATA FOR 1964

Transmission lines, 100 kv+ (km): 6950
Households served (thousands): --
Revenues per kwh (U.S. cents) — Total: 0.7*
  Residential: 2.1   Railways: 1.1
  Industry: 0.6+   Lighting:
Population (thousands): 17457
*Including bulk purchases.

Other characteristics of plants and systems:
    The bulk of South Africa's electricity is produced by the publicly-owned Electricity Supply Commission, which distributes power through seven regional networks. The remainder of the supply is produced and distributed largely by municipal systems. Only a fraction of South Africa's population is supplied with electricity.

Sources of data:
  UN. *Stat. yrbk.*   UNIPEDE. *Statistiques.*
  Bureau of Statistics. *Statistical yearbook of South Africa.* ———. *Union statistics for fifty years, 1910-1960.*
  Department of Mines. *Annual report.*   Electricity Supply Commission. *Annual report.*
  World Power Conference. Tokyo Sectional Meeting. "Power generation in South Africa with special reference to the introduction of nuclear power," by R. L. Straszacker, A. J. A. Roux, G. R. D. Harding and W. L. Grant.
  Bureau of Statistics. Data communicated to N. B. Guyol, by letter dated October 13, 1967 from the Director of Statistics.

SUPPLY AND USE (million kwh)	1958	1959	1960	1961	1962	1963	1964	1965
PRODUCTION (Utilities & industries)								
Total (Gross)	157	169	190	208	210	215	220	
(Net)	--	--	--	--	--	--	--	
Hydro	—	—	—	—	—	—	—	
Conventional thermal	157	169	190	208	210	215	220	
Nuclear	—	—	—	—	—	—	—	
Geothermal	—	—	—	—	—	—	—	
PRODUCTION (Utilities only)								
Total (Gross)	56	65	74	86	89	--	--	
(Net)	--	--	--	--	--	--	--	
Hydro	—	—	—	—	—	—	—	
Conventional thermal	56	65	74	86	89	--	--	
Nuclear	—	—	—	—	—	—	—	
Geothermal	—	—	—	—	—	—	—	
NET IMPORTS	—	—	—	—	—	—	—	
SUPPLY (Gross)	157	169	190	208	210	215	220	
(Net)	--	--	--	--	--	--	--	
CONSUMPTION	--	--	--	--	--	--	--	
Transport	—	—	—	—	—	—	—	
Domestic sector	--	--	--	--	--	--	--	
Industry	--	--	--	--	--	--	--	
LOSS AND USE	--	--	--	--	--	--	--	
PLANT (thousand kw)								
CAPACITY (Utilities & industries)								
Total	51	59	64	84	79	79	79	
Hydro	—	—	—	—	—	—	—	
Conventional thermal	51	59	64	84	79	79	79	
Nuclear	—	—	—	—	—	—	—	
Geothermal	—	—	—	—	—	—	—	
CAPACITY (Utilities only)								
Total	21	29	30	38	38	38	38	
Hydro	—	—	—	—	—	—	—	
Conventional thermal	21	29	30	38	38	38	38	
Nuclear	—	—	—	—	—	—	—	
Geothermal	—	—	—	—	—	—	—	
FUEL CONSUMPTION (Utilities only)								
Coal (mmt)	--	--	--	--	54	--	--	
Diesel oil (mmt)	--	--	--	--	6	--	--	
Total (Tcals)	--	--	--	--	--	--	--	
RESERVOIR STORAGE CAPACITY (million kwh)	—	—	—	—	—	—	—	

SUPPLEMENTARY DATA FOR 1964

Transmission lines, 100 kv+ (km) : --
Households served (thousands) :   --
Revenues per kwh (U.S. cents) — Total:
   Residential: Railways:
   Industry: Lighting:
Population (thousands) :   564

Other characteristics of plants and systems:

The principal source of electricity in Southwest Africa appears to be the Windhoek Municipality, which, in 1961, supplied current to something over 7,000 customers in Windhoek and vicinity.

Sources of data:
UN. *Stat. yrbk.*
US. FPC. *World power data.*
South Africa. Bureau of Statistics. *Industrial census, 1962-63; report #302.*

SPAIN

SUPPLY AND USE (million kwh)	1958	1959	1960	1961	1962	1963	1964	1965
PRODUCTION (Utilities & industries)								
Total (Gross)	16350	17353	18614	20879	22905	25897	29526	
(Net)	15845	16928	18170	20275	22156	25206	28444	
Hydro	11285	14256	15625	15981	16073	21139	20646	
Conventional thermal	5065	3097	2989	4898	6832	4758	8880	
Nuclear	—	—	—	—	—	—	—	
Geothermal	—	—	—	—	—	—	—	
PRODUCTION (Utilities only)								
Total (Gross)	15147	15900	16955	19058	20998	24009	27733	
(Net)		15563	16574	18530	20346	23438	26772	
Hydro	10542	13438	14713	15096	15192	20170	19774	
Conventional thermal	4605	2462	2242	3962	5806	3839	7959	
Nuclear	—	—	—	—	—	—	—	
Geothermal	—	—	—	—	—	—	—	
NET IMPORTS	−17	−201	−163	−255	−255	−839	−1563	
SUPPLY (Gross)	16333	17152	18451	20624	22650	25058	27963	
(Net)	15828	16727	18007	20020	21901	24367	26881	
CONSUMPTION	12798	13492	14625	16317	18276	20088	22479	
Transport	893	665	722	758	783	853	950	
Domestic sector	2949	3161	3429	4106	4267	4781	5301	
Industry	8956	9666	10474	11453	13226	14454	16228	
LOSS AND USE	3030	3235	3382	3703	3625	4279	4402	

PLANT (thousand kw)

	1958	1959	1960	1961	1962	1963	1964	1965
CAPACITY (Utilities & industries)								
Total	6073	6384	6567	7011	7488	8387	9766	
Hydro	4195	4436	4600	4768	5190	5895	7059	
Conventional thermal	1878	1948	1967	2243	2298	2492	2707	
Nuclear	—	—	—	—	—	—	—	
Geothermal	—	—	—	—	—	—	—	
CAPACITY (Utilities only)								
Total	5555	5806	5964	6398	6846	7737	9063	
Hydro	3952	4192	4343	4508	4924	5628	6789	
Conventional thermal	1603	1614	1621	1890	1922	2109	2274	
Nuclear	—	—	—	—	—	—	—	
Geothermal	—	—	—	—	—	—	—	

FUEL CONSUMPTION (Utilities only)

	1958	1959	1960	1961	1962	1963	1964	1965
Coal (mmt)	547	259	305	527	729	249	1003	
Low grade coal (mmt)	832	680	734	895	944	670	1097	
Lignite (mmt)	1176	605	531	1225	1417	967	1569	
Distillate fuel oil (mmt)	--	13	14	15	8	4	16	
Residual fuel oil (mmt)	600e	263	188	175	697	583	920	
Total (Tcals)	17532	9941	9057	13331	19207	12705	23964	
RESERVOIR STORAGE CAPACITY (million kwh)	3854	4201	5994	4789	5277	5895	7139	

SUPPLEMENTARY DATA FOR 1964

Transmission lines, 100 kv+ (km): 19350
Households served (thousands): 6500
Revenues per kwh (U.S. cents) — Total:
    Residential: 2.0   Railways: 0.7
    Industry: 1.1   Lighting: 4.6
Population (thousands): 31506

Sources of data:
    UCPTE. *Réseau.* UN. *Stat. yrbk.*
    UN. ECE. *Ann. bull. of elec. energy stat.*
    ———. *Org. of elec. power services.*
    UNIPEDE. *L'écon. élec.* ———. *Statistiques.*
    Sindicato Nacional de Agua, Gas y Electricidad. *Datos estadísticos tecnicos de las centrales eléctricas españolas.*

Other characteristics of plants and systems:

Private interests, of which the largest are Iberduero, S. A. and Union Electrica Madrileña, S. A., own the bulk of Spain's generating capacity. Much of Spain's capacity is interconnected by a network which is tied also to the networks of France and Portugal. On the basis of the number of meters in service, it is estimated that roughly two-thirds of the Spanish population was supplied with electricity in 1964. Spain boasts western Europe's largest hydroelectric plant, Aldeadavila, which has a capacity of 718 MW.

SUDAN

SUPPLY AND USE (million kwh)	1958	1959	1960	1961	1962	1963	1964	1965
PRODUCTION (Utilities & industries)								
Total (Gross)	--	--	--	--	--	--	--	
(Net)	--	--	--	--	--	--	--	
Hydro	—	—	—	—	—	—	—	
Conventional thermal	--	--	--	--	--	--	--	
Nuclear	—	—	—	—	—	—	—	
Geothermal	—	—	—	—	—	—	—	
PRODUCTION (Utilities only)								
Total (Gross)	67	84	94	103	132	163	167	
(Net)	--	--	--	--	--	--	--	
Hydro	—	—	—	—	—	—	—	
Conventional thermal	67	84	94	103	132	163	167	
Nuclear	—	—	—	—	—	—	—	
Geothermal	—	—	—	—	—	—	—	
NET IMPORTS	—	—	—	—	—	—	—	
SUPPLY (Gross)	67	84	94	103	132	163	167	
(Net)	--	--	--	--	--	--	--	
CONSUMPTION	--	--	--	93	--	124	132	
Transport	—	—	—	—	—	—	—	
Domestic sector	--	--	--	--	--	--	--	
Industry	--	--	--	--	--	--	--	
LOSS AND USE	--	--	--	10	--	39	35	

PLANT (thousand kw)

	1958	1959	1960	1961	1962	1963	1964	1965
CAPACITY (Utilities & industries)								
Total	--	--	--	--	--	--	--	
Hydro	—	—	—	—	—	—	—	
Conventional thermal	--	--	--	—	—	--	--	
Nuclear	—	—	—	—	—	—	—	
Geothermal	—	—	—	—	—	—	—	
CAPACITY (Utilities only)								
Total	30	43	43	51	61	59	59	
Hydro	—	—	—	—	—	—	—	
Conventional thermal	30	43	43	51	61	59	59	
Nuclear	—	—	—	—	—	—	—	
Geothermal	—	—	—	—	—	—	—	

FUEL CONSUMPTION (Utilities only)

	1958	1959	1960	1961	1962	1963	1964	1965
Total (Tcals)	--	--	--	--	--	--	--	
RESERVOIR STORAGE CAPACITY (million kwh)	—	—	—	—	—	—	—	

SUPPLEMENTARY DATA FOR 1964

Transmission lines, 100 kv+ (km): (1961) 180
Households served (thousands): 56
Revenues per kwh (U.S. cents) — Total: (1961) 6.0
  Residential: Railways:
  Industry: 4.0   Lighting:
Population (thousands): 13180

Other characteristics of plants and systems:

Most of Sudan's power is generated by the Central Electric and Water Administration, Government of Sudan. The country is served mainly by the Burri Steam Plant (30 MW) and isolated diesel plants with capacities of less than 5 MW. Service appears to be available to only a small fraction of Sudan's population.

Sources of data:
UN. *Stat. yrbk.* UN. ECA. *Situation, trends & prospects.*
US. *Foreign serv. desp.*
Department of Statistics. *Internal statistics.*

SUPPLY AND USE (million kwh)	1958	1959	1960	1961	1962	1963	1964	1965
PRODUCTION (Utilities & industries)								
Total (Gross)	66	72	79	95	112	119	128	
(Net)	--	--	--	--	--	--	--	
Hydro	—	—	—	—	—	—	—	
Conventional thermal	66	72	79	95	112	119	128	
Nuclear	—	—	—	—	—	—	—	
Geothermal	—	—	—	—	—	—	—	
PRODUCTION (Utilities only)								
Total (Gross)	29	33	39	47	55	61	67	
(Net)	--	--	--	--	--	--	--	
Hydro	—	—	—	—	—	—	—	
Conventional thermal	29	33	39	47	55	61	67	
Nuclear	—	—	—	—	—	—	—	
Geothermal	—	—	—	—	—	—	—	
NET IMPORTS	—	—	—	—	—	—	—	
SUPPLY (Gross)	66	72	79	95	112	119	128	
(Net)	--	--	--	--	--	--	--	
CONSUMPTION	--	--	--	--	--	--	--	
Transport	—	—	—	—	—	—	—	
Domestic sector	--	--	--	--	--	--	--	
Industry	--	--	--	--	--	--	--	
LOSS AND USE	--	--	--	--	--	--	--	

PLANT (thousand kw)

	1958	1959	1960	1961	1962	1963	1964	1965
CAPACITY (Utilities & industries)								
Total	--	--	29	35	37	39	--	
Hydro	—	—	—	—	—	—	—	
Conventional thermal	--	--	29	35	37	39	--	
Nuclear	—	—	—	—	—	—	—	
Geothermal	—	—	—	—	—	—	—	
CAPACITY (Utilities only)								
Total	10	--	11	15	17	20	21	
Hydro	—	—	—	—	—	—	—	
Conventional thermal	10	--	11	15	17	20	21	
Nuclear	—	—	—	—	—	—	—	
Geothermal	—	—	—	—	—	—	—	

FUEL CONSUMPTION (Utilities only)

	1958	1959	1960	1961	1962	1963	1964	1965
Total (Tcals)	--	--	--	--	--	--	--	
RESERVOIR STORAGE CAPACITY (million kwh)	—	—	—	—	—	—	—	

SUPPLEMENTARY DATA FOR 1964

Transmission lines, 100 kv+ (km): —
Households served (thousands): --
Revenues per kwh (U.S. cents) — Total:
  Residential: Railways:
  Industry: Lighting:
Population (thousands): 324

Other characteristics of plants and systems:

The N. V. Overzeese Gas- en Electriciteit Maatschappij is the principal producer of electricity in Surinam. The public supply is produced in diesel plants and distributed entirely on a local basis.

Sources of data:
EEC. *Yrbk. Overseas Assoc.*
UN. *Stat. yrbk.*
UN. ECLA. *Estud. econ.*

SWEDEN

SUPPLY AND USE (million kwh)	1958	1959	1960	1961	1962	1963	1964	1965
PRODUCTION (Utilities & industries)								
Total (Gross)	30354	32230	34740	38324	40624	40672	45247	
(Net)	30099	31972	34412	38014	39944	39978	44482	
Hydro	28829	28880	31090	36537	39099	37924	43022	
Conventional thermal	1525	3350	3650	1787	1525	2748	2225	
Nuclear	—	—	—	—	—	—	—	
Geothermal	—	—	—	—	—	—	—	
PRODUCTION (Utilities only)								
Total (Gross)	--	--	--	--	--	--	--	
(Net)	--	--	--	--	--	--	--	
Hydro	--	--	--	--	--	--	--	
Conventional thermal	--	--	--	--	--	--	--	
Nuclear	—	—	—	—	—	—	—	
Geothermal	—	—	—	—	—	—	—	
NET IMPORTS	−541	−552	−766	−997	−797	48	−205	
SUPPLY (Gross)	29813	31678	33974	37327	39827	40720	45042	
(Net)	29558	31420	33646	37017	39147	40026	44277	
CONSUMPTION	25704	27449	29330	32222	34348	35467	39383	
Transport	1614	1606	1669	1689	1753	1766	1759	
Domestic sector	7687	7938	8710	9366	10243	11697	12443	
Industry	16403	17905	18951	21167	22352	22004	25181	
LOSS AND USE	3854	3971	4316	4795	4799	4559	4894	

PLANT (thousand kw)

	1958	1959	1960	1961	1962	1963	1964	1965
CAPACITY (Utilities & industries)								
Total	7860	8455	8957	9750	10617	11040	11304	
Hydro	6290	6620	7005	7471	8285	8872	9069	
Conventional thermal	1570	1835	1952	2279	2332	2168	2235	
Nuclear	—	—	—	—	—	—	—	
Geothermal	—	—	—	—	—	—	—	
CAPACITY (Utilities only)								
Total	--	--	--	--	--	--	--	
Hydro	--	--	--	--	--	--	--	
Conventional thermal	--	--	--	--	--	--	--	
Nuclear	—	—	—	—	—	—	—	
Geothermal	—	—	—	—	—	—	—	

FUEL CONSUMPTION (Utilities only)

	1958	1959	1960	1961	1962	1963	1964	1965
Coal (mmt)	67e	193	216	25	10	32	2	
Wood & wood wastes (mm^3)	--	178	308	308	362	355	521	
Coke (mmt)	--	--	23	18	20	12	6	
Diesel oil (mmt)	32	13	9	5	7	8	12	
Fuel oil (mmt)	--	669	621	190	256	513	428	
Gasoline (mmt)	--	5	5	5	6	5	5	
Gases (mil m^3)	--	--	--	200	332	346	371	
Total (Tcals)	--	--	--	--	--	--	--	
RESERVOIR STORAGE CAPACITY (million kwh)	10060	10565	10992	12785	14350	15760	16230	

SUPPLEMENTARY DATA FOR 1964

Transmission lines, 100 kv+ (km) : 18663
Households served (thousands) : 2790
Revenues per kwh (U.S. cents) — Total: –
  Residential: 1.3 Railways: 0.8
  Industry: 0.8 Lighting: 2.3
Population (thousands) : 7661

Other characteristics of plants and systems:

The State Power Board and various municipalities own the bulk of Sweden's generating capacity - - privately-owned utilities something more than half as much. Substantial quantities of electricity are also produced and consumed by private industry. Power is supplied to most of the people of Sweden by a national network which includes one of the world's great high-tension lines, extending from Harspranget to Hallsverg, a distance of nearly 1000 kilometers, at 400 KV. The Swedish system is interconnected with the systems of Norway, Finland and, by submarine cables, Denmark. Most of the fuel required to generate thermal electric power in Sweden is imported.

Sources of data:
UN. *Stat. yrbk.* UN. ECE. *Ann. bull. of elec. energy stat.*
_____. *Org. of elec. power services.*
UNIPEDE. *L'écon. élec.* _____. *Réseaux de transport.*
_____. *Statistiques.*
Central Bureau of Statistics. *Industri.*
Swedish State Power Board and Swedish Water Power
  Association. *Power supply in Sweden.*

SWITZERLAND

SUPPLY AND USE (million kwh)	1958	1959	1960	1961	1962	1963	1964	1965
PRODUCTION (Utilities & industries)								
Total (Gross)	16878	18181	19072	22302	21342	22013	22864	
(Net)	--	--	--	--	--	--	--	
Hydro	16703	18078	18826	22177	21154	21678	22663	
Conventional thermal	175	103	246	125	188	335	201	
Nuclear	—	—	—	—	—	—	—	
Geothermal	—	—	—	—	—	—	—	
PRODUCTION (Utilities only)								
Total (Gross)	14056	14975	15834	18580	17865	18708	19465	
(Net)	--	--	--	--	--	--	--	
Hydro	13951	14951	15693	18557	17790	18507	19405	
Conventional thermal	105	24	141	23	75	201	60	
Nuclear	—	—	—	—	—	—	—	
Geothermal	—	—	—	—	—	—	—	
NET IMPORTS	–1117	–1918	–1316	–3478	–1649	–1024	–1164	
SUPPLY (Gross)	15761	16263	17756	18824	19693	20989	21700	
(Net)	--	--	--	--	--	--	--	
CONSUMPTION	13724	14196	15499	16602	17335	18312	19090	
Transport	1289	1363	1452	1509	1599	1634	1649	
Domestic sector	6322	6705	7338	7743	8264	8842	9273	
Industry	6113	6128	6709	7350	7472	7836	8168	
LOSS AND USE	2037	2067	2257	2222	2358	2677	2610	

PLANT (thousand kw)

	1958	1959	1960	1961	1962	1963	1964	1965
CAPACITY (Utilities & industries)								
Total	4980	5430	5840	6210	7160	7690	8100	
Hydro	4780	5240	5640	6010	6960	7490	7870	
Conventional thermal	200	190	200	200	200	200	230	
Nuclear	—	—	—	—	—	—	—	
Geothermal	—	—	—	—	—	—	—	
CAPACITY (Utilities only)								
Total	4315	4772	5160	5530	6480	6985	7395e	
Hydro	4150	4607	4995	5365	6315	6820	7230e	
Conventional thermal	165	165	165	165	165	165	165	
Nuclear	—	—	—	—	—	—	—	
Geothermal	—	—	—	—	—	—	—	

FUEL CONSUMPTION (Utilities only)

	1958	1959	1960	1961	1962	1963	1964	1965
Total (Tcals)	--	--	--	--	--	--	--	
RESERVOIR STORAGE CAPACITY (million kwh)	3460	3750	4080	4450	5220	5760	5970	

SUPPLEMENTARY DATA FOR 1964

Transmission lines, 100 kv+ (km): 4252
Households served (thousands): 1700
Revenues per kwh (U.S. cents) — Total: –
  Residential: Railways: 1.2
  Industry: Lighting: 1.6
Population (thousands): 5892

Other characteristics of plants and systems:

Public authorities generate slightly more than half of Switzerland's electricity. The remainder is provided, in roughly equal shares, by private and mixed enterprises. Services are completely integrated, and interconnected with the systems of all of Switzerland's neighbors, to whom Switzerland exports something over a billion kwh of electricity per annum. Practically all of the people of Switzerland are supplied with electricity.

Sources of data:
UCPTE. Réseau. UN. Stat. yrbk.
UN. ECE. Ann. bull. of elec. energy stat.
——. Org. of elec. power services.
UNIPEDE. L'écon. élec.
——. Statistiques.

SYRIA

SUPPLY AND USE (million kwh)	1958	1959	1960	1961	1962	1963	1964	1965
PRODUCTION (Utilities & industries)								
Total (Gross)	293	346	368	431	502	525	574	
(Net)	--	--	--	--	--	--	--	
Hydro	—	—	—	—	—	—	—	
Conventional thermal	293	346	368	431	502	525	574	
Nuclear	—	—	—	—	—	—	—	
Geothermal	—	—	—	—	—	—	—	
PRODUCTION (Utilities only)								
Total (Gross)	191	235	232	279	313	339	379	
(Net)	--	--	--	--	--	--	--	
Hydro	—	—	—	—	—	—	—	
Conventional thermal	191	235	232	279	313	339	379	
Nuclear	—	—	—	—	—	—	—	
Geothermal	—	—	—	—	—	—	—	
NET IMPORTS	—	—	—	—	—	—	—	
SUPPLY (Gross)	293	346	368	431	502	525	574	
(Net)	--	--	--	--	--	--	--	
CONSUMPTION	260	302	323	386	448	460	502	
Transport	4	4	4	4	3	2	2	
Domestic sector	102e	125e	121e	163e	177e	189e	220e	
Industry	154	173	198	219	268	269	280	
LOSS AND USE	33	44	45	45	54	65	72	
PLANT (thousand kw)								
CAPACITY (Utilities & industries)								
Total	103	117	119	138	186	220	208	
Hydro	—	—	—	—	—	—	—	
Conventional thermal	103	117	119	138	186	220	208	
Nuclear	—	—	—	—	—	—	—	
Geothermal	—	—	—	—	—	—	—	
CAPACITY (Utilities only)								
Total	71	79	76	89	123	149	148	
Hydro	—	—	—	—	—	—	—	
Conventional thermal	71	79	76	89	123	149	148	
Nuclear	—	—	—	—	—	—	—	
Geothermal	—	—	—	—	—	—	—	
FUEL CONSUMPTION (Utilities only)								
Total (Tcals)	--	--	--	--	--	--	--	
RESERVOIR STORAGE CAPACITY (million kwh)	—	—	—	—	—	—	—	

SUPPLEMENTARY DATA FOR 1964

Transmission lines, 100 kv+ (km) :   —
Households served (thousands) :   --
Revenues per kwh (U.S. cents) — Total:
  Residential: Railways:
  Industry: Lighting: 5.5
Population (thousands) :   5200

Other characteristics of plants and systems:

The principal suppliers of electricity in Syria are the Damascus Electricity Establishment, and the Aleppo Electricity and Transport Establishment. The bulk of Syria's power is generated in nationalized establishments.

Sources of data:
UN. *Stat. yrbk.*
US. *Foreign serv. desp.*
Directorate of Statistics. *General bulletin of current statistics.*
———. *Statistical abstract of Syria.*

TANZANIA

SUPPLY AND USE (million kwh)	1958	1959	1960	1961	1962	1963	1964	1965
PRODUCTION (Utilities & industries)								
Total (Gross)	--	--	--	--	--	--	--	
(Net)	--	--	--	--	--	--	--	
Hydro	--	--	--	--	--	--	--	
Conventional thermal	--	--	--	--	--	--	--	
Nuclear	—	—	—	—	—	—	—	
Geothermal	—	—	—	—	—	—	—	
PRODUCTION (Utilities only)								
Total (Gross)	141	146	156	164	179	186	192	
(Net)	--	--	--	--	--	--	--	
Hydro	92	91	94	93	99	97	131	
Conventional thermal	49	55	62	71	80	89	61	
Nuclear	—	—	—	—	—	—	—	
Geothermal	—	—	—	—	—	—	—	
NET IMPORTS	−28	−26	−25	−22	−21	−16	−6	
SUPPLY (Gross)	113	120	131	142	158	170	186	
(Net)	--	--	--	--	--	--	--	
CONSUMPTION	96	102	112	120	135	147	162	
Transport	—	—	—	—	—	—	—	
Domestic sector	31	33	37	39	43	47	52e	
Industry	65	69	75	81	92	100	110e	
LOSS AND USE	17	18	19	22	23	23	24	

PLANT (thousand kw)

	1958	1959	1960	1961	1962	1963	1964	1965
CAPACITY (Utilities & industries)								
Total	--	--	--	--	--	--	--	
Hydro	--	--	--	--	--	--	--	
Conventional thermal	--	--	--	--	--	--	--	
Nuclear	—	—	—	—	—	—	—	
Geothermal	—	—	—	—	—	—	—	
CAPACITY (Utilities only)								
Total	40	43	41	47	49	49	70	
Hydro	20	20	20	20	20	20	41	
Conventional thermal	20	23	21	27	29	29e	29	
Nuclear	—	—	—	—	—	—	—	
Geothermal	—	—	—	—	—	—	—	

FUEL CONSUMPTION (Utilities only)

	1958	1959	1960	1961	1962	1963	1964	1965
Total (Tcals)	--	--	--	--	--	--	--	
RESERVOIR STORAGE CAPACITY (million kwh)	--	--	--	--	--	--	--	

SUPPLEMENTARY DATA FOR 1964

Transmission lines, 100 kv+ (km): --
Households served (thousands): --
Revenues per kwh (U.S. cents) — Total:
  Residential: Railways:
  Industry: Lighting: 2.0
Population (thousands): 9990

Other characteristics of plants and systems:
    Most of Tanganyika's power is generated by the Tanganyika Electricity Supply Company, Ltd., privately owned, mainly at Dar-es-Salaam. There is a separate system on the island of Zanzibar which was taken over by the State Fuel and Power Cooperative.

Sources of data:

UN. *Stat. yrbk.* ———. ECA. *Situation, trends & prospects.*
East African Common Services Organization. *Economic and statistical review.*
Statistics Division. The Treasury. *Monthly statistical bulletin.*
  ———. *Statistical abstract of Tanganyika.*
United Republic of Tanganyika and Zanzibar. Central Bureau of Statistics.
  Census of industrial production in Tanganyika.

SUPPLY AND USE (million kwh)	1958	1959	1960	1961	1962	1963	1964	1965
PRODUCTION (Utilities & industries)								
Total (Gross)	490	477	608	674	775	906	1107	
(Net)	--	--	580	635	733	855	1051	
Hydro	—	—	—	—	—	—	288	
Conventional thermal	490	477	608	674	775	906	819	
Nuclear	—	—	—	—	—	—	—	
Geothermal	—	—	—	—	—	—	—	
PRODUCTION (Utilities only)								
Total (Gross)	408	420	516	602	700	804	1028	
(Net)	--	--	488	563	658	753	972	
Hydro	—	—	—	—	—	—	288	
Conventional thermal	408	420	516	602	700	804	740	
Nuclear	—	—	—	—	—	—	—	
Geothermal	—	—	—	—	—	—	—	
NET IMPORTS	—	—	—	—	—	—	—	
SUPPLY (Gross)	490	477	608	674	775	906	1107	
(Net)	--	--	580	635	733	855	1051	
CONSUMPTION	--	--	472	526	606	732	883	
Transport								
Domestic sector	--	--	214	295	311	425	478	
Industry	--	--	258e	231	295	307	405	
LOSS AND USE	--	--	108	109	127	123	168	
PLANT (thousand kw)								
CAPACITY (Utilities & industries)								
Total	167	174	191	282	313	362	548	
Hydro	—	—	—	—	—	—	140	
Conventional thermal	167	174	191	282	313	362	408	
Nuclear	—	—	—	—	—	—	—	
Geothermal	—	—	—	—	—	—	—	
CAPACITY (Utilities only)								
Total	150	160	178	256	273	331	518	
Hydro	—	—	—	—	—	—	140	
Conventional thermal	150	160	178	256	273	331	378	
Nuclear	—	—	—	—	—	—	—	
Geothermal	—	—	—	—	—	—	—	
FUEL CONSUMPTION (Utilities only)								
Coal (mmt)	14	14	10	4	--	--	--	
Lignite (mmt)	98	86	93	92	95e	102	96	
Charcoal (mmt)	28	--	48	--	--	--	--	
Diesel oil (mmt)	63.4	64.5	80.6	61.3	47.7	50	50	
Fuel oil (mmt)	80	80	85	122	--	103	140	
Total (Tcals)	2163	2016	2506	2352	2247	2107	2366	
RESERVOIR STORAGE CAPACITY (million kwh)	—	—	—	—	—	—	—	

SUPPLEMENTARY DATA FOR 1964

Transmission lines, 100 kv+ (km) : 1377
Households served (thousands) : 477
Revenues per kwh (U.S. cents) — Total: 3.7
   Residential: 5.3   Railways:
   Industry: 2.4   Lighting: 3.8
Population (thousands): 29700

Sources of data:
  UN. Stat. yrbk. UN. ECAFE. Elec. power.
  Central Statistical Office. Quarterly bulletin of statistics.
  ———. Statistical yearbook.
  International Atomic Energy Agency. Report of an IAEA
    Mission to Thailand.
  World Power Conference. Tokyo Sectional Meeting.
    "Electrical power survey in Thailand," by Athorn
  Patumasoota and Archamphon Khambanoda.

Other characteristics of plants and systems:
    Most of the country's power is distributed in Bangkok by the Metropolitan Electricity Authority, which obtains the bulk of its power (via the Yanhee Electricity Authority) from a steam plant (150 MW) at Bangkok and from the Bhumiphol hydro plant (140 MW). Outside the Bangkok area, responsibility for distribution of electricity rests with the Provincial Electricity Authority. Data on the number of customers in Thailand, related to the total population of the country, indicate that less than ten per cent of the people are supplied with electricity. Domestic lignite provides part of Thailand's electricity, but the bulk of the thermal electric power is generated from imported distillate and residual fuel oils.

TRINIDAD

SUPPLY AND USE (million kwh)	1958	1959	1960	1961	1962	1963	1964	1965
PRODUCTION (Utilities & industries)								
Total (Gross)	383	429	470	499	569	624	820	
(Net)	--	--	--	--	--	--	--	
Hydro	—	—	—	—	—	—	—	
Conventional thermal	383	429	470	499	569	624	820	
Nuclear	—	—	—	—	—	—	—	
Geothermal	—	—	—	—	—	—	—	
PRODUCTION (Utilities only)								
Total (Gross)	187	221	261	285	335	369	538	
(Net)	--	--	--	--	--	--	--	
Hydro	—	—	—	—	—	—	—	
Conventional thermal	187	221	261	285	335	369	538	
Nuclear	—	—	—	—	—	—	—	
Geothermal	—	—	—	—	—	—	—	
NET IMPORTS	—	—	—	—	—	—	—	
SUPPLY (Gross)	383	429	470	499	569	624	820	
(Net)	--	--	--	--	--	--	--	
CONSUMPTION	360	388	--	441	501	554	741	
Transport	—	—	—	—	—	—	—	
Domestic sector	61	74	--	78	110	124	142	
Industry	299	314	--	363	391	430	599	
LOSS AND USE	23	41	--	58	68	70	79	
PLANT (thousand kw)								
CAPACITY (Utilities & industries)								
Total	109	117	129	129	152	152	223	
Hydro	—	—	—	—	—	—	—	
Conventional thermal	109	117	129	129	152	152	223	
Nuclear	—	—	—	—	—	—	—	
Geothermal	—	—	—	—	—	—	—	
CAPACITY (Utilities only)								
Total	61	61	81	81	102	102	173	
Hydro	—	—	—	—	—	—	—	
Conventional thermal	61	61	81	81	102	102	173	
Nuclear	—	—	—	—	—	—	—	
Geothermal	—	—	—	—	—	—	—	
FUEL CONSUMPTION (Utilities only)								
Natural gas (mil m^3)	--	--	--	--	--	--	207	
Total (Tcals)	--	--	--	--	--	--	--	
RESERVOIR STORAGE CAPACITY (million kwh)	—	—	—	—	—	—	—	

SUPPLEMENTARY DATA FOR 1964

Transmission lines, 100 kv+ (km) : —
Households served (thousands) : 107
Revenues per kwh (U.S. cents) — Total: 2.2
   Residential: 4.3   Railways:
   Industry: 1.3   Lighting:
Population (thousands) : 952

Other characteristics of plants and systems:
   The Trinidad and Tobago Electricity Commission, a public agency, supplies most of the country's power. Trinidad's largest plant is the Penal Colony steam plant, with a capacity of 70 MW. Power appears to be supplied to about half of the island's population.

Sources of data:
  UN. *Stat. yrbk.* UN. ECLA. *Estud. econ.*
  Central Statistical Office. *Quarterly economic report.*
  ———. *Annual statistical digest.*
  Electricity Supply Commission. *Annual report.*
  Ministry of Petroleum and Mines. *Monthly bulletin on the Trinidad and Tobago petroleum industry.*
  World Power Conference. "An investigation of methods to reduce fuel cost in the island of Tobago," by K. F. Seheult.

SUPPLY AND USE (million kwh)	1958	1959	1960	1961	1962	1963	1964	1965
PRODUCTION (Utilities & industries)								
Total (Gross)	2.8	3.4	5.0	10	14	22	27	
(Net)	- -	- -	- -	- -	- -	- -	- -	
Hydro	–	–	–	–	–	–	3	
Conventional thermal	2.8	3.4	5.0	10	14	22	24	
Nuclear	–	–	–	–	–	–	–	
Geothermal	–	–	–	–	–	–	–	
PRODUCTION (Utilities only)								
Total (Gross)	2.8	3.4	5.0	6.9	8.5	11	12	
(Net)	- -	- -	- -	- -	- -	- -	- -	
Hydro	–	–	–	–	–	–	3	
Conventional thermal	2.8	3.4	5.0	6.9	8.5	11	9	
Nuclear	–	–	–	–	–	–	–	
Geothermal	–	–	–	–	–	–	–	
NET IMPORTS								
SUPPLY (Gross)	3	3	5	10	14	22	27	
(Net)	- -	- -	- -	- -	- -	- -	- -	
CONSUMPTION	2	3	5	9	13	20	24e	
Transport	–	–	–	–	–	–	–	
Domestic sector	1	2	3	4	5	6	7e	
Industry	1	1	2	5	8e	14	17	
LOSS AND USE	1	–	–	1	1	2	3	
PLANT (thousand kw)								
CAPACITY (Utilities & industries)								
Total	3.0	3.1	4.1	10.8	10.8	12.5	12.7	
Hydro	–	–	–	1.6	1.6	1.6	1.6	
Conventional thermal	3.0	3.1	4.1	9.2	9.2	10.9	11.1	
Nuclear	–	–	–	–	–	–	–	
Geothermal	–	–	–	–	–	–	–	
CAPACITY (Utilities only)								
Total	1.6	2e	2e	2.1	2.2	4.2	4.2	
Hydro	–	–	–	1.6	1.6	1.6	1.6	
Conventional thermal	1.6e	2e	2e	0.5	0.6	2.6	2.6	
Nuclear	–	–	–	–	–	–	–	
Geothermal	–	–	–	–	–	–	–	
FUEL CONSUMPTION (Utilities only)								
Total (Tcals)	- -	- -	- -	- -	- -	- -	- -	
RESERVOIR STORAGE CAPACITY (million kwh)	–	–	–	–	–	–	–	

SUPPLEMENTARY DATA FOR 1964

Transmission lines, 100 kv+ (km): –
Households served (thousands): 4.0
Revenues per kwh (U.S. cents) — Total: (1961) 10.0
    Residential: Railways:
    Industry: Lighting: 12.9
Population (thousands): 1602

Other characteristics of plants and systems:

Union Electrique d'Outre-Mer, a privately-owned company, is the principal supplier of electricity to the public in Togo. La Cie. Togolaise des Mines du Bénin operates the country's largest hydro plant, a 6 MW installation at Kpémé. Electricity is supplied to only a very small fraction of the country's population.

Sources of data:
EEC. *Yrbk. Overseas Assoc.*
Inst. de la Stat. *Données statistiques.* UN. *Stat. yrbk.*
Electricité de France. *Survey of the future electricity demand in Togo and Dahomey.*

TUNISIA

SUPPLY AND USE (million kwh)	1958	1959	1960	1961	1962	1963	1964	1965
PRODUCTION (Utilities & industries)								
Total (Gross)	276	298	316	329	345	403e	487e	
(Net)	258	279	297	305	312	367	447	
Hydro	32	60	47	19	19	30	38	
Conventional thermal	244	238	269	310	326	373	449	
Nuclear	—	—	—	—	—	—	—	
Geothermal	—	—	—	—	—	—	—	
PRODUCTION (Utilities only)								
Total (Gross)	235	257	274	282	288	307	333	
(Net)	--	--	--	--	--	--	--	
Hydro	32	60	47	19	19	30	38	
Conventional thermal	203	197	227	263	269	277	295	
Nuclear	—	—	—	—	—	—	—	
Geothermal	—	—	—	—	—	—	—	
NET IMPORTS	10	—	—	—	—	—	—	
SUPPLY (Gross)	286	298	316	329	345	403e	487e	
(Net)	268	279	297	305	312	367	447	
CONSUMPTION	229	239	257	263	271	314	392	
Transport	11	11	9	8	8	7	7	
Domestic sector	80	90	90	102	103	108	117	
Industry	138	138	158	153	160	199	268	
LOSS AND USE	39	40	40	42	41	53	55	
PLANT (thousand kw)								
CAPACITY (Utilities & industries)								
Total	135	136e	139e	139e	140	151	175	
Hydro	27	27	27	27	27	28	28	
Conventional thermal	108	109	112	112	113	123	147	
Nuclear	—	—	—	—	—	—	—	
Geothermal	—	—	—	—	—	—	—	
CAPACITY (Utilities only)								
Total	113	112	115	115	116	117	138	
Hydro	27	26	26	27	28	28	28	
Conventional thermal	86	86	89	88	88	89	110	
Nuclear	—	—	—	—	—	—	—	
Geothermal	—	—	—	—	—	—	—	
FUEL CONSUMPTION (Utilities only)								
Coal (mmt)	1	—	—	—	—	—	—	
Diesel oil (mmt)	5	6	6	7	6.4	7.7	8.7	
Fuel oil (mmt)	68	66	79	96	99	101	108	
Total (Tcals)	784	756	889	1029	1113	1141	--	
RESERVOIR STORAGE CAPACITY (million kwh)	45	45	45	44	44	20	20	

SUPPLEMENTARY DATA FOR 1964

Transmission lines, 100 kv+ (km): —
Households served (thousands): (1963) 213
Revenues per kwh (U.S. cents) — Total: (1961) 3.6
    Residential: Railways:
    Industry: Lighting:
Population (thousands): 4361

Other characteristics of plants and systems:

    La Société Tunisienne de l'Electricité et du Gaz, nationalized in 1962, operates a limited high-tension network of 90 KV in the northern part of the country. The remainder of the country is served by local facilities, but only about a quarter of the population is supplied with electricity.

Sources of data:

Inst. de la Stat. *Données statistiques.* UN. *Stat. yrbk.*
UNIPEDE. *Statistiques.* US. *Foreign serv. desp.*
Secretariat d'Etat au Plan et aux Finances. Service des
    Statistiques. *Annuaire statistique de la Tunisie.*
————. *Bulletin de statistique et d'études économiques.*
————. *Bulletin mensuel de statistique.*

TURKEY

SUPPLY AND USE (million kwh)	1958	1959	1960	1961	1962	1963	1964	1965
PRODUCTION (Utilities & industries)								
Total (Gross)	2303	2586	2815	3011	3560	3983	4435	
(Net)	2163	2435	2675	2910	3372	3824	4220	
Hydro	657	691	1002	1265	1124	2099	1652	
Conventional thermal	1646	1895	1813	1746	2436	1884	2783	
Nuclear	—	—	—	—	—	—	—	
Geothermal	—	—	—	—	—	—	—	
PRODUCTION (Utilities only)								
Total (Gross)	1911	2160	2383	2603	3085	3486	3858	
(Net)	1808	2044	2273	2505	2928	3367	3681	
Hydro	624	660	966	1229	1082	2061	1609	
Conventional thermal	1287	1500	1417	1374	2003	1425	2249	
Nuclear	—	—	—	—	—	—	—	
Geothermal	—	—	—	—	—	—	—	
NET IMPORTS	—	—	—	—	—	—	—	
SUPPLY (Gross)	2303	2586	2815	3011	3560	3983	4435	
(Net)	2163	2435	2675	2910	3372	3824	4220	
CONSUMPTION	1962	2171	2396	2610	3087	3466	3800	
Transport	43	41	39	40	55	56	60	
Domestic sector	473	537	606	681	782	846	920	
Industry	1446	1593	1751	1889	2250	2564	2820	
LOSS AND USE	201	264	279	300	285	358	420	
PLANT (thousand kw)								
CAPACITY (Utilities & industries)								
Total	1031	1161	1272	1324	1369	1381	1434	
Hydro	222	318	412	445	468	478	498	
Conventional thermal	809	843	860	879	901	903	936	
Nuclear	—	—	—	—	—	—	—	
Geothermal	—	—	—	—	—	—	—	
CAPACITY (Utilities only)								
Total	740	840	939	979	1009	1027	1057	
Hydro	210	305	400	433	456	466	486	
Conventional thermal	530	535	539	546	553	561	571	
Nuclear	—	—	—	—	—	—	—	
Geothermal	—	—	—	—	—	—	—	
FUEL CONSUMPTION (Utilities only)								
Coal (mmt)	633	619	566	616	802	493	812	
Lignite (mmt)	441	610	476	235	404	403	700	
Peat & fuelwood (mmt)	6	1	—	—	—	—	—	
Fuel oils (mmt)	39	40	42	44	46	48	70	
Total (Tcals)	4597	5145	4823	4695	6624	4744	7926	
RESERVOIR STORAGE CAPACITY (million kwh)	829	706	918	918	918	918	918	

SUPPLEMENTARY DATA FOR 1964

Transmission lines, 100 kv+ (km): 2712
Households served (thousands): - -
Revenues per kwh (U.S. cents) — Total: (1962) 3.0
  Residential: (1962) 3.5   Railways: 1.5
  Industry: (1962) 2.4   Lighting: 2.6
Population (thousands): 30635

Other characteristics of plants and systems:
    Practically all generating capacity in Turkey is owned by municipalities or by the State. An extensive network serves the northwestern part of the country. Elsewhere, service is mainly regional or local in nature. Only about a third of the Turkish population enjoys the benefits of electricity.

Sources of data:
  UN. *Stat. yrbk.* UN. ECE. *Ann. bull. of elec. energy stat.*
  Electrical Power Resources Survey Department. *Annual electric power survey.*

UGANDA

SUPPLY AND USE (million kwh)	1958	1959	1960	1961	1962	1963	1964	1965
PRODUCTION (Utilities & industries)								
Total (Gross)	--	--	--	--	--	--	--	
(Net)	--	--	--	--	--	--	--	
Hydro	--	--	--	--	--	--	--	
Conventional thermal	--	--	--	--	--	--	--	
Nuclear	—	—	—	—	—	—	—	
Geothermal	—	—	—	—	—	—	—	
PRODUCTION (Utilities only)								
Total (Gross)	279	346	396	435	453	497	521	
(Net)	--	--	--	--	--	--	--	
Hydro	278	346	396	435	451	496	521	
Conventional thermal	1	—	—	—	2	1	—	
Nuclear	—	—	—	—	—	—	—	
Geothermal	—	—	—	—	—	—	—	
NET IMPORTS	−90	−129	−160	−192	−189	−190	−178	
SUPPLY (Gross)	189	217	236	243	264	307	343	
(Net)	--	--	--	--	--	--	--	
CONSUMPTION	163	186	203	209	228	270	293	
Transport	—	—	—	—	—	—	—	
Domestic sector	60	63	67	68	68	72	73	
Industry	103	123	136	141	160	198	220	
LOSS AND USE	26	31	33	34	36	37	50	

PLANT (thousand kw)

	1958	1959	1960	1961	1962	1963	1964	1965
CAPACITY (Utilities & industries)								
Total	--	--	--	--	--	--	--	
Hydro	--	--	--	--	--	--	--	
Conventional thermal	--	--	--	--	--	--	--	
Nuclear	—	—	—	—	—	—	—	
Geothermal	—	—	—	—	—	—	—	
CAPACITY (Utilities only)								
Total	117	133	132	132	133	133	134	
Hydro	106	121	121	121	122	122	122	
Conventional thermal	11	12	11	11	11	11	12	
Nuclear	—	—	—	—	—	—	—	
Geothermal	—	—	—	—	—	—	—	

FUEL CONSUMPTION (Utilities only)

	1958	1959	1960	1961	1962	1963	1964	1965
Total (Tcals)	--	—	—	—	--	--	—	
RESERVOIR STORAGE CAPACITY (million kwh)	(1051)	(1051)	(1051)	(1051)	1051	1051	1680	

SUPPLEMENTARY DATA FOR 1964

Transmission lines, 100 kv+ (km) : (1961) 265
Households served (thousands) :   24
Revenues per kwh (U.S. cents) — Total: 1.7
  Residential: 4.4   Railways:
  Industry: 3.1   Lighting:
Population (thousands) :   7367

Sources of data:
  UN. *Stat. yrbk.*
  UNIPEDE. *Statistiques.*
  East African Common Services Organization. *Economic and statistical review.*
  Electricity Board. *Annual report and accounts.*

Other characteristics of plants and systems:

   All power is produced and distributed by the Uganda Electricity Board, a government agency, which operates a partially integrated system extending into Kenya, to which power is exported. The principal source of electricity is the Owens Falls hydro plant of 120 MW.

SUPPLY AND USE (million kwh)	1958	1959	1960	1961	1962	1963	1964	1965
PRODUCTION (Utilities & industries)								
Total (Gross)	235351	265112	292274	327611	369275	412418	458902	
(Net)	--	--	--	--	--	--	--	
Hydro	46478	47630	50913	59122	71944	75859	77361	
Conventional thermal	188873	217482 ·	241361	268489	297331	336559	381541	
Nuclear			(included in conventional thermal)			(1000)	(2000)	
Geothermal	—	—	—	—	—	—	—	
PRODUCTION (Utilities only)								
Total (Gross)	179190	205177	224490	249933	285196	322418	358902	
(Net)	--	--	--	--	--	--	--	
Hydro	44649	45804	49105	57181	69840	73859	75361	
Conventional thermal	134541	159373	175385	192752	215356	247559	281541	
Nuclear			(included in conventional thermal)			(1000)	(2000)	
Geothermal	—	—	—	—	—	—	—	
NET IMPORTS	—	—	-30	-74	-209	-800	-1300	
SUPPLY (Gross)	235351	265112	292244	327537	369066	411618	457602	
(Net)	--	--	--	--	--	--	--	
CONSUMPTION	206066	231740	255771	286804	323094	384500	426400	
Transport	11418	13977	16784	19187	22349	29200	32900	
Domestic sector	32665	36424	40477	46125	53587	67900	75700	
Industry	161983	181339	198510	221492	247158	287400	317800	
LOSS AND USE	29285	33372	36473	40733	45972	27118	31202	

PLANT (thousand kw)								
CAPACITY (Utilities & industries)								
Total	53641	59267	66721	74098	82461	93050	103584	
Hydro	10863	12710	14781	16366	18622	20830	21251	
Conventional thermal	42773	46552	51935	57727	63834	71915	82028	
Nuclear	5	5	5	5	5	305	305	
Geothermal	—	—	—	—	—	—	—	
CAPACITY (Utilities only)								
Total	35429	39442	44383	49336	56240	65050E	73584e	
Hydro	10105	11927	14071	15675	17919	19830e	20251e	
Conventional thermal	25319	27510	30307	33656	38316	44915	53028	
Nuclear	5	5	5	5	5	305	305	
Geothermal	—	—	—	—	—	—	—	

FUEL CONSUMPTION (Utilities only)								
Coal (mmt)	28097	33295	35980	37356	--	--	--	
Low grade coal (mmt)	7970	6075	7050	8785	--	--	--	
Lignite (mmt)	40880	50502	54924	56733	--	--	--	
Peat & fuelwood (mmt)	17718	19750	19500	17203	--	--	--	
Fuel oils (mmt)	2165	2003	2247	2474	--	--	--	
Natural gas (Tcals)	60742	62333	68091	88410	--	--	--	
Manufactured gas (Tcals)	1240	1038	646	700	--	--	--	
Total (Tcals)	412099	478268	521544	555032	--	--	--	
RESERVOIR STORAGE CAPACITY (million kwh)	--	--	--	--		--	--	

SUPPLEMENTARY DATA FOR 1964

Transmission lines, 100 kv+ (km): 167300
Households served (thousands): --
Revenues per kwh (U.S. cents) — Total:
    Residential: 4.4   Railways:
    Industry: Lighting:
Population (thousands): 227687

Sources of data:
  UN. *Stat. yrbk.*
  UN. ECE. *Ann. bull. of elec. energy stat.*
  EEI. *Rept. on elec. power dev. in the U.S.S.R.*

Other characteristics of plants and systems:
All electricity undertakings, except certain small plants supplying Kolkhozes, belong to the State. In 1963 there were some 55 power systems in the Soviet Union. Interconnections of systems and remote power plants are under way, some at very high voltages, including an 800 KV DC transmission line connecting the Volgograd Hydroelectric Station in the Central Power System with the Donbas in the Southern Power System. Although electrification has moved forward rapidly, it appears that a significant share of the population has yet to receive electricity. Among the more notable features of the Soviet system are some of the world's largest hydroelectric plants, including Kuibyshev (2300 MW) and Bratsk (now 4500 MW). Other features include large peat-burning plants and extensive development of combined heat-and-power stations.

SUPPLY AND USE (million kwh)	1958	1959	1960	1961	1962	1963	1964	1965
PRODUCTION (Utilities & industries)								
Total (Gross)	1905	2125	2639	3723	4110	4460	5106	
(Net)	--	--	--	--	--	--	--	
Hydro	8	9	260	1012	1172	1280	1670	
Conventional thermal	1897	2116	2379	2711	2938	3180	3436	
Nuclear	—	—	—	—	—	—	—	
Geothermal	—	—	—	—	—	—	—	
PRODUCTION (Utilities only)								
Total (Gross)	1347	1508	1991	3041	3359	3668	4257	
(Net)	--	--	--	--	--	--	--	
Hydro	8	9	260	1012	1172	1280	1670	
Conventional thermal	1339	1499	1731	2029	2187	2388	2587	
Nuclear	—	—	—	—	—	—	—	
Geothermal	—	—	—	—	—	—	—	
NET IMPORTS	—	—	—	—	—	—	—	
SUPPLY (Gross)	1905	2125	2639	3723	4110	4460	5106	
(Net)	--	--	--	--	--	--	--	
CONSUMPTION	1683	--	2388	3287	--	--	--	
Transport	85	100	122	117	--	--	--	
Domestic sector	506	--	675	760	--	--	1200	
Industry	1092	1100e	1591	2410	--	--	--	
LOSS AND USE	222	--	251	436	--	--	--	
PLANT (thousand kw)								
CAPACITY (Utilities & industries)								
Total	785	828	1167	1292	1289	1205	1335	
Hydro	5	5	350	350	350	353	353	
Conventional thermal	780	823	817	942	939	852	982	
Nuclear	—	—	—	—	—	—	—	
Geothermal	—	—	—	—	—	—	—	
CAPACITY (Utilities only)								
Total	593	606	944	1048	1037	950e	1069	
Hydro	5	5	350	350	350	353	351	
Conventional thermal	588	601	594	698	687	597e	718	
Nuclear	—	—	—	—	—	—	—	
Geothermal	—	—	—	—	—	—	—	
FUEL CONSUMPTION (Utilities only)								
Fuel oil (mmt)	617	--	953	--	--	--	--	
Diesel oil (mmt)	72	--	71	--	--	--	--	
Total (Tcals)	--	--	--	--	--	--	--	
RESERVOIR STORAGE CAPACITY (million kwh)	--	--	--	--	--	--	--	

SUPPLEMENTARY DATA FOR 1964

Transmission lines, 100 kv+ (km): --
Households served (thousands): --
Revenues per kwh (U.S. cents) — Total:
 Residential: 3.6 Railways:
 Industry: 1.0 Lighting: 6.9
Population (thousands): 28900

Other characteristics of plants and systems:
 Egypt's electricity supply is provided mainly by the government via the Hydroelectric Administration and the Cairo Electricity and Gas Administration. Alexandria is served primarily by Lebon et Cie. A high-tension network which will deliver power from the High Dam to the consuming centers is under construction. Only a very small fraction of Egypt's population is supplied with electricity.

Sources of data:
Federation of Industries in U.A.R. *Industrial Egypt.*
——. *Yearbook.*
US. Department of Commerce. "Basic data on the economy of the United Arab Republic." *Overseas business reports.*
World Power Conference. Tokyo Sectional Meeting. "Coordination of operating thermal power plants in the U.A.R. with hydro-electric Aswan High Dam Power Plant (SAAD EL AALI) to cover load requirements of the country as from 1967." Dr. K. H. Khalil and Dr. A. K. Mohamed.
——. Melbourne. "Electric power generation and distribution in the United Arab Republic." Dr. M.A.B. El-Koshairy.

SUPPLY AND USE (million kwh)	1958	1959	1960	1961	1962	1963	1964	1965
PRODUCTION (Utilities & industries)								
Total (Gross)	113350	121172	136970	145958	160452	173647	182848	
(Net)	107303	114539	129818	138273	151766	163935	172418	
Hydro	2707	2706	3133	3852	3925	3663	4022	
Conventional thermal	110338	117265	131758	139707	152868	163514	170480	
Nuclear	305	1201	2079	2399	3659	6470	8346	
Geothermal	–	–	–	–	–	–	–	
PRODUCTION (Utilities only)								
Total (Gross)	99813	106565	120481	129407	143581	156002	164597	
(Net)	93929	100259	113427	121783	134962	146356	154237	
Hydro	2110	2175	2539	3196	3252	3074	3420	
Conventional thermal	97703	104390	117942	126211	139385	149442	155838	
Nuclear	–	–	–	–	944	3486	5339	
Geothermal	–	–	–	–	–	–	–	
NET IMPORTS	–1	–1	–1	1	87	–15	–211	
SUPPLY (Gross)	113349	121171	136969	145959	160539	173632	182637	
(Net)	107302	114538	129817	138274	151853	163920	172207	
CONSUMPTION	97355	104198	117466	125387	137697	149840	157015	
Transport	2166	2251	2261	2311	2421	2422	2372	
Domestic sector	43560	46897	53762	59752	70474	79563	80873	
Industry	51629	55050	61443	63324	64802	67855	73770	
LOSS AND USE	9947	10340	12351	12887	14156	14080	15192	
PLANT (thousand kw)								
CAPACITY (Utilities & industries)								
Total	32412	34709	36702	38862	42221	44458	45236	
Hydro	1111	1163	1171	1294	1544	1713	1760	
Conventional thermal	31190	33231	35171	37208	39588	41607	41973	
Nuclear	111	315	360	360	1089	1138	1503	
Geothermal	–	–	–	–	–	–	–	
CAPACITY (Utilities only)								
Total	28534	30615	32488	34611	37884	40035	40711	
Hydro	1001	1053	1061	1184	1434	1603	1650	
Conventional thermal	27533	29562	31427	33427	35874	37856	38185	
Nuclear	–	–	–	–	576	576	876	
Geothermal	–	–	–	–	–	–	–	
FUEL CONSUMPTION (Utilities only)								
Coal & coke (mmt)	47811	48029	52989	56558	62299	68414	69620	
Diesel oil (mmt)	29	31	36	40	44	44	43	
Fuel oil (mmt)	2577	4228	5422	5571	5811	5097	5719	
Total (Tcals)	304000	320279	356910	374670	409139	439335	456194	
RESERVOIR STORAGE CAPACITY (million kwh)	1121	1196	1222	1060	1100	1183	1183	

SUPPLEMENTARY DATA FOR 1964

Transmission lines, 100 kv+ (km): 29796
Households served (thousands): 16620
Revenues per kwh (U.S. cents) — Total: 1.9
   Residential: 2.1   Railways: 1.6
   Industry: 1.6   Lighting: 2.3
Population (thousands): 54213

Sources of data:
  UN. Stat. yrbk. UN. ECE. Ann. bull. of elec. energy stat.
  _____ . Org. of elec. power services.
  UNIPEDE. L'écon. élec. _____ . Statistiques.
  _____ . Réseaux de transport.
  Ministry of Power. Statistical digest.

Other characteristics of plants and systems;

In England and Wales, electricity is produced and transmitted by the Central Electricity Generating Board, and distributed by twelve Area Electricity Boards. In Scotland, it is produced and distributed, in the southern part of the country, by the South of Scotland Electricity Board, with headquarters in Glasgow, and in the northern part of the country by the North of Scotland Hydro Electric Board, which has headquarters in Edinburgh. In Northern Ireland, the Electricity Board for Northern Ireland, the Belfast Corporation Electricity Department, and the Londonderry Corporation Electricity Department are responsible for the electricity supply. Integrated service is available throughout each of the four Board areas. Electricity is supplied to almost all the people of the United Kingdom through one of the largest integrated networks in the world. The United Kingdom is currently the leader, by a rather considerable margin, in the development and utilization of nuclear power.

UNITED STATES

SUPPLY AND USE (million kwh)	1958	1959	1960	1961	1962	1963	1964	1965
PRODUCTION (Utilities & industries)								
Total (Gross)	--	--	--	--	--	--	--	
(Net)	726750e	797567	844188	881496	946526	1011417	1083741	
Hydro	143815	141501	149515	155630	172086	168990	180302	
Conventional thermal	582770	655878	694122	724080	772070	839047	899892	
Nuclear	165	188	518	1692	2270	3212	3343	
Geothermal	—	—	33	94	100	168	204	
PRODUCTION (Utilities only)								
Total (Gross)	--	--	--	--	--	--	--	
(Net)	647000e	711821	755374	794273	854797	916792	983990	
Hydro	140462e	138028	145796	152158	168579	165755	177073	
Conventional thermal	506373e	573605	609027	640329	683848	747657	803370	
Nuclear	165	188	518	1692	2270	3212	3343	
Geothermal	—	—	33	94	100	168	204	
NET IMPORTS	3317	3607	4535	2254	536	−121	1955	
SUPPLY (Gross)	--	--	--	--	--	--	--	
(Net)	730067e	801174	848723	883750	947062	1011296	1085696	
CONSUMPTION	666067	732861	777853	809801	868940	928520	999125	
Transport	5777	5567	5425	5276	5234	5043	5030	
Domestic sector	301590e	331443	357231	380797	414848	446380	485360	
Industry	358700e	395851	415197	423728	448858	477097	508735	
LOSS AND USE	64000e	68313	70870	73949	78122	82776	86571	

PLANT (thousand kw)	1958	1959	1960	1961	1962	1963	1964	1965
CAPACITY (Utilities & industries)								
Total	160651	175001	186534	199216	209575	228756	240471	
Hydro	30089	31884	33180	36302	38163	40928	42899	
Conventional thermal	130457	143012	153045	162460	170727	187052	196639	
Nuclear	105	105	297	442	672	749	906	
Geothermal	—	—	12	12	13	27	27	
CAPACITY (Utilities only)								
Total	142597	157347	168569	181312	191747	210549	222285	
Hydro	29359	31132	32423	31557	37418	40213	42188	
Conventional thermal	113133	126110	135837	149301	153644	169560	179164	
Nuclear	105	105	297	442	672	749	906	
Geothermal	—	—	12	12	13	27	27	

FUEL CONSUMPTION (Utilities only)	1958	1959	1960	1961	1962	1963	1964	1965
Coal & lignite (mmt)	141261	152785	160238	165232	175302	191716	204505	
Diesel oil (mmt)	744	692	656	574	567	574	570e	
Fuel oil (mmt)	11629	12417	12900	13274	13331	13838	14709e	
Natural gas (mil m³)	38894	46146	48866	51699	55693	60735	65806	
Total (Tcals)	1418448	1578188	1657170	1713067	1820240	1982177	2126249	
RESERVOIR STORAGE CAPACITY (million kwh)	--	--	--	--	--	--	--	

SUPPLEMENTARY DATA FOR 1964

Transmission lines, 100 kv+ (km): 263945
Households served (thousands): 56307
Revenues per kwh (U.S. cents) — Total: 1.6
  Residential: 2.4   Railways: 1.3
  Industry: 0.9   Lighting:
Population (thousands): 192120

Other characteristics of plants and systems:

The electric power industry comprises some 3600 systems, most of which are associated with at least one of five major networks. The largest single undertaking is the federally owned and operated Tennessee Valley Authority, with a capacity now in excess of 14,000 MW, but the bulk of the U. S. industry is privately owned. Most systems are vertically integrated, from production through distribution. Electricity is supplied to practically the entire population of the U.S.

Sources of data:
UN. *Stat. yrbk.* UN. ECE. *Ann. bull. of elec. energy stat.*
Department of Commerce. Bureau of the Census. *Annual survey of manufactures.*
———. *Statistical abstract of the United States.*
EEI. *Historical statistics of the elec. utility industry.*
———. *Yearbook of the electric utility industry.*
Federal Power Commission. *National power survey, 1964.*

SUPPLY AND USE (million kwh)	1958	1959	1960	1961	1962	1963	1964	1965
PRODUCTION (Utilities & industries)								
Total (Gross)	4.8	6.3	7.8	9.9	14	16	19	
(Net)	- -	- -	- -	- -	- -	- -	- -	
Hydro	–	–	–	–	–	–	–	
Conventional thermal	4.8	6.3	7.8	9.9	14	16	19	
Nuclear	–	–	–	–	–	–	–	
Geothermal	–	–	–	–	–	–	–	
PRODUCTION (Utilities only)								
Total (Gross)	4.8	6.3	7.8	9.9	14	16	19	
(Net)	- -	- -	- -	- -	- -	- -	- -	
Hydro	–	–	–	–	–	–	–	
Conventional thermal	4.8	6.3	7.8	9.9	14	16	19	
Nuclear	–	–	–	–	–	–	–	
Geothermal	–	–	–	–	–	–	–	
NET IMPORTS	–		–		–		–	
SUPPLY (Gross)	4.8	6.3	7.8	9.9	14	16	19	
(Net)	- -	- -	- -	- -	- -	- -	- -	
CONSUMPTION	4	5	6.5	8.2	10	(12)	16	
Transport	–	–	–	–	–	–	–	
Domestic sector	3	3	4.5	5.6	6.6	7e	9	
Industry	1	2	2.0	2.6	3.4	5	7	
LOSS AND USE	1	1	1.3	1.7	4.0	4	3	
PLANT (thousand kw)								
CAPACITY (Utilities & industries)								
Total	2.8	3.2	4.4	4.4	5.1	5.8	11	
Hydro	–	–	–	–	–	–	–	
Conventional thermal	2.8	3.2	4.4	4.4	5.1	5.8	11	
Nuclear	–	–	–	–	–	–	–	
Geothermal	–	–	–	–	–	–	–	
CAPACITY (Utilities only)								
Total	2.8	3.2	4.4	4.4	5.1	5.8	11	
Hydro	–	–	–	–	–	–	–	
Conventional thermal	2.8	3.2	4.4	4.4	5.1	5.8	11	
Nuclear	–	–	–	–	–	–	–	
Geothermal	–	–	–	–	–	–	–	
FUEL CONSUMPTION (Utilities only)								
Diesel oil (mmt)	1.6	- -	- -	- -	- -	- -	- -	
Total (Tcals)	17	- -	- -	- -	- -	- -	- -	
RESERVOIR STORAGE CAPACITY (million kwh)	–		–		–		–	

SUPPLEMENTARY DATA FOR 1964

Transmission lines, 100 kv+ (km) : - -
Households served (thousands) :   3.7
Revenues per kwh (U.S. cents) — Total:
  Residential: Railways:
  Industry: Lighting:
Population (thousands) :   4763

Other characteristics of plants and systems:

Société Africaine d'Electricité, privately owned, operates two isolated plants which generate most of the country's electricity. Electricity is supplied to only a very small fraction of the country's population.

Sources of data:
EEC. *Yrbk. Overseas Assoc.*
Inst. de la Stat. *Données statistiques.*
UN. *Stat. yrbk.*
US. *Foreign serv. desp.*

SUPPLY AND USE (million kwh)	1958	1959	1960	1961	1962	1963	1964	1965
PRODUCTION (Utilities & industries)								
Total (Gross)	1237	1176	1244	1327	1559	1578	1724	
(Net)	1210	1150e	1214e	1297e	1515	1544	1690	
Hydro	760	259	676	1046	829	1102	1267	
Conventional thermal	477	917	568	281	730	476	457	
Nuclear	—	—	—	—	—	—	—	
Geothermal	—	—	—	—	—	—	—	
PRODUCTION (Utilities only)								
Total (Gross)	1237	1176	1244	1327	1559	1578	1724	
(Net)	1210	1150e	1214e	1297e	1515	1544	1690	
Hydro	760	259	676	1046	829	1102	1267	
Conventional thermal	477	917	568	281	730	476	457	
Nuclear	—	—	—	—	—	—	—	
Geothermal	—	—	—	—	—	—	—	
NET IMPORTS	—	—	—	—	—	—	—	
SUPPLY (Gross)	1237	1176	1244	1327	1559	1578	1724	
(Net)	1210	1150e	1214e	1297e	1515	1544	1690	
CONSUMPTION	1018	948e	1015e	1139e	1252e	1281	1388	
Transport	36	34e	35	34e	32	29	29	
Domestic sector	520	475	510e	600e	720e	762e	805e	
Industry	462	439	470e	505e	500e	490e	554e	
LOSS AND USE	192	202	199	158	263	263	302	

PLANT (thousand kw)

	1958	1959	1960	1961	1962	1963	1964	1965
CAPACITY (Utilities & industries)								
Total	337	332	406	427	432	451	477	
Hydro	128	128	236	224	224	224	225	
Conventional thermal	209	204	170	203	208	227	252	
Nuclear	—	—	—	—	—	—	—	
Geothermal	—	—	—	—	—	—	—	
CAPACITY (Utilities only)								
Total	337	332	406	427	432	451	477	
Hydro	128	128	236	224	224	224	225	
Conventional thermal	209	204	170	203	208	227	252	
Nuclear	—	—	—	—	—	—	—	
Geothermal	—	—	—	—	—	—	—	

FUEL CONSUMPTION (Utilities only)

	1958	1959	1960	1961	1962	1963	1964	1965
Coal (mmt)	1	--	--	--	--	--	--	
Diesel oil (mmt)	--	--	26	--	--	34e	36e	
Fuel oil (mmt)	126	--	176	--	--	132	128	
Total (Tcals)	--	--	--	--	--	--	--	
RESERVOIR STORAGE CAPACITY (million kwh)	--	--	--	--	600	--	705	

SUPPLEMENTARY DATA FOR 1964

Transmission lines, 100 kv+ (km): --
Households served (thousands): 515
Revenues per kwh (U.S. cents) — Total: 1.6
  Residential: 1.5   Railways:
  Industry: (1962) 2.7   Lighting: 2.4
Population (thousands): 2682

Other characteristics of plants and systems:

Usinas y Teléfonos del Estado, an agency of the Uruguayan government, is responsible for the production and distribution of electric power. The principal plants and markets are interconnected by a single network, but communities outside this network depend mainly on isolated diesel stations for their electricity. It is estimated that close to two-thirds of the population of Uruguay is supplied with electricity.

Sources of data:

UN. *Stat. yrbk.* UN. ECLA. *Estud. econ.*
———. *Estud. sobre la elec.* UNIPEDE. *Statistiques.*
US. *Foreign serv. desp.*
Administración General de las Usinas Eléctricas y los Teléfonos del Estado (UTE). *Power expansion program, 1961-1968.*
———. *Producción de energía eléctrica.*

VENEZUELA

SUPPLY AND USE (million kwh)	1958	1959	1960	1961	1962	1963	1964	1965
PRODUCTION (Utilities & industries)								
Total (Gross)	3791	4310	4651	5217	5923	6771	7597	
(Net)	--	--	--	--	--	--	--	
Hydro	138	100	95	151	651	1106	1223	
Conventional thermal	3653	4210	4556	5066	5272	5665	6374	
Nuclear	—	—	—	—	—	—	—	
Geothermal	—	—	—	—	—	—		
PRODUCTION (Utilities only)								
Total (Gross)	2250	2724	2972	3445	4021	4870	5324	
(Net)	--	--	--	--	--	--	--	
Hydro	138	100	95	151	651	1106	1223	
Conventional thermal	2112	2624	2877	3294	3370	3764	4101	
Nuclear	—	—	—	—	—	—	—	
Geothermal	—	—	—	—	—	—	—	
NET IMPORTS								
SUPPLY (Gross)	3791	4310	4651	5217	5923	6771	7597	
(Net)	--	--	--	--	--	--	--	
CONSUMPTION	3506	3925	4200e	4417	4949	5865	6721	
Transport	—	—	—	—	—	—	—	
Domestic sector	1175	1401	1600e	1789	2025	2143	2272e	
Industry	2331	2524	2600e	2628	2924	3722	4449	
LOSS AND USE	285	385	451e	800e	974	906	876e	
PLANT (thousand kw)								
CAPACITY (Utilities & industries)								
Total	1121	1277	1347e	1883	1977	2034	2078	
Hydro	35e	35	--	387e	387	380	380	
Conventional thermal	1086e	1242	--	1496	1590	1654	1698	
Nuclear	—	—	—	—	—	—	—	
Geothermal	—	—	—	—	—	—	—	
CAPACITY (Utilities only)								
Total	656	724	794	1447	1507	1527	1547	
Hydro	35	35e	35e	--	387	380	380	
Conventional thermal	621	689e	759e	--	1120	1147	1167	
Nuclear	—	—	—	—	—	—	—	
Geothermal	—	—	—	—	—	—	—	
FUEL CONSUMPTION (Utilities only)								
Total (Tcals)	--	--	--	--	--	--	--	
RESERVOIR STORAGE CAPACITY (million kwh)	--	--	--	--	--	--	--	

SUPPLEMENTARY DATA FOR 1964

Transmission lines, 100 kv+ (km):   --
Households served (thousands):   --
Revenues per kwh (U.S. cents) — Total: 3.6
   Residential: 6.3   Railways:
   Industry: 3.5   Lighting:
Population (thousands):   8427

Sources of data:
UN. *Stat. yrbk.*   UN. ECLA. *Estud. econ.*
———. *Estud. sobre la elec.*
Banco Central de Venezuela. *Informe económico.*
Dirección General de Estadística y Censos Nacionales.
   Anuario estadístico de Venezuela.
———. *Boletín mensual de estadística.*
UN. ECLA. Data communicated to N. B. Guyol.

Other characteristics of plants and systems:

     Venezuela's electricity is generated in part by private companies, such as La Electricidad de Caracas, C. A., and publicly-owned companies, some belonging to the central government and some to municipalities. In addition, substantial quantities of electricity are generated by the petroleum industry. Power is distributed in part through regional networks, in part through local systems, but appears to reach only a fraction of the population - - probably no more than one-quarter.

SUPPLY AND USE (million kwh)	1958	1959	1960	1961	1962	1963	1964	1965
PRODUCTION (Utilities & industries)								
Total (Gross)	--	405	429	474	530	585	574	
(Net)	--	385e	409	456	508	560	551	
Hydro	--	5	7	10	17	—	56	
Conventional thermal	--	400	422	464	513	585	518	
Nuclear	—	—	—	—	—	—	—	
Geothermal	—	—	—	—	—	—	—	
PRODUCTION (Utilities only)								
Total (Gross)	244	287	304	329	374	418	523	
(Net)	--	267e	284	311	359	393	500	
Hydro	3	5	7	10	17	—	56	
Conventional thermal	241	282	297	319	357	418	467	
Nuclear	—	—	—	—	—	—	—	
Geothermal	—	—	—	—	—	—	—	
NET IMPORTS	—	—	—	—	—	—	—	
SUPPLY (Gross)	--	405	429	474	530	585	574	
(Net)	--	385e	409	456	508	560	551	
CONSUMPTION	--	347	364	416	463e	494	504	
Transport	—	—	—	—	—	—	—	
Domestic sector	151	150	172	235	260e	284	400	
Industry	--	197	192	181	203e	210	104	
LOSS AND USE	--	38	45	40	45	66	47	

PLANT (thousand kw)

	1958	1959	1960	1961	1962	1963	1964	1965
CAPACITY (Utilities & industries)								
Total	--	136	137e	137	151	228	325	
Hydro	2	4	4	4	4	84	164	
Conventional thermal	--	132	133	133	147	144	161	
Nuclear	—	—	—	—	—	—	—	
Geothermal	—	—	—	—	—	—	—	
CAPACITY (Utilities only)								
Total	84	98	99	102	115	189	274	
Hydro	2	4	4	4	4	84	164	
Conventional thermal	82	94	95	98	111	105	110	
Nuclear	—	—	—	—	—	—	—	
Geothermal	—	—	—	—	—	—	—	

FUEL CONSUMPTION (Utilities only)

	1958	1959	1960	1961	1962	1963	1964	1965
Coal (mmt)	29	17	16	22	--	--	25	
Diesel oil (mmt)	5.8	21.8	20.6	26.7	36.2	58	41	
Fuel oil (mmt)	73.2	85.9	94	100	--	--	106	
Total (Tcals)	1029	1197	1253	1449	1645	--	1266	
RESERVOIR STORAGE CAPACITY (million kwh)	—	—	—	—	—	--	--	

SUPPLEMENTARY DATA FOR 1964

Transmission lines, 100 kv+ (km):   263
Households served (thousands):   115
Revenues per kwh (U.S. cents) — Total: 10.3
  Residential: Railways:
  Industry: Lighting: 6.2
Population (thousands): 15715

Sources of data:
  UN. *Stat. yrbk.*
  UN. ECAFE. *Elec. power.*

Other characteristics of plants and systems:

    Vietnam's electricity was still generated, in 1964, almost entirely by private companies, including especially the Cie. des Eaux et de l'Electricité de l'Indochine, the Société Centrale d'Eclairage et d'Energie, and the Union Electrique d'Indochine. Electricité du Vietnam was scheduled to take the entire business over at the end of 1967. The country's output of thermal electricity is about equally divided between steam and diesel plants, the former concentrated largely in a single 49 MW plant at Choquan, the latter distributed in isolated units throughout the country. Electrical service appears to have been available to only a very small fraction of the total population in 1964, probably less than five per cent. Practically all of Vietnam's thermal electricity is obtained from imported distillate and residual fuel oils.

VIRGIN ISLANDS

SUPPLY AND USE (million kwh)	1958	1959	1960	1961	1962	1963	1964	1965
PRODUCTION (Utilities & industries)								
Total (Gross)	25	29	34	44	51	69	76	
(Net)	--	--	--	--	--	--	--	
Hydro	—	—	—	—	—	—	—	
Conventional thermal	25	29	34	44	51	69	76	
Nuclear	—	—	—	—	—	—	—	
Geothermal	—	—	—	—	—	—	—	
PRODUCTION (Utilities only)								
Total (Gross)	24	28	33	43	50	62	75	
(Net)	--	--	--	--	--	--	--	
Hydro	—	—	—	—	—	—	—	
Conventional thermal	24	28	33	43	50	62	75	
Nuclear	—	—	—	—	—	—	—	
Geothermal	—	—	—	—	—	—	—	
NET IMPORTS	—	—	—	—	—	—	—	
SUPPLY (Gross)	25	29	34	44	51	69	76	
(Net)	--	--	--	--	--	--	--	
CONSUMPTION	21	25	31	36	44	53	62	
Transport	—	—	—	—	—	—	—	
Domestic sector	15	18	23	27	31	36	43	
Industry	6	7	8	9	13	17	19	
LOSS AND USE	4	4	3	8	7	16	14	

PLANT (thousand kw)								
CAPACITY (Utilities & industries)								
Total	7.7	12	12	13	18	20	23	
Hydro	—	—	—	—	—	—	—	
Conventional thermal	7.7	12	12	13	18	20	23	
Nuclear	—	—	—	—	—	—	—	
Geothermal	—	—	—	—	—	—	—	
CAPACITY (Utilities only)								
Total	6.7	11	11	12	17	19	22	
Hydro	—	—	—	—	—	—	—	
Conventional thermal	6.7	11	11	12	17	19	22	
Nuclear	—	—	—	—	—	—	—	
Geothermal	—	—	—	—	—	—	—	

FUEL CONSUMPTION (Utilities only)								
Total (Tcals)	--	--	--	--	--	--	--	
RESERVOIR STORAGE CAPACITY (million kwh)	—	—	—	—	—	—	—	

SUPPLEMENTARY DATA FOR 1964

Transmission lines, 100 kv+ (km) :   —
Households served (thousands) :   13
Revenues per kwh (U.S. cents) — Total:
  Residential: Railways:
  Industry: Lighting: 7
Population (thousands) :   41

Sources of data:
  UN. *Non-self-gov. terr.; summaries.*
  ———. *Stat. yrbk.*
  US. FPC. *Power system statement.*

Other characteristics of plants and systems:

Electricity is produced and distributed by the Virgin Islands Water and Power Authority, which is publicly owned. Each of the two islands is served by its own network, and power is provided to virtually the entire population. A small part of the power supply of St. Croix is generated in a combined power and desalination plant, with an electrical capacity of 3 MW and a water output of 275,000 U.S. gallons per day.

WESTERN SAMOA

SUPPLY AND USE (million kwh)	1958	1959	1960	1961	1962	1963	1964	1965
PRODUCTION (Utilities & industries)								
Total (Gross)	4.0	4.3	4.4	4.9	5.7	5.9	6.4	
(Net)	--	--	--	--	--	--	--	
Hydro	3.8	4.0	4.2	4.3	4.9	4.5	5.0	
Conventional thermal	0.2	0.3	0.2	0.6	0.8	1.4	1.4	
Nuclear	—	—	—	—	—	—	—	
Geothermal	—	—	—	—	—	—	—	
PRODUCTION (Utilities only)								
Total (Gross)	4.0	4.3	4.4	4.9	5.7	5.9	6.4	
(Net)	--	--	--	--	--	--	--	
Hydro	3.8	4.0	4.2	4.3	4.9	4.5	5.0	
Conventional thermal	0.2	0.3	0.2	0.6	0.8	1.4	1.4	
Nuclear	—	—	—	—	—	—	—	
Geothermal	—	—	—	—	—	—	—	
NET IMPORTS	—	—	—	—	—	—	—	
SUPPLY (Gross)	4	4	4	5	6	6	6	
(Net)	--	--	--	--	--	--	--	
CONSUMPTION	--	--	--	4	4	5	6	
Transport	—	—	—	—	—	—	—	
Domestic sector	--	--	--	4	4	5	6	
Industry	—	—	—	—	—	—	—	
LOSS AND USE	--	--	--	1	2	1	—	

PLANT (thousand kw)

	1958	1959	1960	1961	1962	1963	1964	1965
CAPACITY (Utilities & industries)								
Total	2.3	2.3	2.0	2.0	2.5	2.5	2.4	
Hydro	1.3	1.3	1.3	1.3	1.3	1.3	1.3	
Conventional thermal	1.0	1.0	0.7	0.7	1.2	1.2	1.1	
Nuclear	—	—	—	—	—	—	—	
Geothermal	—	—	—	—	—	—	—	
CAPACITY (Utilities only)								
Total	2.3	2.3	2.0	2.0	2.5	2.5	2.4	
Hydro	1.3	1.3	1.3	1.3	1.3	1.3	1.3	
Conventional thermal	1.0	1.0	0.7	0.7	1.2	1.2	1.1	
Nuclear	—	—	—	—	—	—	—	
Geothermal	—	—	—	—	—	—	—	

FUEL CONSUMPTION (Utilities only)

	1958	1959	1960	1961	1962	1963	1964	1965
Diesel oil (mmt)	—	—	—	—	0.2	0.4	0.4	
Total (Tcals)	--	--	--	--	2	4	4	
RESERVOIR STORAGE CAPACITY (million kwh)	--	--	--	--	--	--	--	

SUPPLEMENTARY DATA FOR 1964

Transmission lines, 100 kv+ (km) :   —
Households served (thousands) :   2
Revenues per kwh (U.S. cents) — Total: 3.5
  Residential: 3.5   Railways:
  Industry: Lighting:
Population (thousands) :   123

Other characteristics of plants and systems:

Power for Western Samoa is produced by the Public Works Department of the government. It appears to be available to only a small fraction of the Samoan population.

Sources of data:
Benn Bros. *Elec. undertakings.*
UN. *Stat. yrbk.*
UN. ECAFE. *Elec. power.*
Acting Government Statistician. *Statistical bulletin.*

YUGOSLAVIA

SUPPLY AND USE (million kwh)	1958	1959	1960	1961	1962	1963	1964	1965
PRODUCTION (Utilities & industries)								
Total (Gross)	7356	8106	8928	9924	11275	13535	14189	
(Net)	7119	7756	8645	9602	10861	13044	13551	
Hydro	4300	4708	5984	5658	6851	8028	7575	
Conventional thermal	3056	3398	2944	4266	4424	5507	6614	
Nuclear	—	—	—	—	—	—	—	
Geothermal	—	—	—	—	—	—	—	
PRODUCTION (Utilities only)								
Total (Gross)	6416	7073	7844	8854	10216	12410	12719	
(Net)	6161	6794	7620	8510	9589	11844	12187	
Hydro	4177	4597	5850	5546	6738	7915	7476	
Conventional thermal	2239	2476	1994	3308	3478	4495	5243	
Nuclear	—	—	—	—	—	—	—	
Geothermal	—	—	—	—	—	—	—	
NET IMPORTS	−175	−100	−93	−53	−142	−295	342	
SUPPLY (Gross)	7181	8006	8835	9871	11133	13240	14531	
(Net)	6944	7656	8552	9549	10719	12749	13893	
CONSUMPTION	5781	6581	7330	8197	9156	11131	11998	
Transport	71	77	90	124	134	158	198	
Domestic sector	1737	2019	1995	2333	2807	3315	3819	
Industry	3973	4485	5245	5740	6215	7658	7981	
LOSS AND USE	1163	1075	1222	1352	1563	1618	1895	
PLANT (thousand kw)								
CAPACITY (Utilities & industries)								
Total	1924	1985	2402	2681	3001	3030	3106	
Hydro	1101	1171	1450	1606	1828	1851	1851	
Conventional thermal	823	814	952	1075	1173	1179	1255	
Nuclear	—	—	—	—	—	—	—	
Geothermal	—	—	—	—	—	—	—	
CAPACITY (Utilities only)								
Total	1544	1601	2000	2267	2588	2657	2721	
Hydro	1061	1131	1400	1556	1778	1801	1801	
Conventional thermal	483	470	600	711	810	856	920	
Nuclear	—	—	—	—	—	—	—	
Geothermal	—	—	—	—	—	—	—	
FUEL CONSUMPTION (Utilities only)								
Coal (mmt)	42	52	35	29	17	24	45	
Low grade coal (mmt)	1137	1466	1041	1562	1434	1936	1901	
Lignite (mmt)	2657	2710	2453	3735	4413	5482	5932	
Fuel oils (mmt)	7	9	5	3	6	7	10	
Manufactured gas (Tcals)	53	64	56	66	5	26	108	
Total (Tcals)	10248	10505	8149	12034	14012	16237	17824	
RESERVOIR STORAGE CAPACITY (million kwh)	456	726	726	936	1289	1289	1289	

SUPPLEMENTARY DATA FOR 1964

Transmission lines, 100 kv+ (km) :   8525
Households served (thousands) :   3000
Revenues per kwh (U.S. cents) — Total:
   Residential: Railways: 1.0
   Industry: Lighting:
Population (thousands) :   19279

Other characteristics of plants and systems:

All power undertakings in Yugoslavia are publicly owned. Much of the country is supplied with electricity by a nationwide network, but it is estimated that only about half the people of Yugoslavia are provided with electricity.

Sources of data:

UCPTE. *Réseau.*   UN. *Stat. yrbk.*
UN. ECE. *Ann. bull. of elec. energy stat.*
———. *Org. of elec. power services.*
UNIPEDE. *L'écon. élec.*
———. *Statistiques.*
Savezni Zavod za Statistiku. *Industrijska preduzeća.*

SUPPLY AND USE (million kwh)	1958	1959	1960	1961	1962	1963	1964	1965
PRODUCTION (Utilities & industries)								
Total (Gross)	967	1194	836	669	642	748	713	
(Net)	960e	1185e	823	659	631	731	694	
Hydro	239	246	256	266	297	311	305	
Conventional thermal	728	948	580	403	345	437	408	
Nuclear	—	—	—	—	—	—	—	
Geothermal	—	—	—	—	—	—	—	
PRODUCTION (Utilities only)								
Total (Gross)	78	122	82	56	33	24	--	
(Net)	--	--	--	--	--	--	--	
Hydro	17	19	22e	23	23	24	--	
Conventional thermal	61	103	60e	33	10	--	--	
Nuclear	—	—	—	—	—	—	—	
Geothermal	—	—	—	—	—	—	—	
NET IMPORTS	662	738	1311	1577	1755	1828	2033	
SUPPLY (Gross)	1629	1932	2147	2246	2397	2576	2746	
(Net)	1622e	1923e	2134	2236	2386	2559	2727	
CONSUMPTION	1535	1871	2013	2104	2220	2366	2518	
Transport	—	—	—	—	—	—	—	
Domestic sector	--	173	194	214	240	254	254	
Industry	--	1698	1819	1890	1980	2112	2264	
LOSS AND USE	87e	52	121	132	166	193	209	
PLANT (thousand kw)								
CAPACITY (Utilities & industries)								
Total	280	281	284	284	264	263	261	
Hydro	40	40	41	43	49	49	49	
Conventional thermal	240	241	243	241	215	214	212	
Nuclear	—	—	—	—	—	—	—	
Geothermal	—	—	—	—	—	—	—	
CAPACITY (Utilities only)								
Total	43	43	46	46	--	--	--	
Hydro	8	8	11	11	--	--	--	
Conventional thermal	35	35	35	35	--	--	--	
Nuclear	—	—	—	—	—	—	—	
Geothermal	—	—	—	—	—	—	—	
FUEL CONSUMPTION (Utilities only)								
Total (Tcals)	--	--	--	--	--	--	--	
RESERVOIR STORAGE CAPACITY (million kwh)	--	--	--	--	--	--	--	

SUPPLEMENTARY DATA FOR 1964

Transmission lines, 100 kv+ (km): --
Households served (thousands): 5.5
Revenues per kwh (U.S. cents) — Total: —
　Residential: 2.3　　Railways: —
　Industry: 1.7　　Lighting: 4.6
Population (thousands): 3600

Sources of data:

UN. *Stat. yrbk.*
Central Electricity Corporation, Ltd. *Annual report and accounts.*
Central Statistical Office. *Monthly digest of statistics.*
Ministry of Finance. *Economic report.*

Most characteristics of plants and systems:

　Most of Zambia's electricity is imported from the Congo (Kinshasa) and Southern Rhodesia. It is distributed principally through the Rhodesia-Congo Border Power Corporation, Ltd., privately owned. Large quantities of power are generated also by mining establishments in Zambia, and small quantities by the Victoria Falls Electricity Board, a government agency.

Appendix

Table 1 ELECTRICITY DISTRIBUTION, 1964

by country and by sector
total and per capita

Total consumption - million kwh
Per capita consumption - kwh

	Population (000)	Electricity Supply		Consumption	
		Gross	Net	Total	Per cap.
EUROPE					
Belgium	9378	20451	19129	18024	1921
France	48434	100987	96158	88361	1823
Germany, West	58290	165396	154031	142360	2441
Italy	51137	77740	75620	66894	1308
Luxembourg	328	2909	2821	1721	5246
Netherlands	12127	22993	21757	20335	1677
EEC	179694	390476	369516	337695	1879
Austria	7215	17655	17176	14841	2057
Denmark	4720	8719e	8254	7160	1517
Faeroe Islands	36	45	(45)	(40)	(1105)
Finland	4580	14332	13076	11964	2612
Iceland	189	681	(681)	573	3032
Ireland	2864	3368	3082	2683	937
Norway	3694	42637	42637	38539	10433
Sweden	7661	45042	44277	39383	5141
Switzerland	5892	21700	21700	19090	3240
United Kingdom	54213	182637	172207	157015	2895
Other [1]	161	--	--	--	--
Other North Europe	91225	336816	323135	291288	3193
Gibraltar	24	39	(39)	(35)	(1458)
Greece	8510	3765	(3765)	3267	384
Malta	324	135	126	112	345
Portugal	9106	4749	4730	4073	447
Spain	31506	27963	26881	22479	713
Yugoslavia	19279	14531	13893	11998	622
Other South Europe	68749	51182	49434	41964	610
West Europe	339668	778474	742085	670947	1975
Albania	1814	288	(268)	(228)	(126)
Bulgaria	8144	8677	7710	6980	856
Czechoslovakia	14058	32685	30314	27654	1967
Germany, East	16991	51179	47765	44385	2612
Hungary	10120	11661	10616	9639	952
Poland	31161	40053	36196	32449	1041
Romania	18927	13855	(13855)	11199	591
East Europe	101215	158398	146724	132534	1309
USSR	227687	457602	(457602)	426400	1872
East Europe/USSR	328902	616000	604326	558934	1699

[1] Channel Islands, Isle of Man

Transport		Domestic Sector		Industry		Lost Used Not acctd.
Total	Per cap.	Total	Per cap.	Total	Per cap.	
700	74	4305	459	13019	1388	1105
4616	95	23906	493	59839	1235	7797
5272	90	41951	719	95137	1632	11671
3357	66	19157	375	44380	867	8726
32	97	176	536	1513	4613	1100
734	61	8982	741	10619	875	1422
14711	82	98477	548	224507	1249	31821
1122	156	5227	724	8492	1177	2335
103	22	5022	1064	2035	431	1094
-	-	(36)	(1000)	(4)	(105)	(5)
32	7	2694	588	9238	2017	1112
-	-	326	1725	247	1307	108
-	-	1836	641	847	296	399
433	117	13054	3534	25052	6782	4098
1759	230	12443	1624	25181	3287	4894
1649	280	9273	1574	8168	1386	2610
2372	44	80873	1491	73770	1360	15192
--	--	--	--	--	--	--
7470	82	130784	1434	153034	1677	31847
-	-	(35)	(1458)	-	-	(4)
42	5	1558	183	1667	196	498
-	-	60	185	52	160	14
176	19	1144	126	2753	302	657
950	30	5301	168	16228	515	4402
198	10	3819	198	7981	414	1895
1366	20	11917	173	28681	417	7470
23547	69	241178	710	406222	1196	71138
-	-	(60)	(33)	(168)	(93)	(40)
242	30	1950	239	4788	587	730
1567	111	4820	343	21267	1513	2660
976	57	10008	589	33401	1966	3380
415	41	2332e	230	6892	681	977
1315	42	5697	183	25437	816	3747
278	14	2234	118	8687	459	2656
4793	47	27101	268	100640	994	14190
32900	145	75700	332	317800	1395	31202
37693	115	102801	312	418440	1272	45392

TABLE 1 (continued)

Total consumption - million kwh
Per capita consumption - kwh

	Population	Electricity Supply		Consumption	
	(000)	Gross	Net	Total	Per cap.
AFRICA					
Algeria	11645	1342	1318	1178	101
Libya	1559	157	(157)	(135)	(87)
Morocco	12959	1356	1326	1129	87
Tunisia	4361	487e	447	392	90
U. A. R. (Egypt)	28900	5106	(5106)	(4536)	(157)
North Africa	59424	8448	8354	7370	124
Angola	5084	260	(260)	232	46
Cameroon	5108	1070	(1070)	1048	205
Central African Republic	1338	20	(20)	(17)	(13)
Chad	3260	15	(15)	13	4
Congo (Brazzaville)	826	43	38	36	44
Congo (Kinshasa)	15300	2237	(2237)	1894	124
Dahomey	2300	20e	(20)	18	8
Gabon	459	36	34	21	46
Gambia	323	7	(7)	(6)	(18)
Ghana	7537	485	(485)	(435)	(58)
Guinea	3420	168	(168)	159e	46e
Ivory Coast	3750	183	(183)	158	42
Liberia	1041	(212)	(212)	(192)	(184)
Mali	4485	25	(25)	19	4
Niger	3237	15	(15)	13	4
Nigeria	56400	1024	(1024)	895	16
Portuguese Guinea	525	(4)	(4)	3	6
Rwanda	3018	12	12	(11)	(4)
St. Thomas & Prince	58	(6)	(6)	5	95
Senegal	3400	(225)	(225)	197	58
Sierra Leone	2332	84	(84)	(74)	(32)
Togo	1602	27	(27)	24e	15e
Upper Volta	4763	19	(19)	16	3
Other[1]	4769	--	--	--	--
West Africa	134335	6197	6190	5486	41

[1]Burundi, Cape Verde Islands, Equatorial Guinea,
Ifni, Mauritania, St. Helena, Spanish Sahara.

Transport		Domestic Sector		Industry		Lost Used Not acctd.
Total	Per cap.	Total	Per cap.	Total	Per cap.	
36	3	405	35	737	63	140
-	-	(120)	(77)	(15)	(10)	(22)
59	5	405	31	665	51	197
7	2	117	27	268	61	55
(120)	(4)	(1200)	(42)	(3216)	(111)	(570)
222	4	2247	38	4901	82	984
-	-	(80)	(16)	(152)	(30)	(28)
-	-	55e	11e	993e	194e	22e
-	-	(10)	(8)	(7)	(5)	(3)
-	-	8	2	5	2	2
-	-	22e	27e	14e	17e	2e
46	3	104	7	1744	114	(343)
-	-	13	6	5	2	(2)
-	-	16	35	5	11	13
-	-	(4)	(12)	(2)	(6)	(1)
-	-	(175)	(23)	(260)	(35)	(50)
-	-	29e	8e	130e	38e	(9)
-	-	83	22	75	20	25
-	-	(50)	(48)	(142)	(136)	(20)
-	-	12	3	7	1	6
-	-	(8)	(2)	(5)	(2)	(2)
-	-	266	5	629	11	129
-	-	2	4	1	2	1
-	-	2	1	9e	3e	1
-	-	3	55	2	40	1
-	-	66	19	131	39	28
-	-	(44)	(19)	(30)	(13)	(10)
-	-	(7)	(4)	17	11	3
-	-	(9)	(2)	7	1	3
-	-	--	--	--	--	--
46	-	1068	8	4372	33	704

TABLE 1 (continued)

Total consumption - million kwh
Per capita consumption - kwh

	Population	Electricity Supply		Consumption	
	(000)	Gross	Net	Total	Per cap.
Ethiopia	22200	208	(208)	(124)	(6)
French Somaliland	81	(20)	(20)	16	198
Kenya	9104	(503)	(503)	426	47
Malagasy	6180	139	(139)	116	19
Malawi	3845	(43)	43	39	10
Mauritius	722	93	(93)	75	104
Mozambique	6872	266e	(266)	242	35
Reunion	384	32	(32)	(27)	(70)
Rhodesia	4140	(2050)	2050	1868	451
Somalia	2420	11	(11)	9	4
South Africa	17457	(32000)	(30000)	(27500)	(1575)
South West Africa	564	220	(220)	(215)	(382)
Sudan	13180	167	(167)	132	10
Tanzania (excl. Zanzibar)	9990	186	(186)	162	16
Uganda	7367	343	(343)	293	40
Zambia	3600	2746	2727	2518	699
Other[1]	2258	--	--	--	--
East and South Africa	110364	39027	37008	33762	306
Africa	304123	53672	51552	46618	153

[1] Botswana, Comoro Islands, Lesotho, Mauritius
dependencies, Seychelles, Swaziland, Zanzibar.

| Transport | | Domestic Sector | | Industry | | Lost Used |
Total	Per cap.	Total	Per cap.	Total	Per cap.	Not acctd.
-	-	(43)	(2)	(81)	(4)	(84)
-	-	11	136	5	62	4
-	-	(250)	(28)	(176)	(19)	77
--	--	59	10	57	9	23
-	-	18	5	21	5	4
-	-	49	68	26	36	18
-	-	68	10	174	25	(24)
-	-	(15)	(39)	(12)	(31)	(5)
-	-	844	204	1024	247	182
-	-	7	3	2	1	2
(1860)	(107)	5140	294	20500	1174	(2500)
-	-	(95)	(169)	(120)	(213)	(5)
-	-	(100)	(8)	(32)	(2)	35
-	-	52e	5	110e	11e	24
-	-	73	10	220	30	50
-	-	254	70	2264	629	209
--	--	--	--	--	--	--
1860	17	7078	64	24824	225	3246
2128	7	10393	34	34097	112	4934

TABLE 1 (continued)

Total consumption - million kwh
Per capita consumption - kwh

	Population	Electricity Supply		Consumption	
	(000)	Gross	Net	Total	Per cap.
ASIA					
Aden	231	205	(205)	(189)	(818)
Bahrain	177	298	(298)	(280)	(1582)
Cyprus	587	306	294	262	446
Iran	23900	2250	(2250)	--	--
Iraq	7910	(1300)	(1300)	1166	147
Israel	2477	3625	(3625)	3098	1251
Jordan	1898	136	(136)	120	63
Kuwait	426	647	(647)	--	--
Lebanon	2345	692	(692)	--	--
Saudi Arabia	6630	273	(273)	218	33
Syria	5200	574	(574)	502	96
Turkey	30635	4435	4220	3800	124
Other[1]	6604	--	--	--	--
Middle East	89020	14741	14514	9635	108
China (mainland)	690000	--	--	--	--
Korea, North	11800	--	--	--	--
Mongolia	1050	--	--	--	--
Vietnam, North	18400	--	--	--	--
Asian Peoples Republics	721250	(68165)	(68165)	(61000)	(84)
Afghanistan	15380	204	(204)	(174)	(11)
Brunei	97	70	(70)	68	700
Burma	24229	570	550	(470)	(19)
Cambodia	6022	(95)	(92)	(59)	(10)
Ceylon	10971	475	467	412	37
China (Taiwan)	12070	6288	6072	5217	432
Hong Kong	3594	2385	2254	2075	577
India	471624	33129	31827	27700	59
Indonesia	102200	(1800)	(1800)	(1175)	(11)
Japan	96906	179592	172103	158014	1631
Korea, South	27631	2966	2818	2309	84
Laos	2570	22	(22)	(19)	(8)
Macao	282	26	(26)	26	92
Malaya	7814	1851	1776	1634	209
Nepal	9920	15	14	(10)	(1)
Pakistan	100753	3220	(3100)	(2500)	(25)
Philippines	31270	4678	(4678)	(4078)	(130)
Ryukyu Islands	923	593	(593)	(220)	(238)
Sabah	507	41	(41)	36	71
Sarawak	818	58	57	51	62
Singapore	1820	914	872	831	457
Thailand	29700	1107	1051	883	30
Vietnam, South	15715	574	551	504	32
Other[2]	2362	--	--	--	--
East and South Asia	975178	240673	231038	208465	214
Asia	1785448	323579	313717	279100	156

[1] Muscat and Oman, Protectorate of South Arabia, Qatar, Trucial Oman, Yemen.
[2] Bhutan, Bonin Islands, Maldive Islands, Portuguese Timor, Sikkim, West Irian.

Transport		Domestic Sector		Industry		Lost Used Not acctd.
Total	Per cap.	Total	Per cap.	Total	Per cap.	
-	-	(90)	(390)	(99)	(428)	(16)
-	-	(116)	(655)	(164)	(927)	(18)
-	-	188	320	74	126	32
-	-	- -	- -	- -	- -	(2250)
-	-	439	55	727	92	(134)
-	-	1890	763	1208	488	527
-	-	(86)	(45)	34	18	16
-	-	- -	- -	- -	- -	(647)
-	-	- -	- -	- -	- -	(692)
-	-	(218)	(33)	-	-	(55)
2	-	220e	42e	280	54	72
60	2	920	30	(2828)	(92)	420
- -	- -	- -	- -	- -	- -	- -
62	1	4167	47	5406	60	4879
- -	- -	- -	- -	- -	- -	- -
- -	- -	- -	- -	- -	- -	- -
- -	- -	- -	- -	- -	- -	- -
- -	- -	- -	- -	- -	- -	- -
- -	- -	(9000)	(12)	(52000)	(72)	(7165)
-	-	(124)	(8)	(50)	(3)	(30)
-	-	13	134	55	566	2
-	-	(170)	(7)	(300)	(12)	(80)
-	-	(55)	(9)	(4)	(1)	(33)
3	-	201	18	208	19	55
-	-	1169	97	4048	335	855
(18)	(5)	1311	365	746	207	179
1440	3	5802	12	20458e	44e	4127
-	-	(850)	(8)	(325)	(3)	(625)
7139	74	55130	569	95745	988	14089
- -	- -	511	19	1798	65	509
-	-	(12)	(5)	(7)	(3)	3
-	-	19	67	7	25	-
-	-	802	103	832	106	142
-	-	(9)	(1)	1	-	(4)
-	-	(1000)	(10)	(1500)	(15)	(600)
-	-	(1600)	(51)	(2478)	(79)	(600)
-	-	(220)	(238)	- -	- -	(373)
-	-	20	39	16	32	5
-	-	28	34	23	28	6
-	-	454	250	377	207	41
-	-	478	16	405	14	168
-	-	400	25	104	7	47
- -	- -	- -	- -	- -	- -	- -
8600	9	70378	72	129487	133	22573
8662	5	83545	47	186893	104	34617

TABLE 1 (continued)

Total consumption - million kwh
Per capita consumption - kwh

	Population	Electricity Supply		Consumption	
	(000)	Gross	Net	Total	Per cap.
OCEANIA					
American Samoa	23	(15)	(15)	(13)	(565)
Australia	11136	32519	(32519)	26880	2414
Fiji Islands	449	93	(93)	(84)	(187)
French Polynesia	82	16	(16)	(13)	(158)
Guam	72	335	(335)	--	--
Nauru	5	11	11	--	--
New Caledonia	89	498	(498)	494	5547
New Guinea	1539	40	(40)	(36)	(23)
New Zealand	2594	9718	(9718)	8189	3157
Papua	562	34	(34)	(30)	(53)
Western Samoa	123	(6)	(6)	6	49
Other[1]	445	--.	--	--	--
Oceania	17119	43285	43285	35745	2088

[1]British Solomon Islands, Gilbert and Ellice Islands, New Hebrides,
Nieu, Norfolk Island, Pacific Islands, Tonga, and others.

Transport		Domestic Sector		Industry		Lost Used Not acctd.
Total	Per cap.	Total	Per cap.	Total	Per cap.	
-	-	(11)	(478)	(2)	(87)	(2)
731	66	13279	1192	12870	1156	5639
-	-	(34)	(76)	(50)	(111)	(9)
-	-	8	97	5	61	(3)
-	-	--	--	--	--	335
-	-	--	--	--	--	11
-	-	31	348	463	5199	4
-	-	(36)	(23)	--	--	(4)
45	17	5821	2244	2323	896	1529
-	-	30	53	--	--	4
-	-	6	49	-	-	-
--	--	--	--	--	--	--
776	45	19256	1125	15713	918	7540

TABLE 1 (continued)

Total consumption - million kwh
Per capita consumption - kwh

	Population	Electricity Supply		Consumption	
	(000)	Gross	Net	Total	Per cap.
AMERICAS					
Canada	19271	(133949)	133949	121220	6290
Greenland	37	38	38	(34)	(919)
St. Pierre-Miquelon	5	4	(4)	(4)	(800)
United States	192120	(1085696)	1085696	999125	5200
North America	211433	(1219687)	1219687	1120383	5299
Bahama Islands	134	123	(123)	(111)	(826)
Barbados	241	60	(60)	49	203
Bermuda	48	133	(133)	(116)	(2417)
British Honduras	103	11	(11)	10	97
Colombia	17485	5916	(5916)	(4690)	(268)
Costa Rica	1387	594	(594)	521e	376e
Cuba	7434	3250	(3250)	(2770)	(373)
Dominican Republic	3498	560e	(560)	476	136
El Salvador	2824	377	(377)	332	117
Guadeloupe	308	40	(40)	33	107
Guatemala	4305	470	(470)	312	72
Haiti	4310	110	(110)	(102)	(24)
Honduras	2209	131	(131)	109	50
Jamaica	1742	715	(715)	664	381
Martinique	314	37	(37)	31	99
Mexico	41253	15869	(15869)	13743	333
Netherlands Antilles	205	1025	(1025)	(990)	(4829)
Nicaragua	1597	281	268	230	144
Panama Canal Zone	54	426	(426)	401	7426
Panama Republic	1205	392	(392)	347	288
Puerto Rico	2578	3638	(3638)	3028	1174
Trinidad and Tobago	952	820	(820)	741	778
Venezuela	8427	7597	(7597)	6721	797
Virgin Islands (U.S.)	41	76	(76)	62	1512
Other[1]	490	--	--	--	--
Caribbean America	103144	42651	(42638)	36589	355
Argentina	22019	13752	(13752)	(11652)	(529)
Bolivia	3647	534	(534)	440e	121e
Brazil	78427	29094	27950	23710	302
Chile	8391	5932	5882	5295	631
Ecuador	4979	551	(551)	(496)	(99)
French Guiana	36	9	(9)	7	195
Guyana	629	171	(171)	159	253
Paraguay	1968	129	(129)	102	52
Peru	11298	3689	(3689)	3095	274
Surinam	324	128	(128)	(121)	(374)
Uruguay	2682	1724	1690	1388	517
Other[2]	2	--	--	--	--
South America	134402	55713	(54485)	46465	345
Latin America	237546	98364	(97123)	83054	350

[1]Cayman Islands, Leeward Islands, Turks and Caicos Islands, Windward Islands.
[2]Falkland Islands.

Transport		Domestic Sector		Industry		Lost Used Not acctd.
Total	Per cap.	Total	Per cap.	Total	Per cap.	
-	-	40415	2097	80805	4193	12729
-	-	(22)	(595)	(12)	(324)	(4)
-	-	(2)	(400)	(2)	(400)	-
5030	26	485360	2526	508735	2648	86571
5030	24	525799	2487	589554	2788	99304
-	-	(111)	(826)	-	-	(12)
-	-	21	87	28	116	11
-	-	(116)	(2417)	-	-	(17)
-	-	(10)	(97)	-	-	(1)
-	-	(2400)	(137)	2290e	131e	(1226)
--	--	390	282	131	94	73
(200)	(27)	(1270)	(171)	(1300)	(175)	(480)
-	-	235	67	241e	69e	(84)
-	-	187	66	145e	51e	45
-	-	21	68	12	39	7
-	-	160	37	152	35	(158)
-	-	(60)	(14)	(42)	(10)	(8)
--	--	59	27	50	23	22
-	-	300	172	364e	209e	51
-	-	19	61	12	38	6
-	-	5358	130	8385	203	2126
-	-	(130)	(634)	(860)	(4195)	(35)
-	-	98	61	132	83	38
112	2074	85	1574	204	3778	25
-	-	229	190	118	98	45
-	-	2148	833	880	341	610
-	-	142	149	599	629	79
-	-	(2272)	(269)	4449	528	(876)
-	-	43	1049	19	463	14
--	--	--	--	--	--	--
312	3	15864	154	20413	198	6049
(400)	(18)	(5300)	(241)	(5952)	(270)	(2100)
-	-	163e	45	277	76	94
783	10	10969	140	11958	152	4240
124	15	1326	158	3845	458	587
-	-	(316)	(63)	(180)	(36)	(55)
-	-	6	167	(1)	(28)	2
-	-	29	46	130	207	12
1	-	(42)	(22)	59	30	(27)
16	1	647	57	2432	216	594
-	-	(54)	(167)	(67)	(207)	(7)
29	11	805	300	554e	206e	302
--	--	--	--	--	--	--
1353	10	19657	146	25455	189	8020
1665	7	35521	150	45868	193	14069

Table 2 INDUSTRIAL USES OF ELECTRICITY, 1964
in 65 countries

(Million kwh)

	All Industry*	Mining	Mfg.	Food Beverage Tobacco
Belgium	13019	1737	11282	662
France	59839	4283	55556	2126
Germany, West	95137	10448	84689	3266
Italy	44380	863	43517	2366
Luxembourg	1513	9	1504	17
Netherlands	10619	691	9928	961
Austria	8492	562	7930	372
Denmark	2035	--	2035	265
Finland	8918	214	8704	296
Iceland	247	--	247	102
Ireland (1963)	884	85	799	240
Norway (1963)	21283	326	20957	531
Sweden	25181	1018	24163	762
Switzerland	8168	37	8131	388
United Kingdom	73799	6887	66912	4096
Bulgaria (1963)	3702	--	3702	292
Czechoslovakia	21267	3100	18167	757
Germany, East	33401	6026	27375	961
Hungary	6826	1051	5775	415
Poland	25437	4507	20930	945
Romania (1963)	7762	878	6884	316
Canada (1961)	63276	4826	58450	1640
United States	508735	(30000)	478735	25858
Japan	92252	4289	87963	1468
South Africa (incomplete)	14426	9927	4499	624
Developed countries	1150598	91764	1058834	49726
Greece (incomplete)	1011	59	952	140
Malta (1963)	12	--	12	7
Portugal	2753	54	2699	152
Spain	16228	1233	14995	924
Yugoslavia	7981	639	7342	423

* Industry totals do not agree in all cases with totals shown elsewhere, "industry," or the use of conflicting sources.

Textiles Clothing Leather	Wood Paper & Products	Chemicals Fuels Rubber	Crude Metals	Non-met. Minerals	Machines & Equipment	Other & Not Acctd.
947	630	3025	3691	1106	1033	188
3082	4222	15603	17766	3427	5512	3818
3778	5588	30949	20541	6752	12409	1406
3744	3011	13248	10171	4756	5228	993
7	2	44	1388	29	17	--
695	1148	4333	1068	460	1169	94
409	1219	1304	3093	707	632	194
125	331	366	468	318	119	43
196	6018	938	501	277	413	65
--	--	133	--	12	--	--
107	123	96	39	121	59	14
262	3286	6403	9177	440	721	137
579	8263	3137	5227	942	2647	2606
677	805	1882	2036	801	1135	407
4924	4787	15049	14101	3672	14510	5773
295	203	1031	1010	401	421	49
1043	1174	3806	4878	1241	3031	2237
1062	1292	15248	3181	1012	2796	1823
547	249	1057	2126	419	872	90
1323	1247	5727	5884	1536	2650	1618
440	698	2604	1280	558	988	--
1139	21845	7721	21104	2191	2430	380
20828	50042	185530	111376	19303	58375	7423
3366	9090	28937	32266	6039	5987	810
--	212	868	1991	447	357	--
49575	125485	349039	274363	56967	123511	30168
151	46	133	132	273	72	5
1	--	1	--	--	2	1
439	222	846	277	321	147	295
897	982	4373	3193	1534	1525	1567
718	869	1292	2499	529	770	242

because of the absence of certain details, differences in the definition of

TABLE 2 (continued)

(Million kwh)

	All Industry*	Mining	Mfg.	Food Beverage Clothing
Cyprus (1962)	89	54	35	12
Iraq	256	1	255	41
Israel	1208	47	1161	186
Kuwait (incomplete)	22	--	22	6
Turkey	2710	291	2419	222
Algeria	506	240	266	79
Cameroon	993	--	993	--
Congo (Kinshasa)	1744	1590	154	--
Ghana	210	210	--	--
Guinea	130	130	--	--
Morocco	665	201	464	--
Mozambique (1963)	156	3	153	34
Rhodesia	1024	413	611	--
Southwest Africa	60	40	20	--
Zambia (1963)	2112	2031	81	--
Afghanistan (1963)	45	-	45	2
Brunei	54	54	--	--
Ceylon	140	--	140	--
China (Taiwan)	4393	260	4133	386
India (incomplete)	13414	576	12838	189
Indonesia (1961)	263	--	263	21
Korea, South	1006	129	877	34
Malaya	996	765	231	1
Philippines (1963) (inc.)	1092	278	814	111
Singapore (1963)	117	1	116	30
Chile	3845	2152	1693	43
Colombia (1963)	1753	--	1753	347
Dominican Republic (1962)	179	2	177	125
Ecuador (1963)	120	7	113	45
El Salvador	142	1	141	34
Honduras (1963)	29	-	29	13
Mexico (1960)	6225	1287	4938	907
Panama (1961)	39	-	39	26
Paraguay (1963)	61	--	61	24
Peru	2129	1160	969	92
Less developed countries	75912	13908	62004	4656
TOTAL (65 countries)	1226510	105672	1120838	54382

* Industry totals do not agree in all cases with totals shown elsewhere, "industry," or the use of conflicting sources.

Textiles Clothing Leather	Wood Paper & Products	Chemicals Fuels Rubber	Crude Metals	Non-met. Minerals	Machines & Equipment	Other & Not Acctd.
2	1	1	--	12	1	6
41	1	43	--	118	10	1
151	78	364	44	180	77	81
--	2	--	--	3	10	1
414	193	255	233	320	56	726
6	31	33	12	91	12	2
--	--	--	970	--	--	23
--	--	--	--	--	--	154
--	--	--	--	--	--	--
--	--	--	--	--	--	--
--	--	--	--	68	--	396
11	2	16	1	21	3	65
--	--	--	--	--	--	611
--	--	--	--	--	--	20
--	--	--	--	--	--	81
35	--	--	--	8	--	--
--	--	--	--	--	--	--
--	10	6	--	14	--	110
275	300	1394	757	357	91	573
3852	603	2718	4392	1084	--	--
52	10	61	--	67	19	33
200	9	374	65	161	30	4
--	1	--	--	14	--	215
218	80	54	--	136	89	126
1	5	36	2	21	12	9
--	388	114	210	181	--	757
412	126	327	99	306	99	37
7	4	8	2	28	1	2
24	3	15	--	22	1	3
28	1	4	3	10	4	57
2	2	4	--	7	1	--
643	585	851	1085	522	250	95
1	2	3	--	3	1	3
14	--	11	--	--	--	12
108	10	117	242	25	26	349
8703	4566	13454	14218	6436	3309	6662
58278	130051	362493	288581	63403	126820	36830

because of the absence of certain details, differences in the definition of

Table 3 SUPPLIES OF ELECTRICITY, 1964

(Million kwh)

	Total Production Gross	Net	Hydro	Conventional Thermal
Belgium	20800	19478	115	20634
France	98759	93930	35218	62886
Germany, West	164436	153071	12102	152230
Italy	76738	74618	39328	32482
Luxembourg	2216	2128	805	1411
Netherlands	22975	21739	-	22975
EEC	385924	364964	87568	292618
Austria	20363	19884	13179	7184
Denmark	7900e	7435	25e	7875
Faeroe Islands	45	45	41	4
Finland	13636	12380	8501	5135
Iceland	681	(681)	656	25
Ireland	3368	3082	784	2584
Norway	44028	(44028)	43864	164
Sweden	45247	44482	43022	2225
Switzerland	22864	22864	22663	201
United Kingdom	182848	172418	4022	170480
Other North Europe	340980	327299	136757	195877
Gibraltar	39	39	-	39
Greece	3780	(3780)	749	3031
Malta	135	126	-	135
Portugal	4761	4742	4220	541
Spain	29526	28444	20646	8880
Yugoslavia	14189	13551	7575	6614
Other South Europe	52430	50682	33190	19240
West Europe	779334	742945	257515	507735
Albania	288	(268)	203	85
Bulgaria	8700	7733	1471	7229
Czechoslovakia	31983	29612	2727	29256
Germany, East	51032	47618	536	50496
Hungary	10580	9535	74	10506
Poland	40611	36754	726	39885
Romania	13851	(13851)	585	13266
East Europe	157045	145371	6322	150723
USSR	458902	--	77361	379541
East Europe/USSR	615947	--	83683	530264

Nuclear	Geothermal	Import	Export	Net Import	Gross Supply
51	-	360	709	-349	20451
655	-	3795	1567	2228	100987
104	-	6272	5312	960	165396
2401	2527	1756	754	1002	77740
-	-	1489	796	693	2909
-	-	50	32	18	22993
3211	2527	13722	9170	4552	390476
-	-	993	3701	-2708	17655
-	-	858	39	819	8719e
-	-	-	-	-	45
-	-	702	6	696	14332
-	-	-	-	-	681
-	-	-	-	-	3368
-	-	116	1507	-1391	42637
-	-	1433	1638	-205	45042
-	-	3518	4682	-1164	21700
8346	-	83	294	-211	182637
8346	-	7703	11867	-4164	336816
-	-	-	-	-	39
-	-	8	23	-15	3765
-	-	-	-	-	135
-	-	43	55	-12	4749
-	-	172	1735	-1563	27963
-	-	429	87	342	14531
-	-	652	1900	-1248	51182
11557	2527	22077	22937	-860	778474
-	-	-	-	-	288
-	-	3	26	-23	8677
-	-	1618	916	702	32685
-	-	835e	688	147	51179
-	-	1159	78	1081	11661
-	-	739	1297	-558	40053
-	-	113	109	4	13855
-	-	4467	3114	1353	158398
(2000)	-	79e	1379	-1300	457602
(2000)	-	4546	4493	53	616000

TABLE 3 (continued)

(Million kwh)

| | Total Production | | Hydro | Conventional Thermal |
	Gross	Net		
Algeria	1342	1318	284	1058
Libya	157	(157)	-	157
Morocco	1356e	1326	1171	185
Tunisia	487e	447	38	449
U.A.R. (Egypt)	5106	(5106)	1670	3436
North Africa	8448	8354	3163	5285
Angola	260	(260)	225	35
Cameroon	1070	1070	1039	31
Central African Republic	20	(20)	20	-
Chad	15	(15)	-	15
Congo (Brazzaville)	43	38	28	15
Congo (Kinshasa)	2435	(2435)	2265e	170
Dahomey	20e	(20)	-	20e
Gabon	36	34	-	36
Gambia	7	(7)	-	7
Ghana	485	(485)	-	485
Guinea	168	(168)	14	154
Ivory Coast	183	(183)	96	87
Liberia	212	(212)	17	195
Mali	25	(25)	1	24
Niger	15	15	-	15
Nigeria	1024	(1024)	126	898
Portuguese Guinea	4	(4)	-	4
Rwanda	12	12	11	1
St. Thomas & Prince	6	(6)	-	6
Senegal	225	(225)	-	225
Sierra Leone	84	(84)	-	84
Togo	27	(27)	3	24
Upper Volta	19	(19)	-	19
West Africa	6395	6388	3845	2550

Nuclear	Geothermal	Import	Export	Net Import	Gross Supply
-	-	-	-	-	1342
-	-	-	-	-	157
-	-	-	-	-	1356
-	-	-	-	-	487e
-	-	-	-	-	5106
-	-	-	-	-	8448
-	-	-	-	-	260
-	-	-	-	-	1070
-	-	-	-	-	20
-	-	-	-	-	15
-	-	-	-	-	43
-	-	-	198	-198	2237
-	-	-	-	-	20e
-	-	-	-	-	36
-	-	-	-	-	7
-	-	-	-	-	485
-	-	-	-	-	168
-	-	-	-	-	183
-	-	-	-	-	(212)
-	-	-	-	-	25
-	-	-	-	-	15
-	-	-	-	-	1024
-	-	-	-	-	(4)
-	-	-	-	-	12
-	-	-	-	-	(6)
-	-	-	-	-	(225)
-	-	-	-	-	84
-	-	-	-	-	27
-	-	-	-	-	19
-	-	-	198	-198	6197

TABLE 3 (continued)

(Million kwh)

| | Total Production | | | Conventional |
	Gross	Net	Hydro	Thermal
Ethiopia	208	(208)	120	88
French Somaliland	(20)	(20)	-	(20)
Kenya	(323)	(323)	(205)	(118)
Malagasy	139	(139)	81	58
Malawi	(43)	43	(4)	(39)
Mauritius	93	(93)	56	37
Mozambique	368e	(368)	(160)	(208)
Reunion	(32)	(32)	(22)	10
Rhodesia	(3801)	3801	3571	(230)
Somalia	11	(11)	-	11
South Africa	(32000)	(30000)	(40)	31960
Sudan	(167)	(167)	-	167
Tanzania	(192)	(192)	131	61
Uganda	(521)	(521)	(521)	-
Zambia	713	694	305	408
South West Africa	220	220	-	220
East & South Africa	38851	36832	5216	33635
Africa	53694	51574	12224	41470
Aden	205	(205)	-	205
Bahrain	298	(298)	-	298
Cyprus	306	294	-	306
Iran	2250	(2250)	270	1980
Iraq	(1300)	(1300)	-	(1300)
Israel	3625	(3625)	-	3625
Jordan	136	(136)	-	136
Kuwait	647	(647)	-	647
Lebanon	692	(692)	375	317
Saudi Arabia	273	(273)	-	273
Syria	574	(574)	-	574
Turkey	4435	4220	1652	2783
Middle East	14741	14514	2297	12444
China (mainland)	55000	--	(11000)	(44000)
Korea, North	12393	(12393)	(12393)	--
Mongolia	224	(224)	-	(224)
Vietnam, North	548	(548)	-	(548)
Asian Peoples Republics	68165	--	23393	(44772)

Nuclear	Geothermal	Import	Export	Net Import	Gross Supply
-	-	-	-	-	208
-	-	-	-	-	(20)
-	-	180	-	180	(503)
-	-	-	-	-	139
-	-	-	-	-	(43)
-	-	-	-	-	93
-	-	-	102	-102	266e
-	-	-	-	-	32
-	-	102	1853	-1751	(2050)
-	-	-	-	-	11
-	-	-	-	-	(32000)
-	-	-	-	-	167
-	-	-	6	-6	186
-	-	-	178	-178	343
-	-	2033	-	2033	2746
-	-	-	-	-	220
-	-	2315	2139	176	39027
-	-	2315	2337	-22	53672
-	-	-	-	-	205
-	-	-	-	-	298
-	-	-	-	-	306
-	-	-	-	-	2250
-	-	-	-	-	(1300)
-	-	-	-	-	3625
-	-	-	-	-	136
-	-	-	-	-	647
-	-	-	-	-	692
-	-	-	-	-	273
-	-	-	-	-	574
-	-	-	-	-	4435
-	-	-	-	-	14741
-	-	-	-	-	55000
-	-	-	-	-	(12393)
-	-	-	-	-	(224)
-	-	-	-	-	(548)
-	-	-	-	-	(68165)

TABLE 3 (continued)

(Million kwh)

	Total Production		Hydro	Conventional Thermal
	Gross	Net		
Afghanistan	204	(204)	(190)	(14)
Brunei	70	(70)	-	70
Burma	570	550	280	290
Cambodia	(95)	(92)	-	(95)
Ceylon	475	467e	338	137
China (Taiwan)	6288	6072	2359	3929
Hong Kong	2385	2254	-	2385
India	33129	31827	14807	18322
Indonesia	(1800)	(1800)	(850)	(950)
Japan	179592	172103	68957	110633
Korea, South	2966	2818	750	2216
Laos	22	(22)	-	22
Macao	26	(26)	-	26
Malaya	1851	1776	544	1307
Nepal	15	14	8	7
Pakistan	3220	(3100)	1635	(1585)
Philippines	4678	(4678)	1554	3124
Ryukyu Islands	593	(593)	-	593
Sabah	41	(41)	-	41
Sarawak	58	57	-	58
Singapore	914	872	-	914
Thailand	1107	1051	-	1107
Vietnam, South	574	551	56	518
Far East	240673	231038	92328	148343
Asia	323579	--	118018	205559
American Samoa	(15)	(15)	-	15
Australia	32519	(32519)	6898	25621
Fiji Islands	93	(93)	-	93
French Polynesia	16	(16)	-	16
Guam	335	(335)	-	335
Nauru	11	11	-	11
New Caledonia	498	(498)	315	183
New Guinea	40	(40)	19	21
New Zealand	9718	(9718)	7753	771
Papua	34	(34)	28	6
Western Samoa	6	(6)	5	1
Oceania	43285	43285	15018	27073

322

Nuclear	Geothermal	Import	Export	Net Import	Gross Supply
-	-	-	-	-	204
-	-	-	-	-	70
-	-	-	-	-	570
-	-	-	-	-	(95)
-	-	-	-	-	475
-	-	-	-	-	6288
-	-	-	-	-	2385
-	-	-	-	-	33129
-	-	-	-	-	(1800)
2	-	-	-	-	179592
-	-	-	-	-	2966
-	-	-	-	-	22
-	-	-	-	-	26
-	-	-	-	-	1851
-	-	-	-	-	15
-	-	-	-	-	3220
-	-	-	-	-	4678
-	-	-	-	-	593
-	-	-	-	-	41
-	-	-	-	-	58
-	-	-	-	-	914
-	-	-	-	-	1107
-	-	-	-	-	574
2	-	-	-	-	240673
2	-	-	-	-	323579
-	-	-	-	-	15
-	-	-	-	-	32519
-	-	-	-	-	93
-	-	-	-	-	16
-	-	-	-	-	335
-	-	-	-	-	11
-	-	-	-	-	498
-	-	-	-	-	40
-	1194	-	-	-	9718
-	-	-	-	-	34
-	-	-	-	-	(6)
-	1194	-	-	-	43285

TABLE 3 (continued)

(Million kwh)

| | Total Production | | | Conventional | |
	Gross	Net	Hydro	Thermal	Nuclear
Canada	134987	134987	113344	21502	141
Greenland	38	(38)	-	38	-
St. Pierre-Miquelon	(4)	(4)	-	4	-
United States	1083741	1083741	180302	899892	3343
North America	1218770	1218770	293646	921436	3484
Bahama Islands	123	(123)	-	123	-
Barbados	60	(60)	-	60	-
Bermuda	133	(133)	-	133	-
British Honduras	11	(11)	-	11	-
Colombia	5916	(5916)	3721	2195	-
Costa Rica	594	594	495e	99	-
Cuba	3250	(3250)	100	3150	-
Dominican Republic	560e	(560)	50e	510e	-
El Salvador	377	(377)	336	41	-
Guadeloupe	40	(40)	1	39	-
Guatemala	470	(470)	120	350	-
Haiti	110	(110)	-	110	-
Honduras	131	(131)	74	57e	-
Jamaica	715	(715)	153	562	-
Martinique	37	(37)	-	37	-
Mexico	15748	(15748)	6866	8882	-
Netherlands Antilles	1025	(1025)	-	1025	-
Nicaragua	281	268	43	238	-
Panama Canal Zone	418	(418)	263	155	-
Panama Republic	400	(400)	31	369	-
Puerto Rico	3638	(3638)	152	3486	-
Trinidad	820	(820)	-	820	-
Venezuela	7597	(7597)	1223	6374	-
Virgin Islands	76	76	-	76	-
Caribbean America	42530	42517	13628	28902	-
Argentina	13752	(13752)	1236	12516	-
Bolivia	534	(534)	421	113	-
Brazil	29094	27950	22097	6997	-
Chile	5932	5882	3723	2209	-
Ecuador	551	(551)	248	303	-
French Guiana	9	(9)	-	9	-
Guyana	171	(171)	-	171	-
Paraguay	129	(129)	-	129	-
Peru	3689	3689	2448	1241	-
Surinam	128	(128)	-	128	-
Uruguay	1724	1690	1267	457	-
South America	55713	54485	31440	24273	-
Latin America	98243	97002	45068	53175	-

Geothermal	Import	Export	Net Import	Gross Supply
-	3121	4159	-1038	(133949)
-	-	-	-	38
-	-	-	-	4
204	6208	4253	1955	1085696
204	9329	8412	917	1219687
-	-	-	-	123
-	-	-	-	60
-	-	-	-	133
-	-	-	-	11
-	-	-	-	5916
-	-	-	-	594
-	-	-	-	3250
-	-	-	-	560e
-	-	-	-	377
-	-	-	-	40
-	-	-	-	470
-	-	-	-	110
-	-	-	-	131
-	-	-	-	715
-	-	-	-	37
-	121	-	121	15869
-	-	-	-	1025
-	-	-	-	281
-	8	-	8	426
-	-	8	-8	392
-	-	-	-	3638
-	-	-	-	820
-	-	-	-	7597
-	-	-	-	76
-	129	8	121	42651
-	-	-	-	13752
-	-	-	-	534
-	-	-	-	29094
-	-	-	-	5932
-	-	-	-	551
-	-	-	-	9
-	-	-	-	171
-	-	-	-	129
-	-	-	-	3689
-	-	-	-	128
-	-	-	-	1724
-	-	-	-	55713
-	129	8	121	98364

Table 4 MONTHLY VARIATIONS IN PRODUCTION OF HYDROELECTRICITY, 1964

Daily averages - million kwh

	Jan.	Feb.	March	April	May
France	85	73	116	133	133
Germany, West	20	24	30	37	37
Italy	116	101	98	115	122
Luxembourg	2.0	1.7	2.0	2.5	2.3
Austria	25	24	26	38	47
Finland	23	23	21	21	26
Iceland	2.0	1.9	1.9	1.8	1.6
Ireland	1.6	1.7	2.4	2.0	2.0
Norway	129	132	125	121	107
Sweden	120	124	115	109	102
Switzerland	61	56	56	54	71
United Kingdom	11	12	11	8	10
Portugal	9.5	10	13	14	11
Spain	71	66	69	73	61
Yugoslavia	22	17	21	25	22
Bulgaria	--	--	--	5.6	5.8
Czechoslovakia	6.0	6.2	6.9	8.4	5.8
Poland	1.3	1.7	1.7	3.3	2.4
Romania	0.9	0.9	1.0	1.4	1.4

June	July	Aug.	Sept.	Oct.	Nov.	Dec.	Max/Min
114	79	62	69	87	85	81	2.14
36	31	31	30	34	37	36	1.85
132	114	86	86	97	98	99	1.54
1.5	2.1	2.5	2.6	2.2	2.1	2.7	1.80
45	41	40	33	38	34	30	1.96
27	23	23	25	24	23	21	1.29
1.6	1.6	1.5	1.5	1.8	2.0	1.9	1.33
0.9	0.7	1.0	1.1	3.2	2.2	4.0	5.72
106	95	101	112	126	137	147	1.55
108	93	112	129	135	135	130	1.45
73	66	60	57	54	53	57	1.38
7	7	8	12	12	12	20	2.86
6.3	6.4	7.5	8.2	12	15	17	2.70
64	52	41	42	43	45	44	1.78
18	15	13	14	22	29	30	2.31
6.2	6.0	6.6	5.2	5.0	4.7	5.2	1.40
5.6	6.4	5.6	5.1	10.8	11.7	10.8	2.29
1.6	1.3	1.8	1.5	2.1	2.6	2.5	2.54
1.6	1.5	1.7	1.5	1.8	2.5	3.1	3.44

TABLE 4

Daily averages - million kwh

	Jan.	Feb.	March	April	May
Algeria	0.8	1.3	1.0	1.0	0.9
Tunisia	0.1	0.2	0.1	0.1	-
Morocco	3.5	3.3	3.0	3.2	3.1
Ivory Coast	0.1	0.1	0.1	0.5	0.5
Nigeria	0.3	0.3	0.3	0.3	0.3
Rhodesia	9.2	9.6	9.4	9.4	9.7
Tanzania	1.3	1.5	1.4	1.4	1.5
Lebanon	0.7	1.0	1.1	1.1	1.0
Turkey	5.8	5.0	4.7	4.5	4.5
Japan	139	147	131	236	192
Korea, South	1.2	1.4	1.4	1.2	1.3
Malaya	1.2	1.0	1.0	1.6	2.0
Philippines	3.4	3.5	3.1	3.1	3.1
Australia	16	16	17	18	19
New Zealand	18	19	22	22	24
Canada	312	313	313	310	310
United States	476	485	524	554	521
Costa Rica	0.7	0.7	0.5	0.4	0.6
Cuba	0.3	0.2	0.2	0.3	0.2
Honduras	0.1	0.2	0.2	0.2	0.2
Mexico	20	21	23	23	23
Venezuela	4.1	3.1	1.6	2.5	3.1
Chile	5.9	5.7	5.9	6.2	6.2
Uruguay	3.3	3.2	3.3	3.5	3.4

June	July	Aug.	Sept.	Oct.	Nov.	Dec.	Max/Min
1.0	0.8	0.8	0.3	1.0	0.7	0.5	4.33
0.1	0.1	0.1	0.2	0.1	0.1	0.1	2.00
3.1	2.7	2.7	2.9	2.9	3.2	3.3	1.30
0.5	0.4	0.4	0.4	0.5	0.6	0.6	6.00
0.3	0.3	0.3	0.3	0.4	0.4	0.4	1.33
10.0	10.4	9.8	9.9	9.6	9.8	9.6	1.13
1.4	1.6	1.5	1.4	1.4	1.4	1.3	1.23
0.8	0.4	0.4	0.4	0.5	0.6	0.8	2.75
4.1	3.9	3.4	4.3	4.4	4.7	4.7	1.71
167	228	172	189	201	161	144	1.80
0.6	2.9	4.9	3.3	1.9	1.3	1.8	8.16
1.3	1.3	1.4	1.9	1.7	2.3	2.5	2.50
3.7	3.7	4.4	4.0	5.2	4.6	4.1	1.68
21	24	27	28	28	25	21	1.75
26	28	27	25	29	29	29	1.61
308	299	292	297	316	322	322	1.10
473	467	456	442	461	479	531	1.25
0.8	0.9	1.0	1.0	1.0	1.0	0.8	2.50
0.4	0.4	0.4	0.4	0.3	0.2	0.2	2.00
0.2	0.2	0.2	0.2	0.2	0.2	0.2	2.00
24	25	25	25	25	25	25	1.25
3.4	3.6	3.8	3.4	3.7	4.1	3.8	2.56
7.3	7.4	6.4	6.2	6.0	5.7	5.5	1.35
3.6	3.6	3.5	3.5	3.8	3.8	3.0	1.27

Table 5 NET IMPORTS OF ELECTRICITY
1958-1964

(Million kwh)

	1958	1959
Belgium	62	-106
France	445	38
Germany, West	2151	2649
Italy	137	189
Luxembourg	7	21
Netherlands	191	75
EEC	2993	2866
Austria	-1364	-1933
Finland	5	124
Norway	-	-
Sweden	-541	-552
Switzerland	-1117	-1918
Denmark	786	-142
Ireland	4	1
United Kingdom	-1	-1
Other North Europe	-2228	-4421
Gibraltar	-	-
Greece	-	-
Portugal	5	1
Spain	-17	-201
Yugoslavia	-175	-100
Other South Europe	-187	-300
Albania	-	-
Bulgaria	16	26
Czechoslovakia	-224	-248
Germany, East	-297	-339
Hungary	333	360
Poland	247	357
Romania	-16	-26
East Europe	59	130
USSR	-	-
Algeria	-5	6
Tunisia	10	-
Congo (Kinshasa)	-308	-744
Kenya	114	151
Mozambique	-	-54
Rhodesia	-	54
Tanzania	-28	-26
Uganda	-90	-129
Zambia	662	738
Canada	-3841	-4081
United States	3317	3607
Mexico	389	462
Panama	-	-
Panama Canal Zone	-	-

1960	1961	1962	1963	1964
37	-236	-473	-520	-349
-98	93	-752	570	2228
4165	4324	3058	2466	960
-128	168	1269	1300	1002
9	-23	154	478	693
118	43	-20	47	18
4103	4369	3236	4341	4552
-1903	-1948	-2099	-1693	-2708
415	180	82	337	696
-162	-101	-334	-945	-1391
-766	-997	-797	48	-205
-1316	-3478	-1649	-1024	-1164
386	997	744	552	819
-	-	-	-	-
-1	1	87	-15	-211
-3347	-5346	-3966	-2740	-4164
-	-	-	-	-
8	-14	-1	-6	-15
1	11	27	-55	-12
-163	-255	-255	-839	-1563
-93	-53	-142	-295	342
-247	-311	-371	-1195	-1248
-	-	-	-	-
28	39	71	87	-23
-263	-322	66	142	702
-378	-359	-179	-2	147
536	498	562	930	1081
302	304	-26	-50	-558
-28	-39	-33	-4	4
197	121	461	1103	1353
-30	-74	-209	-800	-1300
7	-	-	-	-
-	-	-	-	-
-522	-463	-468	-293	-198e
181	211	208	205	180
-59	-61	-70	-88	-102
-743	-1053	-1215	-1478	-1751
-25	-22	-21	-16	-6
-160	-192	-189	-190	-178
1311	1577	1755	1828	2033
-5155	-2763	-1333	-729	-1038
4535	2254	536	-121	1955
604	532	536	605e	121
-	-	-	-	-8
-	-	-	-	8

Table 6 MONTHLY VARIATIONS IN NET IMPORTS OF ELECTRICITY, 1964

Daily averages - million kwh

	Jan.	Feb.	March	April	May
Denmark	2.0	1.6	1.8	1.8	2.9
Finland	2.4	2.2	2.0	2.1	0.3
Norway	-4.1	-5.3	-5.8	-6.2	-3.4
Sweden	0.1	1.1	1.9	2.1	0.2
Belgium	-0.7	-1.0	-1.4	-0.9	-0.3
France	5.8	7.9	5.6	3.2	5.7
Germany, West	-1.0	-6.3	-3.6	5.2	19.4
Italy	6.8	7.1	4.3	2.0	2.1
Luxembourg	1.7	1.6	1.9	2.0	1.8
Netherlands	0.2	0.1	0.2	-	-
Austria	-3.4	-4.8	-2.8	-8.5	-11.4
Spain	-6.2	-5.9	-6.6	-6.9	-3.4
Switzerland	-0.9	3.2	1.8	3.3	-14.1
United Kingdom	-0.5	-0.7	-0.2	-0.1	-0.2
Greece	-	-	-	-0.3	-0.3
Portugal	-	-	-	-	-
Yugoslavia	-0.6	-	-0.4	-	-
Czechoslovakia	0.5	1.5	1.6	2.8	4.4
Hungary	2.6	2.9	2.8	3.2	2.7
Poland	-0.7	-3.8	-1.6	-2.4	-1.9
Romania	0.7	0.6	0.3	-0.5	-0.6
Kenya	0.5	0.6	0.5	0.5	0.6
Uganda	-0.5	-0.5	-0.5	-0.5	-0.5
Canada	-7.3	-4.7	-4.0	-5.4	-3.0
United States	5.9	3.6	2.8	3.7	1.3
Mexico (1965)	0.1	0.2	0.1	0.2	0.2
Congo (Kinshasa)	-	-	-	-	-
Zambia	-	-	-	-	-
Rhodesia	-4.7	-4.9	-4.6	-4.7	-4.6
Mozambique	-0.2	-0.2	-0.3	-0.3	-0.3

June	July	Aug.	Sept.	Oct.	Nov.	Dec.
2.5	3.8	2.2	1.9	1.9	1.9	2.5
0.1	1.3	2.4	2.5	2.3	2.3	2.5
-1.8	-0.4	-2.5	-1.2	-2.2	-4.9	-5.3
-1.0	-4.9	-1.8	-3.2	-2.2	0.6	0.5
-0.3	-0.9	-0.7	-2.1	-1.4	-0.9	-0.9
10.0	12.1	4.8	6.1	3.5	3.8	5.0
22.4	7.8	3.9	-4.2	-4.7	-4.4	-3.3
0.3	0.7	1.0	1.8	3.7	2.8	4.4
1.7	1.8	2.1	1.9	1.8	2.1	2.1
-	-	-	-	-	-	0.1
-12.0	-10.9	-9.0	-5.0	-6.8	-5.9	-7.3
-5.7	-3.7	-0.8	-1.6	-2.6	-4.1	-3.7
-19.1	-6.9	-1.9	1.8	6.8	7.7	3.8
-0.3	-1.7	-0.8	-1.8	-0.3	-0.8	-
-0.2	-	-	-	-	-	-
-	-	-	-	-0.5	0.6	0.6
0.4	0.8	1.8	1.7	2.5	1.7	1.0
3.6	3.7	1.9	3.6	0.1	-1.3	0.5
2.7	2.8	2.5	2.8	3.6	3.8	3.0
-1.8	-1.8	-	-1.7	-1.5	-1.8	-0.9
0.9	0.3	-0.1	0.1	-0.4	-0.4	-1.1
0.5	0.5	0.5	0.5	0.5	0.5	0.4
-0.5	-0.5	-0.6	-0.5	-0.5	-0.5	-0.4
0.1	-1.9	-2.1	-3.4	-2.9	-4.1	-1.1
-2.3	-0.8	-0.5	1.2	1.5	3.1	0.8
0.2	0.3	0.3	0.2	0.2	0.2	0.2
-	-	-	-	-	-	-
-	-	-	-	-	-	-
-4.7	-4.9	-4.8	-4.8	-4.7	-4.8	-5.0
-0.3	-0.3	-0.3	-0.3	-0.3	-0.3	-0.2

Table 7 UTILIZATION OF INSTALLED CAPACITY, 1964

	Capacity* (000 kw)	Total Production (mil kwh)
EUROPE		
Belgium	4872	20800
France	25602	98759
Germany, West	33977	164436
Italy	21193	76738
Luxembourg	886	2216
Netherlands	6332	22975
Austria	5031	20363
Denmark	2255	7900e
Finland	3596	13636
Iceland	166	681
Ireland	852	3368
Norway	8351	44028
Sweden	11040	45247
Switzerland	7690	22864
United Kingdom	44458	182848
Gibraltar	11	39
Greece	827e	3780
Malta	25	135
Portugal	1495	4761
Spain	8387	29526
Yugoslavia	3030	14189
Bulgaria	1493	8700.
Czechoslovakia	7287	31983
Germany, East	8894	51032
Hungary	1785	10580
Poland	8463	40611
Romania	2356	13851
USSR	93050	458902
AFRICA		
Algeria	509	1342
Libya	62	157
Morocco[1]	399	1160
Tunisia	151	487e
U.A.R. (Egypt)	1205	5106

*Capacity as of year-end, 1963
[1]Capacity as of year-end, 1962; production, 1963.

	Hydro		
Utilization (hrs/kw)	Capacity* (000 kw)	Production (mil kwh)	Utilization (hrs/kw)
4269	54	115	2129
3857	11868	35218	2967
4839	3566	12102	3393
3620	13737	39328	2862
2501	623	805	1292
3628	-	-	-
4047	3320	13179	3969
3503e	10	25	2500
3791	1851	8501	4592
4102	126	656	5206
3953	219	784	3579
5271	8210	43864	5342
4098	8872	43022	4849
2973	7490	22663	3025
4112	1713	4022	2347
3545	-	-	-
4570e	260e	749	2881e
5400	-	-	-
3184	1204	4220	3504
3520	5895	20646	3502
4682	1851	7575	4092
5827	545	1471	2699
4389	1472	2727	1852
5737	320	536	1675
5927	20	74	3700
4798	349	726	2080
5879	327	585	1788
4931	20830	77361	3713
2637	134	284	2119
2532	-	-	-
2907	319	1080	3385
3225e	28	38	1357
4237	353	1670	4730

TABLE 7 (continued)

	Capacity* (000 kw)	Total Production (mil kwh)
Angola	334	260
Cameroon	168	1070
Central African Republic	8.3U	20U
Chad	5.3U	15U
Congo (Kinshasa)	900	2435
Dahomey[1]	6.3	18U
Gabon	11	36
Gambia	4.8	7.4
Ghana	143	485
Guinea	68	168
Ivory Coast	52	183
Liberia	63	212
Mali [1]	10U	21U
Niger	7	15
Nigeria	256	1024
Rwanda	9.0	12e
St. Thomas & Prince	2.2	6
Senegal	68U	197U
Sierra Leone	33	84
Togo	12.5	27
Upper Volta	5.8	19
Ethiopia	111	208
French Somaliland	6.2U	20U
Kenya	102U	323U
Malagasy	74	139
Malawi	13	43
Mauritius	81	93
Mozambique	211	368e
Reunion	8.4U	32U
Rhodesia	1188	3801
Somalia	3.2U	10.6U
South Africa[2]	5970	29399
Southwest Africa	79	220
Sudan	59U	167U
Tanzania	49U	192U
Uganda	133U	521U
Zambia	263	713

*Capacity as of year-end, 1963
[1]Capacity as of year-end, 1962; production, 1963
[2]Capacity as of year-end, 1962; production, 1963 (fiscal
U Utilities only

Utilization (hrs/kw)	Hydro Capacity* (000 kw)	Production (mil kwh)	Utilization (hrs/kw)
778	262	225	858
6369	152	1039	6836
2410U	6.6U	20U	3030U
2830U	-	-	-
2706	810	2265e	2796e
2857U	-	-	-
3272	-	-	-
1541	-	-	-
3391	-	-	
2470	20	14	700
3519	19	96	5052
3365	4	17	4250
2100U	-	-	-
2142	-	-	-
4000	21	126	6000
1333e	7.4	11e	1486e
2727	0.5	-	-
2897U	-	-	-
2545	-	-	-
2160	1.6	3	1875
3275	-	-	-
1873	64	120	1875
3225U	-	-	-
3167U	28U	205U	7321U
1878	28	81	2892
3307	-	-	-
1148	16	56	3500
1740e	66	160e	2424e
3809U	3.8U	22U	5789U
3199	705	3571	5065
3312U	-	-	-
4924	14	40e	2857e
2785	-	-	-
2830U	-	-	-
3918U	20U	131U	6550U
3917U	122U	521U	4270U
2711	49	305	6224

years)

TABLE 7 (continued)

	Capacity* (000 kw)	Total Production (mil kwh)
ASIA		
Aden	51	205
Bahrain	65	298
Cyprus	98	306
Iran	845	2250
Iraq[1]	430U	1120U
Israel	665e	3625
Jordan	41	136
Kuwait	163U	647U
Lebanon	285	692
Saudi Arabia	87	273
Syria	220	574
Turkey	1381	4435
Afghanistan[2]	61	181
Brunei	20	70
Burma	252	570
Cambodia[2]	34	99
Ceylon	145	475
China (Taiwan)	1118	6288
Hong Kong	499	2385
India	7623	33129
Indonesia[1]	311U	1335U
Japan	34295	179592
Korea, South	622	2966
Laos	5.8U	13U
Macao	8.9	26
Malaya	387	1851
Nepal	7	15
Pakistan	859U	3553U
Philippines	958	4678
Ryukyu Islands	142	593
Sabah	14	41
Sarawak	20	58
Singapore	224	914
Thailand	362	1107
Vietnam, South	228	574

*Capacity as of year-end, 1963.
[1] Capacity as of year-end, 1961; production, 1962.
[2] Capacity as of year-end, 1962; production, 1963.
U Utilities only

	Hydro		
Utilization (hrs/kw)	Capacity* (000 kw)	Production (mil kwh)	Utilization (hrs/kw)
4019	-	-	-
4584	-	-	-
3122	-	-	-
2663	233e	270	1158e
2605U	-	-	-
5451e	-	-	-
3317	-	-	-
3969U	-	-	-
2428	126	375	2976
3140	-	-	-
2609	-	-	-
3211	478	1652	3456
2967	48	169	3520
3500	-	-	-
2261	85	280	3294
2911	-	-	-
3275	63	338	5365
5624	539e	2359	4376e
4779	-	-	-
4346	3170	14807	4671
4293U	166U	777U	4681U
5236	15106	68957	4564
4768	143	750	5244
2241U	-	-	
2921	-	-	-
4782	81	544	6716
2142	3	8	2667
4136U	347U	1710U	4928U
4883	291	1554	5340
4176	-	-	-
2928	-	-	-
2900	-	-	-
4080	-	-	-
3058	-	-	-
2517	84	56	666

TABLE 7 (continued)

	Capacity* (000 kw)	Total Production (mil kwh)
OCEANIA		
American Samoa[1]	2.5	11
Australia	7983	32519
Fiji Islands	32	93
French Polynesia	7.3	16
Guam	70	335
Nauru	6.1	11
New Caledonia	101	498
New Guinea	13	40
New Zealand	2006	9718
Papua	8	34
Western Samoa	2.5	6.4
AMERICAS		
Canada	26300	134987
Greenland	21	38
United States	228756	1083741
Bahama Islands	33	123
Barbados	13	60
Bermuda	36	133
British Honduras	3.7U	11U
Colombia	1371	5916
Costa Rica	140	594
Cuba	976	3250
Dominican Republic	134	560e
El Salvador	106	377
Guadeloupe	11	40
Guatemala	88	470
Haiti	27	110
Honduras[2]	37	116
Jamaica	186	715
Martinique	9.8	37
Mexico	4243	15748
Netherlands Antilles	243	1025
Nicaragua	84	281
Panama Canal Zone	86	418
Panama Republic	94	400
Puerto Rico	738	3638
Trinidad & Tobago	152	820
Venezuela	2034	7597

*Capacity as of year-end, 1963
[1] Capacity as of year-end, 1961; production, 1962.
[2] Capacity as of year-end, 1962; production, 1963.
U Utilities only

Utilization (hrs/kw)	Hydro Capacity* (000 kw)	Hydro Production (mil kwh)	Hydro Utilization (hrs/kw)
4400	-	-	-
4074	2073e	6898	3327e
2906	-	-	-
2191	-	-	-
4785	-	-	-
1803	-	-	-
4930	68	315	4632
3076	5.9	19	3220
4844	1580	7753	4906
4250	5.5	28	5090
2560	1.3	5	3846
5132	20100	113344	5639
1810	-	-	-
4737	40928	180302	4405
3727	-	-	-
4615	-	-	-
3694	-	-	-
2972U	-	-	-
4315	773	3721	4813
4243	105	495e	4714e
3329	--	--	--
4179e	8	50e	6250e
3557	87	336	3862
3636	--	--	--
5340	31e	120	3870e
4074	-	-	-
3135	5	20e	4000e
3844	21	153	7285
3775	-	-	-
3711	1573	6866	4364
4218	-	-	-
3345	9	43	4777
4860	46	263	5717
4255	7	31	4428
4929	107	152	1421
5395	-	-	-
3735	380	1223	3218

TABLE 7 (continued)

	Capacity* (000 kw)	Total Production (mil kwh)
Argentina	4686	13752
Bolivia	158	534
Brazil	6355	29094
Chile	1336	5932
Ecuador	166	551
French Guiana	4.2U	8.7U
Guyana	74	171
Paraguay	50	129
Peru	999	3689
Surinam	39	128
Uruguay	451	1724

* Capacity as of year-end, 1963.
U Utilities only.

		Hydro	
Utilization (hrs/kw)	Capacity* (000 kw)	Production (mil kwh)	Utilization (hrs/kw)
2935	363	1236	3404
3797	92	421	4576
4578	4480	22097	4932
4440	683	3723	5450
3319	67	248	3701
2071U	-	-	-
2310	-	-	-
2580	-	-	-
3692	551	2448	4442
3282	-	-	-
3822	224	1267	5656

Table 8 ELECTRICITY CONSUMED IN
PUMPED-STORAGE PLANTS
1958 - 1964

(Million kwh)

	1958	1959
Austria	689	587
Brazil	878	992
Bulgaria	7	16
Czechoslovakia	210	114
France	172	184
Germany , West	1315	1393
Italy	295	355
Japan	88	38
Luxembourg	-	-
Poland	17	28
Sweden	79	47
Switzerland	191	175
United Kingdom	-	-
United States	-	-
Uruguay	-	-
Yugoslavia	2	4

1960	1961	1962	1963	1964
747	661	776	841	667
1037	993	1044	981	954
13	12	19	15	15
119	123	106	125	194
186	152	158	226	151
1370	1424	1628	1692	1466
405	403	469	513	509
92	126	179	209	161
-	-	89	624	1040
37	21	28	32	32
62	44	51	64	95
270	196	308	392	390
-	-	212	488	589
-	-	358	610	(728)
-	-	-	-	49
1	3	10	3	3

Table 9 MONTHLY VARIATIONS IN CONSUMPTION OF ELECTRICITY, 1964
grouped by regions*

Daily averages - million kwh

	Jan.	Feb.	March	April	May
Belgium	54.6	52.6	52.5	52.6	46.8
France	279.7	268.0	262.1	260.0	236.7
Germany, West	437.4	428.9	413.5	414.9	378.4
Italy	216.8	213.3	202.7	200.1	189.5
Luxembourg	7.7	7.2	7.6	8.4	7.7
Netherlands	65.7	62.5	60.2	58.0	51.7
EEC	1061.9	1032.5	998.6	994.0	910.8
Denmark	24.3	24.0	22.4	21.0	19.1
Finland	38.4	39.0	36.7	35.4	34.6
Norway	125.6	127.6	120.6	116.0	104.0
Sweden	128.3	132.8	123.5	119.1	107.7
Nordel	316.6	323.4	303.2	291.5	265.4
United Kingdom	570.3	551.8	528.4	472.2	391.8
Ireland	10.0	9.9	9.2	8.4	7.0
Iceland	2.0	2.0	1.8	1.8	1.7
Austria	50.7	48.8	48.3	45.4	44.7
Switzerland	60.8	59.6	57.9	58.0	57.1
Other North Europe	693.8	672.1	645.6	585.8	502.3
Spain	78.7	79.4	73.3	75.7	69.2
Yugoslavia	40.3	36.4	38.5	39.7	37.6
Greece	10.6	10.5	9.8	10.0	9.4
Portugal	13.6	13.5	14.3	14.5	13.2
South Europe	143.2	139.8	135.9	139.9	129.4
West Europe	2216	2168	2083	2011	1835
Bulgaria	21.6	21.8	21.6	21.5	21.9
Czechoslovakia	93.5	92.6	90.2	86.8	82.5
Germany, East	148.6	145.7	140.9	135.9	126.8
Hungary	32.1	32.0	30.9	29.9	29.4
Poland	105.3	101.7	99.8	95.2	88.1
Romania	35.9	36.7	36.5	35.0	34.0
East Europe	437.0	430.5	419.9	404.3	382.7

* Regional totals include only the countries listed.
**

$$\text{Countries north of the Equator} = \frac{\text{January} + \text{December}}{\text{July} + \text{August}}$$

$$\text{Countries south of the Equator} = \frac{\text{July} + \text{August}}{\text{January} + \text{December}}$$

June	July	Aug.	Sept.	Oct.	Nov.	Dec.	Winter/Summer Index**
50.2	44.0	47.2	53.0	56.7	57.5	59.5	1.25
246.6	232.1	190.6	246.6	272.0	278.5	286.1	1.34
397.6	401.0	391.5	424.8	447.5	458.0	457.3	1.13
196.8	204.4	176.5	204.4	211.1	212.6	218.1	1.14
7.1	7.9	8.2	8.6	8.2	8.0	8.6	1.01
53.5	50.0	50.5	58.3	64.4	68.0	70.1	1.35
951.8	939.4	864.5	995.7	1059.9	1082.6	1099.7	1.20
19.2	17.8	20.6	22.5	23.9	25.6	26.5	1.32
32.6	32.3	35.4	40.1	41.1	42.4	38.9	1.14
104.6	95.2	98.8	111.2	124.0	132.4	141.2	1.38
111.3	91.2	115.4	130.7	138.4	142.1	136.9	1.28
267.7	236.5	270.2	304.5	327.4	342.5	343.5	1.30
414.9	354.8	353.4	394.9	483.6	530.1	593.6	1.65
6.9	6.7	6.3	7.4	8.9	9.8	11.1	1.62
1.6	1.6	1.6	1.6	1.9	2.0	2.0	1.25
46.5	45.6	47.3	48.7	50.4	51.8	51.1	1.10
61.8	59.3	58.3	60.3	62.0	62.2	62.6	1.05
531.7	468.0	466.9	512.9	606.8	655.9	720.4	1.51
72.4	70.2	66.8	72.2	73.5	77.6	80.0	1.16
35.9	35.7	36.3	39.1	41.0	46.3	46.9	1.21
9.5	9.6	9.4	10.0	10.3	10.9	11.5	1.16
12.3	12.1	12.4	12.8	13.5	15.9	17.5	1.27
130.1	127.6	124.9	134.1	138.3	150.7	155.9	1.18
1881	1772	1727	1947	2132	2232	2320	1.30
23.1	25.4	25.9	24.2	25.5	25.5	27.0	0.95
85.4	81.7	82.3	88.1	92.0	98.2	98.1	1.17
130.6	124.6	137.8	137.9	143.0	148.1	152.8	1.15
29.6	29.3	29.6	31.8	33.1	33.7	34.6	1.13
89.1	87.6	91.4	97.1	104.6	111.6	113.5	1.22
34.4	35.0	36.3	39.6	40.0	43.2	46.2	1.15
392.2	383.6	403.3	418.7	438.2	460.3	472.2	1.15

TABLE 9 (continued)

Daily averages -   million kwh

	Jan.	Feb.	March	April	May
Algeria	3.4	3.2	3.0	2.9	2.9
Central African Rep.	0.05	0.06	0.06	0.06	0.06
Chad	0.03	0.03	0.04	0.05	0.05
Ghana	1.3	1.3	1.3	1.4	1.2
Morocco	3.5	3.5	3.3	3.3	3.2
Nigeria	2.7	2.7	2.7	2.8	2.8
Senegal	0.5	0.5	0.5	0.5	0.5
Sierra Leone	0.2	0.2	0.2	0.2	0.2
Togo	0.03	0.03	0.03	0.03	0.03
Tunisia	1.0	1.0	0.9	0.8	0.8
Upper Volta	0.04	0.05	0.06	0.06	0.06
Africa No. of Equator	12.8	12.6	12.1	12.1	11.8
Angola	0.2	0.3	0.2	0.2	0.2
Malagasy	0.2	0.2	0.2	0.3	0.3
Malawi	0.1	0.1	0.1	0.1	0.1
Mauritius	0.2	0.2	0.2	0.2	0.3
Rhodesia	5.1	5.3	5.3	5.6	5.7
South Africa	74.3	78.0	78.2	77.6	84.2
Tanzania	0.5	0.5	0.5	0.5	0.5
Africa So. of Equator	80.6	84.6	84.7	84.5	91.3
Cyprus	0.9	0.8	0.7	0.7	0.7
Israel	9.1	8.6	8.1	8.3	9.7
Jordan	0.4	0.3	0.3	0.3	0.4
Kuwait	1.9	1.5	1.2	1.2	2.0
Lebanon	1.5	1.4	1.4	1.4	1.4
Syria	0.9	0.9	0.9	0.8	0.8
Turkey	12.3	11.7	11.7	11.3	11.3
Middle East	27.0	25.2	24.3	24.0	26.3
Burma	0.9	0.9	0.9	0.9	0.9
Cambodia	0.2	0.2	0.2	0.2	0.2
China (Taiwan)	14.9	14.7	15.6	16.3	16.0
Hong Kong	4.9	4.8	4.5	5.1	5.3
India	75.1	77.5	75.8	77.2	75.8
Japan	443.9	471.8	461.6	459.4	455.9
Korea, South	6.7	6.4	6.7	6.8	6.7
Malaya	4.8	4.6	4.9	4.9	5.0
Pakistan	8.5	8.7	8.9	8.7	9.4
Philippines	9.5	10.1	10.2	10.3	10.8
Sarawak	0.1	0.1	0.1	0.1	0.1
Singapore	2.3	2.3	2.4	2.5	2.5
Thailand	2.9	2.7	2.8	2.9	2.9
Vietnam, South	1.1	1.1	1.1	1.2	1.2
Far East	575.8	605.9	595.7	596.5	592.7

*Regional totals include only the countries listed.
**

$$\text{Countries north of the Equator} = \frac{\text{January} + \text{December}}{\text{July} + \text{August}}$$

$$\text{Countries south of the Equator} = \frac{\text{July} + \text{August}}{\text{January} + \text{December}}$$

June	July	Aug.	Sept.	Oct.	Nov.	Dec.	Winter Summer Index**
3.0	2.9	2.9	3.2	3.0	3.1	3.4	1.17
0.05	0.05	0.04	0.05	0.06	0.06	0.06	1.22
0.05	0.04	0.03	0.04	0.04	0.04	0.04	1.00
1.1	1.3	1.3	1.3	1.3	1.4	1.3	1.00
3.2	3.1	3.0	3.2	3.3	3.5	3.7	1.18
2.4	2.7	2.7	2.8	2.9	3.1	3.1	1.07
0.6	0.6	0.5	0.6	0.6	0.6	0.5	0.91
0.2	0.2	0.2	0.2	0.2	0.2	0.3	1.25
0.03	0.02	0.02	0.02	0.02	0.03	0.03	1.50
0.8	0.9	0.9	0.9	0.9	0.9	1.1	1.17
0.05	0.05	0.04	0.04	0.06	0.05	0.05	1.00
11.5	11.9	11.6	12.4	12.4	13.0	13.6	1.12
0.2	0.2	0.2	0.2	0.2	0.2	0.2	1.00
0.3	0.3	0.2	0.3	0.3	0.3	0.3	1.00
0.1	0.1	0.1	0.1	0.1	0.1	0.1	1.00
0.3	0.3	0.3	0.3	0.3	0.3	0.3	1.20
6.0	6.1	5.9	5.8	5.7	5.6	5.2	1.16
90.0	90.3	89.2	85.8	84.6	84.3	80.6	1.16
0.5	0.5	0.5	0.5	0.5	0.6	0.5	1.00
97.4	97.8	96.4	93.0	91.7	91.4	87.2	1.15
0.8	0.8	0.8	0.8	0.8	0.8	0.8	1.06
11.2	11.5	11.4	10.3	11.0	10.4	9.9	0.83
0.4	0.4	0.4	0.4	0.4	0.4	0.4	1.00
2.4	2.4	2.5	2.3	1.7	1.0	1.3	0.65
1.7	1.8	1.7	1.9	1.7	1.6	1.6	0.89
0.8	0.9	0.9	0.9	0.9	0.9	1.1	1.11
11.5	11.2	11.3	12.5	13.0	13.8	13.9	1.16
28.8	29.0	29.0	29.1	29.5	28.9	29.0	0.97
0.9	0.9	0.9	0.9	1.0	1.0	0.9	1.00
0.2	0.2	0.2	0.2	0.2	0.2	0.2	1.00
16.0	16.8	16.7	16.8	16.8	16.3	17.0	0.95
6.0	6.5	6.2	6.6	6.1	6.7	5.3	0.80
80.0	78.9	76.8	77.3	77.8	78.8	79.5	0.99
472.4	495.7	493.5	497.5	494.5	500.6	518.4	0.97
7.4	7.6	7.6	7.4	8.0	8.5	8.6	1.01
5.0	5.0	5.1	5.3	5.4	5.4	5.4	1.01
10.2	9.7	8.4	10.3	9.7	9.3	10.1	1.03
10.7	10.3	10.7	10.9	11.0	10.7	10.7	0.96
0.1	0.1	0.1	0.1	0.1	0.2	0.2	1.50
2.6	2.4	2.5	2.5	2.7	2.7	2.6	1.00
3.0	3.0	3.1	3.2	3.3	3.4	3.4	1.03
1.2	1.2	1.2	1.2	1.3	1.5	1.6	1.13
615.7	638.3	633.0	640.2	637.9	645.3	663.9	0.96

TABLE 9 (continued)

Daily averages - million kwh

	Jan.	Feb.	March	April	May
Australia	76.3	84.5	83.2	89.9	94.8
New Zealand	20.6	22.3	22.9	25.4	28.0
Oceania	96.9	106.8	106.1	115.3	122.8
Canada	370	384	362	358	344
United States	2929	2921	2840	2821	2814
North America	3299	3305	3202	3179	3158
Colombia	10.6	11.6	10.8	11.5	11.3
Cuba	7.1	7.3	7.5	7.4	7.6
El Salvador	1.0	1.0	0.9	0.9	0.9
Guatemala	1.0	1.1	1.1	1.0	1.0
Mexico	39.1	41.5	40.5	43.8	42.5
Panama	0.8	0.7	0.8	0.9	0.8
Panama Canal Zone	1.2	1.2	1.2	1.2	1.2
Puerto Rico	8.9	9.1	9.3	9.6	9.8
Trinidad	1.9	2.2	2.1	2.1	2.2
Venezuela	20.6	20.1	18.3	20.5	20.0
Caribbean America	92.2	95.8	92.5	98.9	97.3
Argentina	27.0	26.9	27.6	28.2	26.8
Brazil	73.0	76.0	74.0	72.6	70.5
Chile	14.7	13.9	14.6	16.3	15.8
Uruguay	3.4	3.5	3.2	3.2	3.5
South America	118.1	120.3	119.4	120.3	116.6

* Regional totals include only the countries listed.

**

$$\text{Countries north of the Equator} \ = \ \frac{\text{January} + \text{December}}{\text{July} + \text{August}}$$

$$\text{Countries south of the Equator} \ = \ \frac{\text{July} + \text{August}}{\text{January} + \text{December}}$$

June	July	Aug.	Sept.	Oct.	Nov.	Dec.	Winter Summer Index**
103.8	107.7	103.2	98.6	93.5	91.5	87.2	1.29
30.6	31.1	30.4	28.5	26.1	25.1	22.7	1.42
134.4	138.8	133.6	127.1	119.6	116.6	109.9	1.32
352	344	346	360	378	392	404	1.12
3017	3086	3062	2983	2884	2935	3088	0.98
3369	3430	3408	3343	3262	3327	3492	0.99
11.5	11.6	11.7	12.2	12.1	12.8	12.5	0.99
7.8	8.1	8.2	8.2	7.9	7.9	7.8	0.92
0.9	0.9	0.9	0.9	0.9	1.0	1.1	1.17
1.0	1.0	1.0	1.0	1.0	1.0	1.0	1.00
43.1	44.5	45.2	44.5	49.3	43.9	43.5	0.92
0.9	0.8	0.8	0.8	0.8	0.8	0.9	1.06
1.2	1.2	1.2	1.2	1.3	1.3	1.3	1.04
10.0	10.2	10.4	10.7	10.7	10.3	10.1	0.92
2.4	2.4	2.1	2.1	2.1	2.4	2.3	0.93
20.6	20.8	21.4	21.4	21.2	22.5	21.8	1.00
99.4	101.5	102.9	103.0	107.3	103.9	102.3	0.95
28.2	28.6	28.0	28.7	28.0	28.4	29.0	1.01
71.8	74.5	73.4	73.8	71.7	72.0	74.0	1.01
17.4	17.4	17.0	15.8	16.4	16.3	16.0	1.12
3.7	3.7	3.5	3.5	3.3	3.5	3.2	1.09
121.1	124.2	121.9	121.8	119.4	120.2	122.2	1.02

351

Guide to Source Abbreviations

Anon. *Rev. Latinoamer. de elec./ Revista Latinoamericano de electricidad.*

Benn Bros. *Elec. undertakings./* Benn Brothers. *Electricity undertakings of the world; the electrical journal red book.*

EEC. *Yrbk. Overseas Assoc./ Yearbook of general statistics. Overseas Associates.*

———. *Energy stat., 1950-1965./ Energy statistics, 1950-1965.*

Inst. de la Stat. *Ann. stat./* Institut National de la Statistique et des Etudes Economiques. *Annuaire statistique des territoires d'outre-mer.*

Inst. de Est./ Instituto Nacional de Estatistica. *Anuário estatístico do ultramar.*

Soc. R. Moreux. *Industries et travaux. No. 122./* La Société René Moreux & Cie. *Industries et travaux d'outre-mer. "L'électricité."* Special number 122.

Energy international./ Miller Freeman Publications. *Energy international.*

OECD. *Elec. ind. survey./ Electricity industry survey.*

———. *Survey of elec. power equipment./ Survey of electric power equipment.*

UNIPEDE./ Union Internationale des Producteurs et Distributeurs d'Energie Electrique./ *L'écon. élec./ L'économie électrique.*

———. *Réseaux de transport./ Réseaux de transport d'énergie électrique d'Europe.* (map)

———. *Statistiques.*

UCPTE./ Union pour la Coordination de la Production et du Transport de l'Electricité. *Réseau./ Réseau d'interconnexion.* (map)

UN. *Non-self-gov. terr.; summaries./ Non-self-governing territories; summaries of information transmitted to the Secretary-General.*

———. *Water desalination./ Water desalination in developing countries.*

———. ECA. *Rept. on econ. coop. in Central Africa./* Economic Commission for Africa. *Report of the ECA mission on economic cooperation in Central Africa.*

———. ———. *Situation, trends & prospects./ Situation, trends and prospects of electric power supply in Africa.*

———. ECAFE. *Elec. power./* Economic Commission for Asia and the Far East. *Electric power in Asia and the Far East.*

———. ———. *Role & application of elec. power./ The role and application of electric power in the industrialization of Asia and the Far East.*

———. ECE. *Ann. bull. of elec. energy stat./* Economic Commission for Europe. *Annual bulletin of electric energy statistics for Europe.*

———. ———. *Elec. power situation./ The electric power situation in Europe and its future prospects.*

———. ———. *Org. of elec. power services./ Organization of electric power services in Europe. 2d. ed.*

———. ECLA. *Estud. econ./* Economic Commission for Latin America. *Estudio económico de América Latina.*

———. ———. *Estud. sobre la elec./Estudios sobre la electricidad en América Latina; Vol. 1: informe y documentos del seminario Latinoamericano de energía eléctrica.*

———. ———. *Stat. bull./Statistical bulletin for Latin America.*

———. ———. Subcom. Centroamer. de eléc. *Estadísticas de energía eléctrica./* Subcomité Centroamericano de Electrificación y Recursos Hidráulicos. *Estadísticas de energía eléctrica de Centroamerica y Panama.*

———. ———. *Estadísticas preliminares./ Estadísticas preliminares de energía eléctrica de Centroamerica y Panama.*

———. ———. *Estudio comparativo de costos./ Estudio comparativo de costos de la energía eléctrica en Centroamerica y Panama.*

————. *Growth of world industry./ The growth of world industry, 1953-1965: National tables.*

————. *Mo. bull. of stat./ Monthly bulletin of statistics.*

————. *Stat. yrbk./ Statistical yearbook.*

————. *World energy supplies./ World energy supplies. Statistical papers, Series J.*

————. *Yrbk. of int. trade stat./ Yearbook of international trade statistics.*

U.S. Foreign serv. desp./ United States Foreign Service despatches.

————. Bur. of Mines. *Int'l coal trade./* Bureau of Mines. *International coal trade.*

————. FPC. *Power system statement./* Federal Power Commission. *Power system statement.* (Report form 12)

————. ————. *Spec. comm./ Special communications to the Federal Power Commission.*

Bibliography

WORLD, INTERREGIONAL, AND REGIONAL SOURCES

Anon. *Revista Latinoamericano de electricidad.* Santiago: quarterly.

Benn Brothers. *Electricity undertakings of the world; the electrical journal red book.* London: annual (to 1963).

European Communities (EEC). Statistical Office. *Energy statistics, 1950-1965.* Brussels: 1967.

———. *Yearbook of general statistics. Overseas Associates.* Brussels: annual.

Institut National de la Statistique et des Etudes Economiques. *Annuaire statistique des territoires d'outre-mer.* Paris: annual.

Instituto Nacional de Estatística. *Anuário estatístico do ultramar.* Lisbon: annual.

International Union of Railways. *International railway statistics.* Paris: annual.

La Société René Moreux & Cie. *Industries et travaux d'outre-mer.* Special number 122: "L'électricité." Paris: January, 1964.

McGraw-Hill, Inc. *Directory of Latin-American electric utilities. Handbook for electrical exporters.* New York: annual.

Miller Freeman Publications. *Energy international.* San Francisco (USA): monthly.

Organisation for Economic Cooperation and Development (OECD). *Electricity industry survey.* Paris: annual.

———. *Survey of electric power equipment.* Paris: annual.

Union Internationale des Producteurs et Distributeurs d'Energie Electrique (UNIPEDE). *L'économie électrique,* 1st quarter 1966. Paris: quarterly.

———. Proceedings of the Madrid Congress, May 1967. *General report of the chairman of the statistics study committee.* Madrid: 1967.

———. ———. "Distribution of electricity consumption through the year: weighting of daily consumptions and seasonal variation." Daniel Jung. Madrid: 1967.

———. *Réseaux de transport d'énergie électrique d'Europe.* (map) Paris: 1961.

———. *Statistiques.* Paris: annual.

Union pour la Coordination de la Production et du Transport de l'Electricité (UCPTE). *Rapport annuel.* Various cities: annual.

———. *Réseau d'interconnexion, 1966.* (map) Heidelberg: 1967.

United Nations publications.

Committee on Information from Non-Self-Governing Territories. *Non-self-governing territories; summaries of information transmitted to the Secretary-General.* New York: irregular.

Department of Economic and Social Affairs. Resources and Transport Division. *Water desalination in developing countries.* New York: 1965.

Economic Commission for Africa (ECA). *Report of the ECA mission on economic cooperation in Central Africa.* Ethiopia: 1966.

———. *Situation, trends and prospects of electric power supply in Africa.* Ethiopia: 1965.

Economic Commission for Asia and the Far East (ECAFE). *Electric power in Asia and the Far East.* Bangkok and New York: annual.

———. *The role and application of electric power in the industrialization of Asia and the Far East.* Bangkok and New York: 1965.

Economic Commission for Europe (ECE). *Annual bulletin of electric energy statistics for Europe.* Geneva: annual.

———. *The electric power situation in Europe and its future prospects.* Geneva: annual.

———. *Half-yearly bulletin of electric energy statistics for Europe.* Geneva: semi-annual.

———. *Organization of electric power services in Europe.* 2nd. ed. Geneva: 1960. and addendum.

Economic Commission for Latin America (ECLA). *Estudio económico de América Latina.* New York: annual.

———. *Estudios sobre la electricidad en América Latina; Vol. 1: informe y documentos del seminario Latinoamericano de energía eléctrica.* Mexico: 1962.

———. *Statistical bulletin for Latin America.* New York: semi-annual.

———. Subcomité Centroamericano de Electrificación y Recursos Hidráulicos. *Estadísticas de energía eléctrica de Centroamérica y Panama.* Mexico: irregular.

———. ———. *Estadísticas preliminares de energía eléctrica do Centroamérica y Panama.*
Mexico: irregular.

———. ———. *Estudio comparativo de costos de la energía eléctrica en Centroamérica
y Panama.* Mexico: irregular.

Statistical Office. *The growth of world industry, 1953 - 1965: National tables.* New
York: 1967.

———. *Monthly bulletin of statistics.* New York: monthly.

———. *Statistical yearbook.* New York: annual.

———. *World energy supplies. Statistical papers, Series J.* New York: annual.

———. *Yearbook of national accounts statistics.* New York: annual.

———. *Yearbook of international trade statistics.* New York: annual.

United States Government publications.

Department of State. *Foreign service despatches.* Washington: irregular.

Department of the Interior. Bureau of Mines. *International coal trade.* Washington:
monthly.

Federal Power Commission. *Power system statement* (Report form 12). Washington:
annual.

———. *Special communications to the Federal Power Commission.* Washington: irregular.

———. *World power data.* Washington: annual.

NATIONAL SOURCES

Albania.

Komisionit të Planit të Shtetit, Drejtoria e Statistikës. (State Planning Commission,
Directorate of Statistics). *Vjetari statistikor i RPSH.* Tiranë: annual.

Algeria.

Directeur Générale des Plan des Etudes Economiques. Service de Statistique
Générale. *Annuaire statistique de l'Algérie.* Alger: annual.

———. *Bulletin mensuel de statistique générale.* Alger: monthly.

Electricité et Gaz de l'Algérie. *Rapport de gestion.* Alger: annual.

American Samoa.

U. S. Department of the Interior. *Annual report, governor of American Samoa.*
Washington, D. C.: annual.

Angola.

Direcção dos Servicos de Economía e Estatística Geral. *Anuário estatístico.* Luanda:
annual.

Argentina.

Dirección General del Gas del Estado. *Boletín estadístico anual.* Buenos Aires:
annual.

———. *Gas del estado; aspectos de su obra presente y futura.* Buenos Aires: 1961.

Dirección Nacional de Energía y Combustibles. *Combustibles.* Buenos Aires: annual.

———. *Energía eléctrica.* Buenos Aires: annual.

Australia.

Commonwealth Bureau of Census and Statistics. *Manufacturing industries.* No. 31,
"Electric light and power works." Canberra: annual.

———. *Yearbook of the Commonwealth of Australia.* Canberra: annual.

Electricity Supply Association of Australia. *Statistics of the electricity supply industry in Australia.* Melbourne: annual.

Austria.

Bundesministerium für Verkehr und Elektrizitätswirtshaft. *Betriebsstatistik.* 2 vols.
Vienna: annual.

———. *Brennstoffstatistik.* Vienna: annual.

Bahamas.

Bahamas Electricity Corporation. *Report and accounts, 1956-1966.*

United Kingdom. Colonial Office. *Bahamas.* London: biennial.

Belgium.
    Fédération Professionnelle des Producteurs et Distributeurs d'Electricité de Belgique
        (FPE). *Annuaire statistique*. Brussels: annual.
    Ministère des Affaires Economiques. Administration de l'Energie. *Répertoire des
        centrales*. Brussels: annual.
    ——. *Statistiques electricité*. 2 vols. Brussels: annual.
Bermuda.
    Bermuda Electric Light Company Ltd. *Annual report*. Bermuda: annual.
    United Kingdom. Colonial Office. *Bermuda*. London: annual.
Brazil.
    Brazilian Embassy, Washington, D. C. *Survey of the Brazilian economy, 1965*.
    Conselho Naçional de Aguas e Energía Elétrica. *Aguas e energía elétrica*. Rio de
        Janeiro: annual.
    Conselho Nacional de Estatística. *Anuário estatístico do Brasil*. Rio de Janeiro:
        annual.
    Petroleo Brasileiro, S.A. *Relatoria das actividades*. Rio de Janeiro: annual.
Bulgaria.
    Edison Electric Institute. *A report on electric power developments in Bulgaria*. New
        York: 1967.
Burma.
    Ministry of Finance and Revenue. *Selected monthly economic indicators*. Rangoon:
        monthly.
    Ministry of National Planning. *Economic survey of Burma*. Rangoon: annual.
British Honduras.
    United Kingdom. Colonial Office. *British Honduras*. London: annual.
Brunei.
    United Kingdom. Colonial Office. *State of Brunei*. London: annual.
Cambodia.
    Direction de la Statistique et des Etudes Economiques. *Annuaire statistique rétro-
        spectif du Cambodge*. Phnom-Penh: annual.
    ——. *Bulletin mensuel de statistique*. Phnom-Penh: monthly.
Cameroon.
    Service de la Statistique et de la Mécanographie. *Quarterly economic bulletin for
        the Federal Republic of Cameroun*. Douala: quarterly.
Canada.
    Department of Northern Affairs and National Resources. Water Resources Branch.
        Electric power in Canada. Ottawa: annual.
    Dominion Bureau of Statistics. *Electric power statistics*. Ottawa: monthly and an-
        nual.
    ——. Industry Division. *General review of the manufacturing industries of Canada*.
        Ottawa: annual.
Central African Republic.
    Service de la Statistique Générale. *Bulletin mensuel de statistique générale*. Banque:
        monthly.
Ceylon.
    Department of Government Electrical Undertakings. *Administration report of the
        Acting General Manager*. Colombo: annual.
Chad.
    Service de la Statistique Générale. *Bulletin mensuel de statistique de la République
        du Tchad*. Fort Lamy: monthly.
Chile.
    Dirección de Estadística y Censos. *Boletín estadístico*. Santiago: bi-monthly.
    ——. *Estadística Chilena, sinopsis*. Santiago: annual.
    Empresa Nacional de Electricidad, S.A. (ENDESA). *Memoria de actividades*.
        Santiago: anuual.
    ——. *Producción y consumo de energía en Chile*. Santiago: annual.
China (Mainland).
    U. S. Congress. Joint Economic Committee. *An economic profile of Mainland China;
        studies prepared for the Joint Economic Committee, Congress of the United
        States*. Vol. 1: Part I. "General economic setting." Part II. "The economic sec-

tors." 90th Congress, 1st Session. February, 1967. Washington, D. C.: 1967.

Wu, Yuan-Li. *Economic development and the use of energy resources in Communist China.* New York: Praeger, 1963.

China (Taiwan).

Directorate-General of Budgets, Accounts and Statistics. Executive Yuan. *Statistical abstract of the Republic of China, 1965.* Taiwan: annual.

Colombia.

Banco de la República. *Informe anual del gerente a la junta directiva.* Bogotá: annual.

Departmento Administrativo Nacional de Estadística. *Anuario general de estadística.* Bogotá: annual.

Empresas Públicas de Medellin. *Informes y balance.* Medellin: annual.

Ministerio de Fomento. *Memoria del Ministerio de Fomento.* Bogotá: annual.

Congo (Brazzaville).

République du Congo. Cabinet du Premier Ministre. Direction de la Service Nationale de la Statistique des Etudes Démographiques et Economiques. *Bulletin mensuel rapide des statistiques* (and supplement). Brazzaville: monthly.

Congo (Kinshasa). (Formerly Leopoldville).

International Union of Railways. *International railway statistics.* Paris: annual.

Ministère du Plan et du Développement. *Bulletin trimestriel des statistiques générales de la République Démocratique du Congo.* Kinshasa: quarterly.

Union Minière du Haut Katanga. *Rapport annuel du Haut Katanga.* Kinshasa: annual.

United Nations Conference on the Application of Science and Technology (UNCAST). "L'énergie au Congo Ex-Belge et au Ruanda-Urundi," by A. Clerfayt. Geneva: 1962.

Costa Rica.

Banco Central de Costa Rica. *Memoria anual.* San Jose: annual.

Instituto Costarricense de Electricidad. *Memoria.* San Jose: annual.

Servicio Nacional de Electricidad. *Informe del Director.* San Jose: annual.

Cuba.

Dirección General de Estadística. Junta Central de Planificación. *Boletín estadística de Cuba.* Havana: 1964.

Cyprus.

Electricity Authority of Cyprus. *Annual report and accounts.* Nicosia: annual.

Ministry of Finance. Statistics and Research Department. *Statistical abstract.* Nicosia: annual.

Czechoslovakia.

Edison Electric Institute. *A report on electric power developments in Czechoslovakia, 1965.* New York: 1966.

Státní úřad statistiky. *Statistická rocenka, C.S.S.R.* Prague: annual.

Dahomey.

Electricité de France. *Survey of the future electricity demand in Togo and Dahomey.* Paris: 1964.

Denmark.

Elektricitetsradet Danske Elvaerkers Forening. *Dansk elvaerksstatistik.* Copenhagen: annual.

Statistiske Departement. *Industriel produktionsstatistik.* Copenhagen: annual.

————. *Statistisk årbog.* Copenhagen: annual.

————. *Tiårs - oversigt.* Copenhagen: annual.

Swedish State Power Board. *Scandinavian co-operation in electric power.* (Blue-White Series No. 32). Stockholm: 1962.

Dominican Republic.

Corporación Dominicana,de Electricidad. *Memoria.* Santo Domingo: annual.

Dirección General de Estadística y Censos. *Estadística industrial de la República Dominicana.* Santa Domingo: annual.

Ecuador.

Banco Central del Ecuador. *Boletín del Banco Central.* Quito: monthly.

Ministerio de Economia. *Síntesis estadística del Ecuador.* Quito: annual.

Ministerio de Fomento. Dirección General de Recursos Hidráulicos y Electrificación. *Primer censo nacional de electrificación, 1962-1963.* Quito: no date.

El Salvador.

    Ministerio de Economia. Dirección General de Estadística y Censos. *Anuario estadístico*. Vol. II. San Salvador: annual.

    ———. *Tercer censo industrial y comercial, 1961*. San Salvador: 1962.

Ethiopia.

    Central Statistical Office. *Statistical abstract*. Addis Ababa: annual.

    Ethiopian Electric Light and Power Authority. *Electricity in Ethiopia*. Special edition. Addis Ababa: October, 1963.

Faeroe Is.

    Elektricitetstrådet Danske Elvaerkers Forening. *Dansk elvaerksstatistik*. Copenhagen: annual.

Fiji Is.

    United Kingdom. Colonial Office. *Fiji Islands*. London: annual.

Finland.

    Central Statistical Office. *Industrial statistics of Finland*. Helsinki: annual.

    ———. *Statistical yearbook of Finland*. Helsinki: annual.

    Voipio, Erkki. "Power generation and transmission system of Finland." Conference paper, Institute of Electrical and Electronics Engineers. New York: 1966.

France.

    Electricité de France. *Rapport d'activité comptes de gestion*. Paris: annual.

    ———. *Résultats techniques provisoires*. Paris: annual.

    ———. *Statistiques de la production et de la consommation*. Paris: annual.

    ———. *Travaux d'investissement*. Paris: annual.

French Guiana.

    Institut National de la Statistique et des Etudes Economiques. *Annuaire statistique de la Guyane*. Paris: biennial.

Gambia.

    United Kingdom. Colonial Office. *Gambia*. London: biennial.

Germany (East).

    Piens, Dr. Heinz. "Die Energiewirtschaft Mitteldeutschlands im Jahre 1964." *Glückauf*, 19 January, 1966. Essen: biweekly.

    Staatlichen Zentralverwaltung für Statistik. *Statistiches Jahrbuch*. Berlin: annual.

    ———. *Statistisches Taschenbuch*. Berlin: annual.

Germany, (West).

    Statistisches Landesamt. *Statistisches Jahrbuch Berlin*. Berlin: annual.

    Vereinigung Deutscher Elektrizitätswerke und Verband der Deutschen Gas- und Wasserwerke (VDEW und VGW). *Ringbuch der Energiewirtschaft*. Frankfurt: irregular.

    Vereinigung Industrielle Kraftwirtschaft. *Tätigkeitsbericht*. Essen: annual.

Ghana.

    Central Bureau of Statistics. *Economic survey*. Accra: annual.

    ———. *Quarterly digest of statistics*. Accra: quarterly.

    ———. *Statistical yearbook*. Accra: annual.

    Electricity Department. *Annual report on Electricity Department*. Accra: annual.

Gibraltar.

    United Kingdom. Colonial Office. *Gibraltar*. London: annual.

Greece.

    Public Power Corporation. *Activities report and balance sheet*. Athens: annual.

Greenland.

    Elektricitetsrådet Danske Elvaerkers Forening. *Dansk elvaerksstatistik*. Copenhagen: annual.

Guadeloupe.

    Institut National de la Statistique et des Etudes Economiques. *Annuaire statistique de la Guadeloupe*. Paris: annual.

Guyana.

    Ministry of Economic Affairs. The Statistical Bureau. *Quarterly statistical digest*. Georgetown: quarterly.

    United Kingdom. Colonial Office. *British Guiana*. London: annual.

Haiti.

    Institut Haïtien de Statistique .*Bulletin trimestriel de statistique*. Port-au-Prince: quarterly.

Honduras.
  Dirección General de Estadística y Censos. Secretaria de Economia y Hacienda. *Anuario estadístico*. Tegucigalpa: annual.
  ———. Consejo Superior de Planificación Economica. *Compendio estadístico*. Tegucigalpa: annual.
Hong Kong.
  Department of Commerce and Industry. *Hong Kong Government gazette*. Hong Kong: monthly.
  United Kingdom. Colonial Office. *Hong Kong Annual Report*. London: annual.
Hungary.
  Central Statistical Office. *Statistical yearbook*. Budapest: annual.
Iceland.
  The State Electricity Authority. *Orkumál frá raforkumálastjóra*. Reykjavik: quarterly.
India.
  Central Electricity Authority. *Annual electric power survey of India*. New Delhi: annual.
  Central Water and Power Commission. *Public electricity supply, all India statistics*. Simla: annual.
Indonesia.
  Central Bureau of Statistics. *Statistical pocketbook of Indonesia*. Djakarta: annual.
  Service de l'Expansion Economique en Indonesie. "Le développement de l'énergie en Indonesie." at Conference de la Pacific-Indonesia Business Association. Djakarta: August, 1967.
Iran.
  Ministry of Industry and Mines. *Industry and mines statistical yearbook*. Teheran: annual.
  U. S. Bureau of Mines. *The petroleum industry of Iran*. By L. Nahai and C. L. Kimbell. Washington, D.C.: 1963.
Iraq.
  Ministry of Planning. Central Bureau of Statistics. *The monthly industrial survey*. Baghdad: monthly.
  ———. *Quarterly bulletin of statistics*. Baghdad: quarterly.
  ———. *Statistical abstract of Iraq*. Baghdad: annual.
Ireland.
  Economic Research Institute. Booth, J. L. *Fuel and power in Ireland*. Part II: "Electricity and turf." Dublin: 1966.
  Electricity Supply Board. *Annual Report*. Dublin: annual.
Israel.
  Central Bureau of Statistics. *Statistical abstract of Israel*. Jerusalem: annual.
  Electricity Corporation, Ltd. *Annual report*. Jerusalem: annual.
Italy.
  United Nations Conference on the Application of Science and Technology (UNCAST). "Data and information on geothermal plants," by Dr. Niccolò Gennai. Geneva: 1962.
Jamaica.
  Department of Statistics. *Annual statistical abstract*. Kingston: annual.
  Electricity Authority. *Electricity in Jamaica*. (Report of the Electric Power Resources Committee, July, 1966.)
Japan.
  Economic Planning Agency. *Economic statistics*. Tokyo: monthly.
  Editions Techniques et Economiques. *Revue française de l'énergie*. Paris: monthly.
  Fédération Professionnelle des Producteurs et Distributeurs d'Electricité de Belgique (FPE). *Annuaire statistique*. Brussels: annual.
  Japan Electric Power Survey Committee. *Semi-annual electric power survey*. Tokyo: semi-annual.
  Office of the Prime Minister. Bureau of Statistics. *Japan statistical yearbook*. Tokyo: annual.
  Overseas Electrical Industry Survey Institute, Inc. *Electric power industry in Japan*. Tokyo: annual.

Jordan.
    Ministry of National Economy. Department of Statistics. *Statistical yearbook of the Hashimite Kingdom of Jordan.* Amman: annual.
Kenya.
    East African Common Services Organization. *Economic and statistical review.* Nairobi: quarterly.
    Office of the Minister of Finance and Economic Planning. Economics and Statistics Division. *Statistical abstract.* Nairobi: annual.
Korea (South).
    Bank of Korea. *Economic statistics yearbook.* Seoul: annual.
    ————. *Monthly statistical review.* Seoul: monthly.
    Economic Planning Board. *Economic survey.* Seoul: annual.
    Korea Electric Company, Ltd. *Electric power in Korea.* Seoul: no date.
Kuwait.
    Kuwait Oil Company. *Annual report.* Kuwait: annual.
    The Planning Board. Central Statistical Office. *Statistical abstract.* Kuwait: annual.
Lebanon.
    Ministère de l'Economie Nationale. Service de la statistique générale. *Bulletin mensuel.* Beyrouth: monthly.
    Office de l'Electricité du Liban. *Statistiques Libanaise.* Beyrouth: quarterly.
    Société et la Presse Economique. "La production et la consommation d'électricité au Liban." *Le Commerce du Levant.* 15 February, 1967. Beyrouth: monthly.
Liberia.
    International Labour Office. *Bulletin of labour statistics.* Geneva: quarterly .
Libya.
    Ministry of Economy and Trade. Department of Census and Statistics. *Statistical abstract of Libya.* Tripoli: annual.
Luxembourg.
    Conseil Supérieur de l'Electricité. *I. Les besoins et resources d'énergie du Grand-Duche de Luxembourg. II. Etude sur l'extension du réseau de transport de l'énergie électrique.* Luxembourg: annual.
    ————. *Rapport sur la production et la consommation de l'énergie électrique dans le Grand-Duche de Luxembourg.* Luxembourg: annual.
Macao.
    Instituto Nacional de Estatística. *Anuário estatístico do ultramar.* Lisbon: annual.
Malagasy.
    Service de la Statistique et des Etudes Socio-Economiques. *Bulletin mensuel de statistique.* Tananarive: monthly.
    ————. *Economie Malagache.* Tananarive: annual.
Malawi.
    Central Statistical Office. *Annual abstract of statistics.* Salisbury: annual.
    Ministry of Finance. *Economic Report.* Salisbury: annual.
    ————. *Quarterly digest of statistics.* Salisbury: quarterly.
Malaya.
    Central Electricity Board of the Federation of Malaya. *Annual report.* Kuala Lumpur: annual.
    Department of Statistics. *Annual bulletin of statistics.* Kuala Lumpur: annual.
    ————. *Monthly statistical bulletin of the States of Malaya.* Kuala Lumpur: monthly.
Mali.
    Chambre de Commerce, d'Agriculture et d'Industrie de Bomako. *Annuaire statistique de la République du Mali.* Bomako: annual.
Malta.
    Central Office of Statistics. *Annual abstract of statistics.* Valletta: annual.
    ————. *Malta statistical handbook.* Valletta: annual.
Mauritius.
    Central Electricity Board. *Annual report and accounts.* Port Louis: annual.
    Central Statistical Office. *Yearbook of statistics.* Port Louis: annual.
    United Kingdom. Colonial Office. *Mauritius.* London: annual.
Mexico.
    Comisión Federal de Electricidad (CFE). *Estadísticas de explotación divisiones*

CFE. Mexico, D.F.: annual.
————. Estadísticas de explotación total federal. Mexico, D.F.: annual.
Comité de Estudios para la Restructurazatión de la Industria Republicana. Informe Anual. Mexico, D.F.: annual.
Dirección General de Estadística. Anuario estadístico. Mexico, D.F.: annual.
————. Censo industrial. Mexico, D.F.: annual.
————. Secretaría de Industria y Comercio. Estadística industrial anual. Mexico, D.F.: annual.
Nacional Financiera, S. A. Informe anual. Mexico, D.F.: annual.
————. Statistics on the Mexican Economy. Mexico, D.F.: 1966.
Mongolia.
  Direction de la Documentation. "Le développement économique de la République Populaire du Mongolie." Notes et études documentaires, no. 3312. Paris: 1966.
Morocco.
  Delegation Générale à la Promotion Nationale et au Plan. Division du Plan et des Statistiques. La situation économique du Maroc. Rabat: annual.
  Ministère du Développment. Service Centrale des Statistiques. Annuaire statistique du Maroc. Rabat: annual.
  ————. Bulletin mensuel de statistique. Rabat: monthly.
  Ministère des Travaux Publics. L'électricité au Maroc. Rabat: annual.
  Société d'Etudes Economiques Sociales et Statistiques. Bulletin économique et social du Maroc, revue trimestrialle. Rabat: quarterly.
Mozambique.
  Direcçao dos Serviços de Economía e Estatística Geral. Provinçia de Moçambique. Anuário estatístico. Lourenço Marques: annual.
  ————. Estatística industrial. Lourenço Marques: annual.
Netherlands.
  Centraal Bureau voor de Statistiek. De Nederlandse energiehuishouding. The Hague: quarterly.
  ————. Statistiek van de elektriciteitsvoorziening in Nederland. Vol. I "Produktie." Vol. II "Distributie." The Hague: annual.
Netherlands Antilles.
  Statistiek- en Planbureau. Statistisch jaarboek. Willemstad, Curaçao: annual.
New Caledonia.
  Institut National de la Statistique et des Etudes Economiques. Annuaire statistique des territoires d'outre-mer. Paris: annual.
  Service des Mines. L'activité minière. Noumea: annual.
New Guinea.
  Commonwealth of Australia. Territory of New Guinea: report to the General Assembly of the United Nations. Canberra: annual.
New Zealand.
  Department of Statistics. New Zealand official yearbook. Wellington: annual.
  ————. Monthly abstract of statistics. Wellington: monthly.
  Farrell, Bryan H. Power in New Zealand. Wellington: 1962.
  New Zealand Electricity Department. Report of the New Zealand Electricity Department. Wellington: annual.
  Public Works Department. Electric power development and operation. Wellington: annual.
  The Electrical Supply Authorities Association of New Zealand. The electrical supply industry in New Zealand, by N. M. Speer. Wellington: 1962.
Nigeria.
  Electricity Corporation of Nigeria. Annual report. Lagos: annual.
  Federal Office of Statistics. Annual abstract of statistics. Lagos: annual.
  ————. Quarterly digest of statistics. Lagos: quarterly.
  Nigerian Coal Corporation. Annual report. Lagos: annual.
Norway.
  Central Bureau of Statistics. Industristatistikk. Oslo: annual.
  ————. Elektrisitetsstatistikk. Oslo: annual.
  Institute of Economics. Norwegian School of Economics and Business Administra-

tion. "Hydro-electricity in the Norwegian economy," by Gunnar K. Sletmo. Bergen: 1963.

Pakistan.
Central Statistical Office. *Census of Electricity Undertakings.* Karachi: annual.

Ministry of Fuel, Power and Natural Resources. Bureau of Mineral Resources. *Annual report of activities.* Karachi: annual.

UN. ECAFE. *Proceedings of the regional seminar on energy resources and electric power development.* New York: 1962.

West Pakistan Water and Power Development Authority. *WAPDA annual report.* Lahore: annual.

Panama.
Dirección de Estadística y Censo. *Estadística Panameña.* Panamá: quarterly.

Papua.
Commonwealth of Australia. *Territory of Papua: report to the General Assembly of the United Nations.* Canberra: annual.

Paraguay.
Ministerio de Industria y Comercio. *Censos económicos.* Asuncion: annual.

Peru.
Empresas Eléctricas Asociadas. *Datos estadísticos.* Lima: annual.

———. *Memoria del Directorio.* Lima: annual.

Instituto Nacional de Investigación y Fomento Mineros. Dirección de Minería. *Anuario de la industria minera del Perú.* Lima: annual.

Instituto Nacional de Planificación. Dirección Nacional de Estadística y Censos. *Boletín de estadística Peruana.* Lima: annual.

Ministerio de Fomento. Dirección de Industrias y Electricidad. *Estadística de los servicios eléctricos del Perú.* Lima: annual.

Philippines.
Bureau of the Census and Statistics. *Economic census of the Philippines, 1961.* Manila: 1961.

International Atomic Energy Agency (IAEA). *Pre-investment study on power including power in Luzon, Republic of the Philippines; general report.* Vienna: 1966.

National Power Corporation. *Annual report.* Manila: annual.

Poland.
Edison Electric Institute. *A report on electric power developments in Poland, 1959.* New York: 1960.

Glówny Urzad Statystyczny. *Rocznik statystyczny.* Warsaw: annual.

Zjednoczenie Energetyki. Statystyka Rozwoju. *Electroenergetyki Polskiej.* Warsaw: annual.

Portugal.
Instituto Nacional de Estatística. *Anuário estatístico.* Vol. I "Metrópole." Lisbon: annual.

———. *Estatística industrial.* Lisbon: annual.

UN. ECE. *The future development potential of reservoir storage and firm hydro-electric capacity in Europe.* New York: 1965.

Puerto Rico.
Bureau of Economics and Statistics. *Anuario estadístico.* San Juan: annual.

———. *Monthly bulletin of statistics.* San Juan: monthly.

Government Development Bank for Puerto Rico. *A special report on Puerto Rico Water Resources Authority.* San Juan: 1966.

Reunion.
Institut National de la Statistique et des Etudes Economiques. *Annuaire Statistique de la Réunion.* Paris: biennial.

Rhodesia.
Central Statistical Office. *Monthly digest of statistics.* Salisbury: monthly.

———. *The Census of production.* Salisbury: annual.

Electricity Supply Commission. *Annual report and accounts.* Salisbury: annual.

Ministry of Economic Affairs. *Economic report.* Salisbury: 1962.

Romania.
Directia Centrală de Statistică, *Anuarul statistic al R.P.R.* Bucharest: annual.

Edison Electric Institute. *A report on electric power developments in Romania, 1964.* New York: 1965.

Rwanda.

République Rwandaise. *Bulletin de statistique.* Kigali: monthly.

Ryukyu Islands.

High Commissioner of the Ryukyu Islands. Civil Administration of the Ryukyu Islands. *Report.* Naha: 1963.

Sabah.

Federation of Malaya. Department of Statistics. *Annual bulletin of statistics.* Kuala Lumpur: annual.

United Kingdom. Colonial Office. *North Borneo.* London: annual.

St. Pierre and Miquelon.

Institut National de la Statistique et des Etudes Economiques. *Annuaire statistique des territoires d'outre-mer.* Paris: annual.

Sarawak.

Electricity Supply Corporation. *Annual Report.* Kuching: annual.

Federation of Malaya. Department of Statistics. *Annual bulletin of statistics.* Kuala Lumpur: annual.

Saudi Arabia.

Ministry of Finance and National Economy. Central Department of Statistics. *Statistical yearbook.* Jedda: annual.

Senegal.

Ministère du Plan et du Développement. Service de la Statistique. *Bulletin statistique et économique mensuel.* Dakar: monthly.

———. *Situation économique du Sénégal.* Dakar: annual.

Sierre Leone.

Central Statistical Office. *Quarterly statistical bulletin.* Freetown: quarterly.

Electricity Department. *Report on the Electricity Department.* Freetown: annual.

Singapore.

City Council. *Annual report of the Electricity Department.* Singapore: annual.

Department of Statistics. *Monthly digest of statistics.* Singapore: monthly.

———. *Report on the census of industrial production.* Singapore: biennial.

Federation of Malaya. Department of Statistics. *Annual bulletin of statistics.* Kuala Lumpur: annual.

Public Utilities Board. Electricity Department. *Annual report.* Singapore: annual.

South Africa.

Bureau of Statistics. *Industrial census: report No. 302.* Pretoria: 1967.

———. *Statistical yearbook of South Africa.* Pretoria: annual.

———. *Union statistics for fifty years, 1910-1960.* Pretoria: 1960.

Electricity Supply Commission. *Annual report.* Johannesberg: annual.

World Power Conference. Tokyo Sectional Meeting. "Power generation in South Africa with special reference to the introduction of nuclear power." R. L. Straszacker, A. J. A. Roux, G. R. D. Harding and W. L. Grant. Tokyo: 1966.

Southwest Africa.

Republic of South Africa. Bureau of Statistics. *Industrial census: report No. 302.* Pretoria: 1967.

Spain.

Instituto Nacional de Estadística. *Anuario estadístico.* Madrid: annual.

———. *Estadística industrial.* Madrid: annual.

Ministerio de Industria. Secretaria General Técnica. *Energía eléctrica.* Madrid: annual.

Sindicato Nacional de Agua, Gas y Electricidad. *Datos estadísticos tecnicos de las centrales eléctricas españolas.* Madrid: annual.

Third United Nations International Conference on the Peaceful Uses of Atomic Energy. "The incorporation of nuclear energy to the Spanish grid." F. Pascual and J. Molina. Geneva: 1964.

Sudan.

Department of Statistics. *Internal statistics.* Khartoum: annual.

Sweden.

Central Bureau of Statistics. *Industri.* Stockholm: annual.

————. *Statistical abstract of Sweden*. Stockholm: annual.

Centrala Driftledningen (CDL). *Elkonsumtionen i Sverige*. Stockholm: annual.

Svenska Elverksforeningens. *Statistik*. Stockholm: annual.

Swedish State Power Board and Swedish Water Power Association. *Power Supply in Sweden*. Stockholm: annual.

Switzerland.

Union Suisse du Commerce et d l'Industrie. *Rapport sur le commerce et l'industrie de la Suisse*. Zurich: annual.

Syria.

Directorate of Statistics. *General bulletin of current statistics*. Damas: quarterly.

————. *Statistical abstract of Syria*. Damas: annual.

Tanzania.

East African Common Services Organization. *Economic and statistical review*. Nairobi: quarterly.

Statistics Division, the Treasury. *Monthly statistical bulletin*. Dar-es-Salaam: monthly.

————. *Statistical abstract*. Dar-es-Salaam: annual.

United Republic of Tanganyika and Zanzibar. Central Bureau of Statistics. *Census of industrial production in Tanganyika*. Dar-es-Salaam: 1962.

Thailand.

Central Statistical Office. *Quarterly bulletin of statistics*. Bangkok: quarterly.

————. *Statistical yearbook*. Bangkok: annual.

International Atomic Energy Agency (IAEA). *Report of an IAEA mission to Thailand*. Vienna: 1964.

World Power Conference. Tokyo Sectional Meeting. "Electrical power survey in Thailand." Athorn Patumasootra and Archamphon Khambanonda. Tokyo: 1966.

Togo.

Electricité de France. *Survey of the future electricity demand in Togo and Dahomey*. Paris: 1964.

Service de la Statistique Générale. *Bulletin de statistique*. Lomé: monthly.

Trinidad and Tobago.

Central Statistical Office. *Annual statistical digest*. Port of Spain: annual.

————. *Quarterly economic report*. Port of Spain: quarterly.

Electricity Supply Commission. *Annual report*. Port of Spain: annual.

Ministry of Petroleum and Mines. *Monthly bulletin on the Trinidad and Tobago petroleum industry*. Port of Spain: monthly.

Sixth World Power Conference. "An investigation of methods to reduce fuel cost in the island of Tobago." K. F. Seheult. Melbourne: 1962.

Tunisia.

Service des Statistiques. *Annuaire statistique de la Tunisie*. Tunis: annual.

————. *Bulletin mensuel de statistique*. Tunis: monthly.

————. *Bulletin de statistique et d'études économiques*. Tunis: quarterly.

Turkey.

Electrical Power Resources Survey Department. *Annual electric power survey*. Ankara: annual.

Electricity Administration. *Annual report*. Ankara: annual.

Institut National de la Statistique. *Annuaire statistique*. Ankara: annual.

Uganda.

East African Common Services Organization. *Economic and statistical review*. Nairobi: quarterly.

Electricity Board. *Annual report and accounts*. Kampala: annual.

U.S.S.R.

Edison Electric Institute. *A report on electric power developments in the U.S.S.R., 1963*. New York: 1964.

————. *U.S.S.R. electric power developments, 1958-1959*. New York: 1960.

United Arab Republic.

Federation of Industries in U.A.R. *Industrial Egypt*. Cairo: quarterly.

————. *Yearbook*. Cairo: annual.

U.S. Department of Commerce. "Basic data on the economy of the United Arab

Republic." *Overseas business reports*. Washington, D. C.: 1967.

World Power Conference. Tokyo Sectional Meeting. "Coordination of operating thermal power plants in the U.A.R. with hydro-electric Aswan High Dam Power Plant (SADD EL AALI) to cover load requirements of the country as from 1967." Dr. K. H. Khalil and Dr. A. K. Mohamed. Tokyo: 1966.

———. Melbourne. "Electric power generation and distribution in the United Arab Republic." Dr. M. A. B. El-Koshairy. Melbourne: 1962.

United Kingdom.

Central Electricity Generating Board. *Annual report and accounts*. London: annual.

The Electricity Council. *Annual report and accounts*. London: annual.

Ministry of Power. *Statistical digest*. London: annual.

United States.

Association of American Railroads. Bureau of Railway Economics. *Operating statistics*. Washington, D. C.: annual.

———. *Statistics of railroads of class I in the United States*. Washington, D. C.: annual.

Department of Commerce. Bureau of the Census. *Annual survey of manufactures*. Washington, D. C.: annual.

———. *Census of mineral industries, 1963*. Washington, D. C.: 1967.

———. *Historical statistics of the United States: continuation to 1962 and revisions*. Washington, D. C.: 1965.

———. *1963 Census of manufactures, fuels and electric energy consumed in manufacturing industries, 1962*. Washington, D. C.: 1964.

Edison Electric Institute. *Historical statistics of the electric utility industry*. New York: 1964.

———. *Yearbook of the electric utility industry*. New York: annual.

Federal Power Commission. *National power survey, 1964*. 2 vols. Washington, D. C.: 1964.

———. *Hydroelectric plant construction cost and annual production expenses*. (Supplement). Washington, D.C.: annual.

Tennessee Valley Authority. *Annual report*. Washington, D. C.: annual.

Uruguay.

Administración General de las Usinas Eléctricas y los Teléfonos del Estado (UTE). *Power expansion program, 1961-1968*. Montevideo: 1961.

———. *Producción de energía eléctrica*. Montevideo: 1964.

Ministerio de Hacienda. *Boletín informativo*. Montevideo: annual.

Venezuela.

Banco Central de Venezuela. *Informe económico*. Caracas: annual.

Dirección General de Estadística y Censos Nacionales. *Anuario estadístico de Venezuela*. Caracas: annual.

———. *Boletín mensual de estadística*. Caracas: monthly.

Vietnam (South).

National Institute of Statistics. *Viet-Nam, 1964-1965*. Saigon: 1967.

Western Samoa.

Acting Government Statistician. *Statistical bulletin*. Apia: August, 1964.

Yugoslavia.

Federal Institute of Statistics. *Indeks*. Belgrade: monthly.

———. *Industrijska preduzeca*. Belgrade: annual.

———. *Statistički godišnjak S.F.R.J.* Belgrade: annual.

Zambia.

Central Electricity Corporation, Ltd. *Annual report and accounts*. Lusaka: annual.

Central Statistical Office. *Monthly digest of statistics*. Lusaka: monthly.

Ministry of Finance. *Economic report*. Lusaka: annual.

Ministry of Labour and Mines. *Annual report of the mines department*. Lusaka: annual.